Paradoxia Epidemica

PARADOXIA
EPIDEMICA

The Renaissance
Tradition of Paradox

ROSALIE L. COLIE

PRINCETON, NEW JERSEY
PRINCETON UNIVERSITY PRESS
1966

Printed in the United States of America
by Princeton University Press, Princeton, New Jersey

TO

BERNARD AND ELINOR BARBER,
AND GEORGE AND SIMONE BOAS,
FOR CLEAR AND DISTINCT REASONS

Preface

Pascal was right: "La dernière chose qu'on trouve en faisant un ouvrage, est de savoir celle qu'il faut mettre la première." At the end of writing, it is at last evident that some apology must come first, some defense of the indefensible—some defense, then, of an attempt to treat systematically a subject designed to deny and to destroy systems. Simply, this study of paradoxy was undertaken in unlearned ignorance, for a pedagogic reason: I could not explain, to my students or to myself, certain recurrent, evidently traditional ambiguities in the literature of the long Renaissance. The students and I had been brought up to read literature according to a critical theory which valued ambiguity, ambivalence, irony, and paradox; we attributed those qualities rather to a given writer's art than to any tradition within which he might have worked. Thinking about this aspect of Renaissance literature in the light of E. R. Curtius' topical method[1] suggested that there was in fact a rich tradition of highly developed paradoxes available for use by Renaissance authors; and suggested, furthermore, that many of the greatest writers of that period systematically exploited the tradition.

This book is an attempt to examine the ways in which some writers made conscious use of the paradoxical tradition and, in two cases, the ways in which paradoxy worked in fields other than literature—in Renaissance scientific inquiry and in one aspect of Renaissance painting. There are many ways in which a book on this subject might have been organized. After many false starts, usually upon an encyclopedic plan, I fixed upon a topical organization. Each chapter, therefore, deals with a general topic—e.g., scientific paradoxes; paradoxes of "nothing"; paradoxes of

[1] Ernst Robert Curtius, *European Literature and the Latin Middle Ages*, trans. Willard Trask (London and New York, 1953).

self-reference—or with a topical paradox sharply focused in the work of a single writer—e.g., Donne, Pascal, Milton —or a group of writers dealing significantly with a given topic—e.g., Petrarca and Sidney; Shakespeare, Donne, and Montaigne. There are (as my massed notes testify) innumerable uninteresting, inept, or failed paradoxes no less "traditional" than those dealt with here (on prison; on debt; how an ugly wife is better than a fair one; how an unfaithful wife is better than a faithful one). Except in a few cases, usually in contrast to "better" examples, I have not dealt directly with this huge mass of paradoxy, so much of it dull and repetitious; but have chosen to indulge myself by concentrating upon a few works of art which with particular ingenuity, particular signature, display the intellectual, structural, or literary possibilities of paradox, works which give back to the tradition of paradoxy at least as much as they take from it. Paradoxy had no special sanction in the Renaissance: what a writer did with the paradoxical tradition, as what he did with any other form, genre, mode, or tradition, is what matters.

The order of the chapters may seem haphazard: I hope their apparent negligence may conceal the effort that went into what is, in fact, a categorical and topical scheme arranged according to intellectual complexity. Insofar as it is possible—the following pages attempt to explain the impossibility of the effort's success—I have tried to begin with the simplest kind of paradox, the rhetorical paradox as illustrated by Rabelais' usage; from this I have passed to a fundamental kind of self-reference in imaginative literature, that involved in lyric poetry; thence, using Petrarca's and Sidney's love poetry as a bridge, to the psychological paradoxes involved in the reality and the poetry of love. Donne's use of love paradox was not restricted to his secular poetry, of course; I have exploited his religious verse to grade into the next section of the book, dealing with various official paradoxes in divinity, those clustered about the ideas of infinity and eternity, and those involved in the *logos* concept. From that preoccupation with divine ontology, I turned to various paradoxes involved in a more worldly ontology, beginning with the rudimentary problem of "nothing." (One privilege relinquished with the completion of this book is that of saying "Nothing," in answer to people who kindly asked me what I was working on.) Because the problem of "nothing" was crucial in Renaissance thought, I have treated it in several different ways—morally, in Chapter 7; physically and morally in Chapter 8; and aesthetically and spiritually in Chapter 9. Since the revolution in physics contributed to the Renaissance reconsideration of ontology, the chapters on natural science and Spenser's view of reality seemed appropriately grouped under the larger rubric of "ontology."

In the last section, all the chapters deal with the self-conscious examination of human knowledge: Chapter 12, relying heavily on Chapter 2, deals with various problems involved in the literary presentation of one's self; Chapter 13, on Donne's Anniversary Poems, picks up the themes of *docta ignorantia*, of self-reference, and of the negative theology, presenting as well, I trust, some new insights into the paradoxes of those complicated pieces of verse. The discussion of Burton's *Anatomy* relies on the *Gargantua and Pantagruel* chapter: my argument here, however, turns on self-references and attempts to persuade readers that Burton's whole book is in fact a large paradoxical box carefully packed with smaller paradoxes all in some measure reflective of their container. It must seem to many readers a work of supererogation to write yet another study of the paradoxy of *King Lear*: the first few pages of my chapter will explain why I had to take my shot at the play; furthermore, *King Lear* is a consummate example of the workings of moral, as well as of rhetorical, paradoxy. The last chapter is another exercise in "matching": that is, it examines some paradoxes on suicide both as moral and as rhetorical paradoxes—as rhetorical paradoxes not merely because they are defenses of an indefensible thing but also because in their strategy and their subject matter they mirror their own paradoxical action.

The predominance of English writers may suggest that I think English a language particularly hospitable to paradox. I don't: my linguistic limitations are responsible for the selection, because English is the only language I can read at the depth required by the ironies, double meanings, and deceptions of paradox. Some paradoxical writers in other languages, however, refused to be passed over—Rabelais and Montaigne, Petrarca and Pascal all claimed their inalienable places in the discussion. In the cases of Rabelais and Montaigne, I used, for convenience' sake only, the great Renaissance translations of their work into English, which have the merit of being readily available to modern readers. Petrarca and Pascal have been less well served, though, and appear here primarily in the original languages.

Some greatly paradoxical authors have not been touched, the most conspicuous of them Giordano Bruno. Like Augustus de Morgan, who "forgot" Bruno in the first edition of his marvelous *Budget of Paradoxes*[2] because Bruno was "all paradox," I must leave that difficult author for another time. The absence of an extended discussion of Erasmus' *Praise of Folly* would be inexcusable if, as this book was taking its final form, Walter Kaiser's *Praisers of Folly*[3] had not appeared, its first section devoted to that mock-oration. In spite of Mr. Kaiser's thorough analysis,

[2] Augustus de Morgan, *A Budget of Paradoxes* (London, 1872).

[3] Walter Kaiser, *Praisers of Folly* (Harvard University Press, 1963).

I have been unable entirely to suppress Folly, who in obedience to her own law frequently appears in the following pages. Don Quixote I have not mentioned, though the omission went hard; that knight, like Falstaff, would have required too much room in a book already overcrowded with famous lodgers. Besides, Mr. Kaiser has promised an extension of his study of paradoxy to cover *Don Quixote*. Jonathan Swift is another matter. His absence is not my fault, but the result of others' intransigence; a study of Swift's uses of paradoxy must await another hand. One naturally paradoxical man, Sir Thomas Browne, the great amphibium, deserves more homage than pillage, but I have borrowed from him only the epigraphs for these chapters.

An inevitable criticism must be met, that this book relies on the notion of a paradoxical *Zeitgeist* as informing, say, as the Burckhardtian *Zeitgeist*, or the mannerist one, or the baroque, or any of the other time-spirits familiar to scholars in the field. I deny the charge: on my field trips, I have never been able to identify a *Zeitgeist* for sure, no matter who pointed it out to me; really, I regard that spirit rather as the *Poltergeist* in scholarship's castle, deliberately increasing intellectual confusion, very far from harmonizing discordant intellectual elements.[4] This book is attempted as a reading of some pieces of Renaissance literature (the very best, to be sure) in a recognizable and overt intellectual and literary tradition. With luck, and at most, it will serve to complement such other readings of the Renaissance as Burckhardt's orderly view;[5] or Love-

---

[4] Stephen Toulmin, introductory essay to *Seventeenth-Century Science and the Arts*, ed. Hedley Howell Rhys (Princeton University Press, 1961).

[5] Jacob Burckhardt, *The Civilization of the Renaissance in Italy* (New York and London, 1951).

joy's scheme of hierarchies;[6] or Cassirer's vision of total cosmic correspondence;[7] or Hiram Haydn's impish "counter-renaissance."[8] Though I am quite sure that the paradoxical mode required of its practitioners certain prior assumptions about transcendence, and as sure that paradox was suitably domesticable within Christianity, I would like to qualify the claim, observable in much modern comment on the subject, that its only sources or only subjects were religious. Some remarks must be made about "the baroque," if only because so many people, on hearing what I was working on, have answered at once, "Oh, the baroque." From the selection of my materials, it should be clear that I regard the mode of paradoxy, though certainly much adopted by writers now classified as "baroque," by no means limited to their work: paradoxy was not limited to the practice of any one style or to the service of any one subject matter, but cut across many critical boundaries. In the case of the works discussed below, the tacit assumption is that the present reading in no sense excludes *all* other readings (though I hope occasionally to reverse Gresham's law and to drive out some clipped interpretations). Sometimes, as, for example, in the chapter on Donne's Anniversary Poems, my reading consciously tries to accommodate certain interpretations which have seemed, though manifestly "correct," magnificently irrelevant to each other.

Clearly, this book relies on the assumption, tested throughout its length, that there was such a thing as a paradoxical tradition, and with it a paradoxical mode of perception which deliberately intermixed material from very

[6] A. O. Lovejoy, *The Great Chain of Being* (Harvard University Press, 1942).

[7] Ernst Cassirer, *Individuum und Kosmos in der Philosophie der Renaissance* (Leipzig, 1927).

[8] Hiram Haydn, *The Counter-Renaissance* (New York, 1950).

different categories—such as, in ontology, "being" and "becoming"; in aesthetics, "imitation" and "invention." In the paradoxical behavior of paradox, such categorical distinctions are challenged and blurred by the curious arrangements which the form sets. For Renaissance aesthetics, this blurring is peculiarly important, since the action of paradox is a simultaneous creation and re creation, a simultaneous invention and imitation, cutting across the regulations of conventional Platonic and Aristotelian critical theory, and resolving some of the troublesome ambiguities that theory turns up. Most paradoxists invoke Socrates, either directly or in Alcibiades' image for him, as their patron; the fuddled remark of Aristodemus at the end of the *Symposium* might be taken as the epigraph for any discussion of the paradoxical theme. The intermingling of mode, tone, genre, and style characteristic of paradox reminds us constantly that "the same man could have the knowledge required for writing comedy and tragedy"— that the fully skilled tragedian could be a comedian as well.[9] Specific examples of very different interminglings are discussed in the book, particularly in the chapters dealing with Rabelais' *Gargantua and Pantagruel*, with Herbert's verse, with still life, and with Renaissance science.

The general topics of paradox and *serio ludere* have interested literary scholars of this generation. Not only Mr. Kaiser, but also Sister M. Geraldine, C.S.J.,[10] Margaret Wiley,[11] A. E. Malloch,[12] Henry K. Miller,[13] and

[9] Plato, *Symposium*, Loeb Classical Library, pp. 244-45.

[10] Sister M. Geraldine, C.S.J., "Erasmus and the Tradition of Paradox," *SP*, lxi (1964), 41-63.

[11] Margaret Wiley, *The Subtle Knot* (Harvard University Press, 1952).

[12] A. E. Malloch, "The Technique and Function of the Renaissance Paradox," *SP*, liii (1956), 191-203.

[13] Henry Knight Miller, "The Paradoxical Encomium with Special Reference to its Vogue in England, 1600-1800," *MP*, liii (1956), 145-78.

Frank J. Warnke,[14] all writing in English, have illuminated aspects of the subject (under the blessing, it would
appear, of Johan Huizinga[15]). Herbert Weisinger[16] has
considered the anthropological and religious backgrounds
of the primary paradox of all tragedy, the "fortunate
Fall." Beyond literary limitation, Edgar Wind[17] and
Gustav-René Hocke[18] have dealt with Renaissance and
"baroque" doubleness and duplicity. Such a groundswell
of interest follows naturally enough upon the work of
existential and linguistic philosophers, of logicians, mathematicians, and psychological and social theorists, all acutely
concerned from different viewpoints with the various manifestations of radical contradiction in the life we think we
live. I am indebted to many thinkers in this area, from
Freud to Sartre, from Russell to Tarski; my chief debt is
to E. H. Gombrich,[19] whose double but stereoptic vision
has thus far never failed to bring into focus not radical
contradictions only, but much other material as well,
usually quite uncontradictory, that brings the reconciliation
of opposites into relation with the rest of life.

Though like Folly, I have tried to point my finger at
"things," so that others may check their perceptions against
mine, I have been so presumptuous as to say, in more than
one case, what a given paradox ultimately "means," to
define and to limit it. In excuse for thus breaking the

[14] Frank J. Warnke, "Sacred Play: Baroque Poetic Style," *JAAC*,
XXII (1964), 455-64; "Play and Metamorphosis in Marvell's Poetry," *SEL*, V (1965), 23-30.

[15] Johan Huizinga, *Homo ludens* (London, 1949).

[16] Herbert Weisinger, *Tragedy and the Paradox of the Fortunate
Fall* (Michigan State University Press, 1953).

[17] Edgar Wind, *Pagan Mysteries in the Renaissance* (Yale University Press, 1958).

[18] Gustav-René Hocke, *Die Welt als Labyrinth* (Hamburg, 1957).

[19] E. H. Gombrich, *Art and Illusion* (London and New York,
1960).

fundamental law of paradoxy, I can only cite the victory of Calvinist conscience over natural hedonism. The temptation to linger forever in the hall of mirrors of paradoxical speculation is always very great. To have stayed there, though, lost in admiration at the infinite alternatives there displayed, would have been to thwart the one natural pleasure in which Calvinist conscience and natural hedonism concur, the acknowledgment of the huge debt piled up during the preparation of this book.

First, I should like to thank the institutions which made possible free time for reading and writing: the Howard Foundation, the John Simon Guggenheim Foundation, and the American Council of Learned Societies. Next, I am grateful to Orville Hitchcock, formerly Acting Dean of the Graduate College at the University of Iowa, and to Professor John C. Gerber, Chairman of the Department of English, for financial help in the preparation of the manuscript; and to Thomas P. Peardon, formerly Dean of the Faculty of Barnard College, for help and support of many kinds. As before, I am grateful beyond saying to the various libraries in which I have worked, as well as to their long-suffering staffs: the Bodleian, the British Museum, the Bibliothèque Nationale, the Bibliothèque Royale in Brussels, the Koninklijke Bibliotheek in The Hague, the University Libraries of Leiden, Amsterdam, and Cambridge, the Laurentian Library, the Library of the Warburg Institute, the Union Theological Seminary Library (especially Mrs. Foster), the Newberry Library, and the Library of the University of Iowa (the last unparalleled in procuring books on interlibrary loan). To the Warburg Institute of the University of London, where an unmethodical method can be learned by sharing it, this book is offered as a payment on account.

More than to institutions, however kindly, my debt is to people, who have over the years made my life more

nearly bearable. For the manifold sins and wickednesses of
this book, I am responsible; to the following is owed
what virtue it may possess: Marjorie Hope Nicolson, un-
tiring reader and sharp critic; at Columbia, Ingrid-Märta
and Julius S. Held, William Nelson, Barry Ulanov,
Bernard and Elinor Barber; at the Warburg Institute,
Frances A. Yates and J. B. Trapp, consistently resource-
ful; at Oxford, Margaret Crum, Helen Gardner, Martha
Kneale, and, above all, Anne Whiteman; at Iowa, Ralph
and Lila Freedman, Arline R. Standley, and Murray
Krieger. I here record my large debt for help and hin-
drance, both creative, to Dorothy Serlin Arndt, Anna Held
Audette, D. M. Barratt, Joan M. Benson, Emily Briney,
Patricia Brown, Anne Daunis, Bridget Gellert, Violet B.
Halpert, Dorothy Mason, Naomi Churgin Miller, Wini-
fred Nowottny, Elizabeth M. Wilkinson, Hannah and
Heinrich Bluecher, Patrick and Helen McCarthy, W. B.
Coley, John Crow (congenitor of the title), Herbert A.
Deane, Frank H. Ellis, Fr. Amadeus Fiore, O.F.M.,
Jonathan E. Freedman, M. M. Goldsmith, W. G. Harris,
James Michael Held, Samuel I. Mintz, Roy Strong, Tom
Tashiro, James M. Wells, Henry H. Wiggins, and L. A.
Willoughby. Barbara Lewalski, Sister M. Geraldine, C.S.J.,
Jackson I. Cope, and A. E. Malloch have all clarified
matters here dealt with. Cynthia Grant, Carol L. Marks,
Brenda S. Webster, John P. Barnes, John B. Jarzavek, and
Max Yeh have helped more than (I hope) they know.
Henry Noble MacCracken saw to the heart of this prob-
lem, as he has of others; Anne K. Dix cheerfully saw
paradoxes everywhere for a time. Dr. and Mrs. Wijmans-
van Dillen, Dr. and Mrs. Brummel-Collard, and Dr. J. A.
Molhuysen taught me more about paradoxes than anyone
else. The following can never be adequately thanked: Lore
Metzger and Margaret A. Waggoner, fierce readers;

George Boas, generous counselor and thinker quicker than thought; Philip Long, who makes much of nothing, and nothing of the impossible; and, most of all, E. H. Gombrich, whose yea is yea; and Curt A. Zimansky, whose nay is nay.

Finally, I should like to thank the editors of *The Huntington Library Quarterly*, *The Philological Quarterly*, *The Journal of the Warburg and Courtauld Institutes*, of Columbia University Press, of the Oxford University Press, and of Routledge Kegan and Paul, for kind permission to use material which, in one form or another, appeared under their aegis. Mrs. James Holly Hanford has been a gentle and firm editor.

R.L.C.

Iowa City
June 1965

Contents

Part IV

Epistemological Paradoxes

Paradoxia Epidemica

Introduction:
Problems of Paradoxes

THE TERM "paradox" covers several meanings legitimately separate in category—though, as this book attempts
to demonstrate, one of the paradoxical qualities of paradox
is that all its categories may ultimately be seen to be
related. To begin with the simplest type of paradox, the
term was applied to the "rhetorical paradox," or the
formal defense, organized along the lines of traditional
encomia, of an unexpected, unworthy, or indefensible
subject. The rhetorical paradox was an ancient form designed as *epideixis*, to show off the skill of an orator and
to arouse the admiration of an audience, both at the out-
landishness of the subject and the technical brilliance of
the rhetorician.[1] Classical examples of the genre (called
"Wonderer" in George Puttenham's domestication of the
Greek term)[2] are Gorgias' praise of Helen (of which more
below: but evidently she was conventionally regarded as
"a thing without honor"), Isocrates' praise of Thersites,

[1] For definitions and descriptions of the rhetorical paradox, see
Theodore C. Burgess, *Epideictic Literature* (Chicago, 1902); A. S.
Pease, "Things without Honour," *CP*, xxi (1926), 27-42; for
logical paradoxes and *aporia*, see Augustus de Morgan, *A Budget of
Paradoxes* (London, 1872), a useful compendium of material, wit-
tily presented; William and Martha Kneale, *The Development of
Logic* (Clarendon Press, 1962), pp. 16-18, 113-15, 652-56;
Bertrand Russell, *The Principles of Mathematics* (London, 1937);
Frank Plumpton Ramsey, *The Foundations of Mathematics and
Other Logical Essays*, ed. R. B. Braithwaite (London, 1931), especially pp. 13-14, 20. Alfred Tarski, *Logic, Semantics, Metamathe-
matics*, trans. J. H. Woodger (Oxford, 1956), discusses the solutions to paradox afforded in the metalanguage.

[2] George Puttenham, *The Arte of English Poesie*, eds. Gladys
Doidge Willcock and Alice Walker (Cambridge University Press,
1936), pp. 225-26.

Synesius' praise of baldness, Lucian's of the fly, Ovid's of the nut, and the pseudo-Vergilian praise of the gnat. In the Renaissance, humanist recovery of ancient texts and imitation of ancient forms led to a revival of such formal paradoxy: some of the major prose pieces (and many more minor ones) are cast in the formal paradoxical mode— Ulrich von Hutten's *Nemo* and Erasmus' *Encomion moriae*, to name only one famous pair.

Related to such enterprises was another, the defense of a proposition officially disapproved in public opinion—such are the *Paradossi* of Ortensio Lando in praise of the virtues of debt, of imprisonment, of exile, and of many more generally disagreeable conditions. Montaigne's "Apologie for Raymond Sebond" belongs to a slightly different category: that is, it misleads its audience because it does the exact opposite of what it claims to do, launches a total attack upon the philosophical position it purports to defend. In the mass of humanist publication there were many collections of paradoxes, ancient and modern, to demonstrate the popularity of paradoxes among the learned who made them up and the educated who were amused by them—defenses of the ant, the flea, the fly, the ass, the fool, and folly; of the pox, of bastardy, of debt, of imprisonment, of tyranny; of hair, of baldness, of drunkenness, of incontinence.[3] The titles of such com-

[3] For material on such paradoxes, see Pease, *op.cit.*; Warner G. Rice, "The *Paradossi* of Ortensio Lando," *Michigan Essays and Studies in Comparative Literature*, VIII (1932), 59-74; Henry Knight Miller, *op.cit.*; A. E. Malloch, *op.cit.*; Alexander Sackton, "The Paradoxical Encomium in Elizabethan Drama," University of Texas *Studies in English*, XXVIII (1949), 83-104; Sister M. Geraldine, C.S.J., *op.cit.* A recent book essential to the subject is Kaiser's *Praisers of Folly*, which studies in close detail the folly paradoxes of Erasmus' *Encomion*, Rabelais' *Tiers Livre*, and the figure of Falstaff in *Henry IV*.

pendia, usually ponderously long,[4] are evidence that paradoxes were undertaken *serio ludere*, as exercises of wit
designed to amuse an audience sufficiently sophisticated in
the arts of language to understand them. One such collection, Caspar Dornavius' *Amphitheatrum sapientiae socraticae joco-seriae*,[5] is the most useful of all to the scholar,
since its paradoxes are organized according to subject
matter, so that one can trace the folly paradoxes, for instance, from antiquity to 1619, the date of the book's
first edition.

The rhetorical paradox as a literary form had duplicity
built into it. As an ancient form—like tragedy or pastoral,
like epic or satire—it set traditional models to be imitated
and improved upon; unlike those mentioned, however, the
rhetorical paradox had no set style, no steady, reliable,
fixed decorum. Its duplicitous intent, honestly proclaimed,
imposed an antic decorum encouraging, in many ways, to
novelty and trickery. Antique and antic, the rhetorical
paradox had a difficult balance to maintain.

Though it is called a "rhetorical" paradox, the paradoxical encomium raises a question in logic which is of the
most profound importance: can a thing unpraisable in fact
be praised? If it can, then it is not unpraisable; if it cannot, then a vast number of pieces of paradoxical prose do
not exist.[6] From this it follows that the rhetorical paradox
is also always a logical paradox, a contradiction within its

[4] E.g., *Argumentorum ludicrorum et amoenitatum scriptores varij*
(Leiden, 1623); *Dissertationum ludicrarum et amoenitatum scriptores varij* (Leiden, 1638, 1644); *Admiranda rerum admirabilium
encomia* (Nijmegen, 1666, 1676); *Jocorum atque seriorum, tum
novorum, tum selectorum atque memorabilium centuriae* . . . (Nürnberg, 1643).

[5] (Hannover, 1619; Frankfurt-am-Main, 1670).

[6] John Donne plays on this point when he says that paradoxes
are "no things": see below, Chapter 7.

own terms, a self-contradiction. In logic (now taken as opposed to rhetoric) there are many such self-contradictions, of which the model is called the "Liar": Epimenides the Cretan said, "All Cretans are liars." If he told the truth, then his statement is a lie, and so he didn't tell the truth; if he lied, then his statement is true, but he did not lie. In terms of logic and of language[7] the statement is a perfect self-contradiction, a perfect equivocation.

In more than one sense, paradox equivocates. It lies, and it doesn't. It tells the truth, and it doesn't. The Liar paradox is a perfect example of equivocation in still another sense, since its negative and positive meanings are so balanced that one meaning can never outweigh the other, though weighed to eternity. The one meaning must always be taken with respect to the other—so that the Liar paradox is, literally, speculative, its meanings infinitely mirrored, infinitely reflected, in each other.

The Liar, in various forms, is one of the most persistent of logical paradoxes, ubiquitous partly because of the economy of its formulation.[8] The problem it presents is a special case of all "speculative," or self-referential operations —a special case, then, of what I call the epistemological paradox, in which the mind, by its own operation, attempts to say something about its operation. Statements by a member of a class about its own class tend to paradox, as does much self-reference—it must be a Cretan who says that all Cretans are liars. If someone else were to formulate the statement, the paradox would dissolve into a simple affirmation, the truth or falsity of which could be more or less

[7] See Kneale, p. 114; and the masterly exposition, "Paradox," by W. V. Quine, in *The Scientific American* (April 1962), pp. 84-96.

[8] See Alexander Rüstow, *Der Lügner. Theorie, Geschichte, und Auflösung* (Leipzig, 1910); and Alexandre Koyré, *Epiménide le menteur* (*Ensemble et catégorie, Actualités scientifiques et industrielles*, Paris, 1946).

accurately tested. Further, the Liar paradox makes a state-ment, not only by a Cretan about the class to which he belongs, but also about itself as a statement, a fact which constitutes another degree of self-reference.

Another way of describing this phenomenon is to say that paradoxes are profoundly self-critical: whether rhe-torical, logical, or epistemological, they comment on their own method and their own technique. The rhetorical para-dox criticizes the limitations and rigidity of argumenta-tion; the logical paradox criticizes the limitations and rigidity of logic; the epistemological paradox calls into question the process of human thought, as well as the categories thought out (by human thought) to express human thought. Paradox deals with itself as subject and as object, and in this respect too may be seen as both tau-tological and paradoxical. Particular paradoxes, especially logical and mathematical paradoxes, are often "fixed" into adamantine hardness, because they mark a regular edge to progressive thinking, a point at which "object" turns into "subject." The thinking process, examining for the "error" which brought it up sharp against paradox, turns back on itself to see how it got stuck upon the paradox, and if that paradox might have been avoided: a paradox generates the self-referential activity. Operating at the limits of discourse, redirecting thoughtful attention to the faulty or limited structures of thought, paradoxes play back and forth across terminal and categorical boundaries —that is, they play with human understanding, that most serious of all human activities.

They play with rational discourse, certainly, and in this respect might be called anti-rational. The most famous such document in paradoxical anti-rationalism is surely the *Parmenides*, the dialogue in which opposites, contradictory opinions, and self-contradictions are exploited almost past bearing. The *Parmenides* became, during a long stage in its complicated history, a document in the history of mysticism,[9] but it is in its construction, with the close dialectical arguments between the Eleatics and the Athenians, entirely rationalistic, its control of the dialectic and of the arts of language marvelously impressive. Most paradoxes do not approach the technical mastery of the *Parmenides*, designed as it is to reduce men to wonder; but all of them share with that mystifying dialogue respect and concern for the techniques they question or defy. Paradoxes earn their right to question technique and method by their demonstration (in that very act of questioning) of their control over the techniques they question. Once more, then, paradoxes turn out to be paradoxical, to do two things at once, two things which contradict or cancel one another.

Sometimes a paradox fails to work as a paradox, to surprise or to dazzle by its incongruities. Gorgias' praise of Helen is a pretty example of such failure: originally a mock-encomium of the woman who was "obviously" unworthy of conventional praise, since she was the cause of the Trojan War and of the train of disasters following it, Gorgias' oration was so effective that Helen became, not a paradoxical, but a proper subject for encomium, a source for many set-pieces on the most beautiful woman in the world. In this case, paradox became orthodox.

Gorgias' encomium of Helen may be worth a sharp look, since the nature of paradoxicality is involved in its use. To deliver a paradoxical encomium, the rhetorician assumed certain values on the part of his audience, values which he would then proceed to question, to undermine, or to overthrow by means of his *epideixis*. Whether or

---

[9] Raymond Klibansky, *The Continuity of the Platonic Tradition* (London, 1939); and "Plato's *Parmenides* in the Middle Ages and the Renaissance," *Medieval and Renaissance Studies*, 1 (1943), 281-330.

not he believed in his argument is not in question: but his audience, representing "received opinion," had to believe in its dialectical opposite. "Helen" was, therefore, a very unsafe topic for Gorgias to defend paradoxically: certainly insignificant compared to the moral and social disasters her elopement set in train, Helen was nonetheless the most beautiful woman in the world. Though received opinion may have officially been that she was a "low thing," it is difficult to believe that received opinion was not in this case a screen for the much more fundamental view that a truly beautiful woman cannot be a low thing, no matter to what low behavior she may stoop. That is, Gorgias may have been trying a double paradox, ironically attributing to his audience views in dispraise of Helen, when he knew perfectly well—and had Homer's *Iliad* to prove it, whatever the *Odyssey* may have said—that men really think the world well lost for the possession of such an ornament. In any case, Gorgias' oration in Helen's praise lost its "paradoxical" qualities very early, itself to become the source for other encomia on Helen.

In another and looser sense, the term "paradox" was often applied, not to a strict logical or rhetorical construction involving some kind of dialectical contradiction, but to a formulation of any sort running counter to received opinion. So novel philosophical or scientific formulations came to be called "paradoxes"—Zeno's Arrow or Achilles, though also logical *insolubilia*, are paradoxes in this simple sense, in that they were formulated against assumptions in physics and metaphysics then prevailing. By the Renaissance, this use of the word is a commonplace: so, for example, the "Copernican paradox," an hypothesis advanced against both the prevailing view in astronomy and the evidence of common-sense experience, lost its paradoxical overtones to harden into orthodoxy until, in their turn, new paradoxical hypotheses were advanced against it.[10] As Hamlet said, in another connection, to Ophelia (III. i. 114-15), "This was sometime a paradox, but now the time gives it proof."[11]

One element common to all these kinds of paradox is their exploitation of the fact of relative, or competing, value systems. The paradox is always somehow involved in dialectic: challenging some orthodoxy, the paradox is an oblique criticism of absolute judgment or absolute convention. The Liar criticizes linguistic and logical limitations; Synesius' praise of baldness is only ostensibly about baldness. Rather he directs moral attention to the triviality of the conventional preference for a full head of hair to a bald pate, suggesting, without saying so, that what counts is not the appearance of the scalp but the reality of the mind within. Equally, one is supposed to ask, what is intrinsically ignoble about a nut, or a flea, or a water closet (the subject of a famous encomium by Sir John Harington)? The subject of a rhetorical paradox is one officially disapproved in received opinion—and what is opinion, received or otherwise, but the dialectical opposite of "truth"? Relying as they do upon relative opinions, upon the concept of relativity, and critical as they are of absolute and fixed conventional judgments, it is odd—or paradoxical—that paradoxes are so often designed to assert some fundamental and absolute truth. Zeno's famous paradoxes are a case in point: both the Arrow and the Achilles depend upon a failure of concurrence between the forms of logic and sense experience—how can an arrow, motionless at

[10] For a discussion of the paradoxy-orthodoxy process in other terms, see Thomas S. Kuhn, *The Structure of Scientific Revolutions* (Chicago, 1962), passim.

[11] All quotations from Shakespeare's works, unless otherwise specified, are to *The Complete Works of William Shakespeare*, ed. George Lyman Kittredge (Boston, 1936).

each *punctum temporis* of its flight time, reach its target? How can Achilles, beginning a race behind a tortoise, ever really make up the tortoise's advantage, since the tortoise always moves even as Achilles takes steps to catch up? These paradoxes handle infinity and infinitesimals;[12] they deal also in the conflict between observed experience and logic, between appearance and reality. Either way, Zeno defeats his pluralist opponents: either the logic by which he (and they) express their ideas is deceptive (in which case, how can they express their ideas?); or the sensible appearance of things is deceptive. Beneath the paradoxes of motion lies Zeno's real point: motion is merely relative and apparent. By his logic, both relativity and appearance can be demonstrated, in their own terms, not to exist; thereby an absolute monism can be demonstrated to be the only truth in existence. In these paradoxes, relativity is (paradoxically) necessary to the proof of Zeno's absolute. As the paradoxes are at once rationalist and anti-rationalist, so are they at once relativist and absolute, equivocally and irrevocably.

Even from these examples, it is obvious how much paradox "implies," folds into itself. Like a tight spring, the implications of any particular paradox impel that paradox beyond its own limitation to defy its own categories. A logical paradox, for instance, is never *merely* logical; it raises questions which force other considerations. Again and again, paradoxes evidently trivial ("It is better to live in a cottage than in a great hall") turn out to be deeply moral: even Lando's list, full of such apparently unpopular opinions, reaches into moral and social areas of utmost importance. Cicero's *Paradoxa Stoicorum* appear to be defenses of the obvious—"only what is morally noble is

---

[12] The classic book on this subject is Bernard Bolzano, *Paradoxes of the Infinite*, trans. Fr. Přihonsky, introduction by Donald A. Steele (London, 1950).

good"—about which official opinion cannot be divided, until we realize that his use of the truism as paradox is profoundly ironic: he criticizes his society for its manifest loss of values, so that the Stoic truism seems a novelty or paradox. Because of its secret reach beyond its own boundaries, boundaries on which it overtly insists, paradox once again works paradoxically, drawing attention to the limitations it questions and denies.

LET us examine certain paradoxes, to see how they work, beginning with some fairly simple ones, then passing to others working on several interrelated levels of paradoxy. In the first place, there are aporetic questions in their nature irresolute or insoluble, puzzles or riddles in logic, such as the Megarian paradoxes of the ancient world, evidently logical exercises to sharpen the wits of young dialecticians.[13] An example is the Bald Man: "Is a man with one hair bald?" Answer: "Yes." "With two hairs?" "Yes." "With three?"—and so on. Another, much like it, is the Heap: "Is one grain of barley a heap?" "No." "Two grains, then?" "No"—and so on. Similar to these, but involving quite different subject matter, are the moral *aporia*, such as the question debated in the *Protagoras*, "Can virtue be taught?" The difficulty of the question is given dramatic force by the behavior of the antagonists, who exchange their argumentative positions in the course of the debate. In fact, the reversal is ironical: Socrates has persuaded Protagoras of the truth of his underlying assumption, that knowledge and virtue are one.

Another kind of paradox deals in *insolubilia*, either experiential, such as those exploited by Zeno in his puzzles, or in the scientific paradoxes collected in the Renaissance,[14]

---

[13] Kneale, pp. 16, 113-15.
[14] For an extended discussion of this subject, see below, Chapter 10.

or intellectual, such as those debated in the *Sophist*, the *Theaetetus*, and the *Euthydemus*. The last group is particularly difficult, involving the questions: are negative statements possible? and, are false statements possible? The long debates in those dialogues deal with the problems arising from the conventional existence of two realms, one of experience and one of discourse; what is real in the second may not be real in the first, with all the intellectual and moral problems thereupon pendant. They raise, really, also questions about the "reality" of the conceptual world and about intellectual creativity; and raise, therewith, the host of questions always present in considerations of matching descriptive language to both experience and concepts.

In the strictest logical sense, what is "not" cannot be discussed: though a host of paradoxical commonplaces exist to demonstrate that it can. One of the simplest of these is the "world upside down,"[15] a more or less familiar environment arranged to contrast with the way the world is commonly experienced. The *topos* runs throughout western literature; in the Renaissance it was often exploited, most notably by Giambattista Marino,[16] Théophile de Viau, and Andrew Marvell. In "Upon Appleton House," Marvell deals in several imaginative inversions—one is the annual flooding of the Nunappleton fields by the River Denton, creating a topsy-turvy world where

> Boats can over Bridges sail;
> And Fishes do the Stables scale.[17]

[15] Curtius, *European Literature and the Latin Middle Ages*, pp. 94-98.

[16] James M. Mirollo, *The Poet of the Marvellous: Giambattista Marino* (Columbia University Press, 1963), pp. 130-31, 155-59; Odette de Mourgues, *Metaphysical, Baroque, and Précieux Poetry* (Clarendon Press, 1953), pp. 93-102.

[17] Andrew Marvell, "Upon Appleton House," *The Poems and Letters*, ed. H. M. Margoliouth (Clarendon Press, 1952), Stanza LIX.

The meadows are both a disrupted world, a world *en-glouti*, and, in the reflecting surface of the flood, a looking-glass world, with everything both upside down and backward to the beholder's view. Similar inversion, or at least reversal, informs a major convention of paradox, nominally an "impossible," the utopia. Literally, "utopia" involves a negative statement of the sort discussed in the *Sophist*, since "nowhere" is, cosmically and geographically, admittedly an *impossibilium*. Utopia is the place which is not; it makes concrete the intellectual impossibilities of the *Sophist*. What "happens" in utopias is made up of elements opposite to the societies in which their authors had to live, looking-glass reflections on the defective real world. Sir Thomas More's book, its title classic for the genre, was apparently written first as a very short book, its contents only the present second part, the utopian section: later, to bring his model commonwealth into higher relief, More added in the first book the description of his actual England.[18] Rabelais' Abbaye de Thélème was remarkable not for itself alone, but also for its overt critique of "normal conventual practice." Without the contrast to a "reality" morally upside down, the Thelemite experiment loses most of its force and all of its fun. Carrying this idea still further, the Ciceronian *Paradoxa Stoicorum* do not present axioms contrary to received opinion, but merely restate the old Stoic moral saws, now "paradoxical" in Cicero's irony because an hypocritical society, though still giving lip service to them, utterly fails to live by them. So John Donne's paradox, "That virginity is a virtue," restates a truism, in order both to point to current libertine practice and to reconsider the precise virtue in being a virgin.

[18] Cf. J. H. Hexter, *More's "Utopia," the Biography of an Idea* (Princeton University Press, 1952), pp. 16ff., for a discussion of the chronology of the book's composition.

One rhetorical paradox particularly rich in variations upon its own theme is Erasmus' *Encomion moriae*, obviously a praise of something conventionally regarded as unworthy of a proper oration. There is irony, if not also comedy, in the display of an author, by common consent the most learned man in Christendom, praising folly— but that oddity is but the beginning of an infinite chain of dependent anomalies.

First of all, what was being praised? We are never quite sure: the speaker, Folly, shifts her ground again and again. Sometimes folly seems a "good," as in the golden world into which Folly was born, a natural arcadia full of harmless pleasures, where children were the proper and properly careless inhabitants. Sometimes folly seems more than a little uncomfortable, as in the second childhood of rheumy old men, or in the self-deceptive world of mortal lovers young, old, and middle-aged. Sometimes folly is not harmless at all, as in the long harangues against the monks and the sharp critiques of secular and ecclesiastical hierarchy. Folly's first golden world, an utterly natural one, was topsy-turvy as utopias are topsy-turvy; but the idyll of the book's beginning soon shades into the darker hatchings of the Christian-Stoical "real" world Folly criticizes (and, ironically, criticizes by the standards set by the Christian Stoicism she criticizes).

Folly introduces herself in a mock-classical mode: she was born, not as her enemy Athena was, out of her author's brain; but "naturally" (like love), the child of Plutus and Penia, into the generous world of Epicurean nature. From an Epicurean position,[19] Folly inveighs against the Stoics

---

[19] Erasmus, *The Praise of Folie*, trans. Sir Thomas Chaloner (London, 1549), Aiii-B. All references are to this edition. For a study of Sir Thomas More's Epicureanism which is very useful to understanding Erasmus' use of the tradition, see Edward L. Surtz, S.J., *The Praise of Pleasure* (Harvard University Press, 1957).

(usually considered the defenders of nature and natural law), whom she interprets as rigorists, bridling by their unrealistic regulations the natural expansiveness and variety of human life, rich as it is in experimental error. During the shifting course of Folly's argument, the Stoical position comes in for considerable criticism, from a Skeptical as well as an Epicurean point of view. Folly herself, skilled in *epideixis* as she is, points to herself as a Sophist leveling her critical gaze at all rigorist positions, asserting her confidence in a life in which to err is not only human but also highly instructive. Folly takes the empirical position, that man is a mistake-maker (or, as she says in various ways, that he is foolish), who learns only from the mistakes he makes (or, that folly teaches wisdom).

Not for nothing had Erasmus elsewhere invoked Socrates, "O sancte Socrate, ora pro nobis." In his *Encomion*, much is made of the classic image for doubleness (and duplicity), Alcibiades' contradictory, paradoxical description of Socrates in the *Symposium*:

For fyrst it is not unknowen, how all humaine thynges lyke the *Silenes or double images of Alcibiades*, have two faces muche unlyke and dissemblable, that what outwardly seemed death, yet lokyng within ye shulde fynde it lyfe: and on the other side what semed life, to be death: what fayre, to be foule: what riche, beggerly: what cunnyng, rude: what stronge, feable: what noble, vile: what gladsome, sadde: what happie, unlucky: what friendly, unfriendly: what healthsome, noysome. Briefely the Silene ones beyng undone and disclosed, ye shall fynde all thyngs tourned unto a new semblance.[20] (Eiij)

[20] In his *Sileni Alcibiadis* (*Adagiorum Opus*, London, 1529, 753-63; separately printed, Paris, 1527), Erasmus lays out the philosophical contradictions reconciled in this figure. His witty exposition identifies the Silenus-figure with Antisthenes, Diogenes, Epictetus, various prophets and apostles, John the Baptist, and Christ Himself.

Folly is as double, as duplicitous, as that Socratic box—
and concerned to "disclose" from that box one of Socrates'
major messages, "Know thyself." *The Praise of Folly* is a
very peculiar exercise in self-knowledge, an exercise inevitably suspect by reason of its self-reference. For what
do we know of Folly? Only what Folly herself tells us,
Folly who all her life had been served by the merry companion Philautia, or self-love. As she tells us, Folly is
accustomed to pointing her finger at things, things themselves, directly, empirically to indicate them as they really
are. And yet that apparently objective gesture turns out
to be subjective, since she, a member of a class, perhaps
even that class itself, points directly at both other members of that class and at a definition for that class. Her
discourse is all of folly: her encomium is a self-praise. She
points her finger always at herself, as subject and object
collapse into tautology, into infinite regression.

This self-reference "matches"[21] the epistemological operation, indeed; and like all reflection, this self-reference
is mirrored again and again in the discourse. Folly confirms the form she has chosen, the paradoxical encomium,
by appeal to ancient authority:

. . . some of theym have not wanted, who with solemne styles,
and much losse of slepe and candell, shewed at lest theyr folie,
what ever theyr mattier was, in commendacion, some of this
notable tyranne, some of that, some in praise of the fever quar-
tane, others in settyng foorth what commoditees be in a flie, in
baldnesse, or such lyke hatefull thyngs.   (Aij)

Paradox may give Folly license, but it does not escape
her strictures. After a long critique of the quibbles of

[21] For a continued discussion of "making" and "matching," see
Gombrich, *Art and Illusion*, especially pp. 29, 73-74, 116-18, 186-
89, 271, 356-58. See also Karl R. Popper, "Self-reference and
Meaning in Ordinary Language," in *Conjectures and Refutations*
(London: Routledge and Kegan Paul, 1965).

scholastic philosophers, Folly lumps the paradox itself in
with those cobwebby time-wasters:

> I maie adde also hereto their *sentences or sawes*, which are so
> estraunge and beyonde all expectacion, as the verie *Stoikes
> sentences* called *Paradoxes*, beyng compared to theyrs [the scho-
> lastics'], seme grosse, and more than vulgar.   (M)

The effect, of course, is to remove all standards by
which the discourse may be measured, to keep the reference wholly internal, so that readers are constantly off
balance, aware only of the infinite progression, or regression, implied in Folly's simplest observation on folly.
Folly does not stop at mocking herself: she mocks her
maker as well, first, by her references to the geographical
locations particularly rich in fools, which of course turn
out to be Erasmus' birthplace, Holland, and the part of
the world where much of his youth was passed, Brabant
(Biiij). In the list of saints idolatrously worshipped by
the foolish and barbarous Christians of Europe, St. Erasmus appears—the saint of riches, therefore a patron particularly irrelevant both to Folly's moral system and to
the scholarly life Erasmus himself led. Again, in the long
list of fools' professions, the long comments upon rhetoricians, grammarians, editors, and Scriptural annotators
point to the great fame of Erasmus as a member of all
these groups. Once more, Folly does not simply dismiss
these activities as worthless, for after having criticized the
fatuity of Scriptural annotation, she praises, ambiguously,
of course, the very "Annotacions" of Erasmus:

> But here (loe) me thynkes I heare how I am hissed at by
> some of these greke professours, who study scripture in that
> tounge, and make as though other doctours at these daies saw
> nothyng, nomore than crowes dooe whan their eies ar peckt
> out, whiles with certaine *Annotacions* of their owne, they goe
> about to duske mens eies as with smoke, amonges whiche

sorte of notemakers, my friende *Erasmus*, whom often for honours sake and good will I dooe mencion, maie be counted the seconde, if not the fyrst. (Qiiij)

Slightly less obvious, though very symmetrical, is the self-reflective irony involved in the invocation by Erasmus, wisest of Christian scholars, of Solomon, wisest of Old Testament sages—in order to praise, not wisdom, but folly.

Folly's passage, so to speak, from Philautia to Solomon is significant in indicating the trend of her curious discourse. Beginning within a fully classical frame of reference, Folly's concern by the end of the encomium has passed to an overwhelmingly Christian preoccupation. Her sharpest strictures, throughout the discourse, were directed against the hypocrisies and deceptions of self-styled Christians. In spite of her skepticism of Scriptural interpretation, she herself cites and explicates passage after passage from Ecclesiastes and Paul's Epistles (the second a particular domain of Erasmus Roterodamus), in order to praise holy foolishness and, therefore, herself. In her own presentation, the classical Epicurean figure changes into the Pauline fool of God: Socrates' self-comment, that his only knowledge was that he knew nothing, becomes Folly's Christian comment upon her own nature. The Silenus-box does turn inside out to reveal Saint Socrates praying for us. In Erasmus' classical world there is a Christian sanctuary.

But even this observation, paradoxical though it is, is too direct a statement for paradox to permit; Folly does not fail us in her final self-contradiction and self-denial. Mocking her audience for its efforts to follow her radically disrupted and distracting discourse, Folly takes her equivocal farewell:

But ones more forgettyng my selfe, *I passe my boundes* [in speaking of salvation]. Howbeit if ought shall seeme unto you to have been saied of me more knappisshely than became me, or with more words than neded, thynke I praie you, that I was the speaker, beyng bothe Folie, and a woman. Yet for all that remembre the Greeke proverbe, that *oftentimes a foole maie speake to purpose*, unless perchaunce ye thinke that this maketh no whitte for women.

I perceive ye loke for an *Epiloge* or knotte of my tale, but than sure ye are verie fooles, if ye wene that I yet remembre what I have spoken, after suche a rablement of wordes powred foorth. The old proverbe saith, *I hate a tale bearer from the boorde*: But I saie, *I hate hym that remembreth what he hath sayd*. Fare ye well therfore, clappe your hands in token of gladnesse, live carelesse, and drink all out, ye the trustie serv-antes and solemne ministers of Folie.   (Tiij)

Her rejection of the value of memory extends to the value of all learning, dependent as it is on the collective memory of the race: she undercuts and undermines her whole argument herself, to leave each reader alone with the unpleasant realization that Folly has been consistent to the last; "on all sydes like unto her selfe," she has abandoned the reader to make his own decisions about value. True to Erasmus' principles of free will, which he was ready to defend even against the blunt pen of Martin Luther, Folly has left it up to each reader to interpret her words as he can and as he must.[22] The fact that each man will, in her view, make mistakes in that interpretation does not concern Folly: mistake-making serves man well, since his salvation depends upon his ultimate realization of his own folly.

A formal aspect of the end of this encomium—and of

[22] In this connection, it is interesting to note how neatly the *Praise of Folly* fits into the categories of ambiguity established by Ernst Kris (an art historian turned psychoanalyst) and Abraham Kaplan: i.e., disjunctive, conjunctive, and integrative ambiguity. Cf. their "Aesthetic Ambiguity," in Kris's *Psychoanalytic Explorations in Art* (New York, 1952), pp. 243-64.

many others in the genre—is that it has no formal ending. The discourse stops, certainly, but in such a way as to stimulate further thought in the reader, even further speculation—Folly cuts off her own discourse, but not discourse in general. Paradox, mocking formal limitation and insisting on the continuity between thought and experience, formally observes the decorum of its content. Erasmus, or Folly, has left his (or her) discourse openended, stretching into infinity. One might risk the further play, to suggest that paradox denies ends to assert the importance of means.

Obviously, Folly (to say nothing of Erasmus) is engaged in *serio ludere*, playing with the crucial problems of intellectual, moral, and spiritual life, playing also with the men who take them too seriously, as well as with the men who do not take them seriously enough. As in the *Protagoras*, Folly's disquisition demonstrates that virtue cannot be taught, even though knowledge and virtue are indissolubly one. John Donne warned an anonymous friend[23] that paradoxes were naturally generative—one paradox led to the making of another. Preoccupation with Erasmus and the problems of Erasmian folly led a later Hollander, Johan Huizinga, to propound his notion of man as characteristically *ludens*, a player of games of chance by rules made up by himself.[24] Paradox, like Sir John Falstaff, is not only witty in itself but the cause of wit in other men. Huizinga was witty in *Homo ludens*, an extraordinarily illuminating book—and there is nearly as much incongruity in Huizinga's brilliant but solemn exposition of his hypothesis as there is in the thin and fastidious Erasmus' praise of eating, drinking, and making love.

[23] Evelyn M. Simpson, *A Study of the Prose Works of John Donne* (Clarendon Press, 1948), pp. 316-17.

[24] Johan Huizinga, *Homo ludens* (London, 1949).

Another way of saying this is that the paradox, involving as it does many different and varying figures of speech —prosopopeia and mock-prosopopeia, irony, hyperbole— is nonetheless primarily a figure of thought, in which the various suitable figures of speech are inextricably impacted. Whatever else it is designed to do to incite its audience's wonder, the paradox dazzles by its mental gymnastics, by its manipulation, even prestidigitation, of ideas, true or false. The rhetorical paradox is, further, paradoxical in its double aim of dazzling—that is, of arresting thought altogether in the possessive experience of wonder—and of stimulating further questions, speculation, qualification, even contradiction on the part of that wondering audience.

The *Praise of Folly* can for a moment be reduced to the paradoxical *topos* of *docta ignorantia* originated by Socrates and developed so brilliantly by St. Paul and a host of Christian thinkers. The complicated and mystifying Socratic dialogue, the *Parmenides*, may be taken as the source of this *topos*, as of so much else in the paradoxical mode; since in the dialogue Socrates himself appears to be defeated by the logical acrobatics of Parmenides and Zeno. Technically, the *Parmenides* is a rhetorical paradox, since it presents two kinds of "unexpected" things. First of all, its material is full of surprises, as Parmenides and Zeno develop and reconcile their contradictory assertions; second, Socrates is, it appears, well and truly shown up by their dialectical subtlety. In the course of the dialogue's action, Zeno brings Socrates to acquiesce in notions quite contrary to those he asserts as his own, notions which, in an almost impenetrable irony, are also contrary to one another. The dialogue has remained a riddle to scholars,[25] and may perhaps be designed as such a riddle, in order to illustrate the pitfalls of purely meta-

[25] Francis Cornford, *Plato and Parmenides* (London, 1939), pp. 102-06.

physical speculation. At its plainest, though, the *Parmenides* is clearly a demonstration of the axiom that paradox necessarily attends upon those men brave enough to travel to the limits of discourse.

The early hypotheses of the *Parmenides*, establishing the identity of the Many and the One, form a bridge to a large province of paradoxy particularly hospitable to religious speculation. Through the middle ages the dialogue was known only as a fragment, the hypotheses expanded into many a Neoplatonic disquisition or rhapsody on the transcendent nature of divine being and of the divine intelligence. From Proclus through Marsilio Ficino,[26] the Renaissance inherited the notion that the *Parmenides* provided the metaphysical corroboration to Christian mystery: as such, the dialogue was a major source for what became known as the negative theology.[27]

The idea behind negative theology is best captured in Tertullian's assertion, in *De carne*, of his own faith in the "impossibility" of transubstantiation: "Certum est, quia impossibile est." As Sir Thomas Browne put it, mystery is the only possible "proof" of divinity. Ordinary events command common sense credulity; religious faith requires far more effort:

I can answer all the Objections of Satan, and my rebellious

[26] See Klibansky, "Plato's *Parmenides* in the Middle Ages and the Renaissance."

[27] The history of the negative theology properly begins with the formulations of the pseudo-Dionysius (Dionysius the Areopagite), in *The Celestial Hierarchies* and *The Mystical Divinity*: his works had a remarkably active life in the tradition of western mysticism. One indication of the importance of his work is given in Lefèvre d'Etaples' edition of the *Opera Dionysii, veteris et nove translationis, etiam novissime ipsius Marsilii Ficini cum commentarijs Hugonis, Alberti, Thome, Ambrosii oratoris, Linconiensis, et Vercellensis*, etc. (Strasburg, 1503). I owe this reference to J. B. Trapp of the Warburg Institute.

reason, with that odde resolution I learned of *Tertullian*, *Certum est quia impossibile est*. I desire to exercise my faith in the difficultest points, for to credit ordinary and visible objects is not faith, but perswasion.[28]

Unavailable to human experience and to human speculation, the transcendent deity deals in *impossibilia*, is itself an *impossibilium*: the appropriate way to express transcendent deity is by tautology (e.g., God's own self-referential comment to Moses, "I am that I am") or by negative affirmations which are by definition paradoxical (e.g., God is incomprehensible, or infinite). That is, there are two ways of avoiding contamination of the divine essence by the implications carried in metaphors from human experience, the one, to use terms of totality about divinity (Omniscience, Omnipotence, Omnipresence); the other, to use negative or "ablative" terms (Infinity, Eternity, Immutability).[29] Of the many practitioners of this sort of language, the two most significant for our purposes are Dionysius the Areopagite and Nicholas of Cusa. Both traveled the *via negativa* to its logical and rhetorical extremes. In Dionysius' work the classic statements appear of the paradoxical "truth" achieved by speaking negatively of God:

For this, as I think, is more appropriate to the divine essence, since, as the secret and sacerdotal tradition taught, we rightly describe its non-relationship to things created, but we do not know its superessential, and inconceivable, and unutterable indefinability. If, then, the negations respecting things Divine are true, but the affirmations are inharmonious, the revelation as regards things invisible, through dissimilar representations,

[28] Sir Thomas Browne, *Religio Medici*, ed. L. C. Martin (Clarendon Press, 1964), p. 9.

[29] For more on this subject, see below, Part II, Chapters 4, 5, 6.

is more appropriate to the hiddenness of things unutterable.[30]

Ingeniously, the "ablative" method avoids lying about God by its method of saying, not what He is, but what He is not:

> . . . and so Divine things should be honoured by the true negations, and by comparisons with the lowest things, which are diverse from their proper resemblance. There is then nothing absurd if they depict even the Heavenly Beings under incongruous dissimilar similitudes, for causes aforesaid.[31]

"Rhopographical" images, that is, images of "insignificant objects, odds and ends," or "rhypological" images, of low and sordid things, as practiced in Hellenistic painting,[32] become by Dionysius' argument appropriate to attempt comprehension of the divine essence. Against this background, several things come clear, among them, the curious habit of devotional poets' using "low things" in immediate juxtaposition to the highest, such as Herbert's likeness of Christ to a bag, or of God to a coconut,[33] and Donne's of the flea's triple life to the Trinity.[34]

The first hypotheses of the *Parmenides*, with their insistence upon the identity of the Many and the One; Plotinus, with his identification of the Many in the One; and Nicholas of Cusa, with his insistent logico-mathematical identification of anything and everything in God, of minimum with maximum (and thus of anything and everything with God) can all be seen to work directly in the tradition of paradox, even at its meanest, or most rhypographical: they seek to elicit an idea of God's transcendent greatness and glory by means of the radical dialectic im-

---

[30] Dionysius the Areopagite, *On the Heavenly Hierarchy*, *Works* trans. John Parker (London, 1897), Part II, pp. 7-8.

[31] *Ibid.*, p. 12. [32] See below, Chapter 9.

[33] See below, Chapter 6.

[34] See below, Chapter 3; for rhypography, see Chapters 1 and 9.

plied in metaphors of extreme contrast.[35] The trick is
nowadays not fashionable, but for Christians it was appropriate to religious utterance in another way, since it illustrated in logical and rhetorical application the orthodox
dictum that the last shall be first.

Nicholas of Cusa exploited paradoxy in many ways. A
skilled logician and mathematician, he pressed the consequences of these techniques to the extreme of questioning
the efficacy of questioning the techniques themselves. Often
classified as one of the fifteenth-century mystics, and certainly preoccupied, as the mystics were, with transcendence, Nicholas was also one of the great masters of rational
discourse. He was, too, playful in his serious presentations
of the divine creation; creation and re-creation conjoin in
his *De ludo globi*.[36] His two books on learned ignorance,
De docta ignorantia and *Idiota*, which insist on the conceptual infinity of deity and utilize the method of persuasion
involved in *coincidentia oppositorum*, offer, even in their
titles, fundamental and irreducible paradoxes. As for *docta
ignorantia*, the oxymoron combines not only opposites but
also impossibles in its unity. Two examples of Nicholas'
prose make "clear" the precision with which he deals in
oxymoron and paradox, the coincidence of contraries in

[35] The basic work on radically contradictory meanings contained
in a single word is Freud's "The Antithetical Sense of Primal
Words," *Collected Papers* (New York, 1959), IV, 184-96. Joseph
A. Mazzeo (in *Renaissance and Seventeenth-century Studies*, Columbia University Press, 1964, pp. 29-59) has considered the subject in relation to the imagery of metaphysical poetry. The critics
Mr. Mazzeo adduces deserve even fuller analysis than he had time
to give them there, as does the whole subject of the connection
between figures of speech and figures of thought. Cf. Mirollo, *Poet
of the Marvellous*, pp. 166-74, for an excellent analysis of material
relating to this question.

[36] Nicholas of Cusa, *De ludo globi*, in *Prohemium in hoc volumine continentur certi tractatus*. . . (Strasburg, 1502).

which maximum being and minimum being, maximum not-being and minimum not-being are all in turn equated with one another:

Maximum truth, besides, is the absolute maximum. All that we can say or think is exhausted by the following propositions which are the maximum truth on the absolute maximum itself: it is or it is not; it is and it is not; it neither is nor is not.[37]

These arguments lead to a further affirmation of learned ignorance, since even "nothing" (which is all the truly wise man knows) can be equated with the infinite God:

For that very reason Denis the Great [Dionysius the Areopagite] says that an understanding of God is not so much an approach toward something as toward nothing; and sacred ignorance teaches me that what seems nothing to the intellect is the incomprehensible Maximum.[38]

As for *Idiota*, the figure in the dialogue is not only one *persona* for learned ignorance, a Pauline cousin-german to Erasmus' Folly, it is also, in the very word of the title a self-reference, a self-confirmation of uniqueness, a tautology, an *idiom*. One can identify in Nicholas' work the fundamental paradox in his attitude toward the mind: he is at once profoundly rational and profoundly anti-rational, profoundly intellectual and profoundly anti-intellectual. His preoccupation with infinity combines with an insistence upon unity; his idiots, like Socrates and like Folly, know that they nothing know—and since "nothing" is, in the equations of transcendence, the same as both "all" and "infinity," they rightly glory in their ignorance, which is also total knowledge, or knowledge at least of the one thing worth knowing.

The doctrine of learned ignorance is an earthbound view

[37] Nicholas of Cusa, *Of Learned Ignorance*, trans. Fr. Germaine Heron (Yale University Press, 1954), p. 17.
[38] *Ibid.*, p. 39.

of transcendent knowledge, taken from the point of view
of human understanding; the *logos* doctrine, that deity is
its own idea as well as all other possible ideas involved in
the idea of divine totality, perceives knowledge as from
inside the mind of God. "In the beginning was the Word":
a Word in which all other words were implicit, a word
totally containing all the other members of the class of
being. The *logos* idea is a very important, and a very confusing one—it allows for both unity and infinite variety
and relates, by a kind of immanence theory, all things to
one surreal essence, the *logos* itself.[39] The *logos* is the idea
of all ideas, implying all other ideas, an idea in its essence
paradoxical, reflexive, at once active and passive, sufficient
to itself and creative of other modes.

In the Renaissance, when so many men worshipped the
logos, Pico della Mirandola nevertheless stands out in his
effort to draw all words, all knowledge however cacopho-
nous, into a single sound system, into, indeed, a single
logos. Pico was a good rhetorician and a self-confident
logician, as his great project suggests, to defend at Rome
the consistency of nine hundred theses drawn from every
philosophical and theological tradition.[40] Pico believed, and

---

[39] For the *logos* doctrine, see, most simply, Jaroslav Pelikan, *The
Light of the World* (New York, 1962), p. 34; and A.A.F. Aall,
*Der Logos, Geschichte seiner Entwicklung in der griechischen
Philosophie und der christlichen Litteratur* (Leipzig, 1896 and
1899); F.F.M. Heinze, *Die Lehre vom Logos* (Leipzig, 1872); E.
Krebs, *Der Logos als Heiland im ersten Jahrhundert* (Freiburg,
1910); Jules Lebreton, "Les théories du Logos au début de l'ère
chrétienne," *Etudes*, CIV (1906); Theodor Simon, *Der Logos. Ein
Versuch erneuter Würdigung einer alten Wahrheit* (Leipzig, 1902);
K. Weiss, "Der Prolog des heiligen Johannes. Eine Apologie in
Antithesen," *Strassburger Theologische Studien*, III (1899); Harry
A. Wolfson, "Extradeical and Intradeical Interpretations of Pla-
tonic Ideas," *JHI*, XXII (1961), 23-32; R. M. Jones, "Ideas as
Thoughts of God," *CP*, XXI (1926), 317-26.

[40] Giovanni Pico della Mirandola, *Conclusiones nonagentae in
omni genere scientiarum* ([Rome?], 1532).

evidently entirely believed, in the power of *logos*, both as
the unifying word from which all other exfoliated words
had been explicated and into which they could be folded
up again; and as the ordering word, the formulation of
words and therefore of truth. Pico was, in the phrase of his
own selection, the Lord of Concord, who could bring all
differences into acquiescence of unity, whose lordship was
exercised by means of intellect and eloquence.[41] The mind
can compose all contradictions: "Contradictoria in natura
intellectuali se compatiuntur," as Pico proudly said.[42]

Pico's chief concern was for intellectual incompatibilities,
anomalies, and contradictions, puzzles soluble by human
wit. His collection of incompatibilities, anomalies, and contradictions implies the further difficulties of ordinary life,
where intellectual control has difficulty in composing opposites. Pico was a man of imagination, a lunatic, lover,
and poet: his love, though passionate in the extreme, was
rather *amor intellectualis* (*dei*) than *amour courtois*. For
most people, denied the transcendence of divine ecstasy or
intellectual rapture, love is the closest they can come to

[41] Avery Dulles, *Princeps Concordiae: Pico della Mirandola and
the Scholastic Tradition* (Harvard University Press, 1941); Edgar
Wind, *Pagan Mysteries in the Renaissance* (Yale University Press,
1958), esp. pp. 39-56.

[42] Pico della Mirandola, *Conclusiones*, title page: "De adscriptis
numero noningentis Dialectis, Moralibus, Physicis, Mathematicis,
Metaphysicis, Theologicis, Magicis, Cabalisticis, cum suis tum sap-
ientum Chaldeorum, Arabum, Hebraeorum, Graecorum, Aegypti-
orum, Latinorumque placitis, disputabit publice, Joannes Picus Mi-
randulus, Concordiae Comes, in quibus recitandis, non Romanae
lingue nitorem, sed celebratissimorum Parisiensium disputatorum,
dicendi genus est imitatus, properea, quod eo nostri temporis philo-
sophi plerique omnes utuntur. Sunt autem disputanda dogmata,
quod ad gentes attinet, et ipsos haeresiarchas, seorsum posita, quod
ad partes philosophiae, promiscue, quasi per satyram omnia simul
mixta."

anything like self-transcendence. Love certainly qualifies as
a psychological paradoxical condition, with its "impossible"
sensations of transport and its sensible *coincidentia oppositorum.*[43] "To enter in these bonds is to be free,"[44] as
every lover agrees during the span of his joy. There are,
too, other kinds of psychological paradoxes in the experiences of love; sooner or later, each lover comes upon the
maddening, descriptive truth of Catullus' opposition, to
face in himself, for better and for worse, the peculiar
mixture of love and hate that love induces.

To review the progress of a love affair is to recast Paul:
"For that which I do I allow not: for what I would, that
do I not; and what I hate, that I do." Paul's emphasis
upon the inward condition of all men demands the same
intense scrutiny that love produces; Paul requires that all
men continually examine themselves in their spiritual love,
that they unceasingly note the contradictions in each human nature: "For the good that I would I do not: but the
evil which I would not, that I do."[45]

The Christian God, in Paul's teaching at least, leads to
moral self-examination, impels men to epistemological consideration. Indeed, in Christian literature, moral self-
examination is of immense importance, invading the literary and visual arts to the psychological enrichment of
them both.[46] Based on so many doctrinal paradoxes inac-

[43] To write about the contradictions of love is an act of *hubris*
(if not of *chutzpah*); some gifted psychoanalysts, as well as some
even more gifted poets, have managed the task. Hiding behind a
figure from the second category, I have tried to lay out some of
these paradoxes in Chapter 3, below.

[44] "Elegy XIX," *The Poems of John Donne*, ed. H.J.C. Grierson (2 vols., Clarendon Press, 1912). Except for the Divine Poems,
all subsequent references are to this edition.

[45] This moral insight is by no means exclusively Christian: cf.
Ovid's "Video melior proboque, / Deteriora sequor" (*Met.* VII. 20).

[46] Recent work in the theory and conventions of moral self-

cessible to "mere" logic (or "mere" experience), Christianity also canonized various moral paradoxes which are the stuff of art.[47] Ralph Venning's little handbook, *Orthodox Paradoxes*,[48] is by no means the most sophisticated presentation of metaphysical and moral paradoxes, but it is a handy reference, with its long list of contradictory epigrams. For example: "The Christian believes that he cannot be saved by his working; and yet he believes that he is *to work out his owne salvation with feare and trembling*,"[49] is more elegantly put by Milton—

> Man shall not quite be lost, but saved who will,
> Yet not of will in him, but grace in me
> Freely voutsaft. . . ;   (*PL*, III. 173-75)

but the moral meaning of the two passages is the same. "He cryes out *what must I do to be saved*, and yet he never expects to be saved by doing," is a dilemma under which all orthodox Christians live. Over and over again, Venning applies Pauline insights to ordinary Christian life: "He is willing to *dye* daily, yet daily prayes to live longer"; "He accounts his life but as a bubble; and yet he priseth it above the whole world"; "He dares not put

---

examination has proved very useful in explicating the literature of the Renaissance: see particularly Georges Poulet, *Etudes sur le temps humain* (Paris, 1950); Louis L. Martz, *The Poetry of Meditation* (Yale University Press, 1954); A. J. Krailsheimer, *Studies in Self-Interest* (Oxford University Press, 1962).

[47] The whole question of moral paradoxy is not directly tackled in this book. The author assumes that moral life is by definition made up of contradictions, their solutions and recombinations, and hopes that that assumption recognizably underlies the argument of the whole book, particularly in Chapters 7, 8, 12, 15, and 16.

[48] Ralph Venning, *Orthodox Paradoxes, Theoreticall and Experimental* (London, 1650 [1st edition, 1647]); the 5th edition, 1652, also contains the "Second Part," frequently printed separately.

[49] Venning (1652 edition), p. 11, paradox 96.

himselfe to *death*, least he *sinne*, and yet he thinkes he
sins if he *dye* not daily."[50]

Self-conscious Christianity imposes the obligation upon
all men to live with contradictions and to compose themselves as best they can, under the eye of an all-seeing but
distant deity; all Christians must take upon themselves
Pico's task, to harmonize their private nine hundred contradictory theses, but the theses are, in psychological terms,
all internal, all coterminous with the self. For Pico the
operations of the human mind, for Ralph Venning or for
John Milton the energies of the human soul, could compose opposites simply because God Himself was the primary compositor of opposites. His creation, ideal and
actual, demonstrated the harmony achievable from the
many sensible and metaphysical contradictions of existence.
In God's world, then, intellectual and moral double meanings were so habituated that man could himself be viewed
as a microcosmic set of intellectual, moral, and psychological contradictions. Christian paradoxes, in an ultimate
oxymoron, are always orthodox, not only in the propriety
of their doctrine but also in the fact that they appear to
describe accurately feelings deeply rooted in human nature.
When God, man, and all things are seen under the aspect
of *concordia discors*, then everything in human experience,
however materially distant from abstract divinity, is nonetheless immediately—without mediation—metaphysical
also. Each thing contains or implies its opposite; each
thing refers to transcendence. Both by correspondence
(all things "match" an aspect of *logos*) and by contradiction (all things coincide in deity), anything in human
experience can be perceived at once in its metaphysical as
well as in its experiential aspect. Folly points her finger

[50] Venning (1650 edition), p. 17, paradox 1; p. 19, paradox 23,
paradox 24, paradox 27.

fearlessly "at things" because by so doing she also points "through" them to their ideal significance.

QUITE CLEARLY, paradoxes are phenomena by no means peculiar to the historical period called the Renaissance, but occur in any period or place where intellectual speculation goes on. They tend to constellate, however, in a period, like the Renaissance, of intense intellectual activity, with many different ideas and systems in competition with one another. The epidemic of paradoxy in the Renaissance coincides with active speculation on the market of ideas; two less general causes may also be cited for the paradoxical epidemic. One is the humanist return to ancient texts as models for both life and art. The classical paradox lay ready to hand, easily imitable—a form easier to imitate, for example, than Greek tragedy or classical epic. The other is the mastery, by the humanists themselves, of the arts of the trivium, which permitted them the linguistic acrobatics required by paradoxy. The earliest, and the most, Renaissance paradoxes were written within the international humanist circle, as a kind of intellectual play practiced by a self-defined coterie. When the rhetorical paradox moved out of the classical languages into the vernacular literatures, it remained a sophisticated form, written for a learned and experienced coterie, an audience of men and women in the know, who could be expected to understand the paradoxists' learned wit and to admire the rhetorical skills demonstrated in the paradoxes themselves. So in that book that is itself a praise of disciplined spontaneity, Castiglione's *Courtier*, the Lady Emilia quite naturally says,

We shal now trie your wit. And if all be true I have heard, there have bene men so wittie and eloquent, that thei have not wanted matter to make a book in the praise of a flie, other in praise of a quartaine fever, an other in the praise of bauldnes, doth not your hert serve you to finde out somwhat to saie for one nyght of courting?[51]

Like the court of Urbino, Castiglione's book offers the proper environment for paradox, concerned as the book is with the rules of "games" for everything in life (from stone-throwing to choosing and living with a wife). The *sprezzatura* that informs the book is the very quality essential to a paradox's life.

For paradox demands of its framers both total control over expression and thought, and the appearance of completely effortless manipulation of expression and thought. Only when disciplines are completely mastered, when learning has become "natural,"[52] can one automatically behave with *sprezzatura*—the concept reconciles much contradiction in itself. The humanists and their pupils were masters and mistresses of the trivial arts, and thus were ideally suited to appreciate and to create paradoxes. As Professor Kristeller has often stressed, in the Renaissance major emphasis within the trivium shifted from logic to rhetoric, to the arts of expression and persuasion. As far as humanists were concerned—Valla, Ficino, Pico, Erasmus, Montaigne—earlier concentration on logic had resulted merely in the sterile barbarity of scholastic logical structures—expressed, furthermore, in a barbaric Latin lacking both the flexibility and grace of the classical language. For the humanists, rhetoric seemed to open anew the possibility of expressive integrity such as the ancients had enjoyed, in which style, form, and matter were inextricably conjoined. For persons with such a preference, the rhetorical paradox offered a specific illustration that what was said, to

---

[51] Baldassare Castiglione, *The Book of the Courtier*, trans. Sir Thomas Hoby, ed. Walter Raleigh (London, 1900), p. 123.

[52] R. L. Colie, "Castiglione's Urban Pastoral," *Greyfriar*, VII (1965), 5-13.

be properly understood, must be said in a particularly appropriate way. Even in the ordering of its sentences, a paradox is paradoxical, contradicting itself as it goes along, so that no one of its statements could be extracted from its contradictory context. As an acute critic of paradox has said, a paradox cannot be paraphrased.[53] If it can, it is flat and dull: if it is flat and dull, then it is not a paradox.

There is a stylistic problem raised by this fact: how does the paradoxist succeed in surprising an audience trained to expect the unexpected? Paradox as an intellectual construct is self-critical, both of its technique and its matter. Though paradoxes are in one sense entirely self-sufficient in their self-reference,[54] in another (and paradoxical) sense, they are also unalterably dependent upon society, upon what E. H. Gombrich has called the "beholder's share."[55] A Berkeleian paradox is an impossibility: paradox demands an audience, and an audience desiring to be surprised. The satisfactions of paradox depend upon the frustration of satisfaction in the ordinary sense, then; the successful paradox can only satisfy by surprise, by its twist, its gimmick. And yet its twists, its gimmicks, were very familiar; since paradoxes are so traditional, in both their form and their subject matter known to sophisticated audiences, they present their composers with terrible difficulties in finding the surprise. Hence, surely, the refusal of so many paradoxes to "end" formally, their abrupt, irrelevant, and indeterminate endings—Folly's sudden farewell, the short choice bluntly presented at the end of Montaigne's "Apologie," the curious close to Harington's *Metamorphosis of Ajax*:

[53] Malloch, "The Techniques and Function of the Renaissance Paradox," p. 193.

[54] See below, especially Chapters 2 and 12.

[55] Gombrich, *Art and Illusion*, Part III, pp. 155-244.

An Apologie
1. Or rather a retraction
2. Or rather a recantation
3. Or rather a recapitulation
4. Or rather a replication
5. Or rather an examination
6. Or rather an accusation
7. Or rather an explication
8. Or rather an exhortation
9. Or rather a consideration
10. Or rather a confirmation
11. Or rather all of them
12. Or rather none of them.[56]

One can perceive in the paradoxy developed in the
Renaissance two major stylistic solutions to the problem
of surprise—one, intensified complexity in a given rhetorical paradox (e.g., *The Praise of Folly, Biathanatos*); the
other, the embedding of individual paradoxes within a
larger cover-form (e.g., *Gargantua and Pantagruel, The
Anatomy of Melancholy, King Lear*) without particular
associations with traditional paradoxy. The surprise, then,
may be said to reside either in extraordinary consistency
of decorum (tautology) or in the incongruous mixture of
paradox with a normally unparadoxical form (contradiction).

To define paradox is, by definition, a self-defeating enterprise. In a letter to an unknown friend, John Donne,
himself a master of paradoxy, pointed his finger directly
at paradoxes, and told what they did, without seeking to
describe, define, delimit, or determine the form in general:

Only in obedience I send you some of my paradoxes; I love
you and myself and them too well to send them willingly for

[56] Sir John Harington, *A New Discourse of a Stale Subject called
the Metamorphosis of Ajax*, ed. Elizabeth Story Donno (Columbia
University Press, 1962), p. 205.

they carry with them a confession of their lightnes. and your trouble and my shame. but indeed they were made rather to deceave tyme then her daughter truth: although they have been written in an age when any thing is strong enough to overthrow her: if they make you to find better reasons against them, they do their office: for they are but swaggerers: quiet enough if you resist them. if perchaunce they be pretyly guilt, that is there best for they are not hatcht: they are rather alarums to truth to arme her then enemies: and they have only this advantadg to scape from being cald ill things that they are no things: therfore take heed of allowing any of them least you make another.[57]

Explication of some of the phrases of this letter may help to confirm some of the generalizations about paradox made here; for instance, that paradoxes flourish in a period with many competitive "truths" ("they have been written in an age when any thing is strong enough to overthrow her"). They deceive time—times—rather than truth, because shifting opinion depends upon shifting times, while truth does not. They are gadflies ("they make you to finde better reasons against them"); and they are self-destructive, consenting in their own destruction ("better reasons against them"). "They are but swaggerers," the *milites gloriosi* among rhetorical forms, making claims they cannot support; like Falstaff, they amuse by the outrageousness of their claims. They are "alarums to truth," trumpets (Folly, as she had said, was her own trumpet) calling truth to battle for herself. They are, because of the formulation of their impossible affirmations, all "nothings": but "nothing" is also precisely what they are not, since they are so generative ("take heed of allowing any of them least you make another"). In this letter, Donne has illustrated the generative power of paradox, since he has him-

self made a paradox about them, balancing the contradictions against one another in the equivocal balance in which
paradoxy excels. That equivocation is the paradoxist's protection, too, against his detractors: to his enemies, for example, Erasmus could answer that it was not he who had
made rude remarks about monks, bishops, cardinals, and
popes, but Folly who had spoken the words. The paradox
does not commit itself, nor does the paradoxist: another
reason why, in the melee of Renaissance ideas, there was
a paradoxical epidemic, affording man the chance to postpone a philosophical or religious choice he might live to
regret. Indeed, the paradoxical form denies commitment:
breaking out of imprisonment by disciplinary forms and
the regulations of schools, it denies limitation, defies "sit-
ing" in any specific philosophical position.

But even that failure to commit itself can be seen, in the
paradox, to be paradoxical. The failure to commit is a kind
of commitment, as the breaking of bounds affords a kind of
limitation. Montaigne's "Apologie" is a beautiful example
of the illusion of freedom in a paradox. Though "everything" seems to be adduced to demonstrate the uncertainty
of human judgment, Montaigne's essay narrows to an
utterly limited choice, a choice furthermore obscured
rather than clarified by the pseudo-data adduced in the
length of the essay. Seeming to open out, the paradox
turns in, acknowledging the wide world of alternatives
and denying autonomy to most of them. The very "in-
finiteness" of paradox, its open-endedness, is balanced by
its tautology, for all paradoxes (especially those of self-
reference) are self-enclosed statements with no external
reference point from which to take a bearing upon the
paradox itself. Self-limited, they deny limitation.

THIS BOOK has been very difficult to write, since the convention of scholarly exposition requires that a certain de-

velopmental order be imposed upon academic discourse. The ideal decorum for a book on paradoxy would require no chapter division whatever, so that the reader is at once naturalized and surprised by the passage from one subject to the "next." So Folly leads us through her own *Encomion*, defying logical construction in her argument, refusing those fences conventionally assigned to the topics she treats, demonstrating in her own oration the point she always insists upon, that all experience is at once both utterly disparate and unbrokenly united. I share with Folly her notorious tendency to rush in, but not, alas, her technical mastery of *epideixis*. Therefore I have attempted *mimesis* of the progression conventionally expected in books of discursive commentary. Part I, primarily concerned with rhetorical and psychological paradoxes, culminates in a discussion of love profane and sacred; the ecstasy of sacred love was designed to carry readers naturally into Part II, about the paradoxes raised by considerations of divine ontology. Part III deals with ontology once more, this time with problems, particularly poignant in the Renaissance, of redefining Being and Becoming. The final section, Part IV, deals with some ostentatious examples of the paradoxes which, in the end, underlie rhetorical, logical, or other perceptual paradoxes: that is, with the paradoxes clustering around the epistemological enterprise, with its inevitable problems of self-reference. This section properly follows, in history at least, upon the material in Part III, since the need for new definitions of Being was a major stimulus to the remarkable burst of epistemological thought which resulted, in the Enlightenment, in the formation of an entirely "new" epistemology.

In the matters discussed there is, necessarily, a great deal of overlap—self-reference is treated twice, once as a rhetorical problem and once as an epistemological problem. Problems of time and eternity are dealt with in three different contexts, aesthetic, theological, and ontological. The chapter on "nothing" depends upon the chapter on totality; the chapters on still life and suicide in turn depend heavily upon "nothing." The last chapter, on suicide, depends as much on the self-reference chapter—but the last chapter depends upon all the preceding ones. Its subject, suicide, is the moral parallel to the self-canceling action of paradox; the particular paradox discussed at the end, Donne's *Biathanatos*, returns to the theme with which the book began, since Donne's essay is a classic mock-oration in praise of what is absolutely the lowest thing in morality. It praises also "nothing," since it deals with the condition of not-being and since, as Donne had said, all paradoxes are "no things." In this book's end is its beginning, its structure an attempt to imitate its theme in the emblematic figure of the circle, the figure traditionally regarded as at once limited and limitless.

The circle-figure is also the figure for zero; the snake with his tail in his mouth may eat around to his head. So this book may destroy itself, though it is intended to come full circle. The risk it takes is within the decorum of paradox; I rely on Folly's one dogmatic statement as protection, that to make mistakes is to be a man. With that apologia, let us begin.

Part I
Rhetorical and Psychological Paradoxes

1

"The Puny Rhypographer":
François Rabelais and His Book

. . . There are no Grotesques in Nature. . . .
Browne, *Religio Medici*, 1. 15

In *Gargantua and Pantagruel*, Rabelais made elaborate use of the traditions of formal paradox. The book as a whole is not cast directly into the paradoxical form, but it contains many different sorts of "official" paradox— almost as many, indeed, as the recreative compendia of paradox collected in the Renaissance. "Recreation" is both the function and the theme of *Gargantua and Pantagruel*: the book is playful, diverting, and amusing; it is, equally, sustaining and nourishing. As far as the literary modes are concerned, *Gargantua and Pantagruel* mingles genres outrageously, with the excuse of parody. It offers critiques and/or parodies of heroic romance, of scholastic debate and discourse, of humanist treatises, of medical expositions: it is classical, medieval, folkish, sophisticated, formal and informal. It is, of course, too large and too various for any of these limiting categories. Written in the high, the middle, and the low styles, it burlesques all of these. Technically and metaphorically, the book is a macaronic, in its linguistic mix and in its mixtures of style, genre, and tone.

"Macaronic" is the name given to literary constructions, usually verse, in more than one language; the genre crudely, often primitively, combines elements from different contexts, thereby invoking certain relativities to its own aid. Though the spoof of macaronic denies its claim to more than cursory reflection, such success as the genre has, derives from its creators' and its hearers' learning in languages. Macaronic involves the kind of wit demonstrated in puns, calembours, conundrums,[1] clerihews, and even limericks: its violation of linguistic convention and expectation depends upon profound control of just that convention. Macaronic is only occasionally *serio ludere*, but its play derives from a great deal of serious application in the past.

The pleasure in macaronic—its "ludic"[2] recreative appeal—results from its sprightly combination of elements from systems conventionally regarded as totally disjunctive. In this sense, *Gargantua and Pantagruel* may be regarded as a macaronic, not only because of its remarkable juxtapositions of languages, but as a ludic combination of different styles, episodes, tones, and genres in addition.

In the first place, the book mingles scales. Grandgousier, Gargamelle, and their issue are distinctly larger than life. In case we forget this fact, since the giants do not always move among pigmies, Rabelais uses "himself," anagrammatized as Alcofribas Nasier, in the ordinary human scale, to demonstrate the "size" of his creation. In his own words for himself, Rabelais was "the puny rhypographer,"[3] a little man, whose vision and whose attention directed his descriptive art to low and sordid things, busy presenting

---

[1] See Leo Spitzer, *Linguistics and Literary History* (New York, 1962), pp. 4-10, for a brilliant linguistic analysis of the word "conundrum."

[2] I apologize for this barbarism. Its widespread use in literary connections, especially since Huizinga's use of the term, I hope, will confer upon it sufficient familiarity, if not sufficient authority, to warrant its appearance here.

[3] François Rabelais, *Gargantua and Pantagruel*, trans. Sir Thomas Urquhart (2 vols., London: Everyman edn. 1653, 1693), II.251; all references are to this edition. For "rhypography," see Introduction, above, and Chapter 9, below.

—what?—a world of giants. The world of those giants is in fact several worlds—a distant, idealized Cloud-cuckoo-land, or Utopia (indeed, Gargantua is ruler of a country by that name), constructed in scale to their needs; the actual world of Europe, tiny in comparison to them—and, thus, seen to be the small things described by the rhypographer; the fictional world of fantastic journey and discovery of the last two books of *Pantagruel*. Sometimes Gargantua and Pantagruel enter the "real" world without reference to any disparity in scale; sometimes one sweep of Gargantua's mare's tail can destroy a forest, or Gargantua will pluck from the towers of Notre-Dame de Paris the bells for his horse's bridle. Only after the event is fully narrated, fully realized, does one know the relative scale of landscape to persons in the episodes, and can one then draw the moral lesson implied by the use of scale.

The book relies upon the simple parodic pattern of the world upside down, the most important instance of which is the utopian Abbaye Thélème. There are other worlds upside down in the later books, such as the world inhabited by Queen Whim and the sovereignty of Entelechy. Abrupt juxtapositions of the frankly fictional with the fictionally real worlds shock the reader into criticism of both, and shock him also into a critical realization of fiction's operation, as in the passage about Gargantua's companionable mare:

> The first day being thus spent, and the bells put up again in their own place, the citizens of Paris, in acknowledgment of this courtesy, offered to maintain and feed his mare as long as he pleased, which Gargantua took in good part, and they sent her to graze in the forest of Biere. I think she is not there now. (1.48)

In the mode of fantasy, the book exploits such "impossibles" as the chess game played by the rules laid down in

Cusanus' mystical geometry (11.308-12); or as the impossible things (many of them deriving from common proverbs)[4] performed by the officers of Queen Whim:

> I then saw a great number of the queen's officers, who made black-a-moors white, as fast as hops, just rubbing their bellies with the bottom of a pannier.
>
> Others, with three couples of foxes in one yoke, ploughed a sandy shore, and did not lose their seed. . . .
>
> Others sheared asses, and thus got long fleece wool.
>
> Others gathered off of thorns grapes, and figs off thistles. . . .
>
> Others pitched nets to catch the wind, and took cock lobsters in them. . . .
>
> Others set carts before the horses, and began to flay eels at the tail; neither did the eels cry before they were hurt, like those of Melun.   (11.302)

Some of Queen Whim's servants emulate the Judaeo-Christian deity, since "out of nothing [they] made great things, and made great things return to nothing." That same miraculous creation appears at intervals throughout the book—on the island of Medamothy, "Epistemon bought another [picture], wherein were painted to the life, the ideas of Plato, and the atoms of Epicurus. Rhizotomus purchased another, wherein Echo was drawn to the life" (11.110). Rhypographers in general, Rabelais in particular, inevitably—and consciously—engaged in the same operation, such as Rabelais' classic library of St. Victor, where impossible titles were attributed to impossible authors or, even odder, attributed to actual authors (to at least one of whom Rabelais alluded later in the book). The parody list of books (1.159-61) became itself a model for other such exercises in the paradoxical imagination,[5]

----

[4] For comparable uses of proverbial material, Bruegel's *Netherlandish Proverbs* is important, as are the utterances of Sancho Panza.

[5] See below, Chapter 7.

all learned and witty projections, all creations sucked out
of their author's thumbs.

The library list, though, tells us more than that François Rabelais knew how to make fun of the pretentious
libraries formed in the sixteenth century. His library catalogue ridicules the separation of the learned world from
the world of everyday life, by turning inside out pretentious intellectual subjects to reveal their seamy—and their
bloody, and their intestinal—side instead.

Turning inside out was Rabelais' specialty. In the Author's Prologue to Book 1, he begins at once with the image
which becomes the crucial metaphor for the whole book:

. . . Alcibiades, in that dialogue of Plato's, which is entitled
The Banquet, whilst he was setting forth the praises of his
schoolmaster, Socrates . . . amongst other discourses to that
purpose said, that he resembled the Sileni. Sileni of old were
little boxes, like those we now may see in the shops of apothe-
caries, painted on the outside with wanton figures . . . to excite people unto laughter, as Silenus himself, who was the
foster-father of good Bacchus, was wont to do; but within
those capricious caskets called Sileni, were carefully preserved
and kept many rich and fine drugs, such as balm, amber-
greese, amomon, musk, civet, with several kinds of precious
stones, and other things of great price. Just such another thing
was Socrates: for to have eyed his outside, and esteemed of him
by his exterior appearance, you would not have given the peel
of an onion for him, so deformed he was in body, and ridiculous in his gesture. He had a sharp pointed nose, with the look
of a bull, and the countenance of a fool; he was in his carriage
simple, boorish in his apparel, in fortune poor, unhappy in his
wives, unfit for all offices in the commonwealth, always laughing, tippling, and merry, carousing to every one, with continual
gibes and jeers, the better by those means to conceal his divine
knowledge. Now, opening this box you would have found
within it a heavenly and inestimable drug, a more than human
understanding, an admirable virtue, matchless learning, in-

vincible courage, inimitable sobriety, certain contentment of
mind, perfect assurance, and an incredible disregard of all that
for which men commonly do so much watch, run, sail, fight,
travel, toil, and turmoil themselves.   (1.3)

The uglier the box, the sweeter its content, precious beyond price, like the mind and spirit of Socrates, miraculously contained in that bald head and bandy-legged
body. Like Socrates' arguments, Silenus-boxes were designed to surprise: and so was Rabelais' book, in this respect like the paradox of rhetorical convention, designed
to confound expectation. Anything in the book may mean
just what it appears to mean; or it may mean something
else altogether, or, best of all, it may mean both what it
appears to mean *and* something else altogether as well.

From the image of the Silenus-box, implying a strict
correspondence of opposites, one might expect a more
dialectical organization to *Gargantua and Pantagruel* than
the total work actually displays. Far from being a balanced
presentation of opposites, the book is a prodigal horn of
plenty (again, an image used in libidinous as well as in
literary context by the multifarious author), mingling its
gifts in a limitless tumble of language, incident, character,
style, tone, and genre, each of which requires intense
scrutiny for its overt, half-concealed, or covert implications.

As for language, Panurge's identification of himself ful-
fills the first requirements of macaronic: he answers Pantagruel's question in German, Arabic, Italian, English,
Dutch, Spanish, Danish, Hebrew, Greek, and Latin, as
well as in several garbled and some altogether invented
tongues. Throughout, Rabelais manages dialect and patois
—Limousin, Parisian, Gascon—as well as languages of
trades and social classes, such as the humanist Ciceronian
style of Eudemon; the scholastic Latinate style of the
Sophister and of the Limousin (who in crisis reverts to

his native dialect); Bridlegoose's judicial droning; the allegorical obscurity of the alchemists. Rabelais' interest in terms of art, the languages by which the professions shaped their existence and their view of the larger world, is evident both from his parodies of such languages (from that of cake-bakers through that of the men-at-law), and from the encyclopedic lists with which the book is punctuated, separate worlds of apprehension included in the universe of his tolerant book. His propensity for lists, parodies of epic catalogue, leads him to many subjects not immediately relevant to the canons of his narrative— for example, in a neat *praeteritio* in Book II, he manages to include the heroic meals of Pantagruel; the vernacular games of Gargantua; the saints called on by the monks and priests when the old Abbaye Thélème was being attacked; the areas of France traveled by Pantagruel; the countries of the world; the pilgrimage places of the Mediterranean world; the military ranks and pieces of artillery of a Renaissance army; the articles of clothing of Renaissance gentlefolk; the parts of armor for man and horse required for tilting; the creatures hunted for sport and food; the spas of Europe; the noises of animals; the sorts of heresy and their punishments; the epithets of men enraged—to say nothing of the materials of Rabelais' own profession, medicine, in the constant references, satiric and direct, to the parts of the body, its processes, diseases and disorders, as well as the medical treatments relevant to those parts and their diseases and disorders. Even a catalogue of the catalogues makes epic reading.

These are only some of the various materials combined and recombined to make up *Gargantua and Pantagruel*, an inclusive, generous, indulgent book. Rabelais manages to ally all kinds of literary genres as well as linguistic modes in his good-humored, sharp-tongued narrative: sermons and scholastic lectures; legal pleas and decisions; epic battles, such as the one between the Utopians and the Dipsodes, or the one between the cake-bakers of Lerné and the shepherds of Grandgousier's country; heroic births, such as that of Gargantua himself; parodies of scholastic and humanist education, in the education Gargantua received and later provided Pantagruel; picaresque, such as the fantastic odyssey of the fourth and fifth books; social criticism in the form of allegorical satire and utopian commentary. And among the many literary genres Rabelais exploited—always with the greatest originality—is the formal paradox.

Indeed, his major social and moral criticism is cast into the form of paradox: the Abbaye Thélème is a utopia (dependent in good part upon Sir Thomas More's),[6] in which an enlightened Epicureanism directs men and women to care for one another in a way at once natural and reasonable. Technically topsy-turvy, the new Abbey, entrusted to the tosspot monk, was reformed on lines precisely opposite to those of existing conventual institutions. Rabelais' utopia was a cheerful convent: the monk

then requested Gargantua to institute his religious order contrary to all others. First then, said Gargantua, you must not build a wall about your convent, for all other abbeys are strongly walled and mured about. . . . Moreover, seeing there are certain convents in the world, whereof the custom is, if any women come in, I mean chaste and honest women, they immediately sweep the ground which they have trod upon; therefore it was ordained, that if any man or woman, entered into religious orders, should by chance come within this new abbey, all the rooms should be thoroughly washed and cleansed through which they had passed. And because in all other monasteries and nunneries all is compassed, limited, and regulated by hours, it was decreed that in this new structure there should be

[6] For a study of Epicureanism in More's *Utopia*, see Edward L. Surtz, S.J., *The Praise of Pleasure*; and Kaiser, *Praisers of Folly*.

neither clock nor dial, but that according to the opportunities and incident occasions, all their hours should be disposed of.

Since in ordinary convents, only women were admitted who were

purblind, blinkards, lame, crooked, ill-favoured, mis-shapen, fools, senseless, spoiled, or corrupt; nor . . . any men, but those that were either sickly, subject to defluxions, ill-bred louts, simple sots, or peevish trouble-houses,

only those were to be admitted to Thélème who were

fair, well-featured, and of a sweet disposition . . . comely, personable, and well conditioned.   (1.119-20)

In all things opposite to the peevish—and commonly, in Rabelais' view, hypocritical—ethos of the Church, the new Abbey was commodious, in its graceful architecture ("a hundred times more sumptuous and magnificent than ever was Bonnivet, Chambourg, or Chantilly"), in decorations within and without pleasing to the senses, in habit, and in government.

Especially in government: "Fay ce que voudras" entrusted the well-born, well-bred ladies and gentlemen with absolute choice. Elsewhere unbridled, Rabelais here shows the decorum of his Epicureanism, for the ladies and gentlemen are governed by the natural limitations of reason from falling into excess or license:

Because all men that are free, well-born, well-bred, and conversant in honest companies, have naturally an instinct and spur that prompteth them unto virtuous actions, and withdraws them from vice, which is called honour. Those same men, when by base subjection and constraint they are brought under and kept down, turn aside from that noble disposition, by which they formerly were inclined to virtue, to shake off and break that bond of servitude, wherein they are so tyrannously en-

slaved; for it is agreeable with the nature of man to long
after things forbidden, and to desire what is denied us.

(1.129-30)

The result of this liberty was not libertinism but creativity—"So nobly were they taught, that there was neither
he nor she amongst them, but could read, write, sing,
play upon several musical instruments, speak five or six
several languages, and compose in them very quaintly,
both in verse and prose" (1.130). The experience of
Thélème had a permanent effect upon the inmates, furthermore: if a man and woman had a mind to marry, they
left the perfections of that unwalled utopia without for-
feiting the advantages gained there:

And if they formerly in Theleme lived in good devotion and
amity, they did continue therein and increase it to a greater
height in their state of matrimony: and did entertain that mutual love till the very last day of their life, in no less vigour and
fervency, than at the very day of their wedding.   (1.130)

By definition, a utopia must be a paradox (since it is
about "nowhere"); "utopias" make positive statements
about a nonexistent thing. In his original version of *Utopia*,
More had stressed the "paradoxical" or imaginary side of
his commonwealth, only later adding the dialogue on an
England recognizably real, to whose political, social, and
moral imperfections the Utopia was designed to be the
corrective.[7] Though technically paradoxes, since they deal
in negation, utopias are the least indeterminate type within
the genre, since they, of all paradoxes, commit themselves
to a doctrinaire, even didactic program. They prescribe
rules, offer models for behavior remarkably unequivocal
compared to other kinds of paradox. There *is* always the

[7] Cf. Hexter, *More's "Utopia," the Biography of an Idea*, for
a careful discussion of this point, in which Hexter comes to an opposite conclusion to this one.

technical escape for the utopist if he is charged with undue levity or undue seriousness, however: he can claim that his Utopia is nowhere, is a cloud-cuckooland in which whatever happens, happens in jest. Had Rabelais' readers chosen to question the moral realism of the Thelemite program, he could, after all, have pointed to a hundred other examples from his work recording the imperfect and exacerbated relations of men and women, conventionally regarded as the more realistic view; he could, always, take refuge in the fact that his model is situated nowhere. Thélème is utopian because topsy-turvy: the here-and-now of ordinary life, even the here-and-now of the book, is always less gracious, less generous than Thélème. Even though brought up in his father's kingdom, officially called Utopia, Pantagruel was forced to leave it in order to know its value. When Utopia marches with other countries, conventional difficulties arise. In the Utopians' colonization of the land of the Dipsodes, for instance, the usual disputes between national states naturally resulted.

There are more conventional, that is, more indeterminate, paradoxes in the book than the utopian passage. The *Tiers Livre* is full of paradox—and, if not a paradox itself, it is at least organized around one of the great subjects of Renaissance paradoxy, the question of woman's nature.[8] Within the *Tiers Livre* there are two paradoxes which at first glance seem to be merely the witty *epideixis* of the extravagantly competent rhetorician, but which on further examination turn out to be generative beyond ordinary expectation.

The first of these is Panurge's praise of debtors and borrowers, one of Lando's paradoxical subjects, with classi-

---

[8] The fullest discussion of the "Querelle des Femmes" in Rabelais' book is that by M. A. Screech, *The Rabelaisian Marriage* (London, 1958); see below, Chapter 3; and Kaiser, *Praisers of Folly*, pp. 103-92.

cal precedent (1.266-74). During the long price-rise of the Renaissance, many men fell into debt, some to their ruin, a few to their great advantage. Many men came to realize, with Panurge, "the Lord forbid that I should be out of debt, as if, indeed, I could not be trusted" (1.266). Pantagruel's embracing morality appears to need persuasion in this respect, so Panurge goes on to explain the merits to the debtor, and thus to all men, of the credit system. Sometimes his examples are clearly ironical, as the explanation that an indebted man always has someone to pray for him; again, he likens the incurring of debt to creation *ex nihilo* (and therefore, by extension, to the form of rhetorical paradox as well):

> For against the opinion of most philosophers, that, of nothing ariseth nothing, yet, without having bottomed on so much as that which is called the First Matter, did I out of nothing become such a maker and creator that I have created,—what? —a gay number of fair and jolly creditors.   (1.267)

Debt ensures the social amenities: politeness, even fawning and flattery, depend upon hope of repayment. A debtless world

> will be no better than a dog-kennel, a place of contention and wrangling, more unruly and irregular than that of the rector of Paris; a devil of an hurly-burly, and more disordered confusion, than that of the plagues of Doüay. Men will not then salute one another; it will be but lost labour to expect aid or succour from any, or to cry fire, water, murder, for none will put to their helping hand. Why? He lent no money, there is nothing due to him. Nobody is concerned in his burning, in his shipwreck, in his ruin, or in his death; and that because he hitherto had lent nothing, and would never thereafter have lent any thing. In short, Faith, Hope, and Charity would be quite banished from such a world. . . .   (1.269)

Debt and lending become the image for circulation and

mutual exchange on all levels, from "the regular motions of the heavens" to the utopian mutual exchanges of a perfectly self-regulated society (1.271). Panurge's model for such perfect regulations is the operation of the human body, as he traces the digestive process (1.272-73) from beginning to end and around again. In other words, he provides a natural model for the circulation of money and credit, which he wishes to regard as a natural process, as beneficent in effects upon the body of society as the digestive process for the whole human body.

The other major paradoxical set-piece of the *Tiers Livre* is one of the most famous in the whole genre, Panurge's praise of the codpiece. The chapter had been promised in the book before:

God keep from hurt, said he, the good fellow whose long codpiece or braguet hath saved his life! God keep from hurt him, whose long braguet hath been worth to him in one day one hundred threescore thousand and nine crowns! God keep from hurt him, who by his long braguet hath saved a whole city from famine! And, by God, I will make a book of the commodity of long braguets, when I shall have more leisure. And indeed he composed a fair great book with figures; but it is not printed as yet that I know of. (1.191)

To praise the codpiece is, as Pantagruel says, " a new kind of doctrine, very paradoxical"; but Panurge holds his own very well, demonstrating by correspondence the natural ubiquitousness of the codpiece, "in pease, beans, fasels, pomegranates," and so on, and so on; and arguing from ancient authority (Moses and Galen: who better?) the moral and medical importance of the codpiece for the precious member it protects (1.281-84).

The paradoxes of both debt and codpiece are related to the large subject of the *Tiers Livre*, that of marriage. Panurge has, he says, "a flea in mine ear, and . . . a mind to marry" (1.279). The debt paradox had ended by demonstrating the physiological point that the whole body was in the service of Venus' member, and that the said service "is done by loans and debts of the one unto the other; and hence have we this word, the debt of marriage" (1.273-74). Marriage increases debt, certainly, both because of the assumed innate improvidence of women and the expense of families; but increases debt also, by Panurge's argument, because it increases different sorts of mutual exchange. As debt is creative, making something of nothing, so is marriage, designed to make additional men where only two people had been before.

Panurge's whole debate about marriage takes place against the background of warfare: his codpiece required to be spectacularly large and strong because he might have to go to war, when men laying about them with swords might do him, and his putative posterity, considerable harm. As in Donne's elegy, "Loves Warre,"[9] this section of the *Tiers Livre* both compares and contrasts love and warfare—marriage *is* a battle, a continual argument, a continual suit at law, a continual game of chance, a continual dream. And because marriages make men while battles unmake them, it is also exactly the opposite of a battle. Somehow the two contradictory meanings are held in balance throughout the *Tiers Livre*, as are two elements of a more serious contradiction, the pursuit of conjugal happiness and the fear of conjugal betrayal. It appears to be in the nature of marriage that, however unhappy it is, no husband wants to be cuckolded; perhaps even that the more unhappy it is, the more he fears cuckoldry. And so Panurge, who fears at once both marriage and cuckoldry; for chapter upon chapter he consults the soothsayers, the

[9] See below, Chapter 3.

oracles, and other wise men for advice on the problem of whether or no he should take a wife.

Generous Pantagruel, who will not abuse Panurge's independence by making up his mind for him, responds to Panurge's see-sawing emotions as they seem to require— "Then do not marry"; "Then marry in the name of God"; "Do not marry then"; "Marry then, in the name of God"; "Do not marry then"; "Marry then, in the name of God. . . ." (1.285-87). Like Montaigne, Pantagruel is sufficiently balanced to endure the idea of the evidently inevitable vicissitudes of the married state—though it is worth noting that in the course of the whole book neither Pantagruel nor Panurge commit themselves to marriage. But unlike Panurge, Pantagruel could manage to contemplate both the joys and the terrors of marriage without losing his wits.

The fact that a whole book of *Pantagruel* was devoted, *ceteris paribus*, to the marriage question may seem in itself rather odd. Since, after all, most men, excepting priests, marry (and all men copulate, according to Rabelais, including priests), why should so long a book be constructed around a debate on a subject which experience seems invariably to settle one way or the other? In debating the marriage question, Rabelais was in a humanist tradition and contributing one more paradox to the line of paradoxes defending (and pretending to defend) women. Like the paradoxes in defense of debt, which turn into discussions of far greater importance than merely that of private indebtedness, the marriage paradoxes reflect a change in larger social conditions and often opened into reflections upon human nature far beyond the sexual context.

Humanist defenses of women are often contrasted to examples of "typical" medieval misogyny; examples of clerical abuse of women, though rare in the New Testament, abound in the pages of the founders of the Christian

Church, until dispraise of women became an accepted convention, with a store of *topoi* drawn upon for didactic purposes by didactic males from cardinals to barnyard cocks. In secular commentators at least, conventional dispraise is often softened by self-critical irony about male hypocrisy in this regard, which blames the complications arising from the sexual drive entirely upon the frailties of women: even Chaunticler did not dare translate his tag accurately for his wife. The humanist defense of women certainly altered, in a self-conscious sophistry, the general tone of official utterance on women. Humanistic paradoxes assumed that women since Eve had been human beings rather than a mixture of succubus and chattel, and that as human beings they had souls as well as their notorious bodies (though the point about souls was debated in Donne's *juvenilia*)—and that they even had, in the view of some observers, minds. Castiglione provides an elevated example of the thoroughly favorable view of women; his book pays them the compliment of including them in the category of courtier, and expounds a system of education and behavior for them as well as for the more obviously familiar male courtier type. But not all humanist defenses were so unequivocally favorable as Castiglione's; most of them were truly paradoxical in that they both defended and did not defend their subject, incorporating elements from the long tradition of misogyny into their general arguments for the relative emancipation of women.

Pantagruel's calm assumption of female frailty, of a piece with his view of masculine propensity to error, exemplifies an important shift in the official literary view of women: regarded neither as a succubus necessarily intent upon destroying men nor as a chilly piece of property, women could be considered as fully human—or, like men, as mixtures of good and bad traits, capable of development or degeneration, different in different relationships.

The gains in commonsense morality are obvious; but the
improvement in the attitude toward women carried with
it the equally obvious disadvantage that once a woman was
regarded as a normal human being, she acquired responsibility for her own social, moral, and spiritual condition.
To enter more fully into humanity was to enter a new and
more difficult bondage, the paradoxical one of general freedom. Pantagruel's mild commentary on Panurge's hopes
and fears makes all this plain. Women share the ambiguousness of men's lives, share its uncertainties, and contribute to the ambiguousness and uncertainty by their own
human nature.

Then why marry, if only to compound the general uncertainty of each human life? Because it *is* better to marry
than to burn. Panurge illustrates what Pantagruel takes
for granted, that men *do* burn, and women too. The son
of Gargantua, the utopian founder of an establishment
where rational marriages could prove to be happy as well,
could assume that the burning, however intense, need not
necessarily destroy; could take for granted that sharing
a life with anyone at all, even with a woman, would have
its natural ups and downs—nothing worse, and nothing
better, than that.

Panurge's search for a sure prognostication about his
chances of marriage led him to abandon the quest for a
wife in favor of the quest for certainty, through *sortes
Virgilianas*, consultations with oracles and sibyls, discourses
by men much married, unsuccessfully married, or never
married at all. His worries over his own condition led him
to become, as the book makes plain, a fool.[10] Not a simple
fool, however: Panurge is both a fool and not a fool, and
a great many men in the *Tiers Livre* are even more foolish
than he. Panurge's fears are, after all, as natural as the

[10] Kaiser, *Praisers of Folly*, pp. 103-92.

drives from which they derive; however headlong his search for reassurance, in the nature of the case impossible, Panurge does come to recognize the idiotic excesses of some of the men he meets, as his long list of epithets to describe fools bears witness. The *Tiers Livre* is a direct and, by definition, therefore an ambiguous praise of folly, in which many sorts of relative folly are measured against Pantagruel's large and tolerant wisdom. Praises of folly can only be ambiguous—the follies held up to ridicule may on examination turn out to be foolish enough; but Folly itself (or herself) turns out in the end to be a natural wisdom too obvious to be noticed by learned and obscurantist fools.

The marriage question is important intrinsically, too, though one tends to overlook that obvious fact. To marry may be foolish, given the particular tendencies of women, but *not* to marry, or not to love women, is more than foolish. It is suicidal. By not loving, men risk extinction of themselves, of their memories and families, and, theoretically at least, of the race altogether. The marriage debate of the *Tiers Livre* in its turn opens into a larger question, for which sexual reference is the constant metaphor: creation and creativity of all sorts. Though he so often seems barren intellectually and spiritually, Panurge *is* well named: he is the creative fool whose ideas and questions are the origin of the book's activity.

By the doctrine of imitation, works of art are "re-creations" of an original always assumed to have had a more mysterious genesis than the product of the human mind. Sometimes such acts of imaginative re-creation were highly prized, sometimes they were derogated as mere aping; but in either case, the mysterious origins of human creativity, of genius, seemed themselves to be in imitation of the original mysterious beginning of things, by which Being, and human life and human perception of that

Being, came to pass. Renaissance literature is full of pre-occupation with Creation—and indeed, all literature is in part the record of man's ideas about the beginning of things. Many a book, poem, or story begins "in the beginning," thus making of itself an image of what it attempts to represent. In the western tradition, to name only the most obvious, two inestimably important books begin so, Genesis and the Gospel according to St. John. In the development of Christian doctrine the importance of the creation was crucial: inspired by doctrinal preoccupation, the literature of the hexaemeral tradition developed, enriched by the accumulation of ideas and details from many non-Christian sources.

The "beginning" of things inevitably presents a puzzle. How did "things," a whole set of ideas that can only with the greatest difficulty be thought away, "begin"? Christian doctrine came to depend, not without conciliar struggles, upon a paradox canonized into orthodoxy, that God created the universe *ex nihilo*; by implication, that act of Creation could not be re-created by any human being. When King Lear warned his tongue-tied daughter that "Nothing can come of nothing," he was expressing what was, in the physical world at least, a truism.[11]

But all the same, all acts of creation by human beings were seen to be imitations of original Creation. Alchemical systems relied upon an elaborate analogy to the Creator's act: musicians and painters soon found themselves likened to the supernatural Creator, and Plato's verb was joyfully expounded to the poet's advantage. The question of imitation and creation became of primary importance in Renaissance literary criticism: George Puttenham manages to accommodate the ambiguities of maker and imitator in his explication of the matter.

[11] See below, Chapters 7, 8, and 9, for a fuller discussion of "nothing."

A Poet is as much as to say as a maker. And our English name well conformes with the Greeke word; for of ποιειν to make, they call a maker *Poeta*. Such as (by way of resemblance and reverently) we may say of God: who without any travell to his divine imagination, made all the world of nought, nor also by any paterne or mould as the Platonicks with their Idees do phantastically suppose. Even so the very Poet makes and contrives out of his owne braine both the verse and the matter of his poeme, and not by any foreine copie or example, as doth the translator, who therefore may well be sayd a versifier, but not a Poet. The premises considered, it giveth to the name and profession no small dignitie and preheminence, above all other artificers, Scientificke or Mechanicall. And neverthelesse without any repugnancie at all, a Poet may in some sort be said a follower or imitator, because he can expresse the true and lively of everything is set before him, and which he taketh in hand to describe: and so in that respect is both a maker and a counterfaitor: and Poesie is an art not only of making, but also of imitation.[12]

"Both a maker and a counterfaitor": both an inventor and an imitator, both a creator and a re-creator. In both senses of the word, *Gargantua and Pantagruel* is a book of recreation, a book to amuse and divert its readers and to restore them to themselves by means of that recreation. It is a fantastic and comical book, but its message is intensely in earnest: it is, like those solemn collections of paradoxes and learned witticisms, designed *serio ludere*. By the image of the Silenus-box on the first page of the first book, Rabelais serves notice of his own intention *serio ludere*: the book is plainly satire and burlesque, it deals constantly in "low things" (sexual organs, excremental processes, and so forth), always to some extraordinarily serious moral aim. In fact *Gargantua and Pantag-*

[12] Puttenham, *The Arte of English Poesie*, p. 3.

ruel praises living, simply being alive, and being conscious of being alive.

"Being alive" means living the life of mind, like the humanists, *and* of body. The body which Rabelais knew so well from his medical study is constantly used as an extended metaphor and epic catalogue, as the reference point for all human activity. Indeed, at one point, Friar John comforts Panurge "in the doubtful matter of cuckoldry" by imaging forth Panurge himself as an anthropomorphic landscape (1.354-55). Once more, Rabelais acts literally the part of rhypographer, translating into verbal tradition the pictorial notion of a double image, coupling landscape and human form: a picture in which the elements of a landscape can be composed into the shape of a recumbent human being.[13] The trick fits Rabelais' sleight-of-hand, but the particular imagery of the body as a natural world is appropriate to the general theme, a praise of the fullness, even the doubleness, of life itself.

To be alive is, *inter alia*, to eat and drink, which everyone in the book does on gigantic scale and which is, from the beginning, the restorative re-creation of human beings and their creative powers—witness Gargamelle's enormous intake just before the birth of her prodigious son. Being alive means drinking (1.3)—"Most noble and illustrious drinkers"—and thus getting inspiration for greater accomplishment than in one's sober state. Drinking leads to copulation—"and you thrice pockified blades"—which leads, often, to generation. In Rabelais' etymology, Pantagruel means "all-thirsty" and, therefore, one assumes, all-inspired. That Pantagruel's wisdom seems more often pure native wit than the product of inspiration by wine or other means merely generalizes the concept of inspiration to

[13] See below, Chapter 10.

include the consciousness of being a thinking and feeling man—the consciousness of being a sensible man.

The relation of eating and drinking to inspiration, to love and creativity, turns out to have been implied from the first sentence of the Author's Prologue to Book 1, when Rabelais refers to "that dialogue of Plato's, which is entitled, *The Banquet*": not for nothing does the sumptuous meal precede discourse on love and spiritual creativity.

The form of the "rhypographical" paradox, praising low things in opposition to things conventionally considered "high," gave Rabelais license for his scatological interests, interests perhaps not exceptional in terms of the psychological "set" of western man, and certainly quite common in the tedious tradition of Latin and vernacular epigram, but surely exceptional in the grand tradition of *belles-lettres*, to which Rabelais' book so patently belongs. For Rabelais, and for the characters in his book, though, the naturalness of all bodily functions, the importance of the body—and therefore of proper elimination—imply the importance of the literary recreation in which he is engaged. *Gargantua and Pantagruel* purges ill-humor, restoring men to their proper balance; and purgation is, correspondingly, celebrated. If the body is to generate properly, it must be in balance. Rabelais was, furthermore, entirely undisturbed by the fact that Celia, or any other man or woman, shits; undisturbed, also, that "love has pitched his mansion in/ The place of excrement." The body is, simply, the body. No need, in his psychology, for an elevated spiritualization, such as the Neoplatonic love theory provided, to gloss over the physiological arrangements for generation.[14]

[14] This is not to say that Rabelais is universally enthusiastic about excretion: when he speaks of the monks consuming the ordure

Much of the book concerns itself with copulation, either in fact or in fantasy; physical copulation and conception become major images for intellectual conception and creation. Like many paradoxists, Rabelais criticizes creation even as he praises it, and even as he creates: to do this, he draws attention to his own artifice, even to his own selection of words. More than one student has been driven to the brink of despair by the abundance of Rabelais' neologisms, so many of which have still escaped, so rhypological are their portmanteaux, confinement in dictionaries. Words are displayed, played with, used in their multiple meanings—and, when the available stock of words runs low, Rabelais never hesitates—once more, in emulation of the divine Creator—to create new ones.

For certainly in this book, in the beginning was the Word, a Word extraordinarily generative of other words and systems of signals. The macaronic aspect of the book is one such use of language: all the ebullience of linguistic alternative is evoked, and with that, a critique of language itself as a means of expressing reality. On the one hand, there is the piling up of words as the legitimate medium of description and communication, for example, in the great passage on Diogenes' treatment of his tub (where the translator added verbs to Rabelais' own list)—

. . . there, I say in great vehemency of spirit, did he turn it, veer it, wheel it, frisk it, jumble it, shuffle it, huddle it, tumble it, hurry it, jolt it, justle it, overthrow it, evert it, invert it, subvert it, overturn it, beat it, thwack it, bump it, batter it, knock it, thrust it, push it, jerk it, shock it, shake it, toss it, throw it, overthrow it, upside down, topsiturvy, arsiversy, tread it, trample it, stamp it, tap it, ting it, ring it, tingle it, towl it, sound it, resound it, stop it, shut it, unbung it, close it, unstopple it. And then again in a mighty bustle he bandied

of the world, for example, he speaks from well within a different tradition (1.93-94).

it, slubbered it, hacked it, whitled it, wayed it, darted it, hurled it, staggered it, reeled it, swinged it, brangled it, tottered it, lifted it, heaved it, transformed it, transfigured it, transposed it, transplaced it, reared it, raised it, hoised it, washed it, dighted it, cleansed it, rinced it, nailed it, settled it, fastened it, shackled it, fettered it, levelled it, blocked it, tugged it, tewed it, carried it, bedashed it, bewrayed it, parched it, mounted it, broached it, nicked it, notched it, bespattered it, decked it, adorned it, trimmed it, garnished it, gaged it, furnished it, bored it, pierced it, trapped it, rumbled it, slid it down the hill, and precipitated it from the very height of the Craneum; then from the foot to the top, (like another Sisyphus with his stone,) bore it up again, and every way so banged it and belaboured it, that it was ten thousand to one he had not struck the bottom of it out.   (1.253)

Other examples are the lists (augmented in Urquhart's enthusiastic translation) of the cake-bakers' epithets or the animal noises uttered to disturb the philosophers. Most important of all in this connection is Rabelais' brilliant transcription of the debate between Panurge and Thaumast, "by signs without speaking" (1.200). One passage must suffice to illustrate Rabelais' artfulness in describing what most people, in the interests of swift communication, merely mime:

He put the nail of his forefinger of his left hand to the nail of the thumb of the same, making in the middle of the distance as it were a buckle, and of his right hand shut up all the fingers into his fist, except the forefinger, which he often thrust in and out through the said two others of the left hand. Then stretched he out the forefinger, and middle finger or medical of his right hand, holding them asunder as much as he could, and thrusting them toward Thaumast. Then did he put the thumb of his left hand upon the corner of his left eye, stretching out his hand like the wing of a bird, or the fin of a fish, and, moving it very daintily this way and that way, he did as much with his right hand upon the corner of his eye. Thaumast began then to wax somewhat pale, and to tremble, and made him this sign. (1.204-05)

Rabelais' inexhaustible imagination supplied hosts of neologisms to re-create whatever he might sense, understand, or conceive of. *Ruach*, the breath of inspiration usually taken as divine, however, he does not acknowledge as the generative source for his imaginative spring of words; the Island of Ruach (II.189-91) was, in a metaphor for sickly enthusiasm, the island of flatulence. In their odyssey, Panurge and Pantagruel sailed into a cold area where they thought they heard words in the air, though they saw no one who might have spoken them. This was the sea of frozen words, then thawing haphazardly and, thus fragmented, sounding in the crisp air. Pantagruel collected some of the words still frozen—

Here, here, said Pantagruel, here are some that are not yet thawed. He then threw us on the deck whole handfuls of frozen words, which seemed to us like your rough sugar plums, of many colours, like those used in heraldry; some words gules, (this means also jests and merry sayings,) some vert, some azure, some black, some or, (this means fair words;) and when we had somewhat warmed them between our hands, they melted like snow, and we really heard them, but could not understand them, for it was a barbarous gibberish. One of them, only, that was pretty big, having been warmed between Friar John's hands, gave a sound much like that of chestnuts when they are thrown into the fire, without being first cut, which made us all start. This was the report of a field piece in its time, cried Friar John— (II.218)

meaning to save "some merry odd words, and . . . preserve them in oil, as ice and snow are kept, and between clean straw." But Pantagruel would not let him, saying,

. . . it is a folly to hoard up what we are never like to want, or have always at hand; odd, quaint, merry, and fat words

of gules, never being scarce among all good and jovial Panta-
gruelists.   (II.219)

The frozen words were heraldically colored according
to their kind, gules, vert, and so forth. Like other men of
the Renaissance, Rabelais was interested in alternative
systems of communication, such as the color language, the
language of flowers, of *imprese*, of emblems, some of them
as elaborate as the secret system then attributed to hiero-
glyphics (1.25-26). In the good contemporary tradition of
dealing with letters, Pantagruel subjected a letter to him
from the Lady of Paris, a blank sheet folded around a
gold ring and a square table-diamond, to every test he
knew for invisible writing. When his experiments failed
to reveal any script, he was forced to interpret the self-
evident message of the two rich gifts (1.215-16), with
which he ought, of course, to have begun. *Am Anfang*,
this time, *war die Tat.*

Panurge and Thaumast carried on their mimic contest
in silence: Panurge defeated his English opponent by his
greater skill in gesture. In the *Tiers Livre*, the rhetoric of
silence is further praised by Panurge in his role of *moro-
soph*, who praised dumb oracles which could never be
misinterpreted

through amphibologies, equivoques, and obscurity of words,
no less than by the brevity of their sentences. For which cause
Apollo, the god of vaticination, was surnamed Λοξίας. Those
which were represented then by signs and outward gestures,
were accounted the truest and the most infallible.   (1.321)

After a brief discourse upon the received history of language and expression, Panurge continued to praise dumb
men and women, until his consultation with the deaf-and-
dumb prognosticator, Goats-nose, who nearly puts out Panurge's eyes and thus sends him back to the world of words,
away from the ideal of unequivocal silence.

The "world in Pantagruel's mouth," as Auerbach so felicitously entitled his chapter on this book,[15] *is* the world of words, and to that world Rabelais gives his own unqualified allegiance. The pilgrims sheltering under a lettuce leaf went into Gargantua's mouth with the salad and suffered considerable fright until Gargantua picked his teeth and got them out again. In Book ii the same conceit is more fully worked: Pantagruel covers a whole army of frightened soldiers with his tongue, whereupon Alcofribas, the author of the work, climbing on the extended tongue, entered Pantagruel's mouth and lived there, he said, for six months.

There he met "a good honest fellow planting coleworts" —the cabbages that good honest Frenchmen are constantly enjoined to plant. The inhabitants of Gargantua's mouth are rather more sophisticated than Plato's cave-dwellers, for they know that there is another world beyond Gargantua's teeth, whence the pigeons come, but they know it only by hearsay. Alcofribas traveled to the market town of Aspharage, where he learned that hard by, at Larynx and Pharynx, men were dying of the plague (caused by Gargantua's garlicky breath, thought Alcofribas); he traveled hither and thither, was robbed, was employed, learned that men of "the countries Cidentine and Tradentine" distrusted one another just as bordering European nations did; composed a travel book about the Gorgians, so called "because they dwell in the gorge of my master Pantagruel." When finally Alcofribas came out and slid down to Pantagruel's feet, the giant asked him, "Whence cometh thou?," to which he answered, "Out of your mouth, my Lord" (1.241-44). The inverted self-reference is in the high tradition of paradox, certainly. Self-reference abounds in the book: Rabelais puts "himself," legitimately,

[15] Erich Auerbach, *Mimesis*, trans. Willard Trask (Garden City: Anchor Books, 1957), pp. 229-49.

into the Author's Prologues, and aslant again and again. His native province of Touraine recurs, most significantly as the birthplace of Panurge; his city of Chinon receives the most loving topographical and mythographical description. His participation, under his own name, in "the moral comedy of him who had espoused and married a dumb wife" (II.21), occurs just after Panurge's praise of dumbness. The Shandean informality of the earlier author's prologues becomes extreme in the Prologue to Book v, in which Rabelais presents himself as an incurable drunkard. That is, Rabelais puts Rabelais into the book, and puts various versions of Rabelais in—a posed literary man in anagram, a drunkard, an actor, a doctor, a Franciscan highly critical of friars, a priest opposed to the corruption of the hierarchy, a pigmy sheltering and exploring in Pantagruel's mouth, whence he takes the words of the book. Rabelais plays back and forth among the sorts of illusion and reality he perceives, fictionalizing himself to force on his readers the realization of how forceful is the fiction that can treat even the author as a piece of fiction, can rearrange even the author by the force of the words in a fictional man's mouth. Of course the world of words that is the book *was* in Pantagruel's mouth, but it was put there by the "puny rhypographer, or riffraff follower of Pyreicus" [Piraikos] (II.251)—put there by Rabelais himself.

In the re-creation of the immense and various world of this book, Rabelais perforce also re-created himself. In turn he re-creates others: as he took the words from Pantagruel's mouth, he offered his book as food for others. The advice he gave was to take books into one's self, to incorporate them as one incorporates meals of food and wine, to take one's recreation from books:

Therefore both dry and hungry souls, pot and trencherman,

fully enjoying these books, perusing, quoting them in their
merry conventicles, and observing the great mysteries of which
they treat, shall gain a singular profit and fame: as in the like
case was done by Alexander the Great, with the books of
prime philosophy composed by Aristotle.

O rare! belly on belly! what swillers, what twisters will
there be!

Then be sure all you that take care not to die of the pip,
be sure, I say, you take my advice, and stock yourselves
with good store of such books, as soon as you meet with them
at the booksellers; and do not only shell those beans, but even
swallow them down like an opiate cordial, and let them be
in you; I say, let them be within you; then you shall find, my
beloved, what good they do to all clever shellers of beans.

(II.251-52)

His book is a feast, and a symposium, with all that follows
after such pleasures.

2

"Pity the Tale of Me":
Logos and Art's Eternity

> Now for my life, it is a miracle of thirty yeares,
> which to relate, were not a History, but a peece
> of Poetry, and would sound to common eares like
> a fable. . . .
>
> Browne, *Religio Medici*, II. 11

GARGANTUA AND PANTAGRUEL solves many of the moral
problems presented in the book by means of paradoxical
device: some human conditions, after all, can best be presented, or "imitated," by means of figural contradiction.
A rhetorical and literary form such as the paradox, which
can play impartial host to moral and psychological contradiction, makes both a descriptive and an interpretative
statement about the condition dealt with. Psychological
ambivalence was by no means an invention of Freud,
though indeed it was he who provided us with some hope
of solving irresolute problems of that sort: Plato's char-
ioteer, attempting to bring the horses of his nature into
step with one another, is one early metaphor for the condition of ambivalence; Paul's complaints about the waywardness of his will speak for most men honest with
themselves. Rabelais was not concerned merely with the
perceptual duplicities of the world: he knew the problems
of psychological ambivalence as well, as in the scene in
which Gargantua is caught in the grip of conflicting passions, grief at the death of his wife, joy in the delivery
of his son.

With these words he did cry like a cow; but on a sudden

fell a laughing like a calf, when Pantagruel came into his mind. Ha, my little son, said he, my childlolly, fedlifondy, dandlichucky, my ballocky, my pretty rogue! O how jolly thou art, and how much I am bound to my gracious God, that hath been pleased to bestow on me a son, so fair, so spriteful, so lively, so smiling, so pleasant, and so gentle! Ho, ho, ho, ho, how glad I am! Let us drink, ho, and put away melancholy! . . .

As he spake this, he heard the litanies and the mementoes of the priests that carried his wife to be buried, upon which he left the good purpose he was in, and was suddenly ravished another way, saying, Lord God, must I again contrist myself? This grieves me.   (1.148-49)

Gargantua was "*hinc et inde* choaked with sophistical arguments, for he framed them very well, *in modo et figura*, but he could not resolve them, remaining pestered and entangled by this means, like a mouse caught in a trap, or a kite caught in a gin" (1.148).

Gargantua resolved his dilemma at last, not by the sophistical arguments of which he was master, but by the appropriate actions of drinking and rocking his son, of turning his attention to the living. In contrast to Gargantua's sensible solution, Panurge, hung between his hopes and fears of marriage, was unable to cast off his fears of life sufficiently to live with a wife, and deserved the two pieces of advice he got from the philosopher Trouillagan: "Both together"; "Neither the one, nor the other." Only Gargantua, experienced in helping himself out of psychological dilemmas, could gloss Trouillagan's utterances:

If I be not mistaken, quoth Gargantua, I understand it very well. The answer is not unlike to that which was once made by a philosopher in ancient time, who being interrogated, if he had a woman, whom they named to him, to his wife?

I have her, quoth he, but she hath not me,—possessing her,
by her I am not possest.   (II.24)

Pantagruel enunciates the lesson of balance in this particular case:

If I thus interpret, quoth Pantagruel, the having and not having of a wife. To have a wife, is to have the use of her in such
a way as nature hath ordained, which is for the aid, society,
and solace of man, and propagating of his race. To have no
wife is not to be uxorious, play the coward, and be lazy about
her, and not for her sake to distain the lustre of that affection which man owes to God; or yet for her to leave those
offices and duties which he owes unto his country, unto his
friends and kindred; or for her to abandon and forsake his
precious studies, and other businesses of account, to wait still
on her will, her beck, and her buttocks. If we be pleased
in this sense to take having and not having a wife, we shall
indeed find no repugnancy nor contradiction in the terms at all.
                                                           (II.25)

Panurge's indecision resulted from his desire to be married: he had no specific mistress, so he cannot be said precisely to have been in love, though he came very near it,
being in love with the idea of love. Francesco Petrarca
may or may not have been in love with a lady named
Laura, or one for whom Laura was a cover-name, but his
fiction at least was that he was in love with such a one, and
that he experienced throughout his long life of love all
sorts of contradictory emotions arising from the psychological condition of loving. Though Petrarca's ways of expressing the contradictions of love are of the utmost
importance historically and poetically, and provide insights
into the nature of loving, it is not with his brilliant presentation of love paradox that I wish to concern myself in
this chapter, but with his solutions to other evidently incompatible literary aims. Because of the extraordinary

effect of Petrarca's sonnet sequence upon the subsequent history of western love poetry, one sometimes fails to consider the magnitude of his invention. As he viewed his own work, he felt that he stood at a point at once of beginning and of continuation; the greatest laureate since antiquity,[1] Petrarca was crowned both for his classical traditionalism and for his classic inventiveness. His debt to ancient poets was very great, as he admits and proclaims. In the *Trionfo d'Amore*, he runs through the sequence of great poets of love:

> l'uno era Ovidio, e l'altro era Catullo,
> l'altro Properzio, che d'amor cantaro
> fervidamente, e l'altro era Tibullo.

(one was Ovid, another Catullus, / another Propertius, who sang of love / intensely, and another was Tibullus.)[2] Behind them stood the shadowy figure of Sappho, and since them, Dante, Cino da Pistoia, Guido Guinicelli, Guido Cavalcante, and a host of Sicilian and Provençal love poets whose names Petrarca cited, to deepen the tradition of which he himself wished to be a part. Though he borrowed much from the *dolce stil nuovo*, Petrarca was chiefly concerned with establishing his literary genealogy from the Roman and Greek poets, as his 186th and 187th sonnets show, where he invokes Vergil, Homer, Ennius, and Orpheus as poets who might be worthy to celebrate the great love he bears for Laura, a love for which his rhetoric is inadequate.[3]

[1] J. B. Trapp, "Owl's Ivy and the Poet's Bays: an Enquiry into Poetic Garlands," *Journal of the Warburg and Courtauld Institutes,* XXI (1958), 227-55.

[2] Francesco Petrarca, *Canzoniere, Trionfi, Rime Varie,* eds. Carlo Muscetta and Daniele Ponchiroli (Milan, 1958), p. 488. Translations are from Anna Maria Armi, *Petrarch, Sonnets and Songs* (New York, 1946).

[3] *Canzoniere,* pp. 244-45.

On that tradition of classical poetry Petrarca determinedly grafts himself, not just by tagging along at the end of the long train of great poets, invoking their names in piety, but as he says, by adapting his style to theirs: writing "tra lo stil de' moderni e 'l sermon prisco" (Sonnet 40). In the first place, Petrarca chose in the two persons for whom and about whom the *Rime* were composed symbolic figures, Colonna and Laura. *Colonna* is not only the name of an ancient Roman family whose fourteenth-century members were friends and patrons of Francesco Petrarca, but was also the word for "column," the architectural support for Roman buildings and one of the rewards for particular triumph. *Colonne* stood all over Italy, and in Petrarca's Provence, as the sensible marks of antique grandeur; however ruined by time, they provided immediate references both to the greatness and the continuity of the classical tradition.

As for Laura, evidently her existence as a real person was subject, even in Petrarca's lifetime, to some doubt, as the injured tone of his letter to Giacomo Colonna[4] makes plain. In that letter, Petrarca cleared himself of the charge of having made up the lady, of having given her that particular name for purely poetical purposes in order to celebrate his own notorious desire for poetic fame. Modern scholarship tends to confirm Petrarca's defense of himself and to assign the lady a father and a husband, as well as the death date Petrarca registered in the *Rime*: but her name, even if hers by baptism, remains, like Colonna's, a most significant piece of luck for Petrarca. In Sonnet 5, where he first anagrammatically introduces her name, Petrarca refers to Apollo's love for Daphne and his subsequent symbolic attachment to the laurel tree; throughout

---

[4] Petrarca, *Lettere . . . delle case familiari*, ed. G. Fracassetti (Firenze, 1892), II. 9. See the observations by Henri Peyre, *Literature and Sincerity* (Yale University Press, 1963), pp. 18-19.

the sequence, he returns again and again to the connection
between the god of lyric poetry and the laurel tree for
whom his lady is so felicitously named (Sonnets 12, 22).
The light green dress that the lady wore fuses with the
eternally green foliage of the laurel tree, as well as with
the eternal greenness of life and of verse itself.[5]

With a name, Petrarca provided Laura with a local
habitation, too: she lives in Avignon, on the Rhone. Near
the beginning of the sequence, Helicon springs up, the
muses' fountain from which all poetry must flow; from that
Helicon Petrarca derives his own stream:

> che per cosa mirabile s'addita
> chi vol far d'Elicona nascer fiume.
>
> (. . . an astounding sight is he who tries
> To draw from Helicon a newborn stream.)
>
> (Sonnet 7)

Sometimes it is the Rhone of which he speaks—

> Rapido fiume, che d'alpestra vena
> rodendo intorno, onde 'l tuo nome prendi,
> notte e dí meco disioso scendi
> ov' Amor me, te sol natura mena,
>   vattene innanzi. . . .
>
> (Swift river that from vein of Alpine blue
> Running around, whence you derive your name,
> Night and day carry your and my claim
> There where Love directs me and Nature you,
> Go on . . .)—   (Sonnet 208)

more often of the miraculous little tributary of the Rhone,
the Sorgue, rising as if spontaneously from the deep pot-
hole at the end of the Vaucluse and flowing down the
enclosed valley into the Rhone past Avignon, fed in fact
by the run-off from Petrarca's windy mountain, Mont

[5] *Canzoniere*, pp. 2, 4.

Ventoux, which he once climbed in the actual company of his brother and the spiritual company of St. Augustine:[6]

> Se 'l sasso and' ò piú chiusa queste valle,
> di che 'l suo proprio nome si deriva. . . .

(If the rock of this valley closed and stable,
From which has been derived its proper name. . . .)

(Sonnet 117)

The Vaucluse and the Sorgue nourish his memories of Laura dead and alive; even when he is in Tuscany, Petrarca longs to be "home," where he can think of his lady in peace:

> e si mia voglia in ciò fusse compita,
> fuor del dolce aere de' paesi toschi
> ancor m'avria tra' suoi bei colli foschi
> Sorga, ch'a pianger a cantar m'aita.

(And if my wish in this were satisfied
Out of the gentle Tuscan country air,
Sorga would still have me along the side
Of its dark hills, weeping and singing there.)

(Sonnet 259)

After her death, he invokes Laura, imploring her to look down on him by the waters of the Sorgue, where he sits to weep at the loss of his love:

> Mira 'l gran sasso donde Sorga nasce
> e vedra' vi un che sol tra l'erbe e l'acque
> di tua memoria e di dolor si pasce:
>   ove giace il tuo albergo e dove nacque
> il nostro amor. . . .

(Look at the rock where Sorga comes to leap,
You will see one, amid water and grass,
Who feeds on memory and pain, forlorn.

[6] Petrarca, *Epistolae Familiares*, IV.

> Where your house stands and where our love
> was born. . . .)   (Sonnet 305)

Petrarca forces the autonomy of his locality upon us: the Vaucluse is of major importance in the emotional economy of the sequence as well as the backdrop against which the passion is played out. When he had to leave Avignon and the Vaucluse, he located himself precisely, as in Sonnets 67 ("on the left shore of the Tyrrhenian Sea") and 69 ("between Giglio and Elba"); even in Tuscany, he longed for the melancholy scenery which he forced to reflect his own mood and to take the form of his emotions, just as the landscape of Arcadia was transformed into the pastoral mood, or Tempe into the lyric mood. His valley recapitulated Apollo's Tempe; his stream, welling so mysteriously at the wall of the valley, sprang from Helicon; his laurel tree was the eternal creation of Apollo's love. Like Helicon and Tempe, his actual Sorgue and Vaucluse became localities informed by the numen of poetic inspiration.

As the revived learning constantly rediscovered, it *was* possible to build in poetry a monument more lasting than bronze: with increased knowledge in the West of Latin and, later, Greek texts, the miracle of their preservation was submerged in the proud *topos* of their permanency. For Petrarca, the task was to ensure the same permanency for his verse—the classicizing and laureateship were all part of his life-long program to establish himself ineradicably in the roster of "classical" poets, poets whose work future poets could never afford to ignore.

In *Il Trionfo della Fama*, Petrarca dealt with the problem, in connection with heroic men and women, stressing the importance of writers on whom, after all, heroes are dependent for whatever fame they enjoy: in the *Rime*, however, Petrarca could rely only on himself to ensure the fame of his heroic love. On nothing but his skill with words (which he continually deprecates in a fine initial self-reference) could his dramatic presentation of himself depend: he was his own lyric subject.

In the very first sonnet, Petrarca gives notice that he writes of his "real" self—

> Voi ch'ascoltate in rime sparse il suono
> di quei sospiri ond' io nudriva 'l core
> in sul mio primo giovenile errore
> quand'era in parte altr' uom da quel ch' i sono. . . .

> (O you who hear in scattered rhymes the sound
> Of that wailing with which I fed my heart
> In my first youthful error, when in part
> I was not the same man who treads this ground.)
>
> (Sonnet 1)

—of a man changed and changing over what he was, from what he at any moment is. The sonnets conventionally record, then, a real man living through a real life of love, not a man held at the idyllic stasis of arcadian love, but a man suffering, lonely, busy, and, always, growing older.

Love is a wearing emotion, as Petrarca set it down, full of the psychological paradoxes of willing and unwilling, of love and distress, of self-hatred and pride:

> S'a mia voglia ardo, onde 'l pianto e lamento?
> s'a mal mio grado, il lamentar che vale?
> O viva morte, o dilettoso male,
> come puoi tanto in me, s'io nol consento? . . .
>   sí lieve di saver, d'error sí carca,
> ch'i' medesmo non so quel ch'io mi voglio,
> e tremo a mezza state, ardendo il verno.

> (If I burn at my will, why do I cry?
> If in spite of myself, what is the use?
> O living death, o delightful abuse,
> How can you conquer me if I deny? . . .
> So light in wisdom, so full of mistake,

That what I want I myself cannot learn,
And freeze in summer and in winter burn.)

(Sonnet 132)

Or, in a famous sonnet, often translated:

Pace non trovo e no ho da far guerra,
e temo e spero, e ardo e son un ghiaccio,
e volo sopra 'l cielo e giaccio in terra,
e nullo stringo e tutto 'l mondo abbraccio . . .
Veggio senza occhi e non ho lingua e grido,
e bramo di perir e cheggio aita,
et ho in odio me stesso e amo altrui.

(I find no peace, and I am not at war;
I fear and hope, and I burn and I freeze;
I rise up to the sky, lie on earth's floor;
And I grasp nothing and I hug the trees . . .
I see and have no eyes; no tongue, and cry;
I wish to perish and call help to fly;
And I abhor myself, and love another.)

(Sonnet 134)

In the paired sonnets, 229 and 230, he begins the first, "Cantai, or piango," and the second, "I' piansi, or canto," to show that wherever he begins his love song, his love is ever the same. Petrarca manages to balance the alternate and simultaneous freezing and burning attendant upon each love affair, but the effect of such tension, as exemplified in his sequence, is actually to wear him out, to wear out such beauty as he had had, to wear out his energy and his poetic talent.

The whole sequence records, always with the careful semblance of verisimilitude, the physical and spiritual changes wrought in the man and in his perception of love. Remarkably enough, the sequence does show that Petrarca was not, as he said in the first sonnet, the man he used to be. Time's wingèd chariot hurries ever nearer, but he does not exploit that fact to argue his lady into bed; rather, time was for him simply the unalterable fact of alteration. Seasons change, spring comes, night succeeds each day; and he can imagine Laura's golden head grey—

> e i cape d'oro fin farsi d'argento. . . .

(The gold head sprinkled with silver. . . .)

(Sonnet 12)

Throughout the sonnets, during Laura's life and after her death, days, nights, seasons, and years pass, with time and the turning skies, in an endless round until, at last, the poet too shall come to the end of his life. There is no one simple time, *edax rerum, edax Laurae et Francisci*, in these sonnets; there are many times, internal times measured by the poet's mood, and a ritual time measured by the anniversaries of his love.

> Benedetto sia 'l giorno e 'l mese e l'anno
> e la stagione e 'l tempo e l'ora e 'l punto
> e 'l bel paese e 'l loco ov'io fui giunto
> da' duo begli occhi che legato m'hanno.

(Blessed may be the day, the month, the year,
And the season, the time, the hour, the point,
And the country, the place where I was joined
By two fair eyes that now have tied me here.)

(Sonnet 61)

From that day,

> Mille trecento ventisette, a punto
> su l'ora prima il dí sesto d'aprile,
> nel labirinto intrai, ne veggio ond'esca.

(In thirteen hundred twenty-seven, I,
At the first hour, in April's sixth day,
Entered the labyrinth, and lost my way.)

(Sonnet 211)

he reckons his real life of service to Laura. The date gives
the verisimilitude to narrative otherwise too pat: and from
that precise date, precisely given, we can reckon with Petrarca the "seven and seven years" (Sonnet 101), enough
to deserve both Leah and Rachel, but not enough for
Laura, as he notes in Sonnet 206; the sixteen years of
Sonnet 118; the seventeenth year of Sonnet 122; the
twentieth of Sonnet 212. And then, suddenly, Laura died,
on the twenty-first anniversary of the day Petrarca first
saw her and fell in love:

> . . . 'n mille trecento quarantotto
> Il dí sesto d'aprile, in l'ora prima,
> Del corpo uscio quell' anima beata.

(Because in thirteen hundred forty-eight,
On the sixth day of April, the first hour,
That blessed soul left here her mortal weight.)

(Sonnet 336)

But he remained faithful, his twenty-first year of service
(Sonnet 271), the twenty-fourth (Sonnet 278), and for
ten years after her death (Sonnet 364).

Death may seem to have triumphed, since death unquestionably carried off the lady, but in reality Laura, like
Beatrice before her, leads her poet to the proper self-
preparation for beatitude and heaven. In imitation of
Beatrice, Laura grants him a vision of heaven (Sonnets
279, 280) and the hope of ultimate reunion there (especially Sonnet 334). The sonnets written after Laura's
death industriously translate Petrarca's earthly love into
spiritual love for his lady now in heaven. In one sense, as
he says, his life ended with her life; his heavenly life
began while he was still on earth, through his contemplation of her. In his last years, he only seemed to live:

> Dunque vien', Morte, il tuo venir m'e caro,
> e non tardar, ch'egli e ben tempo omai,

e se non fusse, e' fu 'l tempo in quel punto
che madonna passo di questa vita.

D'allor innanzi un dí non vissi mai:
seco fui in via e seco al fin son giunto
e mia giornata ho co' suoi pie' fornita.

(Then, come on, Death; your coming is my good.
Do not delay, because it is high time;
If it is not, it was the moment when
My lady from this life vanished away.

I have not lived a single day since then:
With her I walked, with her I end my climb,
With her feet I accomplished my workday.)

(Sonnet 358)

As the *Trionfi* ended with the *Trionfo dell' Eternità*, triumphing over Love, Chastity, Death, Fame, and Time, so all these themes in the *Rime* fuse into another kind of triumph of eternity: Laura, faithful Petrarca, love, fame, death, and time are all gathered into the divine artifice of eternity, which subsumes without losing the eternities of fame and art which Petrarca sought for himself and the lady he sang.

The Petrarca who is gathered into that artifice was, in the *Rime* at least, a real man: as he dealt precisely with the passage of time, so Petrarca dealt unsparingly with the effects of time on him. He was always "altr'uom da quel ch'i sono": his moods shift with the passing seasons and years as his external appearance changes. After eleven years of love, he can ask on Good Friday for relief from his own minor crucifixion:

miserere del mio non degno affanno,
reduci i pensier vaghi a miglior luogho:
rammenta lor come oggi fusti in croce.

(Have pity on my guilty pain and loss,

Lead my distracted thoughts to better state,
Tell them today you were nailed to the cross.)
                                        (Sonnet 62)

As his hair grows grey, he notes the fact—

Se bianche non son prima ambe le tempie
Ch'a poco a poco par che 'l tempo mischi,
securo non saro. . . .

(Until the temples of my brow are white,
That slowly time is mixing with grey hair,
I shall not go secure. . . .)   (Sonnet 83)

Di dí in dí vo cangiando il viso e 'l pelo. . . .

(Day after day I change my face, my hair. . . .)
                                        (Sonnet 195)

e vo sol in pensar cangiando il pelo,
quale ella e oggi e 'n qual parte dimora,
qual a vedere il suo leggiadro velo.

(And in thinking of this my hair turns white,
What she is like today, where she did soar,
As when I looked at her enchanting veil.)
                                        (Sonnet 319)

And, greatest of all:

Quel foco e morto e 'l copre un picciol marmo,
che se col tempo fossi ito avanzando
come gia in altri in fino a la vecchiezza,

di rime armato ond' oggi mi disarmo,
con stil canuto avre fatto, parlando,
romper le pietre e pianger di dolcezza.

(That fire is dead, in a small marble press.
Ah, if with time, it had increased in rage
As in the past, until my oldest age,

Armed with my rhymes that now I leave alone,

My grey-haired style would have broken a stone
With words, and made it weep from tenderness.)

(Sonnet 304)

The passions of his "grey-haired style" can break stone,
where the passions of his youthful style could not; the endless practice in versifying which his long love afforded
him, as well as the inevitable deepening of his emotions,
served to increase the power of his language. In the "Tran-
quillo porto" sonnet, he imagines Laura alive, talking to
him late in life, both of them realistically aged:

> Pur, vivendo, veniasi ove deposto
> in quelle caste orecchie avrei parlando
> de' miei dolci pensier l'antiqua soma,

> et ella avrebbe a me forse resposto
> qualche santa parola sospirando,
> cangiati i volti e l'una e l'altra coma.

(Had she lived, very soon I could afford
In talking to entrust to her dear care
The ancient load of my passionate thought;

And she perhaps would have answered and brought
To me her sighing and her holy word,
Our faces altered, and altered our hair.)   (Sonnet 317)

Laura, too, who changed like the real woman she was during her lifetime, would have been still more changed had
she survived her illness; would have become, like her
lover, unequivocally old (Sonnet 361).

All through the "lunga e torbida tempesta" which lasted
until "gli anni de la eta matura onesta" (Sonnet 317),
Petrarca's praise of Laura was so constant and so renowned
that he feared, as he said in the first sonnet, that

> al popol tutto
> favola fui gran tempo, onde sovente

di mi medesmo meco mi vergogno. . . .

(. . . in this land
To the whole people like a tale I seem,
So that I feel ashamed of my own name. . . .)

(Sonnet 1)

And yet this is surely what he was, and what he wanted to
be: a "fable" and a "fiction" for other people, something
more than simply himself, Francesco Petrarca. As he recorded the "real" Petrarca, growing thin and grey, he
made an ideal Petrarca, a poet fabulous in his fidelity and
endurance, remarkable even for his very reality, a poet
whose life took on the air—"l'aura," as he said himself—
of the laureateship of love.

The Vaucluse landscape became famous as the abode of
love because Petrarca, probably borrowing from Vergilian
techniques in the *Eclogues* which he knew so well, filled
his familiar landscape with his own emotions, presented
it as the projection of his own moods. In Sonnet 35, "Solo
e pensoso," Petrarca makes plain that love is always with
him, however hostile to love the environment may seem:

si ch' io mi credo omai che monte e piagge
e fiumi e selve sappian di che tempre
sia la mia vita ch' e celata altrui.

Ma pur si aspre vie ne si selvagge
cercar non so, ch' Amor non venga sempre
ragionando con meco, et io con lui.

(. . . I think now mountain and plain
And woods and rivers must know of what stuff
My life is made, that is congealed and dim.

Yet there is not a wild or rough terrain
Where I am not accompanied by Love
Always talking to me, and I to him.)   (Sonnet 35)

Petrarca pours his love into the landscape, and the love

thereafter resides in the landscape forever, its natural objects to remind him constantly of his love:

> Io amai sempre e amo forte ancora
> e son per amar piu di giorno in giorno
> quel dolce loco ove piangendo torno
> spesse fiate quando Amor m'accora. . . .

> (I always loved and I love dearly still,
> And to love even more each day I learn,
> That darling place where weeping I return
> Time and again when Love disrupts my will.)
>
> (Sonnet 85)

When he is in Florence, he longs for the Sorgue, where the landscape answers to his needs. Sonnet 301, written to the Vaucluse and the Sorgue, combines most fully the themes of the lady who had actually been in that landscape, the changing of the landscape with the poet's memories, and the recreative powers for the poet of the familiar places:

> Valle che de' lamenti miei se' piena,
> fiume che spesso del mio pianger cresci,
> fere selvestre, vaghi augelli e pesci
> che l'una e l'altra verde riva affrena;
>   aria, de' miei sospir calda e serena,
> dolce sentier, che si amaro riesci,
> colle che mi piacesti, or mi rincresci,
> ov'ancor per usanza Amor mi mena;
>   ben riconosco in voi l'usate forme,
> non, lasso, in me, che da si lieta vita
> son fatto albergo d'infinita doglia.
>   Quinci vedea 'l mio bene, e per queste orme
> torno a veder ond'al ciel nuda e gita
> lasciando in terra la sua bella spoglia.

> (Vale that is filled with my lamenting words,
> River that swells with all the tears I pour,

Beasts of the woods, fishes, and pretty birds
That are contained between either green shore,

Warm, serene air exhaling from my sighs,
Sweet lanes that all too bitter have become,
Hill that pleased me and that now can leave me numb,
Where my old custom Love can still entice,

I recognize in you the usual traces,
But not in me, who from that happy soil
Have been set in a dwelling of despair.

From here I used to see her; in these places
I come to see whence she ascended, bare,
Leaving inside the earth her lovely spoil.)   (Sonnet 301)

The lady, the lover, and the landscape—all are inseparable in the poet's mind and in the operation of the poetry.
Laura becomes one of those classical ladies to whom Petrarca likened her in Sonnet 260; the Helicon does rise
to make the Sorgue; the vale of Tempe is transformed
into the Vaucluse; Petrarca comes crowned with laurel
in the train of the classical poets he hoped to emulate. All
at once, lady, poet, poetic inspiration, and the award of
poetic eternity fuse: local time has been marked until it
passed into eternity.[7]

Once Petrarca had established the conventions of the
sequence of sonnets, the challenge shifted for poets imitating him: Ronsard and Spenser, for example, followed
Petrarca's idealism and attempted the eternization of
ladies frankly real and subject to the real ravages of time;
Shakespeare and Drayton pursued Petrarca's psychological
and metaphysical explorations of the state of love without
reference to a christened lady or any specific sojourn for
love. Sir Philip Sidney's sequence, *Astrophil and Stella*,
was composed on the Petrarchan model, with himself and
his lady thoroughly identifiable—in one sonnet, he sets

[7] For another treatment of this theme, see below, Chapter 5.

the riddle of her name and answers it again and again;[8] situations are given locality, and the poet's variable moods are recorded. The Petrarchan scheme shows through the surface of Sidney's style, in the punctuation of sonnets with songs, in the kind of imagery and conceit, such as the antithesis in the very last sonnet of the sequence:

> Ah what doth *Phoebus'* gold that wretch availe,
> Whom iron doores do keepe from use of day?
> So strangely (alas) thy workes in me prevaile,
> That in my woes for thee thou art my joy,
> And in my joyes for thee my only annoy.
>
> (Sonnet 108)

But the sequence is also very deliberately anti-Petrarchan, poking fun at conventional utterances of love dependent upon Petrarca's own idiom, poking fun even at itself when it follows that idiom too closely.

Sidney's originality in this sequence, chiefly, lies in his brilliant and self-conscious manipulation of language and ideas about language. He expands Petrarca's relatively few references to his own style into one of the major themes of *Astrophil and Stella*, a theme which works, often, ironically and even paradoxically to call into question assertions made in the very language Sidney examines.

The first sonnet, in which Sidney bewails his poetic clumsiness—

> But words came halting forth, wanting Invention's
>   stay,
> Invention, Nature's child, fled step-dame Studie's
>   blowes,
> And others' feete still seem'd but strangers in my
>   way—   (Sonnet 1)

introduces a metrical innovation into the sonnet conven-

[8] Philip Sidney, "Sonnet 37," *Poems*, ed. William A. Ringler (Clarendon Press, 1962). All references are to this edition.

tion. As Sidney's climax resounds, in the most blatant sincerity, " 'Foole,' said my Muse to me, 'looke in thy heart and write'!," the fact that the evident sincerity derives from Ronsard emphasizes the conventional nature of poetic honesty, or emphasizes that sincerity is a poetical *topos* like most thematic elements of poetry.

Throughout the sonnets, the critical theme recurs, ostensibly to underline the simple truth in the expression of Astrophil's love. In Sonnet 6, Sidney points to the artificiality of various poetic conventions—oxymoron, mythologizing, pastoralism, repetition of adjectives, the personification of pen and paper—contrasting such self-conscious versifying with his own "trembling voice" that "brings forth that I do Stella love"; though in Sonnets 19, 60, and 87, his language provides examples of just the sort of thing he deplored in this straight-talking sonnet.

Sonnet 15 criticizes "stepdame Studie," particularly the imitation of ancient poets and of "poore Petrarch's long-deceased woes." Sonnet 28 criticizes borrowing false allegories from other poets; Sonnet 74 rejects "Aganippe's well" and the "shade of Tempe"; although in Sonnet 55, Sidney thanks the muses for the "choicest flowers" of rhetoric they have granted him "to engarland" the "trew but naked shew" of his love. Indeed, in all these sonnets of literary criticism, Sidney belies his protestations of natural awkwardness and sincerity, for each sonnet performs variations on a far more daring, and more outrageously artificial, conceit than those he so pointedly denounces. Sonnet 15 ends, "*Stella* behold, and then begin to endite"; Sonnet 28 asserts that simply by saying "Stella," the poet reveals the richest source of the fullest love imaginable— that the real Stella is, in short, the personification of all that all poets might wish to say of love. Stella's name becomes for Sidney the very name of love:

> For let me but name her whom I do love,
>   So sweete sounds straight mine eare and heart do hit,
>   That I well find no eloquence like it.   (Sonnet 55)

From the *logos* of Stella's name, especially when confirmed by the kiss of her mouth, all necessary words can be unfolded, in perfect measure and meaning:

> How falles it then, that with so smooth an ease
> My thoughts I speake, and what I speake doth flow
> In verse, and that my verse best wits doth please?
> Guesse we the cause: 'What, is it this?' 'Fie no:
>   'Or so?' Much lesse: 'How then?' Sure thus it is:
>   My lips are sweet, inspired with Stella's kisse.
>   (Sonnet 74)

The more one examines the poems, the more brilliantly can Sidney be seen to operate within self-contradiction— Sonnet 90, "*Stella* thinke not that I by verse seeke fame," reverses the stock theme of the poet's gift of immortality to the beloved, an idea used, to comfort and to threaten, by Petrarca, by Ronsard, by Shakespeare and the rest. Rather, in Sidney's case, since "love doth hold my hand, and bid me write," it is the lady who gives fame to the poet. Of course, this is in fact nonsense: exceptional as Penelope Devereux was as an historical example of extramarital fidelity, it is not for her real life, but for her life in Sidney's poems, her life as Stella, that she is celebrated. She has her eternity from the man who could say, patently untruthfully,

> In truth I sweare, I wish not there should be
> Graved in mine Epitaph a Poet's name . . . .
>   (Sonnet 90)

In other words, Sidney is engaged in an artifice more artful than most of the poet's tricks, in contradicting his expressed statement by the operation of the poem in which that statement occurs. Sonnet 34, "Come let me write, 'And to what End?,'" plays on the poet's desire for fame, to be got by his wit; ostensibly Sidney rejects both the desire and the wit, in a line about wit, written in the most rhetorically compressed wit: "Peace, foolish wit, with wit my wit is mard." "Mard," then, belies itself: "mard" is what makes the conceit work. In the next Sonnet, 35, he asks,

> What may words say, or what may words not say,
> Where truth it selfe must speake like flatterie?

only to return to the *logos*-theme of Stella's name, which, since it names her who is infinitely rich, opens out into an infinity of words to express that infinite richness:

> Wit learnes in thee perfection to expresse,
>   Not thou by praise, but praise in thee is raisde:
>   It is a praise to praise, when thou art praisde.

Since Stella is all perfection, the poet's grief at her unkindness must turn to joy in the expression of itself—when his words reach her, which "well set forth his mind" and misery,

>   The sobs of mine annoyes
> Are metamorphosed straight to tunes of joyes.
>   (Sonnet 44)

The truth is that even grief caused by Stella is joy, so that when her voice reads his verse, "th'anatomy of all his woes,"

> O voice, o face, maugre my speech's might,
> Which wooed wo, most ravishing delight
> Even those sad words even in sad me did breed.
>   (Sonnet 58)

In the Ciceronian terminology with which the octave began, her voice "delivers" the delight from the grief.

Sonnet 63 most beautifully exploits the self-contradiction of all language, as Sidney interprets the grammar rules to invert the sense of what is, plainly, a perfectly simple utterance:

> O Grammer rules, o now your vertues show;
> So children still reade you with awfull eyes,
> As my young Dove may in your precepts wise
> Her graunt to me, by her owne vertue know.
> For late with heart most high, with eyes most low,
> I crav'd the thing which ever she denies:
> She lightning *Love*, displaying *Venus'* skies,
> Least once should not be heard, twise said, No, No.
> Sing then my Muse, now *Io Pean* sing,
> Heav'ns envy not at my high triumphing:
> But Grammer's force with sweet successe confirme,
> For Grammer sayes (o this deare *Stella* weighe,)
> For Grammer sayes (to Grammer who sayes nay)
> That in one speech two Negatives affirme.

The argument is sound enough, but it is not true. It cannot be made to work, except as a conceit: words will not be ruled by rules made out of words. Words do triumph, even over "real life," however, in this sequence praising sincerity: the artlessness which Sidney praises throughout the book yields at last to the emotional power of art. In Sonnet 45, the poet must become something other than a man to receive Stella's pity: he must become himself, a figure of tragedy.

> *Stella* oft sees the verie face of wo
> Painted in my beclowded stormie face:
> But cannot skill to pitie my disgrace,
> Not though thereof the cause her selfe she know:
> Yet hearing a fable, which did show
> Of lovers never knowne, a grievous case,
> Pitie thereof gate in her breast such place
> That, from that sea deriv'd, teares' spring did flow.

Alas, if Fancy drawne by imag'd things,
Though false, yet with free scope more grace doth breed
Then servant's wracke, where new doubts honor brings;
Then thinke my deare, that you in me do reed
Of Lover's ruine some sad Tragedie:
I am not I, pitie the tale of me.

The paradoxical "I am not I" can be taken as the motto for the whole sequence, perhaps for any such set of poems where the writer is both subject and creator: Sidney is, but also he is not the "I" that is Astrophil—although, of course, Astrophil's words must come from Sidney's mouth as Pantagruel's do from Rabelais'; words which create the truth and can therefore uncreate it, since they made it in the beginning; words which can at once, in triumph, assert and deny the truth of what they say.

3

John Donne and the Paradoxes of Incarnation

There are wonders in true affection, it is a body
of *Ænigmaes*, mysteries and riddles, wherein two
so become one, as they both become two. . . .
　　　　　　Browne, *Religio Medici*, ii. 6

Love being what it is, it is a subject excellently suited
to the paradoxical rhetoric. In the first place, "what it is"
is far from clear: love encourages that state of nescience so
congenial to paradoxes. For all the precision of physiological and psychological description and analysis of love,
love itself remains an intransigent mystery to those in its
grip, or even to those out of it. It is the world's most widespread wonder, and it persuades, every time, of its uniqueness. Love gives the illusion of solving, for a time at least,
the fundamental metaphysical problem of the one and
the many, since love so obviously supplies an example, not
of the unification of the "many," that is, of two, only, but
of the unification of opposites, male and female, as well.
Love provides the alogical illustration, plain to the plainest
sense, of identity in diversity.

　　Furthermore, love may be alogical, but its peculiar logic
persuades any lover of the truth of various psychological
miracles—that he and another human being are "one,"
that he knows another human being, that he at once understands and transcends "himself." Love heightens awareness
of the body and consciousness of one's self as an experi-
encing being; paradoxically, by this physical intensification
love induces the sensation of *ecstasis*: the articulation of

the body's most intense sensations results in the sensation of bodilessness, of physical as well as emotional transcendence.

Sensations of transcendence tax traditional languages. Mystics and theologians, worshippers of *logos* that they are, come to terms with the experience of deity by identifying it with the divine *logos*, the word for all words obviating the necessity of other words.[1] For them, it is axiomatic that the experience of the divine can be expressed only by the fundamental word for words that recollects, fits back all subsidiary words into itself, the *logos*. For most human beings, barred from mystical experience of deity, love is the school in which to learn the inadequacy of all words to express experience. In most situations of ordinary life, words are by convention regarded as adequate, are taken as "matching" reality, and verbal language is usually regarded as the proper medium into which experience is to be translated or transliterated. Love questions all these assumptions: love forces us back upon the fundamental autonomy of experience, subject to its own rules and inexpressible in any other medium. Love offers sensible conviction of the transcendence and therefore of the indescribability of any ordinary experience.[2]

For these and other profound social reasons, love itself becomes a traditional metaphor for other sorts of intense experience, particularly religious experience. The vicissitudes of lover and lass, elevated to King and Princess in the Canticles, provide the classic example of the holy mar-

---

[1] For *logos*, see Introduction, n. 38.

[2] See L. A. Willoughby, " 'Name ist Schall und Rauch,' " *German Life and Letters*, N.S. xvi (1963), 294-307; Elizabeth M. Wilkinson, "The Inexpressible and the Un-speakable: Some Romantic Attitudes to Art and Language," *ibid.*, 308-20; and "The Theological Basis of Faust's Credo," *German Life and Letters*, N.S. x (1956), 229-39.

riage of love to religion—and in the glosses to the Song of Solomon, even to religious institutions—a marriage forced upon transcendent religion because of the common nature of human love, which since it is part of ordinary human experience need never be "explained" as a metaphor for any other intense or transcendent experience.[3] Actually, to use love as a metaphor for transcendence is to evade the problem of expression: one inexpressible experience is simply evoked to enlarge or to identify a second.

In this sense, love has, like religion, its language of negatives—love is by definition indefinable, unidentifiable, inexpressible, and alogical.[4] Love provides, further, an experience of tautology: in the first place, through the intense consciousness it provides of the self as an entity; further, through the illusion it gives to lovers of their self-sufficiency. For all lovers, love "makes one little room an everywhere";[5] all lovers know that

[3] On this and related points, I owe much to my colleague Barry Ulanov, who is at work on an extended study of the "rhetoric of love" and Canticles.

[4] For this truism, one second-rate reference must suffice:

A Sonnet

Who can define, this all things, nothing love,
Which hath so much of every thing in it?
Which watry, with the planets oft doth move,
And with the zoane it hath a fiery fit;
Oft seizes men, like massy stupid earth,
And with the aire, it filleth every place;
Which had no midwife, nor I think no birth,
No shrine, no arrowes, but a womans face.
A god he is not, for he is unjust;
A boy he is not, for he hath more power;
A fiction 'tis not, all will yeeld I trust;
What is it then, that is so sweetly sowre?
No law so nice, that can his absence prove?
But (ah) I know there is a thing call'd love.

(*Facetiae* [London, 1817], II. 323.)

[5] John Donne, "The Good-morrow." Except for the Divine

> Shee is all States, and all Princes, I.
> Nothing else is.

Love in flood is, of all human (and animal)[6] experiences, sovereign over all others, as the *Phaedrus* makes plain, exploiting love as the metaphor for all other forms of "possession," of raptness. Perfect love casts out fear, certainly, but at its peak it casts out also every other emotion, activity, society, preoccupation, casts out even time itself.

> Love is a growing, or full constant light;
> And his first minute, after noone, is night.[7]

Love strives toward a condition of stasis which daily experience exists to deny; love at its best succeeds in the illusion that there is but one single eternal moment, even as the clocks tick, and hearts beat, to mark the passage of actual time.[8]

Love induces the concept of "perfection," of being fully present and fully experienced. Precisely by reason of its transcendent psychology, love is also readily felt as imperfection, as defect and defection, as suffering. In the mutable world to which human beings are consigned, all

---

Poems, all references are to *The Poems of John Donne*, ed. H. J. C. Grierson (Clarendon Press, 1912).

[6] "The Sunne Rising," ll. 21-22.

[7] "A Lecture upon the Shadow," ll. 25-26.

[8] For a complicated astrological and astronomical argument supporting the view that one of Donne's conscious aims in his love poetry was the establishment of stasis within or beyond the flux of experience, see John Freccero, "Donne's 'Valediction: Forbidding Mourning,'" *ELH*, xxx (1963), 335-76. Also above, Chapter 2. I am indebted for clarification of this point to Max Yeh's examination of stasis in the poetry of Louise Labé. For a discussion of the opposite problem for painting, the problem of movement, see E. H. Gombrich, "Moment and Movement in Art," *Journal of the Warburg and Courtauld Institutes*, xxvii (1964), 293-306; and the forthcoming study of *ecphrasis* by Murray Krieger.

too often love's first minute after noon *is* night; or, the flood of love ebbs to leave behind a litter of decay. Love provides rich materials for disquisitions upon contrast, contrariety, and contradiction, upon the difference between illusion and reality, between truth and falsehood. Love impels toward philosophical considerations, toward epistemological and ontological questions which other experience does not require. Like birth, to which it is so sensibly allied, love induces thoughts of death, as if intense experience of being must, to be fully felt, invoke its opposite, death or nonbeing. Seventeenth-century love poetry provides one record of the closeness of the ideas of love and death, since in the voluptuary's slang, "death" was the act of love: as we shall see, Donne made new combinations out of the common juxtaposition of love with death. Since love is mixed with the flux of everyday life, arises from it, and returns to it, however pure, distilled, and self-sufficient love may seem, it is necessarily compromised if it is to endure beyond the moment that seems eternal.

Nor is it just the pressures of the external world that compromise love: made up of "the many," a minimum of two, love's unity is always precariously maintained, always threatened by imbalance, if not by anarchy or secession. By the old physiology perfect balance could never long be maintained in a single body, still less in a corporation formed of two single bodies; by the new psychology, unmixed "love" is an impossibility; life is understood to be made up by the interplay of dialectically opposite emotions.

Freud's observations were, as he himself observed, far from new; literature provided him with clues and data often concealed by the disorder of ordinary inarticulate life. The pleasure-pain principle is, classically, observable in love. *Odi et amo* cannot be bettered as a plain statement of the anomalous substratum of human love. Out of

Catullus' perception of his simultaneous love and hate, of self-loathing precisely because of love borne, grew a great love rhetoric of oxymoron, antithesis, contradiction, and paradox exploited particularly in the Petrarchan tradition of Renaissance love poetry, indeed, exploited so widely as to become cliché. The lover's consciousness of a simultaneous present, past, and future; his sense of future hazards implicit in immediate choice; his awareness of joy remembered, experienced, or anticipated, even in his greatest frustration, make up a dialectical aesthetics of contradictory emotions "matched" by the rhetoric of paradox.

The word "passion" itself provides an example of the dialectic of love. Primarily "suffering," or being acted upon, "passion" has come to mean something quite opposite—a drive or force, impelling a human being to the most intense activity, thus combining in its meanings the whole of love's interchange, the acting and the being acted upon, the getting and the giving, and the getting and giving, furthermore, of both pleasure and pain, and both at once.

All of which is merely to say that love, especially as explored in the Petrarchan rhetoric of Renaissance love poetry, is by its nature a primary subject for paradoxical expression. In the work of John Donne, eminently a poet of love and eminently a paradoxist,[9] I wish to explore some of the functions and effects of love paradoxes. In his youthful *Paradoxes and Problemes*,[10] Donne sets the con-

[9] Of the many critical commentaries on Donne's ostentatious paradoxicality, I cite only Hansruedi Faerber, *Das Paradoxe in der Dichtung von John Donne* (Zürich, 1950), because it attempts a typological classification of all the paradoxes Donne used.

[10] John Donne, *Paradoxes, Problemes, Essays, Characters . . .* (London, 1652); Evelyn M. Simpson, *A Study of the Prose Works of John Donne*, pp. 17-19, 132-48.

vention for much in his *Songs and Sonets*: that is, both books are predominantly *outré*, arch, challenging, arbitrary, and independent, but through all the clang and clatter of the man-about-town rings still the soft serenade of the devoted lover.

In the first place, Donne's *Paradoxes and Problemes* is directly in the paradoxical line: he mocks the Stoical paradox, from Zeno to Cicero, in attacking the merits of the One and in defending the Many—"A Defense of Women's Inconstancy"; "That Good is More Common than Evil" (which, though it does not begin as such, ends up as a defense of the arts of the prostitute); "That it is Possible to Finde Some Vertue in Some Women"; "That the Gifts of the Body are Better than those of the Minde."[11] In contradistinction to the official misogyny of the schoolmen, who glibly blamed all male failures—to themselves, to their callings, to their God—upon the defenseless daughters of Eve, the humanists amused themselves with writing paradoxes, specifically so-called, in defense of woman—this time paradoxes because their argument ran counter to popular conventions of disesteem for the poor creatures. Erasmus, More, Agrippa, Rabelais, Du Plessis Mornay all tried their hand at defending the weaker sex with the serious moral purpose of installing woman in a higher social position than she had appeared to occupy.[12]

[11] *Paradoxes, Problemes*, pp. 1, 18, 33.

[12] There are many humanist defenses of women, of which I cite only some of the best-known: Henry Cornelius Agrippa, *De nobilitate fœminei sexus. The Commendation of Matrimony*, trans. David Clapam (London, 1545); Alexandre de Pont-Aymery, *Paradoxe apologétique, où il est fidèlement demonstré que la femme est beaucoup plus parfaicte que l'homme en toute action de vertu* (Paris, 1596); Desiderius Erasmus, *Christiani matrimonii institutio* (Basel, 1526); Joannes Ludovicus Vives, *De institutione fœminae Christianae* (Antwerp, 1524). Philippe du Plessis Mornay, Pierre de la Primaudaye, Sir Thomas More, Girolamo Cardano all defend the

Even in these exercises of his early years, Donne's equivocation emerges: he manages to exploit both the tradition of derogation and the tradition of praise—his "Defense of Women's Inconstancy" is a parody of the Stoical defense of immutability, a defense of frequent change, both of heart and of body. Women, of course, appear overtly as the more fickle sex: the changes of men's minds are considered only by implication. Women, for Donne, are properly described by paradox, since their deceptions can be likened to the conventional deception of formal paradox: "Are not your wits pleased with those jests, which cozen your expectation?"[13]

Love is in the fullest sense "common": women are "like *Flies*, which feed among us at our Table, or *Fleas* sucking our very blood, who leave not our most retired places free from their familiarity, yet for all their fellowship will they never be tamed nor commanded by us."[14] Each woman is a science past knowing:

---

moral and spiritual value of women in their works, as do a host of minor humanists. The point of course is that this opinion is a paradox, since whatever honor may have been paid women thitherto, they were "officially" regarded as inferior, dangerous, and even worthless.

[13] *Paradoxes, Problemes*, p. 2.

[14] *Paradoxes, Problemes*, p. 4. Fleas and flies in connection with sexual love are recurrent themes in the literature of paradox: see Lucian's fly (on which, see below, n. 41); Calcagnini's *Pulex*; Heinsius' *Pediculus*; and *Floia, De magna humani genesis floga . . . Authore Scharreo Schabhutio ex Flolandia . . .* [Bodley Shelfmark Antiq. e. X. 27]; that Donne knew Vergil's *Culex* may be assumed, but is established by his marginal notes to the Bodley copy of Pithou's *Epigrammata et poemata vetera* (Paris, 1550; Bodley Shelfmark 8° E. 4. Art. Seld.; see Simpson, p. 54). The common use of insects and "low" material in paradoxes is traditional in the praise of things without honor. In *Facetiae facetiarum* (Frankfurt-am-Main, 1615), p. 443, there is a macaronic poem on the flea; in

Learning affords us no rules to know, much less knowledge to rule the minde of a Woman: For as *Philosophy* teacheth us, that *Light things do always tend upwards*, and *heavy things decline downward*; Experience teacheth us otherwise, that the disposition of a *Light Woman*, is to fall down, the nature of women being contrary to all Art and Nature.[15]

Women ought to paint, for the superbly inconsequential reason that men "with more pleasure behold the *painted* shape of Monsters and Devils, whom true, we must not regard."[16] And women, though they are poison, follow the Paracelsan medical axiom, and provide their own physic with the disease, since they infect the lecherous with the pox and thus are at once the occasioners and avengers of one and the same sin.

The Paracelsan therapy, as opposed to the more "paradoxical" oppositional therapy of Galen, appears in another agile paradox, in which Donne argues the case for the puritan, platonic, Spenserian-Miltonic condition of love, that of a chaste and faithful marriage. "That Virginity is a Vertue" argues against its initial premise: virginity, merely the state of nature in girls, is in fact not a virtue (by the *carpe diem* argument) and is likely furthermore to "degenerate into a *Vice* (for *Virginity* ever kept is ever lost)." By the Paracelsan medicine, ("curing like by like"), "femal *Virgins* by a discreet marriage should swallow down into their *Virginity* another *Virginity*, and devour such a life and spirit into their womb, that it might make them, as it were, immortall here on earth, besides their

---

Dornavius' collection alone, there are fifty-five pages of flea encomia (Dornavius, I. 21-76). Nearer home, Robert Heath had a defense of the louse: "That next to Man, the Lous is the Noblest Creature," *Paradoxical Assertions and Philosophical Problems* (London, 1659), pp. 28-31.

[15] *Paradoxes, Problemes*, p. 3.   [16] *Ibid.*, p. 9.

perfect immortality in heaven: And that *Vertue* which otherwise would putrifie and corrupt, shall then be compleat; and shall be recorded in Heaven, and enrolled here on Earth; and the name of *Virgin* shal be exchanged for a farre more honorable name, A *Wife.*"[17]

At this point, the paradox doubles back on itself to escape into a new kind of declaration, one contrary to the expectation aroused by its own title, which had suggested an indefensible opinion addressed to an audience posing as libertines and light-minded men. So, again and again, do the *Songs and Sonets*. Like the *Paradoxes and Problemes*, libertinism is a dominant mode in the lyrics, cheerful in "The Indifferent," cynical in "The Communitie" and "Loves Usury," to name only a couple of examples. Sometimes Donne plays with "simple" impossibilities, as in "Song":

> Goe, and catch a falling starre,
>   Get with child a mandrake roote,
> Tell me where all past yeares are,
>   Or who cleft the Divels foot,
> Teach me to heare Mermaides singing,
>   Or to keep off envies stinging,
>   And finde
>   What winde
> Serves to advance an honest minde.   (ll. 1-9)

No man can catch a falling star and live—except George Herbert, who had immunities rarely granted to lesser men[18]—and no man can father, try as he will, a child upon a mandrake. Nor will the sophisticated Londoner of the late Renaissance seriously attempt explication of the scholastic riddles of the third and fourth lines. He might,

[17] *Ibid.*, p. 86.
[18] "Artillerie," *Works*, ed. F. E. Hutchinson (Oxford, 1953), p. 139.

however, if he traveled, have a chance at a mermaid; in the log of Hudson's northern voyage of 1608, the following entry appears:

This morning, one of our companie looking over boord saw a Mermaid, and calling up some of the companie to see her, one more came up, and by that time shee was come close to the ships side, looking earnestly on the men; a little after, a Sea came and overturned her: from the Navill upward, her backe and breasts were like a womans, (as they say that saw her) her body as big as one of us; her skin very white; and long haire hanging downe behind, of colour blacke: in her going downe they saw her tayl, which was like the tayle of a Porposse, and speckled like a Macrell. Their names that saw her, were *Thomas Hilles* and *Robert Rayner*.[19]

As for the next pair of lines, their propositions were a bit less "impossible" to believe, at least for the Stoic, who *could* ward off envy and *did* expect good men to achieve some advancement.

From accepted impossibilities, Donne moves into his personal (and courtly) system of impossibilities, in which all men know envy and all good men by definition fail of advancement. In the second and third stanzas, he swings between his derogation and idealization of woman: but the cynic is victorious. Even the uniquely faithful woman discovered by his traveling friend is, must be, unstable in time:

> Though shee were true, when you met her,
> And last, till you write your letter,
>   Yet shee
>   Will bee
> False, ere I come, to two, or three.[20]

[19] Henrie Hudson, *Divers Voyages and Northerne Discoveries, Purchas his Pilgrimes* (London, 1625), v. 575. To this I should like to add that I too, at the age of four, saw a mermaid in the ocean off Bay Head, New Jersey.

[20] "Song," ll. 23-27.

The libertine sings last, in a song sung, as its surviving setting indicates, to as sweet and soothing a tune as the heart could desire.

In a curious way, Cicero's *Paradoxa Stoicorum* provides a model for this particular pattern of paradox: evidently satires upon the behavior current in Cicero's time, his paradoxes ran counter to public opinion in their ultimate affirmation of the official—and ignored—Stoic morality. Cicero comments upon accepted manners and on accepted hypocrisy; his paradoxes affirm a simpler, truer morality than was possible in sophisticated Roman society. In the same way, beneath his libertine affirmations, Donne laments the fact that women are unfaithful, longs for a simpler morality of love; he is, in short, in this poem, the self-critical libertine.

"The Flea," so often cited to show Donne's extraordinary originality, is actually in the direct tradition of paradox, a discussion of something conventionally accepted as "without honor," something utterly beneath the rhetorician's or the moralist's notice. In the ancestry of that flea are the uncanonical Vergilian *Culex* and many paradoxical poems on other insects—the louse, the fly, and, precisely, the flea.

Donne's flea, like Burns's louse, is no respecter of persons: unromantically, it has bitten both the poet and his coy mistress, to become, in the poem, "you and I," "our marriage bed, and marriage temple," in spite of the lady's coyness and her parents' opposition. In the second stanza, the lady moves to kill the flea: the poet then invokes the guilt to be incurred by such triple crime (of murder, suicide, and sacrilege). It is paradox enough, surely, to turn a flea into a temple; a lesser man might have rested at that witticism, but Donne of course went recklessly on. The lady does kill the flea, does purple her "naile, in blood of innocence"; and denies that its death has lessened either her or her lover, who then turns her argument against her, from the triviality of the death of the flea to the slightness of the loss of maidenhead:

> 'Tis true, then learne how false, feares bee;
> Just so much honor, when thou yeeld'st to mee,
> Will wast, as this flea's death tooke life from thee.
>
> (ll. 25-29)

The real trick is not the poet's turning the flea into a temple, and into the lovers' legitimate child; it is permitting the flea in the poetic love affair in the first place, and then making the reader forget the realities of flea existence by means of the outrageous ratiocinations of the lover.

For the flea hops out of the harsh world of Renaissance realism, or reality, which intrudes in fact even upon the world lovers construct and set beneath a glass bell, out of time and circumstances, for the duration of the ecstasy. Donne himself, the author of the *Paradoxes and Problemes*, comes into love from that world of libertine realism: "Womans Constancy," "The Indifferent," "Loves Usury," "Communitie," "Confined Love" and "Elegie III: Change" are all variations upon the theme of inconstancy, itself a theme parodying official Stoical paradoxes. Change is a virtue and a natural state:

> Change is the nursery
> Of musicke, joy, life, and eternity.[21]

Furthermore, change is "useful," and in the stoical precept, usefulness is by definition a virtue:

> Who e'er rigg'd faire ship to lie in harbors,
> And not to seeke new lands, or not to deale withall?
> Or built faire houses, set trees, and arbors,
> Only to lock up, or else to let them fall?
> Good is not good, unlesse

[21] "Elegy III," ll. 35-36.

> A thousand it possesse,
> But doth wast with greedinesse.[22]

Sometimes the "change" is simply contradictory, as in "Elegie II," counterspeaking the Petrarchan ideal:

> Marry, and love thy Flavia, for, shee
> Hath all things, whereby others beautious bee,
> For, though her eyes be small, her mouth is great,
> Though they bee ivory, yet her teeth be jeat. . . .
>
> (ll. 1-4)

Flavia's truth is that of "witches, which impossible's confesse"—parodied love, like its great original, must deal in "impossibles" too. In "Womans Constancy" the lady can be true to herself only by being untrue to the poet, since her nature is untruth—she must play him false, and she must lie about playing him false. The serpent-beloved in "Twicknam Garden" kills her lover by her cruel persecution: but in the topsy-turvy propriety of this kind of love, she does right, since she is "therefore true, because her truth kills me." In "The Indifferent" Venus sentences the libertine poet to be true only to those ladies who are untrue to him. In "Love's Deitie" he accepts his fate:

> Falshood is worse then hate; and that must bee,
> If shee whom I love, should love mee.
>
> (ll. 27-28)

This particular poem simplifies the Catullan dilemma by dividing the love and the hate psychologically between the two persons of the poem; the lady hates the poet, who naturally loves her. The bitter-sweetness of love, Catullus' reductive *odi et amo*, ramified into thousands of Renaissance songs and sonnets, is characterized by the contradictions of oxymoron. Spenser provides a pleasant example:

---

[22] "Confined Love," ll. 15-21.

> Sweet is the Rose, but growes upon a brere;
>   Sweet is the Junipere, but sharpe his bough;
>   Sweet is the Eglantine, but pricketh rough. . . ,

he wrote, beginning a long catalogue of botanical oppositions culminating in the lover's expectations of reward:

> Why then should I accoumpt of little paine,
>   That endlesse pleasure shall unto me gaine.[23]

Figures of oxymoron and contradiction are, obviously, appropriate to any rhetorical exploitation of oppositions,
particularly appropriate to paradox. In love poetry dealing
with mixed emotion as its primary subject matter, such
figures of speech are designed to imitate, to match, the
psychological situation assumed or described in the poem.
They set the tone by describing confusion and contradiction; they do not necessarily, although they may, impel
the reader into further analysis of his own. Like Petrarca,
Spenser solves his problem by referring to a future in
which fidelity must be rewarded: but not all poets escaped
so easily from this contradictory situation. Sidney's state,
for instance, was miserable; like Petrarca, in love with
his living mistress, whatever he tried to do resulted only in
opposition to his hopes:

> Since shunning paine, I ease can never find:
> Since bashfull dread seekes where he knowes me harmed:
> Since will is won, and stopped eares are charmed:
> Since force doth faint, and sight doth make me blind. . . .

We might expect the poet to abandon a love which so evidently reaches but to dust: but this poem cheats our expectation. On the contrary, the poet says:

> I yeeld, ô Love, unto thy loathed yoke,

[23] Edmund Spenser, *Amoretti*, Sonnet XXVI, ll. 1-3; 13-14,
Poetical Works, ed. J. C. Smith and E. de Selincourt (Oxford,
1963).

demanding only that love enslave him by the law of arms.[24]

There are, unlike most Renaissance sonnets, very few oxymora in Donne's verse of this kind, where the ambiguities of love are not rendered static, but are, rather, explored actively. Donne does not seek (as poets of oxymoron tend to do) to describe the frustration induced by the mixed emotions of love; he attempts its evocation. So, I think, he tended to move from oxymoron, with its static formal balance, into the more abstract language of poetic pseudo-logic—or, he moves from figure of speech into figure of thought.

In "The Prohibition," for example, Donne deals in the love-hate dilemma, forbidding his lady to love him, since his joy in satisfaction may kill him and thus frustrate her: "If thou love me, take heed of loving mee." Nor must she hate him, though, since her hate must surely kill him, when

> thou wilt lose the stile of conquerour,
> If I, thy conquest, perish by thy hate.
> Then, lest my being nothing lessen thee,
> If thou hate mee, take heed of hating mee.
>
> (ll. 13-16)

If she love him, she must not love him; if she hate him, she must not hate him. The antithesis can be resolved, for the purposes of this poem at least, only by an arrangement of the two emotions which does not so much fuse as balance them. Literally, the poet equivocates:

> Yet, love and hate mee too,
> So, in these extreames shall neithers office doe;
> Love mee, that I may die the gentler way;
> Hate mee, because thy love is too great for mee;

[24] Philip Sidney, "Certain Sonnets, 1," ll. 1-4, 9. *Poems,* ed. William A. Ringler.

> Or let these two, themselves, not mee decay;
> So shall I live, thy Stage, not triumph bee;
> Lest thou thy love and hate and mee undoe,
> *To let mee live, O love and hate mee too.*
>
> (ll. 17-24)

Life itself results from the antithesis, which is contradictory in that it does not, this time, cancel, but creates.

Usually, of course, the lover cannot endure these pressures, and is consumed by such antithesis—

> When I dyed last, and, Deare, I dye
>   As often as from thee I goe,
> Though it be but an houre agoe . . . .[25]

>   and then thou shouldst, till I returne,
>   Since I dye daily, daily mourne.[26]

In "The Computation" the poet is reduced to a ghost; in "The Expiration" both he and his mistress become ghosts. Separation is death ("Soe thou and I are nothing, then, when on a divers shore"); for a lady to say "Go" is to order her lover's death, and his bidding her to go causes hers.

> Goe; and if that word have not quite kil'd thee,
>   Ease mee with death, by bidding mee goe too.
> Oh, if it have, let my word worke on mee,
>   And a just office on a murderer doe.
> Except it be too late, to kill me so,
>   Being double dead, going, and bidding, goe.[27]

And yet the poet cannot die, already dead: a paradox Donne exploited in other ways, in other poems.

But normally, to be "many"—that is, to be separate, apart, denied love—is by Parmenides' argument not to

---

[25] "The Legacie," ll. 1-3.
[26] "A Valediction: Of my Name in the Window," ll. 41-42.
[27] "The Expiration," ll. 7-12.

have "real" existence. So when lovers are separated, are "many," they too do not exist. Full of impossibles as it is, physical love neatly provides the sensation and the sense of oneness: it is an emblem of the many-in-one, in which to be "one" is, for lovers, to transcend the earthly state and to dispense with earthly things. By such a paradox, even the One can be dual: "Let us possess one world, each hath one, and is one,"[28] Donne says in one poem; and in another:

> Shee is all States, and all Princes I,
> Nothing else is.[29]

"The Extasie," whether the poem be serious or parody, certainly expresses the sensations of both exchanged and fused personality:

> Love, these mixt soules, doth mixe again,
> And makes both one, each this and that.[30]
>
> (ll. 35-36)

Time must be controlled, even annihilated, to achieve either *ecstasis* or *stasis*: in "The Computation," time is both an endless succession of hours and a single eternal moment, and both these things simultaneously. Perfect love reaches superlunary perfection, to transcend itself and earthly limitations to partake of immortality—when two people

> Love so alike, that none doe slacken, none can die.

Neither Parmenides nor Zeno could have disapproved of the conclusion of "The Anniversarie":

> Only our love hath no decay;
> This, no to morrow hath, nor yesterday,

---

[28] "The Good-morrow," l. 14.
[29] "The Sunne Rising," ll. 21-22.
[30] "The Good-morrow," l. 21.

Running it never runs from us away,
But truly keepes his first, last, everlasting day.
                                        (ll. 7-10)

The problems of sublunary love, even when it is "perfect," are, that things change, not merely lovers, as Donne
so grimly warned in a surrealist passage in The Second
Anniversary,[31] but all things about them, conspiring to
destroy the momentary balance that love attempts to maintain. Even in the world of timeless love, the mutable
effects Donne celebrated in his libertine passages threaten
every gain, as the sad poet must instruct his lady in "A
Lecture upon the Shadow":

Love is a growing, or full constant light;
And his first minute, after noone, is night.[32]
                                        (ll. 25-26)

Mutability threatens the existence of love, but it can also
be twisted to augment the idea of love, resulting in paradoxes of totality, as in "Love's Growth":

Me thinkes I lyed all winter, when I swore,
My love was infinite, if spring make it more—
                                        (ll. 5-6)

and that love *was* infinite, as proved by the fact that spring
can "make it more." "Lovers Infinitenesse"[33] combines

---

[31]   Poore cousened cousenor, *that* she, and *that* thou,
        Which did begin to love, are neither now;
        You are both fluid, chang'd since yesterday;
        Next day repaires, (but ill) last dayes decay. (ll. 391-94)

[32] The shadow is itself a regular subject of the paradoxist, because the shadow appears to be something that both is and is not.
Janus Dousa's "In laudem umbrae" and Erycius Puteanus' "Bruma"
are among the most famous humanist paradoxes of this sort; Martinus Schoock, the mathematician, later produced a "Fumi encomium."

[33] This poem plays upon a common subject of paradox, namely,

various tautologies, various paradoxes, to make it seem possible that love can simultaneously be complete and grow toward infinity:

> If yet I have not all thy love,
> Deare, I shall never have it all . . .
> Or, if thou gavest me all,
> All was but All, which thou hadst then—
>
> (ll. 1-2; 12-13)

or, the totality *then*, which seemed so utter, was but partial. Relativity can resolve this particular problem: the lovers' little room was for them "an everywhere" in which, by an easy miracle, they

> shall
> Be one, and one anothers All.

"A Valediction: Of Weeping" leaps wonderfully from nothing, of which only God could make a world, to "all." Lovers separated are "nothing," but if their love be strong enough, even their tears, round like the greater world, can become "all":

> On a round ball
> A workeman that hath copies by, can lay
> An Europe, Africke, and an Asia,
> And quickly make that, which was nothing, All.
>
> (ll. 9-12)

In his "nocturnal" upon the shortest day of the year (with its concomitant long lovers' night),[34] Donne depends upon

---

"omnis," or "all." The concept of totality presents logical paradoxes immediately upon its manipulation; Dornavius' great collection of paradoxes has a whole section of them, immediately preceding a section on "nothing." Cf. Shakespeare, Sonnet 40: "Take all my loves, my love, yea, take them all. . . ."

[34] "A Nocturnall upon St. Lucies Day" also has its connections with official paradoxy, since St. Lucy's day, so niggardly with its

the imagery of alchemical medicine to bear his paradoxical, contradictory meanings of creation and annihilation. The year is at its nadir—darkness controls light; the world is entirely dead, and the poet deader than the world, for

> all these seeme to laugh,
> Compar'd with mee, who am their Epitaphe.
>
> (ll. 8-9)

The death of the beloved has killed the poet, not outright, obviously, but impossibly, metaphorically, paradoxically:

> For I am every dead thing,
> In whom love wrought new Alchimie.
>   For his art did expresse
> A quintessence from nothingnesse,
> From dull privations, and leane emptinesse:
> Hee ruin'd mee, and I am re-begot
> Of absence, darknesse, death; things which are not.
>
> (ll. 12-18)

Regarded seriously and with respect, the alchemist's operation was analogous to the creative process of God Himself: the homunculus the alchemist sought to create was a direct copy of God's own creation. Only God, or the alchemist, or the poet can create out of absence, darkness, and death, can make something where nothing was before: can make light out of darkness, or raise the dead to a new life.

The second stanza deals, quite simply, with uncreation,

---

light, obligingly presents to lovers what they allege most to desire, a long uninterrupted night. J. C. Scaliger's "Brevissimae noctis felicitas" (Dornavius, i. 719), plays on the notion of the intensity of passion involved in a short summer night and (contrariwise) denigrates the slackness of long winter nights. Donne utilizes all these commonplace notions in his praise-dispraise of the year's most lightless day. Further, the poem is a witty variation on the Petrarchan "Zefiro torna," in which spring returns to the world but cannot reanimate the despairing lover.

with the reduction of creation to its components and, finally, to nothing once more: by their love the lovers have undone their world, which is to say, have undone their love and themselves.

> Oft a flood
> Have wee two wept, and so
> Drown'd the whole world, us two; oft did we grow
> To be two Chaosses, when we did show
> Care to be aught else; and often absences
> Withdrew our soules, and made us carcasses.

(ll. 22-27)

The Flood, however, drowned the world to remake it better. Chaos was, according to some doctrines, the matter of creation, originally unflawed: and "often absences" implies some sort of reconciliation, some sort of revival. So the poet can be "the grave/ Of all, that's nothing," and still live to tell the tale and to hope for a resurrection. Indeed, the image itself is ambiguous: he is the grave of all that is nothing, i.e., of all that is not, or has no existence (such as absence, darkness, and death), which, because they have no existence, cannot die and be laid in a grave; and he is the grave of a "nothing" nihilistically made up of all things.

But since the lady has died, the poet is robbed of his essence—or, his essence *is* nothing: he has become the elixir, the absolute essence of nothingness. He is entirely not-being; he has not even a shadow, that appearance at once of something and of nothing. The last stanza raises the alchemical imagery to something greater, turns from a possible imagery for God to God Himself:

> But I am None; nor will my Sunne renew.
> You lovers, for whose sake the lesser Sunne
> At this time to the Goat is runne

> To fetch new lust, and give it you,
> Enjoy your summer all. . . .   (ll. 37-41)

For him, there is a better occupation, to "prepare toward her" for a greater resurrection, for the permanent re-creation of himself out of the "things which are not" into an eternal reconciliation with love.

This "Nocturnall upon St. Lucies Day," is, in spite of its title, far more serious than most night-pieces, trading as it does in being and not-being and entirely abandoning the sphere and the language of the ordinary world of "becoming." In "The Will," Donne practices another kind of annihilation, this time brought to pass not by subtraction by the "ablative method," but by works of supererogation. He leaves his qualities to those who least require them:

> My faith I give to Roman Catholiques;
> All my good works unto the Schismaticks
> Of Amsterdam: my best civility
> And Courtship, to an Universitie. . . .   (ll. 19-22)
> To Schoolemen I bequeath my doubtfulnesse;
> My sicknesse to Physitians, or excesse. . . .
>   And to my company my wit.   (ll. 30-33)

The gifts, so deliberately useless, shall be useless in another sense, since he is determined to "undoe/ The world by dying," and to cause all graces, all beauties to become no more than "a Sundyall in a grave." This particular destruction is an emblem of more, for

Thou love taughtst mee, by making mee
Love her, who doth neglect both mee and thee,
    To invent, and practice this one way, to' annihilate all three.
                                        (ll. 52-54)

Poetry can create love, and uncreate it as well—but in jest, poems do but annihilate in jest.

"Negative Love" exploits direct paradox: love, like

God, cannot be reached directly, but only by the *via negativa*.

> If that be simply perfectest
> Which can by no way be exprest
> But *Negatives*, my love is so.   (ll. 10-12)

The poet's love is higher than all other loves, more refined and rarefied: "To All, which all love, I say no," denying the commonplaces of love's resort. He himself is a strange figure, however:

> If any who deciphers best,
> What we know not, our selves, can know,
> Let him teach me that nothing. . . .   (ll. 14-16)

If it were possible to know one's self in this poem, then that knowledge would be merely "nothing"—and that the poet knows already. The "decipherer" of one's self, who translates the "ciphers," the secret nothingness of one's self into another and clearer language, comes out with nothing all the same. The poem ends in a libertine paradox of unknowing:

> This
> As yet my ease, and comfort is,
> That though I speede not, I cannot misse.
>
>   (ll. 16-18)

He makes no effort, and comes to his satisfactions by his (Stoical) apathy, by his (Skeptical) ataraxy: Zeno's lessons are brought home to the situation of love. In this poem by equivocation the poet confirms himself instead of annihilating himself, as in the "Nocturnall." However "negative" his love may be, he is rewarded by being unable to "misse" whatever it is that he is deliberately *not* aiming at.

Sometimes Donne exploits paradoxical tradition more integrally than in patently rhetorical paradoxes. In the poem called "The Paradox" he relies on the Liar paradox of

Epimenides the Cretan, but makes that paradox his own, to express not simply the difficulty of expressing any truth about existence, but to justify the libertine's notorious unreliability in love:

> No lover saith, I love, nor any other
> Can judge a perfect lover;
> Hee thinkes that none else can, nor will agree
> That any loves but hee. . . . (ll. 1-4)

The proper lover is too busy loving to stop and declare his state of love: he will therefore disdain to accept the declarations of another lover who *can* interrupt the business of loving long enough to announce his love. In any case, the proper lover, even if he does not stop to do so, naturally believes that only he is capable of expressing love fully: believes, really, that no one knows love but himself. In this psychological context, Donne suggests a kind of answer to the Liar paradox, that conditions inexpressible in words are nonetheless expressible in experience; but in this poem, he does not stay to solve the riddle. Instead, he keeps the tone light, developing conventional paradoxes about love and death:

> I cannot say I lov'd, for who can say
> Hee was kill'd yesterday?
> Love with excesse of heat, more yong than old,
> Death kills with too much cold;
> Wee dye but once, and who lov'd last did die,
> Hee that saith twice, doth lye. . . . (ll. 5-10)

After the act of love, lovers' bodies are not really alive, have the semblance of life merely; their mouths have, therefore, no authority to make any assertion about their condition. The poet himself is in this predicament:

> Once I lov'd, and dy'd; and am now become
> Mine Epitaph and Tombe, (ll. 17-18)

a fine and familiar paradox of self-destruction, to which Donne often reverted, here given the final libertine twist:

> Here dead men speake their last, and so do I;
> Love slaine, loe, here I lye.   (ll. 19-20)

The pun is also the paradox; in the play on words lies not just the point of the poem, its epigrammatic moment of wit, but the poem itself. Take it away, and the poem disintegrates altogether.

"The Calme," the great verse-letter about the Islands Voyage, paints a picture of life in total suspension, of existence without change, a still life in which the laws of the natural world are transcended so that a man becomes "his own Priest, and owne sacrifice," to "lose his end" in the unpredictable absence of context—

> for here as well as I
> A desparate man may live, and a coward die.
>   (ll. 43-44)

Man had been "nothing," and is now "for nothing fit": he is undone, literally, has "no power, no will, no sense" and cannot therefore know his existence. "The Calme" is about the terrors of calm and the nightmares of nonbeing, but as in the "Nocturnall upon St. Lucies Day," the poet reverses the poem's whole proposition in the last couplet:

> I lye,
> I should not then thus feele this miserie.
>   (ll. 55-56)

The poem arrives at its conclusions by negatives: by identifying the state of uncreating described in the poem, the poet finds himself again, in the end re-creates the thinking, feeling, and willful man. The liar concept, instead of denying the assertions of the poem, as in "The Paradox," and therefore calling the whole poem into question, in "The Calme" reverses the apparent argument of the poem precisely to show the intensity with which the poet recovers his being.

In "A Valediction: Of my Name in the Window," Donne gives a brilliant display of interpenetrating logical imagery drawn from the macrocosm, from nominalism, as well as from a realistic but entirely invented projection of the behavior of his beloved in his absence. The poem ends:

> Neere death inflicts this lethargie,
> > And this I murmure in my sleepe;
> > Impute this idle talke, to that I goe,
> > > For dying men talke often so.
> > > > (ll. 63-66)

What precisely is "this idle talke"? The poet's protestations of love? Evidently he *does* love his mistress, at least for the poem's purposes, since the poem exists and he has, at least in the poem, written his name in her window. Does he expect to love her on his return? Not so certain by any means—if the "idle talke" is merely his speculations on her possible tendency to infidelity, then he will on his return love his still-loving mistress. But if the "idle talke" *is* the whole poem, then he will not.

In the Ovidian elegy called "Loves Warre"[35] the poet tries something different with paradoxes. The analogy of love to war is too common in western poetry to require comment: not in poetry only, but in ordinary speech the relations of courtship and consummated love are described in terms of battle, siege, and conquest. Petrarca had reformed the classical idiom in his sonnets to Laura as *bella guerriera* and the sonneteers after him exercised their ingenuity in perfecting the comparison. "Loves Warre"

---

[35] A famous humanist paradox, often reprinted in the collections, was Marcus Zuerius Boxhoorn's "Allocutio Nuptialis" written in honor of the marriage of a Goes to a Heinsius, in which the entire marriage episode is translated directly into military terms.

provides a fine example of the fusion of figure of speech
with figure of thought: Donne's use of the traditional
imagery relies upon our knowing the ways in which poets
assume love to be like war and exploits certain other likenesses not conventionally taken for granted. That is, he
passes from the analogy as a figure of speech to a figure
of thought, turning the one into the other. The poem
begins with the conventional image:

> Till I have peace with thee, warr other Men,
> And when I have peace, can I leave thee then?
>
> (ll. 1-2)

This war with his lady gives him a *raison d'être*. Their
warfare, too, is metaphorical, that is, both like and unlike
life at arms, and Donne exploits not just the analogies,
but the dissimilarities of his image:

> Heere let mee warr; in these armes lett mee lye;
> Here lett mee parlee, batter, bleede, and dye.
> Thine armes imprison me, and myne armes thee,
> Thy hart thy ransome is, take myne for mee.
> Other men war that they their rest may gayne;
> But wee will rest that wee may fight agayne.
>
> (ll. 29-34)

Conventional expectation is reversed in their war—"There
lyes are wrongs; her selfe uprightly ly"; "there men kil
men, we' will make one by and by." And, in this warfare,
cowardice is more useful, more delightful, and more creative than courage, cowardice is "braver" than courage:

> And shall not I do then
> More glorious service, staying to make men?
>
> (ll. 45-46)

This poem does more than exploit the metaphor of love
and war; it is also made up of the metaphor of that metaphor, made up of the antitheses and oppositions, conven-

tionally ignored by both poet and reader, involved in these metaphors. The lovers' "warfare" in "Elegy XX" is not destructive but constructive: where other men must wear themselves out traveling to wars, the lover travails at home with better, more civil, and more creative results. One way in which "Loves Warre" turns its figure of speech into a figure of thought is to "unmetaphor" it: the poet speaks as if there were a real war going on, which he has opted out of in order to dally with his lady. By exploiting aspects of the analogy other than those conventional in verse, Donne manages to have it both ways, forcing us to consider his title both as a figure of speech and as a figure of thought because the one is constantly played against the other, and neither can stand alone.

In another, and justly more famous poem, the imagery once more transcends the ornament to "become" the poem itself: in this case, too, the image in question is based upon a spiritual paradox. The circle is, officially in several traditions, the image of eternity, the paradoxical snake with its tail in its mouth, the emblem of totality, perfection, and thus of God. George Puttenham praised the verse-form, the "Roundell or Spheare," because it supplied the poetic counterpart to the circle emblem:

The most excellent of all the figures geometricall is the round for his many perfections. First because he is even and smooth, without any angle, or interruption, most voluble and apt to turne, and to continue motion, which is the author of life: he conteyneth in him the commodious description of every other figure, and for his ample capacitye doth resemble the world or univers, and for his indefiniteness having no special place of beginning nor end, beareth a similitude to God and eternity.[36]

[36] Puttenham, "The Roundell or Spheare," in *The Arte of English Poesie*, pp. 98-99. The passage continues:
"This figure hath three principall partes in his nature and use

The "Valediction: Forbidding Mourning" tries to answer the riddle set in so many of Donne's poems, of the One and the Many in love. What happens to love when lovers are separated, to lovers who

> by a love, so much refin'd
> That our selves know not what it is?
>
> (ll. 15-17)

---

much considerable: the circle, the beame, and the center. The circle is his largest compasse or circumference: the center is his middle and indivisible point: the beame is a line stretching directly from the circle to the center, & contrariwise from the center to the circle. By this description our maker may fashion his meetre in Roundel, either with the circumference, and that is circlewise, or from the circumference, that is, like a beame, or by the circumference, and that is overthwart and dyametrally from one side of the circle to the other." Then follows "A generall resemblance of the Roundell to God, the world and the Queene":

> All and whole, and ever, and one,
> Single, simple, eche where, alone,
> These be counted as Clerkes can tell,
> True properties, of the Roundell.
> His still turning by consequence
> And change, doe breede both life and sence.
> Time, measure of stirre and rest,
> Is also by his course exprest.
> How swift the circle stirre above,
> His center point doeth never move:
> All things that ever were or be,
> Are closde in his concavitie.
> And though he be, still turnde and tost,
> No roome where wants nor none is lost.
> The Roundell hath no bonch or angle,
> Which may his course stay or entangle.
> The furthest part of all his spheare,
> Is equally both farre and neare.
> So doth none other figure fare
> Where natures chattels closed are:
> And beyond his wide compasse,

The separation is a death, but a death like that of virtuous men, who pass mildly away. The lovers' two souls are either two or one: if one, then like a thin leaf of gold, "to ayery thinnesse beate"; if two, then like the joined legs of the geometer's compass. According to the poem's logic, the compass answer is correct. "Gold, to ayery thinnesse beate" is too formless an image for the poet's needs; lovely as it is, the gold governs but one stanza, while the compass governs not just the three final stanzas, but the whole poem.

> If they be two, they are two so
> > As stiffe twin compasses are two,
> Thy soule the fixt foot, makes no show
> > To move, but doth, if the other doe.
>
> And though it in the center sit,
> > Yet when the other far doth rome,
> It leanes, and hearkens after it,
> > And growes erect, as that comes home.
>
> Such wilt thou be to me, who must
> > Like the' other foot, obliquely runne;
> Thy firmnes drawes my circle just,
> > And makes me end where I begunne.

> (ll. 25-36)

As God has made the spheres of the third stanza perfect

> There is no body nor no place,
> Nor any wit that comprehends,
> Where it begins, or where it ends:
> And therefore all men doe agree,
> That it purports eternitie.
> God above the heavens so hie
> Is this Roundell, in world the skie,
> Upon earth she, who beares the bell
> Of maydes and Queenes, is this Roundell:
> All and whole and ever alone,
> Single, sans peere, simple, and one."

in their unchanging circles, so does the lady make him
"end" where he "begunne," in a perfect circle, too.
"Where first I ended, then I first began,"[37] wrote Drayton
in a marvelous sonnet of theological and logical antitheses
addressed to his lady; in this different context, both more
macabre and more optimistic, Donne asserts the same antithesis. For "in my beginning is my end," both in the
paradoxology of love and of Christian existence: man's
conception is the beginning of his dying; in life as in love
he dies daily;[38] and if a man is either virtuous or lucky he
dies to live, and his end *is* his beginning. The lady's firm-
ness draws the poet's circle just, makes him end where he
began—which in this poem was with the mild death of
virtuous men, who die into their life so quietly that their
friends cannot tell when their breath fails and their souls
depart.

In the first death in "The Valediction"—

> As virtuous men passe mildly away,
>   And whisper to their soules to goe,
> So that their sad friends do say,
>   The soule goes now, and some say, No,
>
> So let us melt, and make no noise . . .   (ll. 1-5)

—the poet contemplates this particular holy dying and
meditates its total meaning for both watcher and watched.
The final image in the poem, that of the circle drawn by
the compasses, is active: it returns, as it should, to itself,
to its beginning. The lover comes back from his travels
to his condition at the beginning of the poem, conjunction with the beloved; however deep his feelings for her,
his return to his lady is as little violent as his quiet de-

[37] Michael Drayton, *Poems*, ed. John Buxton (London, 1953),
Sonnet 32 (62).

[38] Ralph Venning, *Orthodox Paradoxes . . . The Second Part*
(London, 1657), pp. 4, 23.

parture, as the soul's departure in the poem's first death. In this poem, action and contemplation have become one, by means of the circle; the love that "was peace, that now is rage" of "The Canonization"; the love that "sometimes would contemplate, sometimes do" of "Loves Growth"; the love of "The Extasie" in which the shift from soul to body is "small change" is the perfectly regular formal love of this "Valediction." The circle image, so "even and smooth," is indeed Puttenham's "author of life" in this poem: it unites beginning and end of the poem to become the poem itself, drawing the various mixed kinds of love and death into one smooth circle-image that makes sense of sense.

These three poems illustrate quite different sorts of paradox—one, the most classical of all logical paradoxes, the next, a paradox that itself derives from a similitude, the third, a visual emblem designed to illustrate a conceptual paradox usually religious in its application. The poems fall into another kind of paradox, for though they spring from what seems an extraordinary lightness of spirit with regard to truth, a "libertine" sophisticated sense of the relativity of all earthly things, they make of the "nothings" of paradox extraordinarily subtle, complicated, and full poems. They are creative in the most daring way, forming of refractory contradiction something smooth, finished, and orderly, making "poems," accomplishments, in the manner of the deity.

To do so, they mix modes often enough—for the paradox, that mixer of the modes of truth, is also a tremendous mixer of literary modes. Donne's verse notoriously deals in mixtures—in the *Songs and Sonets* he runs from conventional vilification of woman ("The Apparition") to her hyperbolical praise ("The Sunne Rising"); his elegies are rarely elegiac and often indistinguishable in tone from his satires. For Donne at least, so deliberately posed in his poetic practice, so devoted to effects of surprise, the mixing and fusing of modes, tones, and genres afforded a congenial game: his considerations of lightness and gravity, of truth and untruth found in paradox a decorum exactly right, since it "exactly" matched inexactness, the shifting contours of his paradoxical subjects. For the poet attempting imitation of a contradictory reality, of contradictory psychological states, paradox meets the formal mimetic requirement.

THAT Donne used the language of religion to celebrate secular love, and the language of bodily passion to celebrate God, is one fact of his poetic practice that everyone knows. He was, of course, working in canonized traditions: in the language of philosophy, Uranian love is often indistinguishable from Aphrodite Pandemos; from the composer of the Canticles through the Middle Ages and the Renaissance, religion had been fortified, intensified, and incorporated in the language of physical love. Donne's love poetry is hallowed by many a religious paradox—in the anti-compliment of "Negative Love," relying upon the negative theology, and in the hyperbolical compliments of "A Lecture upon the Shadow," "The Good-morrow," and "A Valediction: Forbidding Mourning," the references are to the miracles and surrealisms of religion. In "Lovers Infinitenesse," where the changes are rung on lovers' vows, the gospel paradox sounds clear:

> Yet I would not have all yet,
> Hee that hath all can have no more,
> And since my love doth every day admit
> New growth, thou shouldst have new rewards in store;
> Thou canst not every day give me thy heart,
> If thou canst give it, then thou never gav'st it:
> Loves riddles are, that though thy heart depart,
> It stayes at home, and thou with losing savest it. . . .
> (ll. 23-30)

Donne often played upon the notion of miraculous resurrection, a primary article of the Christian faith. In "The Relique," for example, he fancies that he and his lady will meet "at the last busie day," since she must collect the bracelet—of her "bright hair about the bone,"—which he intends to wear into his grave. "The Canonization"[39] is the most famous of Donne's exploitations of profane and sacred love: the poet and his lady, quite obviously profane, became saints in the calendar of love. The first two stanzas deal in worldly imagery—of the court, the universities, commerce, law, medicine, and war—and all are rejected as irrelevant to the hermetic world of lovers. *Contemptus mundi*, normally invoked in a religious context, is demanded, not for God's sake, but for love's. By the involutions of the poetic logic, we learn that God's

---

[39] "The Canonization" has proved almost irresistible to explicators of Donne's work. I cite only some of the most distinguished: Cleanth Brooks, *The Well-Wrought Urn* (New York, 1947), pp. 3-20; Clay Hunt, *Donne's Poetry* (Yale University Press, 1954), pp. 72-95; Murray Krieger, *The New Apologists for Poetry* (Indiana University Press, 1963), pp. 10-28. The phoenix has a long history in encomiastic work, especially as a type for the resurrected Christ: cf. *inter alia*, Michael Maier, *Jocus severus, hoc est tribunal aequum, quo noctua, regina avium, phoenice arbitro* (Frankfurt, 1617) and a whole section of phoenix poems and prose passages in Dornavius. For phoenixes and urns, see *TLS*, 22 April 1965, p. 220. The fly has been slighted, I think: though all that was said about the fly's inordinate sexual appetite was an antique commonplace, and therefore, by the paradoxical logic, makes the low and physical fly a proper contrast to the elevated phoenix, the fly nonetheless has qualities in common with the phoenix, as Lucian testifies (*The Fly, Works*, ed. A. M. Harmon, 1. 82-95 [Loeb Classical Library]). The fly has immortality and rises from its own body to new life: when ashes are sprinkled on it, it rises and takes a new beginning; furthermore, says Lucian, some flies are bisexual (or perhaps hermaphroditic), like the phoenix and the contracted lovers of the poem. For the flea *topos*, see also Curtius, *European Literature and the Latin Middle Ages*, p. 84.

sake and love's are the same: and with that statement, of course, the poem began—

> For Gods sake hold your tongue, and let mee love. . . .

By the third stanza, the poet has rejected all the aspects of the public world to withdraw with his mistress into an entirely private world, profanely spiritual and spiritually profane:

> Call us what you will, we are made such by love;
> Call her one, mee another flye,
> We' are Tapers too, and at our own cost die,
> > And wee in us finde th' Eagle and the Dove.
> > The Phoenix ridle hath more wit
> > > By us, we two being one, are it.
> > So to one neutrall thing both sexes fit,
> > > Wee dye and rise the same, and prove
> > > Mysterious by this love.   (ll. 19-27)

First of all, names do not matter, as the images prove: the lovers are lovers, however anyone chooses to characterize them. Flies were, in the Renaissance at least, notoriously industrious sexually, shortening their lives with the incessance of their concupiscence. "Tapers," a word with more religious connotations than mere "candles," seems to be thematically utterly opposite to "flies"—but the two have in common that they consume themselves with their own burning. The eagle and the dove combine sacred and profane action, combine action and passion, though in a mixture different from that of the self-destructive flies and tapers. The eagle represents action in the secular sphere and St. John in the spiritual; the dove, passion as well as the Holy Ghost. Only in symbol, of course, not in nature, can the characteristics of eagle and dove be joined; only in poetry will their union produce a phoenix, the unique author of its own death and resurrection and therefore the symbol for Christ Himself. This image transcends the others and yet gathers them all, fly, taper, eagle, and dove, into one.

The phoenix is a paradoxical creature, and a sign for paradox too, since that bird unites birth and death, time and eternity, and at once partakes of and transcends the natural world. On the whole, the phoenix image is an elevated one, a fiction of the high tone—necessarily, Donne sets its sacred function in juxtaposition to the vernacular sexual reference, "Wee dye and rise the same." The whole stanza turns out upon examination to be made up of various "official" subjects for paradox, culminating in "the Phoenix ridle" which straddles the sacred and profane worlds, is neither sacred nor profane exclusively, but both at once. "Low things," or lovers' deaths, are made to stand for the greatest death of all; erection becomes a symbol for resurrection. Since the phoenix was so unequivocally an emblem for Christ, the riddle is and must be sacred also: in the paradoxical phoenix, the world of body is fused with that of spirit, but the two are also kept apart. Depending upon which perception we permit, we "oscillate" between the body and the spirit, aware of both, aware that each is a metaphor for the other, and that a metaphor makes a mutual comparison between things at once like and unlike. We are always conscious that the world of lovers is in fact different from that of saints—that lecherous flies, for instance, may not enter the universe of saints, but must remain recognized inhabitants of the lovers' world; that candles are more common images for *vanitas* and the life of the senses than tapers, reserved to sacred use: we are conscious, in short, that the phoenix image is not one image but two images acting simultaneously.[40] The paradox in this stanza is in the image itself—that is, the intrinsically paradoxical nature of the

[40] In Elizabethan practice, there was one conventional mode of

phoenix—and in the mutually indebted parts of the analogy, distinct even under the cover of the single set of words chosen to make up the meter and the rhyme.

In "A Valediction: Of my Name in the Window," Paul's words to the Corinthians appear in Donne's injunction to his lady, "Since I dye daily, daily mourne." In "The Computation," death, either in its colloquial or its common sense, makes the poet immortal, a conceit invoking both classical and Christian antecedents. "A Nocturnall upon St. Lucies Day" plays upon notions of creation *ex nihilo* which, though mediated by the mimetic imagery of alchemy, was the prerogative of God, a prerogative merely usurped by the creative artist. Oddly enough, the "Nocturnall" is indeterminate, again in a way out of official paradoxology: as the poet tells us, he is reduced first to nothing, then to something more nothing even than that first nothing. He is an extraordinary nothing—

> All, all some properties invest;
> If I an ordinary nothing were,
> As shadow, a light and body must be here—
> (ll. 34-36)

---

expressing two contradictory images simultaneously, in the madrigal settings. The verses set regularly exploit paradoxical or contradictory notions and metaphors (e.g., Chidiock Tichborne's "My Prime of youth is but a frost of cares," many times set); the musical arrangements accommodated the simultaneous utterance of, for example, "grief" and "joy" (Wilbye's "I live, and yet methinks I do not breathe," *English Madrigal Verse 1588-1632*, ed. E. H. Fellowes, Oxford, 1929, I. 239-45). Cf. Wilbye's work in *The English Madrigal School*, ed. E. H. Fellowes (London, 1924), II. 224 (pains/joys); 229 (rejoice/lament); 231 (tormented/contented); 233 (high/fall); VI. 37 (sigh/smile); 46-47 (comes/goes); 58 (fall/bound); 110 (glad/sorry); 124 (life/death); 133 (sweet/bitter); VII. 35 (thirst/drink; dream/wake); 43 (little/nought // all/little // all/nought). See also John Hollander, *The Untuning of the Sky* (Princeton University Press, 1961), pp. 26-31.

he is the "nobody" of a series of paradoxes descended from the quick-witted Odysseus.[41] Since he is both "nobody" and "nothing," it may be that all the assertions he makes in the poem are thereby nullified. Like the ambiguously religious "Valediction: Of my Name in the Window," "A Nocturnall" does not make its use of religious paradox entirely plain. The paradox is of course too open to be ignored, but too true a paradox to be defined. "A Nocturnall" is self-sufficient, turns in upon itself, completes its own self-sufficient mystery, whatever that dark mystery may be. "The lesser Sunne" that went in at the beginning of the poem does come out at the end, although the poem "ends" where it "began," at "the yeares, and the dayes deep midnight."

When Puttenham sought English words for classical terms of rhetoric, he chose for paradox "The Wondrer," since all paradoxes always attempted to command wonder and amazement. "Paradox" was, like Miranda, always a wonder, a miracle, an impossibility, a contradiction, or a mystery. More than this, the term "Wondrer" implies something fundamental about paradox—that it is only *apparently* self-sufficient, only *apparently* an independent work of art, circumscribed and sufficient to itself. In reality, paradox requires an audience, demands attention, solicits reactions on the part of hearers or readers, and, if successful, elicits specifically admiration, amazement, and wonder. Though directed toward frustrating conventional expectation, at unsettling "normal" reactions and normal constellations of thought and feeling, the paradox is itself paradoxical in requiring the cooperation of the audience it

[41] See below, Chapters 7 and 9; and Gerta Calman, "The Picture of Nobody," *The Journal of the Warburg and Courtauld Institutes*, XXIII (1960), 60-104.

seeks to frustrate. For its own existence, paradox requires active social participation among men.

FOR the love poems of Donne, so careful a constructor of his works, so social a man in his many tones and combinations of tones, Puttenham's term, "Wondrer," is particularly suitable, since Donne himself so often associated love, wonder, and divinity—in "The Anagram," he said, "All love is wonder"; in "A Valediction: of the Booke," "all Divinity/ Is love or wonder." Love's mysteries are unfathomable, can never be unperplexed by the mind alone, but only by the imaginative recreation of art, or by more love. All God's mysteries, including human love, are designed to perplex—how much more so, then, the metaphysical mysteries of divinity. God, "All changing unchang'd Ancient of dayes"; His Son, "Which cannot die, and cannot chuse but die"; the Virgin, addressed as "Thy Makers maker, and thy Fathers mother"; the Cross, which, "When it beares him, he must beare more and die" —all these, and more, subjects of divinity provided Donne with witty opportunities to bear witness to his own faith. Sometimes he managed independent and brilliant paradoxical plays in addition to the conventional ones, as in "The Crosse"—

>   the losse
> Of this Crosse, were to mee another crosse;
> Better were worse, for, no affliction,
> No Crosse is so extreme, as to have none.   (ll. 11-14)

In the combination of holy contraries Donne saw the chance to contribute paradoxical variations of his own. In 1609 the feasts of the Annunciation and of Good Friday fell upon the same day; for this coincidence of opposites, Donne composed a poem of antithesis piled upon tremendous antithesis. The circle plays its part: his soul

> sees him man, so like God made in this,
> That of them both a circle embleme is,
> Whose first and last concurre, this doubtfull day
> Of feast and fast, Christ came and went away.[42]

The calendar of the church provides, or provided in 1609 at least, a temporal and sublunary illustration of the concurrence in divinity of all temporally linear events. "Feast and fast" are compressed into one day, as if to confuse the true worshipper: which should he choose? should he observe both feast and fast? feasting, should he think of fasting, and of feasting in his fast? Both acts are appropriate, and simultaneously so, since Christ is always present, though no longer bodily on earth as an historical personage: on that particular day, He also "came, and went away." The figural tradition of Christianity, glossing Scripture always *sub specie aeternitatis*, stresses the simultaneity of all significant spiritual events, however disjunctive chronologically. The peculiarities of the 1609 calendar permitted Donne to exploit the trick, familiar enough in Christian rhetoric and doctrine, of compressing linear time into a single deeply significant point. That point then becomes less a *punctum temporis* than a *punctum ex tempore*.

These paradoxes of divinity are witty enough, but are also entirely conventional—had Donne been a less witty poet,[43] he still could not have avoided paradox in these

---

[42] "Upon the Annunciation and Passion falling upon one day. 1608," ll. 3-6; quotations from the Divine Poems are from the edition by Helen Gardner (Clarendon Press, 1952).

[43] An example of relevant "inevitable" paradox is Francis Quarles' epigram:

> I follow'd rest, rest fled and soon forsook me;
> I ran from grief, grief ran and over-took me.
> What shall I do? lest I be too much tost
> On worldly crosses, Lord, let me be crost.

poems, since the choice of a paradoxical subject is almost
automatic for any man engaged in writing about doctrine.
But there is opportunity for deployment, for independence
and poetic wit, in another kind of paradox inherent in the
practice of religion: that is, the psychological conditions of
the Christian state offer paradoxes of their own. Drayton's
great sonnet, "When first I ended, then I first began," is
a handy introduction to Donne's religious sonnets, since
Drayton's poem combines the worlds of religion and love
so that one is not certain to which the poem refers:

> When first I ended, then I first began,
> Then more I traveld, further from my rest,
> Where most I lost, there most of all I wan,
> Pined with hunger, rising from a feast.
> Me thinkes I flie, yet I lack legges to goe,
> Wise in conceit, in act a very sot,
> Ravish'd with joy amidst a hell of woe,
> What most I seeme, that surest I am not.
>   (Sonnet 32 [62], ll. 1-8)

The first, third, and eighth lines of this octave contain
paradoxes generally referring to man's spiritual condition;
the others may, but need not exclusively, deal with the
problems of earthly love. As the sonnet continues, its
spiritual preoccupations become clearer—

> I build my hopes a world above the skie,
> Yet with the mole I creepe into the earth,
> In plentie I am starv'd with penurie,
> And yet I surfet in the greatest dearth.
>   I have, I want, despaire, and yet desire,
>   Buried in a sea of yce, and drown'd amidst a fire.

The sextet seems to have settled on a religious theme, but
the final couplet is of course a familiar trope out of Petrarca.

(*Emblemes*, Book ii. xii, in *Complete Works*, ed. Alexander B.
Grosart [Chertsey Worthies Library, London, 1881], iii. 65).

Out of the long tradition of sonnet-celebrations of the painful delights of love, from Petrarca's "Pace non trovo, e non ho da far guerra," comes Donne's Holy Sonnet, "Oh, to vex me, contraryes meet in one," a sonnet which at first glance may seem more autobiographical and less traditional than it is. This poem not only develops the "contraryes," that is, the antitheses, of his situation, but becomes true paradox as well:

> Inconstancy unnaturally hath begott
> A constant habit—   (ll. 2-3)

a conceit invoking many of Donne's poems of the "humorous" behavior in "prophane Love." Like the old, profane love, this holy love is also "ridlingly distemper'd, cold and hott." It is no easier to love God than to love a mistress, in many ways, indeed, far more difficult. The courtship is chancy, too:

> I durst not view heaven yesterday; and to day
> In prayers, and flattering speaches I court God:
> To morrow I quake with true feare of his rod.

As the courtly lover had burnt and frozen in his fits of love, so now the poet suffers from holy chills and fever:

> So my devout fitts come and go away
> Like a fantastique Ague; save that here
> Those are my best dayes, when I shake with feare.
>   (ll. 12-14)

The "best dayes" are measured by moral necessity: if the poet cannot be secure from fear, contented in God's love, then he is surely safest fearing God, and fearing his own damnation. The transformation of a figure of speech into a figure of thought is perhaps best illustrated in this sonnet: Donne does not use oxymora, but stretches out the contradiction into full sentences—"Inconstancy unnaturally hath begott / A constant habit . . ."; "Those are my best dayes when I shake with feare"—stretched it out, indeed, into the poem's whole theme of the psychological double-ness required for "true" Christian experience.

"Batter my Heart, three-person'd God" is another love sonnet to the Lord, this time through the means of the familiar secular metaphor likening love to war: the octave bears out the triune oppositions of the struggle between God and the besieged soul of man. The sestet seizes on the other half of the usual metaphor: that is, the poet's rela-tions with God are not likened to a battle, but to the siege and seizure of profane love—

> Yet dearely I love you, and would be loved faine,
> But am betroth'd unto your enemie:
> Divorce mee, untie, or breake that knot again,
> Take mee to you, imprison mee, for I
> Except you enthrall mee, never shall be free,
> Nor ever chast, except you ravish mee.   (ll. 9-14)

Siege will not do: God must act precipitately, must abduct the poet from his earlier entanglement, by which he was contracted ("betroth'd unto your enemie") to sin. And only with God can a bridal be both consummated and re-main still to be consummated—the only chastity possible is confirmed by spiritual ravishment. That particular line unfolds to an interpretation literally true: that is, that the poet can be withheld from unchastity, in the worldly sense, only by being filled, totally occupied, by love of God, Who thus protects him against the physical temptations of the flesh. In this sonnet, also, one notes that the poet must play the woman's part: God is the ravisher, the enthraller, the powerful initiator of love, and the poet must remain passive, must be possessed as a woman is.

Donne's secular love poetry does not often express an-other great paradox of love, the fusion of roles of lover and beloved; only in "Breake of Day" is the person a woman.

In this Holy Sonnet he casts himself in the woman's part, but exploits the feminine sensation of oneness with the lover. God is of course the husband: all marriages are made in heaven with one Bridegroom, to whom men as well as women must be joined and to whom they must all submit. Not merely individual men, but also the Church, must submit to ravishment by the Lord, as the gloss on the Song of Solomon early announced. Donne's sonnet on the Church of England relies on traditions of chivalric romance as well as the imagery of the Canticles, resolved in and by a paradox:

> Dwells she with us, or like adventuring knights
> First travaile we to seeke and then make Love?

The Church's "kind husband," however, God Himself, acts very differently from the courtly husband: this husband cannot be cuckolded by his "Spouse so bright and clear":

> Betray kind husband thy spouse to our sights,
> And let myne amorous soule court thy mild Dove,
> Who is most trew, and pleasing to thee, then
> When she is embrac'd and open to most men. [44]

The world of love is, in one sense, a world of faith, too, though of faith constantly breached by human weakness. Husbands demand total fidelity; lovers demand the same: ladies make all sorts of impositions upon both husbands and lovers—and all of them know that this sort of vow exists to be broken. There are courtly codes of faithfulness within infidelity; and faithlessness, so deplored by the poets, has its bittersweet solace, if those same poets are to be believed. In the realm of human love, values are always at hazard; even where the sternest code of conduct has been set by lovers for themselves and scrupulously ob-

[44] "Show me deare Christ," ll. 9-14.

served, that code is merely a private one, liable under the public law—in other words, the firm values love tries to set are doomed from the start in a mutable, often topsy-turvy world. In the world of divine love, however, one partner never breaks faith: whatever mutable men and women may do, God never betrays, except into a love greater than before. Faith is always a wonder, in love or in divinity, so that the psychological paradoxes of conditional love readily translate into the spiritual paradoxes of Christian psychology. God's creative problem was to make flesh of the Word; the poet's, to make word and words of the mortal flesh—in other words, God's incarnation must be reworked, worked the other way, so that the transient experiences of the mutable body may lay some claim to immortality. Both unions of word and flesh are incomprehensible: in life, as well as in literature, one must resort to figurative language to express psychological states, especially those induced by sacred and profane love, marked by such significant intensity. The genre and rhetoric of paradox, since it exists, like love, in order to conjoin disjunctive elements and states of being, and to elicit the wonder appropriate to such states of being, are proper manipulations of the lame language by which men attempt to approximate their sensations of love's transcendence, whether that transcendence be momentary or eternal.

Part II
Paradoxes in Divine Ontology

4

Affirmations in the Negative Theology: the Infinite

> As for those wingy mysteries in Divinity, and ayery
> subtilties in Religion, which have unhindg'd the
> braines of better heads, they never stretched the
> *Pia Mater* of mine; me thinkes there be not im-
> possibilities enough in Religion for an active
> faith. . . .
>
> Browne, *Religio Medici*, I. 9

O F THE many Renaissance poets who dared to tackle the problem of God's nature in their art, and who there-fore turned to poetic account the traditions of the nega-tive theology, I shall discuss only two. As suggested in the introduction,[1] the idea that God cannot and should not be described in positive terms, but only in negative ones, derives from the first hypotheses of the *Parmenides* and was subsequently developed in the Christian tradition from the remarkably seminal writings of the pseudo-Dionysius. In the seventeenth century, discussion of God was by no means limited to negative definition, as the warring sec-tarians, unable to come to any consensus over the nature of His nature, had reason to learn. Though the *via nega-tiva* may have seemed a safe way to refer to God, it proved a difficult turnpike for writers to take, since its necessary paradoxicality endangered the substance and communicability of every utterance about the Deity. In the work of the two poets dealt with in this consideration, Thomas Traherne and John Milton, I wish to examine

[1] See Introduction, notes 9, 26-27.

manipulations of two of God's "negative" attributes—in Traherne's case, God's infinity;[2] in Milton's, His eternity. The word "infinity" might well be selected as the key to Traherne's total devotion, but no single word can be detached from Milton's vocabulary as "the" key to his thought: eternity is but one of the many subjects to which he gave his close poetic attention. Nonetheless, in their very different styles, both poets found solace in the negative theology, exploited it with a creative ingenuity worthy of the divine Creator whose works both poets praised throughout their writings. In Traherne's work, so often criticized for its looseness and aimlessness,[3] the many references to the infinite, infinity, and infinitude may seem merely the obvious preference of a man in love with the large, and consequently careless of stylistic details. His preoccupation, however, is not accidental but the result of deliberate choice; the idea of infinity informs his style, his

[2] For the paradoxical problem of infinity, see Bernard Bolzano, *Paradoxes of the Infinite.*

[3] Helen C. White, in *The Metaphysical Poets* (New York, 1936), is an exception; Gladys I. Wade (*Thomas Traherne*, Princeton University Press, 1946), Queenie Iredale (*Thomas Traherne*, Oxford, 1935), Gladys Willett (*Traherne, an Essay*, Cambridge University Press, 1919), Rufus M. Jones (*Spiritual Reformers of the 16th and 17th Centuries*, London, 1914) all assume that Traherne's spiritual life was made easy by his mysticism. E.N.S. Thompson ("The Philosophy of Thomas Traherne," *PQ*, VIII, 1929, 97-112) remarks on Traherne's likeness to Vaughan and to the Cambridge Platonists, whose philosophical systems were indeed much like his. John M. Wallace, "Traherne in Meditation," *ELH*, XXV (1958), 79-89, describes Traherne's meditative patterns, which are definitively dealt with by Louis L. Martz, in *The Paradise Within* (Yale University Press, 1964), pp. 35-102. See also A. L. Clements, "On the Mode and Meaning of Traherne's Mystical Poetry: 'The Preparative,' " *SP*, LXI (1964), 500-521; Harold G. Ridlon, "The Function of the 'Infant-Ey' in Traherne's Poetry," *SP*, LXI (1964), 627-39.

psychology, his cosmology, his metaphysics, and his theology. As for *Paradise Lost*, I suggest that the idea of eternity, ordinarily regarded as an unclassical idea, disruptive to firm poetics and narrative structure, played a major part in the arrangement of Milton's epic events and in the presentation of his idiosyncratic doctrine. In other words, as in the other chapters of this book, I stress the relation of particular paradoxes to the meaning and structure of the works in which they appear.

Thomas Traherne's glad affirmations of the bounty of his God border upon an attitude in singular disfavor in the period when he wrote—bordered, in fact, upon "enthusiasm."[4] "*Lukewarmness* is Profane," he wrote in his *Christian Ethicks*,[5] and certainly his imaginative writing demonstrates his repugnance to all indifference, all mere "contentment."[6] At a time increasingly emphasizing order and "reasonableness," there were few legitimate outlets for the *furor divinus*; Traherne is one of the few poets— with Henry More, in his unbridled speculations, and John Milton, in his extraordinary imagery—who found outlets for the exuberance and intensity of their love for God.

The "new space," the indefinite or infinite reaches of atmosphere beyond the earth and the planets, provided Traherne with the ground he required for his praise of

[4] Henry More, for example, deplored his own tendency toward enthusiasm, and thanked God that he could subdue it to the appropriate moderation. See Richard Ward, *The Life of the Learned and Pious Henry More* (London, 1710), p. 43.

[5] Thomas Traherne, *Christian Ethicks* (London, 1675), p. 169. Quotations are from this edition, abbreviated as *C.E.*

[6] The material and ideas of the next two paragraphs may be found discussed in far greater detail in Marjorie Hope Nicolson, *The Breaking of the Circle* (Evanston, 1950), specifically on Traherne, pp. 173-179; passim for the effect upon poets of their expanding universe. See also below, Chapter 6, "*Logos* in *The Temple*."

God. Like many of his contemporaries, he was always in search of metaphors for the Deity; and he laid hold upon one of the most daring, upon the idea of abstract infinity, together with its variations both of infinite cosmological space and of the infinite variety of all created things.[7]

[7] For an astonishing parallel to Traherne's joy in infinity, now demonstrated to be an actual influence by Dr. Carol L. Marks, see Thomas Jackson, *A Treatise of the Divine Essence and Attributes* (London, 1628). For the development of space theory in general see Max Jammer, *Concepts of Space* (Harvard University Press, 1954) [to be used with caution]; John Tull Baker, *An Historical and Critical Examination of English Space and Time Theories from Henry More to Bishop Berkeley* (Bronxville, 1930), and his "The Emergence of Space and Time in English Philosophy," *Studies in the History of Ideas*, III (New York, 1935), 273-93; E. A. Burtt, *The Metaphysical Foundations of Modern Physical Science* (Garden City: Anchor Books, 1954); Alexandre Koyré, *From Closed World to Infinite Universe* (Johns Hopkins University Press, 1957). There were two kinds of space theory open to Thomas Traherne: he might have adopted the Epicurean-Lucretian atomist theory, to devout believers ultimately deterministic and even atheistic, or he might have fallen back upon the combined Platonic and Judaeo-Christian theory of absolute space. The second plainly governed in the Renaissance; in England a Platonic and theological absolute theory, first suggested by More and later canonized by Locke and Newton, became the official space theory of the period. It was so much an "English" theory that Leibnitz, a relativist in space theory, called it "an *Idol* of some Modern Englishmen," because the notion had become so interlocked with the prevailing theological ideas. See Samuel Clarke, *A Collection of Papers, Which passed between the late Learned Mr. Leibnitz, and Dr. Clarke* (London, 1717), p. 55. For developing space theory, see Henry More, *Enchiridion metaphysicum* (London, 1671), p. 71; John Locke, *An Essay Concerning Human Understanding*, ed. John W. Yolton (London: Everyman, 1961), Book I, xiii, xvii; Isaac Newton, *Mathematical Principles of Natural Philosophy*, ed. Florian Cajori (University of California Press, 1934), p. 545; and Nicolson, *Breaking of the Circle*, p. 178; E. L. Tuveson, "Space, Deity, and the 'Natural Sublime,'" *MLQ*, XII (1951), 20-38.

For Traherne, the infinite cosmological space apparently "demonstrated" by the new astronomy offered a proper habitation for a God long recognized, in the metaphysics of theology, as "infinite." For such a God to be genuinely infinite, as Traherne saw, an infinite cosmos, or an infinite creation, was the only appropriate physical manifestation of that infinite, eternal, omnipotent, and omnipresent Deity. The infinite world was, Traherne declared well before Leibnitz, "the Best of all possible Works."[8]

By his own account, Thomas Traherne came "naturally" upon the idea of infinity:

Once I remember (I think I was about 4 yeer old, when) I thus reasoned with my self. sitting in a little Obscure Room in my Fathers poor House. If there be a God, certainly He must be infinit in Goodness. And that I was prompted to, by a real Whispering Instinct of Nature.   (*CM*,III.16)

The "real Whispering Instinct of Nature" had gifted that child with a metaphysical imagination which early framed speculations in his mind:

Som times I should be alone, and without Employment, when suddainly my Soul would return to it self, and forgetting all Things in the whole World which mine Eys had seen, would be carried away to the Ends of the Earth: and my Thoughts would be deeply Engaged with Enquiries, How the Earth did End? Whether Walls did Bound it, or Suddain Precipices. or Whether the Heavens by Degrees did com to touch it; so that the face of the Earth and Heaven were so neer, that a Man with Difficulty could Creep under?   (*CM*,III.17)

Som times I should Soar above the Stars and Enquire how

8 Thomas Traherne, *Centuries, Poems, and Thanksgivings*, ed. H. M. Margoliouth (Oxford, 1958). All references to the *Centuries of Meditation* are by number and lines, as in this case: *CM*, II.10.10; references to poems are to title and line numbers as given in Margoliouth's edition.

the Heavens Ended, and what was beyond them? concerning
which by no means could I receiv satisfaction. som times my
Thoughts would carry me to the Creation, for I had heard
now, that the World which at first I thought was Eternal,
had a Beginning: how therefore that Beginning was, and Why
it was; Why it was no sooner, and what was before; I mightily
desired to Know.   (*CM*,iii.18)

As Traherne passed from his childhood to Brasenose,
in the 1650's, he met with many new ideas of the "new
philosophy," and learned "Logick, Ethicks, Physicks,
Metaphysicks, Geometry, Astronomy, Poesie, Medicine,
Grammer, Musick, Rhetorick, all kinds of Arts Trades and
Mechanicismes that Adorned the World" (*CM*,iii.36).
He studied Albertus Magnus, Galileo, Hevelius, Galen,
and Hippocrates, and was thus introduced into a rich
world of traditional learning. But neither the new science
nor the old provided Thomas Traherne with a system by
which he could organize his extraordinary perceptions of
the plenitudinous universe:

Natural Philosophy teaches us the Causes and Effects of all
Bodies simply and in them selvs. But if you extend it a little
further, to that indeed which its Name imports, signifying the
Lov of Nature, it leads us into a Diligent inquisition into all
Natures, their Qualities, Affections, Relations, Causes and
Ends, so far forth as by Nature and Reason they may be
Known.   (*CM*,iii.44)

All these things—natures, qualities, affections, relations,
causes and ends—must of course be known by any God-
seeker, but so also, and much more, must "Humanity and
Divinity." When one has learned all this, he has reached
Felicity and knows enough, or knows all. "He that Knows
them for Valu, and Knows them His own: shall profit
infinitly" (*CM*,iii.41).

For his own infinite profit, which he then communicated

to anyone who would attend him, Traherne set about studying and expressing what infinity was. "Infinity," "infinite," "infinitely": these words echo throughout his *Poems*, his *Centuries of Meditation*, and his *Thanksgivings*. To understand Traherne's concept of "infinity" is to understand his metaphysical and moral universe, always seen *sub specie infinitatis*, or, *sub specie Dei*.

> His Omnipresence is an Endless Sphere,
> Wherin all Worlds as his Delights appear.
> His Beauty is the Spring of all Delight,
> Our Blessedness, like His, is infinit.
> His Glory Endless is and doth Surround
> And fill all Worlds, without or End or Bound.[9]

Positive discussion of God's negative attributes necessitated the language of Dionysius the Areopagite, Nicholas of Cusa, and Giordano Bruno, whose works indeed Traherne may have known.[10] In many of his poems, Traherne discusses the failure of the formal disciplines of learning to provide him with the "felicity" for which he yearned (*CM*,III.36,44); in one, he may even have been paraphrasing Nicholas' *Docta Ignorantia*:

> A learned and a Happy Ignorance
>   Divided me,
>   From all the Vanitie,
> From all the Sloth Care Pain and Sorrow that advance,
>   The madness and the Miserie
> Of Men. No Error, no Distraction I
> Saw soil the Earth, or overcloud the Skie.[11]

Like all three mystical writers (and many others), Traherne made use of the hermetic image of the infinite circle,

---

[9] "Thoughts IV," ll. 29-34.
[10] See Nicolson, *Breaking of the Circle*, p. 107; Iredale, *Traherne*, pp. 52-53.
[11] "Eden," ll. 1-7.

whose center was everywhere and whose circumference was nowhere. As he expressed it in the *Centuries of Meditation*, "for Being wholy evry where, His omnipresence was wholy in evry Centre: and He could no more, then that would bear: Communicat Himself wholy in evry Centre" (*CM*,II.82).

By this image, God was central to and immanent in every aspect of His creation, however various and dispersed. Traherne certainly rejoiced in the plenitude of the creation, and was entirely unafraid of its variousness and multitudinousness:

When I heard of any New Kingdom beyond the seas, the Light and Glory of it pleased me immediatly, enterd into me, it rose up within me and I was Enlarged Wonderfully. I entered into it, I saw its Commodities, Rarities, Springs, Meadows, Riches, Inhabitan[t]s, and became Possessor of that New Room, as if it had been prepared for me, so much was I Magnified and Delighted in it.   (*CM*,III.24)

When I heard any News I received it with Greediness and Delight, becaus my Expectation was awakend with som Hope that My Happiness and the Thing I wanted was concealed in it. . . . Thus also when any curious Cabinet, or secret in Chymistrie, Geometry, or Physick was offered to me, I diligently looked in it, but when I saw it to the Bottom and not my Happiness I despised it. These Imaginations and this Thirst of News occasioned these Reflexions.   (*CM*,III.25)

Ultimately he was able to see that although his felicity did not reside in the recesses of any specific "news," or in the ciphers of information new to him, he could find the mystery of God in all things—

> And every Thing is truly Infinite,
> In its Relation deep and exquisite. . . ;[12]

and all things finally in God:

[12] Poems from *Christian Ethicks IV* printed in Margoliouth, II. 187.

> From One, to One, in one to see *All Things*
>   To see the King of Kings
> At once in two; to see his Endless Treasures
>   Made all mine own, my self the End
> Of all his Labors! Tis the Life of Pleasures!
>   To see my self His friend!
> Who all things finds conjoynd in Him alone,
>   Sees and enjoys the Holy one.[13]

Traherne's exhilarated perceptions of the union of Many and One owes something to Ficino's commentaries on Plato and Plotinus,[14] still more to the dithyrambic outpourings of Pico della Mirandola upon both the miraculous manifold singularity of God's Creation and the glories of the human intellect which could, and did, encompass that Creation. Among the treasures of the *"Bodleian Library*, which is the Glory of *Oxford*, and this *Nation*,"[15] Traherne found Pico della Mirandola's tract, *De dignitate hominis*, from which he quotes in *Centuries* (iv.74-76, 81). Pico's enormous confidence in human powers and divine unity reinforced the conviction of Traherne's enlarged Platonic speculations. Like Pico, Traherne was able to attribute natural goodness to man and to mankind, even himself:

> How like an Angel came I down!
>   How bright are all Things here!
> When first among his Works I did appear
>   O how their GLORY me did Crown!
> The World resembled his *Eternitie*,
>   In which my Soul did Walk;
> And evry Thing that I did see,
>   Did with me talk.[16]

---

[13] "The Vision," ll. 49-56.

[14] Marsilio Ficino, *Opera omnia*, ed. M. Sancipriano and P. O. Kristeller (Torino, 1959), Vol. i: see especially *De creatione rerum*, *De divino furori*, *De lumine*.

[15] *Centuries, Poems*, i. xxix.

[16] "Wonder," ll. 1-8.

Only what Adam in his first Estate,
        Did I behold;
    Hard Silver and Drie Gold
As yet lay under Ground; my Blessed Fate
    Was more acquainted with the Old
And Innocent Delights, which he did see
In his Original Simplicitie.

Those Things which first his Eden did adorn,
            My Infancy
    Did crown.[17]

And like Pico also, in his confident Platonic epistemology:

Tis more to recollect, then make. The one
Is but an Accident without the other.[18]

Pico's Pelagianism struck a chord in Traherne, with his astonishing trust in the purity of human children.[19] Like a child, interested always in the novel and the exciting, Traherne responded to the variety of God's creation, "Beauty," as he said, "being a thing consisting of Variety" (*CM*,II.20); and,

Were all your Riches here in som little place: all other Places would be empty. It is necessary therfore for your Contentment, and true Satisfaction, that your Riches be dispersed evry where. Whether is more Delightfull; to have som few privat Riches in one, and all other Places void, or to hav all places evry where filled with our Proper Treasures? Certainly to hav Treasures in all Places.   (*CM*,II.77)

In "Shadows in the Water," a remarkably peaceful poem

---

[17] "Eden," ll. 29-38.

[18] "The Improvement," ll. 1-2.

[19] See Anne Davidson [Ferry], "Innocence Regained: Seventeenth-century Interpretations of the Fall of Man," unpublished doctoral dissertation, Columbia University, 1956; and Martz's comments, *The Paradise Within*, pp. 80-85.

in the tradition of the world upside down, Traherne reported how in his "unexperienc'd Infancy" he had made "a sweet Mistake":

> Thus did I by the Water's brink
> Another World beneath me think;
> And while the lofty spacious Skies
> Reversed there abus'd mine Eys,
>   I fancy'd other Feet
>   Came mine to touch and meet;
> As by som Puddle I did play
> Another World within it lay.
>
>   .   .   .   .
>
> Within the Regions of the Air,
> Compass'd about with Hev'ns fair,
> Great Tracts of Land there may be found
> Enricht with Fields and fertil Ground;
>   Where many num'rous Hosts,
>   In those far distant Coasts,
> For other great and glorious Ends,
> Inhabit, my yet unknown Friends.[20]

Traherne could stand not only the total plenitude of Creation, but was ever ready to imagine "more": plenitude for him was never "enough." He required an infinite God and an infinite space. Child and man, Traherne had experienced the meaning of infinity:

> . . . Infinity we know and feel by our Souls: and feel it so Naturaly, as if it were the very Essence and Being of the Soul. The truth of it is, It is individualy in the Soul: for GOD is there, and more near to us than we are to our selvs. So that we cannot feel our Souls, but we must feel Him, in that first of Properties infinit Space.   (*CM*,ii.81)

Given the idea, his mind could enlarge upon it infinitely: "Suppose it Millions of Miles from the Earth to the

---

[20] "Shadows in the Water," ll. 9-16, 49-56.

Heavens, and Millions of Millions above the Stars, both here and over the heads of our Antipodes: it is surrounded with infinit and Eternal Space" (*CM*,i.19). Obviously, such an idea can rest neither upon empirical test nor upon mathematical logic: its verification depended upon a psychological and philosophical axiom, the Platonic doctrine of innate ideas. Infinite space existed because Traherne's mind conceived of it; he would not, could not, have conceived of it if it had not been true—and been, furthermore, serviceable to the Lord.[21]

In general, Traherne's attitude to the creation, to God, and to space has seemed unqualifiedly happy, entirely uncritical. His space, infinitely extensive and infinitely filled with a beautiful and increasing plenitude of being, has seemed utterly different from the "eternal silence of infinite spaces" that so terrified the solitary Pascal.[22] In spite of his customary cheerfulness, however, Traherne had known, with Pascal, the *horror vacui*, had known as a small child the intuition of total loneliness, a self-conscious experience of the same intensity as his happier intuitions of infinity and purity.

Another time, in a Lowering and sad Evening, being alone in the field, when all things were dead and quiet, a certain Want and Horror fell upon me, beyond imagination. The unprofitableness and Silence of the Place dissatisfied me, its Wideness terrified me, from the utmost Ends of the Earth fears sur-

---

[21] Cf. Ward, pp. 7-8, for Henry More's similar experience. For the idea of infinity as necessarily innate, see Traherne, *CM*, ii. 80-81; "Sight," *Poems*, ii. 32-34; and Henry More, *An Antidote against Atheism* (London, 1654), p. 17. Ralph Cudworth, More's colleague and friend, was of the two more restrained in his idea of infinite space; he concluded that there was a potential rather than an actual infinity (*The True Intellectual System of the Universe* [London, 1678]), pp. 643-44.

[22] See below, Chapter 8.

rounded me. How did I know but Dangers might suddainly arise from the East, and invade me from the unknown Regions beyond the Seas? I was a Weak and little child, and had forgotten there was a man alive in the Earth.   (*CM*,III.23)

In a poem about the same experience far less powerful than his prose passage, Traherne experienced the natural world "As if no Kings/ On Earth there were, or living Things"; as if the world were inanimate, or neutral, like Pascal's world without secondary qualities, entirely indifferent to sensitive man:

> Ye Sullen Things!
> Ye dumb, ye silent Creatures, and unkind . . . .
>
> They silent stood;
> Nor Earth, nor Woods, nor Hills, nor Brooks, nor Skies,
>   Would tell me where the hidden Good,
>   Which I did long for, lies:
>   The shady Trees,
>   The Ev'ning dark, the humming Bees,
> The chirping Birds, mute Springs and Fords, conspire,
> To giv no Answer unto my Desire.[23]

Occasionally, when in this mood of alienation, Traherne accepted the notion that the world was inanimate—"The Material World is Dead and feeleth Nothing," as he wrote once, though he was quick to add: "But this Spiritual World tho it be Invisible hath all Dimensions, and is a Divine and Living Being, the Voluntary Act of an Obedient Soul" (*CM*,II.90). Only at very rare moments did Traherne record his feeling that the world was neutral; overwhelmingly, for him, the glittering, shining, variable world was an angel of the Lord, carrying the message of its divinity openly for every man to read:

> That all we see is ours, and evry One

[23] "Solitude," ll. 41-42, 49-56.

Possessor of the Whole; that evry Man
Is like a God Incarnat on the Throne,
Even like the first for whom the World began. . . .[24]

Like Pico's glorious man, Traherne's could not only perceive the intrinsic excellencies of the natural world, but could also internalize them so thoroughly that he could not be certain whether the natural world *had* intrinsic qualities or was fused with him: Nature's store

Was all at once within me; all her Treasures
Were my Immediat and Internal Pleasures,
Substantial Joys, which did inform my Mind.
        With all she wrought,
        My soul was fraught,
And evry Object in my Soul a Thought
        Begot, or was; I could not tell,
        Whether the Things did there
        Themselves appear,
Which in my Spirit *truly* seemd to dwell;
        Or whether my conforming Mind
        Were not alone even all that shind.[25]

Traherne's intense appreciation of the wonders of Creation re-created that Creation in his own mind—literally, epitomized the creation by his own imagination. In his optimistic mood, even emptiness, which had so frightened him as a child, became a ground for the works of his worshipping imagination:

But yet there were new Rooms, and Spaces more,
Beyond all these, Wide Regions ore and ore,
And into them my pent-up-Soul like fire
Did break, Surmounting all I here admire . . .
The Empty, like to large and Vacant Room
For Fancy to enlarge in, and presume

[24] "Ease," ll. 17-20.
[25] "My Spirit," ll. 40-51.

A Space for more, removd, but yet adorning
These neer at hand, that pleasd me evry Morning.[26]

Actually, as he considered the subject, Traherne came to fill "empty" space with "something," usually with God. In his *Democritus Platonissans*, another conspicuous space poem of the seventeenth century, Henry More postulated a "wide and wast Vacuitie" lying "even equall with the Deitie."[27] Henry More had his difficulties with the notion of space, the properties of which he for a time identified with the properties of God;[28] and his "heroine pupil," Anne Conway, followed that aspect of her teacher's thought when she wrote, "Neither is God said to exist in imaginary Spaces, because no place plainly agrees with God; but he may be said to operate there by his simple activity."[29]

Traherne also concluded that no space, however small or large, was in fact "empty," but must be always pervaded by God's immanence:

[26] "Nature," ll. 71-74, 77-80.

[27] *The Complete Poetical Works of Henry More*, ed. Alexander B. Grosart (Chertsey Worthies Library, London, 1878), p. 95.

[28] Henry More, *Enchiridion metaphysicum*, p. 71: "Unum, simplex, Immobile, Aeternum, Completum, Independens, a se existens, Per se subsistens, Incorruptibile, Necessarium, Immensum, Increatum, Incircumscriptum, Incomprehensibile, Omnipraesens, Incorporeum, Omnia permeans et complectens, Ens per essentiam, Ens actu, Purus Actus." Isaac Barrow, More's pupil and in turn the teacher of Isaac Newton, used more restrained language but made the same point in his *Usefulness of Mathematical Learning* (London, 1734), p. 171: "Nor can any infinity of Matter be deduced hence, but such Extension will follow as God shall please to assign it. Neither does this at all derogate from the *Divine Ubiquity*, which only figures that God is present in all *Space*, or that something may exist everywhere."

[29] [Anne Conway], *The Principles of the most Ancient and Modern Philosophy* (London, 1692), p. 22. Her "simple activity" agrees with More's "*Purus Actus*" in the preceding footnote.

> No empty Space; it is all full of Sight,
> All Soul and Life, an Ey most bright,
> All Light and Lov. . . .[30]

He was to be supported, later, in the official English space theory represented by Isaac Newton (the pupil of Isaac Barrow, who had been the pupil of Henry More), for whom infinite space was the "Sensory of God";[31] and who spoke of God in the *Principia* as "all eye, all ear, all brain, all arm, all power to perceive, to understand, and to act."[32] "Our little Sensoriums," as Newton called the human senses, comprehended God through the medium of His great sensory. For Traherne as well, God's "Essence also is the Sight of Things. For He is all Ey and all Ear" (*CM*,ii.84). Newton had been careful to qualify his metaphor of the sensory, by saying that God sensed "in a manner not at all human, in a manner utterly unknown to us."[33] Traherne disengaged the human sense also from its normal modes of perception into a "nakedness," a condition of apperception so purified that it was possible for a human being to die of a rose in aromatic pain.

> Then was my Soul my only All to me,
> 　　A Living Endless Ey . . .

> For *Sight* inherits Beauty, *Hearing* Sounds,
> 　　The *Nostril* Sweet Perfumes,
> 　　All *Tastes* have hidden Rooms
> Within the *Tongue*; and *Feeling Feeling* Wounds
> 　　With Pleasure and Delight: but I
> Forgot the rest, and was all Sight, or Ey. . .[34]

In that poem, the poet became "A Disentangled and a

[30] "Felicitie," ll. 19-21.
[31] Isaac Newton, *Opticks* (New York, 1952), p. 370.
[32] Newton, *Mathematical Principles*, p. 545.
[33] *Ibid.*, p. 545.
[34] "The Preparative," ll. 11-12, 31-36.

Naked Sense," utterly open to the sensations of God's creation, until his whole self was consumed in the act of sense perception:

> My Naked Simple Life was I.
>> That Act so Strongly Shind
> Upon the Earth, the Sea, the Skie,
> That was the Substance of My Mind.
>> The Sence it self was I.[35]

Traherne has managed to combine in one stanza two different philosophical traditions and psychological states, the optimistic mystical openness which perceives by the undefended senses, and the contemplative intellectual recreation which sufficiently internalizes external objects until, as the poet wrote a few stanzas later,

> I could not tell,
> Whether the Things did there
> Themselves appear,
> Which in my Spirit *truly* seemd to dwell;
> Or whether my conforming Mind
> Were not alone even all that shind.[36]

Traherne's contemplations were always active—in one poem, for example, the title "Walking" is a metaphor for thinking about the works of God.[37] The pressure in his head is realized in his question,

> Can all the Sky,
> Can all the World, within my Brain-pan ly?[38]

For Traherne, the answer was always in the affirmative. God was active like him, and demanded responsive human activity. Far from having absconded, Traherne's immanent and vigorous Deity constantly re-created Being and thus affirmed external nature and Himself in it. God's "Vol-

[35] "My Spirit," ll. 1-5.   [36] "My Spirit," ll. 46-51.
[37] "Walking," ll. 1-54.   [38] "Dreams," ll. 13-14.

untary Act" was not simply a sole historical gesture by
which the cosmos came into being, but was His continuous
creativity throughout the existence of the conceivable universe. As a constant actor, God appears in "The Anticipation":

> His Essence is all Act: He did, that He
>   All Act might always be.
>   His Nature burns like fire;
> His Goodness infinitly doth desire,
>   To be by all possest;
>   His love makes others Blest.
> It is the Glory of his High Estate,
> And that which I for ever more Admire,
> He is an Act that doth Communicate.[39]

"His Essence is all Act": for the acts of an infinite God, an
inconceivably large scene is required, which, for Traherne,
was very simply supplied by the newly confirmed marvelous "fact" of an infinite physical universe. Indeed, as the
"container" for the infinite God, only an infinite universe
was fit—God could not "dwell" in a less commodious
dwelling. However distant from the finite infinity might
be, God's activity was to "communicate" with his creatures, so that somehow they might come to "know" His
infinite greatness. Pico's cheerful conviction that man
could understand all things depended upon the preponder-
ant idealism of his philosophy: in a way, Pico's optimism
was easier than Traherne's. Pico was concerned with ab-
straction, rather than with Traherne's concrete "things";
the divine aspiration with which Pico assumed man was
endowed was directed toward ideas and the unification
of all ideas, however disparate they might seem. Traherne's aspiration was involved with real things, not
merely with the things themselves but also with thoughts
about what was, and with sensuous apperceptions of all

[39] "The Anticipation," ll. 91-99.

things as well: for him, space was actual, existent, extended, and fused infinitely with an infinite variety of things. Thus space could be perceived, somehow or other, by the human senses and the human mind. Moreover, infinite space existed not merely as the medium by which an infinite Deity communicated with His creation but also as the locus for God's own aspiration. Pico's divinized aspiration, the *furor divinus* with which man was to hurl himself upon the idea of God, was extended in Traherne's philosophy to become an attribute, not of man only, but also of God Himself. "Wants are the Bands and Cement between God and us," he wrote early in the "First Century" (*CM*,1.51), and went on to describe the desire of God that had prompted His acts of creation. Though it might at first seem "very strange that GOD should Want" (*CM*, 1.42), nonetheless His holy desires were the reason for the creation and the model on which man was to construct his ethics.

Critics have regularly commented on Thomas Traherne's bare considerations of the conventional sins and errors of Christian life: his ethics, like that of Ficino and Pico, pointed toward an intellectual and spiritual reconstruction rather than to any mundane program of daily behavior. The "acts" and "works" with which Traherne concerned himself were "metaphysical" in the literal sense of the word; he devoted himself to understanding the strenuous "want" by which man reached understanding of his God. In "Insatiableness," Traherne wrote:

> No walls confine! Can nothing hold my Mind?
> Can I no Rest nor Satisfaction find?
> > Must I behold Eternity
> > > And see
> > What Things abov the Hev'ns be? . . .
> > This busy, vast, enquiring Soul
> > > Brooks no Controul,

> No Limits will endure,
> Nor any Rest: It will all see . . .

> This busy, vast, enquiring Soul
> Brooks no Controul:
> 'Tis hugely curious too.
> Each one of all those Worlds must be
> Enricht with infinit Variety
> And Worth; or 'twill not do.[40]

And God had provided him with sufficient power to grasp what his "busy, vast, enquiring Soul" wanted:

> A vast and Infinit Capacitie,
> Did make my Bosom like the Deitie,
> In Whose Mysterious and Celestial Mind
> All Ages and all Worlds together shind.[41]

The enlightened soul "by Understanding becometh All Things" (*CM*,II.78) and so unites with the deity; and all the emotions become identified in one transcendent human act, imitative of the divine act: love is perception and understanding, and both are impelled by aspiration, desire —"Wants are the Ligatures between God and us" (*CM*, I.51). In Traherne's vocabulary, so little concerned with sin and so innocent of evil, words for qualities normally considered "bad" become meritorious: the poet "flagrantly Burned" with his desire for God (*CM*,III.38). And again,

It is the Glory of man, that his *Avarice* is insatiable, and *Ambition* infinite, that his *Appetite* carries him to innumerable Pleasures, and that his Curiosity is so Endless, that were he Monarch of the World, it could not satisfie his Soul, but he would be curiously inquisitive into the original and End of Things, and be concerned in the Nature of those that are beyond the Heavens. For having met with an infinite Bene-

[40] "Insatiableness," I, ll. 1-5; II, ll. 1-4, 13-18.
[41] "Silence," ll. 75-78.

factor, he would not be fit for his Bounty, could any finite Object satisfie his Desire.[42]

God's infinite gifts to man not only left him with an infinite cosmos, filled with an infinite plenitude of created things, to enjoy and through which to arrive at God Himself again; but also left man with a will infinitely free: "God made Man a free Agent for his own Advantage; and left him in the hand of his own Counsel, that he might be the more Glorious" (*CM*,iv.42.2-4). God's confidence in human good will equaled Traherne's, and that confidence could only elicit full human response:

O Adorable and Eternal GOD! hast thou made me a free Agent! And enabled me if I pleas to offend Thee infinitly! What other End couldst Thou intend by this, but I might please Thee infinitly! (*CM*,iv.43)

Like his will, man's thoughts have "An endless Liberty"[43] also to speculate fittingly upon the grandeur of God.

Literally, to "speculate": for man's mind with its infinite capacity was the proper mirror of the richness and extent of God's continued act, that is, the mirror of the whole material and physical creation. Such recreation was "the Voluntary Act of an Obedient Soul" (*CM*,ii.90), and could not fail to bring that soul to bliss. One of Traherne's most famous meditations is a successful example not only of his art—which was of course considerable—but also of his idea of the infinitely aspiring vision:

The Corn was Orient and Immortal Wheat, which never should be reaped, nor was ever sown. I thought it had stood from everlasting to everlasting. The Dust and Stones of the Street were as Precious as GOLD. The Gates were at first the End of the World. The Green Trees when I saw them first through one of the Gates Transported and Ravished me;

---

[42] *C.E.*, p. 93.
[43] "Consummation," l. 10.

their Sweetnes and unusual Beauty made my Heart to leap, and almost mad with Extasie, they were such strange and Wonderfull Thing: The Men! O what Venerable and Reverend Creatures did the Aged seem! Immortal Cherubims! And yong Men Glittering and Sparkling Angels and Maids strange Seraphick Pieces of Life and Beauty! Boys and Girles Tumbling in the Street, and Playing, were moving Jewels. I knew that they were Born or should Die. But all things abided Eternaly as they were in their Proper Places. Eternity was Manifest in the Light of the Day, and som thing infinit Behind evry thing appeared; which talked with my Expectation and moved my Desire. The Citie seemed to stand in Eden, or to be Built in Heaven. The Streets were mine, the Temple was mine, the People were mine, their Clothes and Gold and Silver was mine, as much as their Sparkling Eys Fair Skins and ruddy faces. The Skies were mine, and so were the Sun and Moon and Stars, and all the World was mine, and I the only Spectator and Enjoyer of it. (*CM*,iii.3)

"[A]ll the World was mine, and I the only Spectator and Enjoyer of it": the psychological condition described in that sentence, as in the whole passage, is exactly opposite to that described in iii.23, the *horror vacui* passage, though the author in each meditation describes himself as the sole inhabitant of a world which he poignantly perceives. In the *horror vacui* passage, the young Traherne's soul, "naturaly very Dark, and Deformed and Empty when Extended through infinit but empty Space," had not yet been filled with the "Amiable Ideas" which the true world provided (*CM*,ii.84). In iii.3, "The Corn was Orient and Immortal Wheat," the whole plenitudinous world appeared before him, shining and glittering in its ineffable beauty, arrested, checked, but at the same time full of motion and potentiality: at once perfect and being perfected. The metaphysics of physical things was, literally, revealed to him: "Eternity was Manifest in the Light of the Day, and som thing infinit Behind evry thing appeared"—as in the perfect still-life painting, where the surrealism of reality is expressed by the very exactness of reality.[44] In his great vision Traherne has caught the full and filling plenitude of variable things in a stasis rarely granted the writer and achieved by the very *process* of writing, in which the true meaning of all things is revealed *as revealing itself*, once and for all, to the poet preoccupied not with writing down his vision simply but with recreating it.

The vision is, specifically, of the infinity in every finite thing, of the fact that "every thing is truly Infinite,/ In its Relation deep and exquisite" because of the infinite grace of the infinitely creating God. God's love is

> an interminable Sphere, which as som say of the Sun, is infinities infinita, in the Extention of its Beams, being equaly vigorous in all Places, equaly near to all Objects, Equaly Acceptable to all Persons, and equaly abundant in all its Overflowings. Infinitly evry where. This of Naked and Divested Lov in its true Perfection . . . It filleth the World, and exceeds what it filleth. It is present with all Objects, and Tasts all Excellencies, and meeteth the Infinitness of GOD in evry Thing. (*CM*,iv.66)

Traherne found that the old images of a contained infinity, the sphere, the circle, the globe, and the ring, would not do: his concept of infinity forced itself beyond the "circle of perfection"[45] to communicate to men the idea of a limitlessly abundant Deity. When he was ready to transcend human limitations, to experience fully his own most intense perceptions of the metaphysics of Deity, Traherne abandoned the circular image of an ordered infinity to insist upon the imaginative re-creation of an infinite infinity:

[44] See below, Chapter 9.
[45] Nicolson, *Breaking of the Circle*.

One would think that besides infinit Space there could be no more Room for any Treasure. yet to shew that God is infinitly infinit, there is Infinit Room besides, and perhaps a more Wonderfull Region making this to be infinitly infinit. No man will believ besides the Space from the Centre of the Earth to the utmost bounds of the Everlasting Hills, there should be any more. Beyond those Bounds perhaps there may, but besides all that Space that is illimited and present before us, and absolutely endles evry Way, where can there be any Room for more? This is the Space that is at this Moment only present before our Ey, the only Space that was, or that will be, from Everlasting to Everlasting. This Moment Exhibits infinit Space, but there is a Space also wherin all Moments are infinitly Exhibited, and the Everlasting Duration of infinit Space is another Region and Room of Joys.   (*CM*,v.6)

"Real" spatial infinity became Traherne's material image for the spiritual infinity of God's goodness: and the infinite variation and stretch of man's speculation was the mirror image of that space. Only by understanding and accepting infinite space might man approach ultimate union with an infinitely infinite Deity. In logic, Traherne's tautology may be nonsense, but in the language of the imagination his obsession with God's greatness demanded tautology and infinite progression. With heroic fury, he insisted upon his paradoxical language until even the "real" infinity with which his perceptions began could not satisfy him; his infinite aspirations bore him not only beyond the physical boundaries of the world but beyond the logical boundaries of discourse as well, into the sphere of divinity itself, whose center was everywhere and whose circumference nowhere; where God's "Omnipresence is infinite wisdom and power; which filling Infinity is able to exert itself beyond all the bounds of Space in an infinite Manner all at once."[46]

[46] *C.E.*, p. 345.

5

Affirmations in the Negative Theology: Eternity

> . . . for who can speake of eternitie without a
> soloecisme, or thinke thereof without an extasie?
>
> Browne, *Religio Medici*, I. 11

PART of the difficulty of *Paradise Lost* lies in its enormous scope, which makes it almost impossible for modern critics to apply their analytical tools; part of its difficulty undeniably lies in its reliant reference to two worlds—the classical and the Biblical—now closed to the common reader. But part of its difficulty, and indeed a concealed difficulty, lies in the paradoxical nature of Christian doctrine. Milton wrote, as he intended, a poem doctrinal to a nation, a poem designed to teach men various lessons—that Christian doctrine is true, that man can and must live by it, that Christian life, though hard, is infinitely worth the effort it demands. Christian belief is not easy, even intellectually: the Christian is regularly required, for instance, to express his belief in a number of essentially paradoxical articles of faith. To begin with an orthodox paradox which Milton himself conspicuously fell away from, the Christian believes in a Trinity which is One and a Unity which is Triune. He believes in an unknowable God and is instructed that his duty is to know that God; he believes in the resurrection of the dead. In fact, every time the Christian affirms his Creed, he formally recapitulates a number of logical or empirical paradoxes. The point of such formulation, of course, is the denial of logic and mundane experience to assert the mystery of faith.[1] Quoting Tertullian, Sir Thomas Browne proclaimed his especial pleasure in believing what was impossible; a whole school of poets contemporary with him and with Milton exploited in rhetorical paradoxes of great brilliance the conventional Christian paradoxes of grace. But Milton was no Donne, no Herbert, no Alabaster: he was not concerned with the verbal pyrotechnics of theological wit so much as with the straight sense of Christian doctrine and Christian history. According to the evidence of his *De doctrina Christiana* he rejected as much of the paradoxical matter of orthodox Christian belief as he was able and used a fairly modern logic to substantiate his own heterodoxies. Nonetheless, some Christian paradox is inevitable, even for so rationalist and classical a poet as Milton. In an article of fundamental importance, "Milton and the Paradox of the Fortunate Fall," Professor Lovejoy discussed the history and demonstrated the function of the doctrinal paradox central to *Paradise Lost*, without which the poem could not have come into existence. There are other "orthodox paradoxes"[2] in *Paradise Lost*: here, I am not concerned to identify them all or to trace their histories among the labyrinths of patristic and conciliar writings, but simply to discuss two related aporetic doctrinal paradoxes directly affecting the poem's structure.

The first of these paradoxes is of major philosophical

---

[1] For interesting comments on this point, see Arthur Barker, "Structural Pattern in *Paradise Lost*," *PQ*, xxviii (1949), 18; Kester Svendsen, *Milton and Science* (Harvard University Press, 1956), pp. 105-107; Jackson I. Cope, *The Metaphoric Structure of Paradise Lost* (Johns Hopkins Press, 1962), pp. 50-71.

[2] See A. O. Lovejoy, *Essays in the History of Ideas* (Johns Hopkins Press, 1948), pp. 277-95; and articles by Clarence C. Green, *MLN*, liii (1938), 557-71; Millicent Bell, *PMLA*, lxviii (1953), 863-83, as well as Mrs. Bell's exchange with Wayne Shumaker, *PMLA*, lxx (1955), 1185-1203.

importance: the existence at once of foreknowledge on the part of God and of free will on the part of man. Generations of students have, like Milton's devils, debated in vain

> Fixt Fate, Free Will, foreknowledge absolute,
> And found no end, in wand'ring mazes lost. (II. 559-60)

The devils could never really hope to find an answer, since alone of God's creatures they were subject to a "fixt Fate" that ruled their existence forever, after their first unwise exercise of free will in heaven. They could never thereafter know good, though they might recognize it; for them the paradox of foreknowledge and free will can only remain unresolved.

Not so for Adam and Eve and Milton's Christian readers. The data of faith are that God foreknows—and since He is perfect, He can foreknow only what is true[3]—and that man's will is incontrovertibly free to make his moral choices in his world. Upon the proper understanding of this paradox Christian salvation may depend; on the mundane plane, to understand the poem at all, readers of *Paradise Lost* must accept the paradox and come to some sort of terms with it.

The paradox of foreknowledge and free will relates to another metaphysical paradox, that of eternity and time. Eternity was one of God's attributes and a condition of perfection, of which in art and poetry the circle was com-

[3] See Ralph Venning, *Orthodox Paradoxes* . . . (London, 1650), p. 7: ". . . God foreknew all things; and whatever he foreknew to be, must needs be, and yet . . . God's foreknowledge was not the cause of their being." Compare Herbert Palmer, *Memorials of Godliness & Christianity* (London, 1657), p. 62: "He [the Christian] knows God's providence orders all things; yet is he so diligent in his business, as if he were to cut out his own fortune." See also Milton, *Of Christian Doctrine, Works*, ed. Frank Allen Patterson, *et al.*, (Columbia University Press, 1933), XIV, 65.

monly the emblem.[4] God has existed from eternity. He has neither beginning nor end; even in his name, Jehovah, He contains all imaginable time, the past, the present, and the future.[5] "God is the *Alpha* and *Omega*, the *beginning* and the *end*," as Ralph Venning put it in his *Orthodox Paradoxes* (p.2); "God had never a *beginning* and shall never have an *end*." Even Beelzebub knows this and tells the devils in hell that

> he, be sure,
> In highth or depth, still first and last will Reign
> Sole King. . . .   (*PL*, II. 323-25)

It is in the medium of His eternity that God has fore-knowledge: because He "is" all things and thus knows all things, God is beyond time and outside it, as well as in it. All things, including the historical events that men experience and identify in time, happen at once and con-tinually in the mind of God.[6] Dionysius the Areopagite dealt with God's relation to time in *On the Divine Names*: "And God we must celebrate as both Eternity and Time, as the Cause of all Time and Eternity and as the Ancient of Days; as before Time and above Time and producing all the variety of times and seasons; and again, as existing before Eternal Ages, in that He is before Eternity and

---

[4] For random examples, see Venning, p. 2; Nicolson, *The Break-ing of the Circle*, Chapter 2; E. H. Gombrich, "Icones Symbolicae," *Journal of the Warburg and Courtauld Institutes*, XI (1948), 163-92.

[5] *Of Christian Doctrine*, p. 41.

[6] *Of Christian Doctrine*, p. 57: "So extensive is the prescience of God, that he knows beforehand the thoughts and actions of free agents as yet unborn, and many ages before those thoughts or actions have their origin"; p. 65: "For the foreknowledge of God is noth-ing but the wisdom of God, under another name, or that idea of every thing, which he had in his mind, to use the language of men, before he decreed any thing."

above Eternity and his Kingdom is the Kingdom of all the Eternal Ages."[7] Augustine's explanation in the *Confessions* is classic for the second point: "Thy yeeres neyther goe nor come; whereas these yeeres of ours, doe both goe and come, that (in their order) they may all come. Thy yeeres are in a standing all at once, because they are still at a stay: nor are those that goe, thrust out by those that *come*, for that they passe not away at all; but these of ours shall all bee, even when they shall not all be. Thy yeeres are one day; and thy day, is not *everyday*, but *today*: seeing thy *To day* gives not place unto *To morrowe*, nor comes in place of *yesterday*. Thy *To day* is Eternity. . . ."[8] For his simpler audience, Ralph Venning (p.10) paraphrased the same thought: "God created all things in time, and yet . . . all which God doth, is done in eternity."

The paradox of time and eternity is involved in the Creation itself. In the mind of God, Creation was instantaneous ("Immediate are the acts of God"; God "in a moment will create/ Another world"), yet it took six days to perform or to be revealed. In God's mind all created time was one, as Browne (p.27) saw it: "Thus God beholds all things, who contemplates as fully his works in their epitome, as in their full volume; and beheld as amply the whole world in that little compendium of the sixth day, as in the scattered and dilated pieces of those five before." In *Paradise Lost*, God speaks of all created time in one sentence:

> I can repair
> That detriment, if such it be to lose
> Self-lost, and in a moment will create
> Another World, out of one man a Race

[7] Dionysius the Areopagite, *On the Divine Names*, trans. and ed. C. E. Rolt (London, 1951), pp. 72-75.

[8] St. Augustine, *Confessions*, trans. William Watts (London, 1631), pp. 753-54.

Of men innumerable, there to dwell,
Not here, till by degrees of merit rais'd
They open to themselves at length the way
Up hither, under long obedience tri'd,
And Earth be chang'd to Heav'n, and Heav'n to Earth,
One Kingdom, Joy, and Union without end. (VII. 152-61)

During the Creation, God kept "an everlasting Sabbath" quite as if He were not simultaneously creating; furthermore, even though His Creation was accomplished on the sixth day, "creation is continued in providence every day."[9] Once the Creation was finally accomplished, as Milton reminds his readers again and again, God is at once in the Creation and out of it, at once in time and beyond it. History and materiality at once are and are not in the mind of God, for whom all history is both one instant and eternity.

Such concepts are natural in theology and quite permissible in metaphysics or mathematics, but they are extremely difficult to deal with in a piece of literature subject to its own laws, where the content, if it is to have relevance, must be presented to its audience concretely and precisely. Milton wrote, certainly, *sub specie aeternitatis* both morally and poetically; his "fit audience" was never allowed to forget the absoluteness of moral and natural law, however particularized the specific situation and character of Adam and Eve. He also wrote, inevitably, as a created human being at a certain recognizable point in history for other human beings of his time and future times—and, most important consideration of all, the narrative art which he practiced in *Paradise Lost* is necessarily governed by chronology. There is no other way to tell a tale, even a tale told with continual reference to abstract theological conceptions of eternity and infinity. Milton says so himself:

[9] Venning, pp. 9, 10.

> Immediate are the Acts of God, more swift
> Than time or motion, but to human ears
> Cannot without process of speech be told,
> So told as earthly notion can receive. (VII. 176-79)

In certain ways Milton's material served him well. Although *Paradise Lost* begins according to the orthodox literary doctrine of Horace, *in medias res*, it could not by its nature begin otherwise: the Christian material it presents outdoes the material of Troy or Latium by its appropriateness. For however precise its focus on man, the whole narrative of *Paradise Lost*, from the elevation of Christ in heaven to the vision of the New Heaven and the New Earth, is *in mediis rebus*, since in the chronology of eternity there is neither beginning nor end, and time is, in Donne's phrase, but a parenthesis in eternity.[10] Nonetheless, though the metaphysical sense in which Milton's material was by its nature *in mediis rebus* may help to explain its extraordinary suitability to the epic pattern he inherited from the ancients, the material itself was not by definition thus made tractable to poetic laws. For the purposes of his narrative, Milton had to establish a chronology of motivation in the events prior to the creation of measured time: after the elevation of Christ, Satan knew jealousy, incited the third part of heaven to rebel, fought the great war in heaven, and fell into hell. All this accomplished, Christ acts as God's instrument in the Creation of the world, taking the necessary narrative "time" to enter His chariot, to depart from heaven, to ride out across chaos, and with His golden compasses to draw, one by one, all the planets and all the worlds.[11]

[10] John Donne, *Devotions upon Emergent Occasions* (University of Michigan Press, 1959), p. 89.

[11] In general, orthodox theologians took the view, with Augustine, that time began with the Creation. See Frank Egleston Robbins, *The Hexaemeral Literature* (University of Chicago Press, 1912),

Only after all this preparation does the central drama of Adam and Eve begin, and even then, the human action of *Paradise Lost* is not limited to the Fall of the first pair and their expulsion from Eden. It involves, on the contrary, the total sum of human history, of what is past and passing and to come. All that is "historical"—and it goes without saying that for Milton the historicity of Scriptural record went unquestioned—is contained in the epic, both from the human point of vision and under the aspect of eternity.[12]

For example, we learn in Book III that the action of the first two books of *Paradise Lost* has all taken place under God's eye, that God has supervised the action of Satan and his legions in hell, and that He foresees, in a tre-

---

pp. 6-7; Arnold Williams, *The Common Expositor* (University of North Carolina Press, 1948), pp. 40, 42. Grant McColley, in *Paradise Lost* (Chicago University Press, 1940), pp. 16-17, makes a "chronology" of the events in heaven before the Creation. On the whole, Milton seems to speak, in the poem, analogically of time before the Creation (cf. the "grateful vicissitude" of night and day in heaven: "Nine times the space that measures day and night") and to distinguish between duration in the natural and supernatural worlds (see *PL*, v. 580-82; vi. 684-85; x. 89-90). In *Of Christian Doctrine* (pp. 181-89), however, he makes plain a crisper view of time, that it could have existed before the Creation and probably existed from the Son. For an interpretation of the time-space imagery of the poem, see Cope, pp. 60-61, 68-69; the definitive view of Milton's theological view of time is Lawrence Stapleton's "Milton's Conception of Time in *Of Christian Doctrine*," *Harvard Theological Review*, LVII (1964).

[12] See F. T. Prince, "On the Last Two Books of *Paradise Lost*," *Essays and Studies* (London, 1958), pp. 40-51; George Wesley Whiting, *Milton and This Pendant World* (University of Texas Press, 1958), pp. 165-200; Barbara Kiefer Lewalski, "Structure and Symbolism in Michael's Prophecy, *Paradise Lost*, Books XI-XII," *PQ*, XLII (1963), 25-35; and F. T. Prince, "Adam Unparadis'd," *The Living Milton* (London, 1960), pp. 85-123; Martz, *The Paradise Within*, pp. 141-48.

mendous vista of history, the whole future of created man.[13] On analysis, Milton's descriptive art is even more remarkable than at first glance it seems. Satan's long views, across the chaos and from the sun down upon the little earth, are magnificent perspectives of that "universe of space" in which Milton lived,[14] but we come to realize that there can be still longer views than Satan's. God's eye, seeing from an infinitely greater distance, always surveys Satan surveying his distant prospects:

> he then survey'd
> Hell and the Gulf between, and *Satan* there
> Coasting the wall of Heav'n on this side Night
> In the dun Air sublime . . .   (III. 69-72)
> Him God beholding from his prospect high,
> Wherein past, present, future he beholds,
> Thus to his only Son foreseeing spoke. (III. 77-79)

God's point of view always dominates: it is through God's eyes that we first meet Adam and Eve; only later do we see them from Satan's point of disadvantage.[15]

Just as Satan has not God's perspective of space, he has not God's perspective of time. Satan cannot have foreknowledge, and thus his attempts on man are true attempts, in that he cannot know, in spite of his supernatural craft, success or failure. So much more powerful and so-

[13] Cf. *Christian Doctrine*, pp. 55, 57, 65, 85-87.

[14] Marjorie H. Nicolson, "Milton and the Telescope," *Science and Imagination* (Cornell University Press, 1956), pp. 80-109.

[15] One might note, further, that Uriel, Raphael, and Michael, all of whom in *Paradise Lost* reveal to the reader supernatural or prophetic events, are among those angels frequently called the "eyes" of God. They operate as such in the poem, where they constantly present their narrative as from God's point of view. See Merritt Y. Hughes, Introduction to *PL*, in his edition of Milton's *Complete Poems and Major Prose* (New York, 1957), p. 182.

phisticated than Adam, Satan knows no more of the future than he.

Indeed, he knows less. For all the grandeur of his superhuman prospects, Satan is not permitted the panoramic revelation of future time vouchsafed to Adam, who is ultimately granted a limited participation in the divine foreknowledge. Such a favor is hard to bear: at the first sight of human experience, Adam asserts the orthodox argument against attempting to know the future:

> O Vision ill foreseen! better had I
> Liv'd ignorant of future, so had borne
> My part of evil only, each day's lot
> Anough to bear: those now, that were dispens't
> The burd'n of many Ages, on me light
> At once, by my foreknowledge gaining Birth
> Abortive, to torment me ere thir being,
> With thought that they must be. (xi. 763-70)

But God has prepared Adam to face the glories of his hard lesson. The way Adam learns his lesson, too, in two long narrative and descriptive books at the end of the poem, also demonstrates the difference between the way God knows time and the way Adam must experience it. Compared with the quick speeches of God in Book iii, where human history is so compressed as to appear almost immediate in God's mind, the length of Books xi and xii makes the long human experience more real, more actual, both to Adam and to the reader. In further contrast to Book iii, a book peculiarly of eternity, Books xi and xii express the long, continuing process of history, the succession of event upon event that is the lot of fallen mankind.

The history of the world is of course prophetic to Adam: not until he has learned his lessons from Raphael, from the tree, from Michael, is he permitted to enter upon the long life of his race. In a process of artistic identification,

Adam's experience is brought abreast of that of Milton's readers, so that both Adam and the reader share the view or review of Scriptural history and the final revelation of the new Heaven and Earth—the only narrated events in the poem inevitably prophetic to Milton's readers. In our last view of Adam and Eve,

> They hand in hand with wand'ring steps and slow
> Through *Eden* took thir solitary way. (xii. 648-49)

The story simply stops, but it does not end. The world lay all before Adam and Eve in double truth, before them in place and before them in time. Their story cannot end so long as place and time are the dimensions of human history, so long as the generation of mankind continues its course in the Creation. The epic ends as it began, *in medias res*, but at the end, in the midst of actual time, seen and experienced from the point of view of man, rather than, as at the beginning, in the midst of an eternity comprehensible only to the Divine Mind. And at the end as at the beginning, we are left doubly in the midst of things, both in historical time and within eternity, to which at the Last Judgment time shall finally be joined forever.

WE MUST be so left, because we ourselves share Adam's expectation of the Judgment and because we are at some point farther along the stretch of history into which at the end of the epic Adam first steps. Man must exercise his free will within that history, and except in very general terms he cannot foreknow the world's end and his own. So Milton's contemporary readers must have felt with Adam and Eve at the end of *Paradise Lost*, for their own errors "sorrowing, yet in peace," able to shed "some natural tears" with Adam and Eve and to wipe them soon and go on with the active business of life.

Milton succeeded in the course of the epic in shifting

the point of view from that of God, dominant in the early books, to that of man; he did so by making Adam enter history understanding it, insofar as man can, from God's point of view. Milton's readers, living at a point in history so far beyond Adam, are recalled by Adam's situation from their purely human occupations to a renewed realization of God's intentions in history. If ever additional proof were needed that it is man, and neither Devil nor Deity, that is the hero of *Paradise Lost*, such proof may be drawn from the reader's acceptance as his own of Adam's predicament, with all the natural worries and rewards attendant upon the human condition. Milton understood such identification well enough and found its ground in another paradox of Christian doctrine: the notion that Adam is, and is in, every man. Venning's aphorism (p.19) puts the idea most simply: "The Christian knows that he was not when *Adam* was, and yet he believes that he sinned when *Adam* did." The life of Adam was for each Christian the classic paradigm of moral life—and more. Each man's experience recapitulated Adam's and was Adam's experience; from Adam, as Augustine explained, the world's "two societies" sprang. John Salkeld, modifying Augustine, made clear that Adam's specific sin was in each Christian:

But if it bee so as *Austine* saith, *that wee were all originally defiled with the sinne of our first father*, if wee had also besides this some other inherent originall sinne, wee should have the two kindes of originall sinnes, the one by imputation, the other by inhesion; the one inherent in *Adam* only, the other in us derived from *Adam*, which is to speak without ground of Scripture, which only maketh mention of one originall sinne, by which all bee truly called sinners, according to that of the Apostle, *Omnes peccaverunt in Adam*; all have sinned in *Adam*, in *Adam* hee saith, not in themselves. . . .[16]

[16] John Salkeld, *A Treatise of Paradise* (London, 1617), p. 250;

Because Adam's last vision is of the Second Coming of Christ and the reception of the saints into bliss, the end of the poem is, appropriately, optimistic. At the beginning of history Adam is brought to realize how God's justice operates with His mercy, and Milton's readers could reaffirm that realization with many more examples from history that Adam could not know. The paradox identifying Adam in each Christian is another way of fusing historical times that no man can literally experience at once, another way of bringing to man's attention the immediacy in God's mind of all the moral choices scheduled across the total duration of the human race.

God grants Adam leave to leave Paradise "not disconsolate"; unlike the despairing couple Masaccio painted, Milton's Adam and Eve go to find a "paradise within" "happier far" than the one they left behind them, go with pride in their human callings both to labor and to God. Adam and Eve depart in full awareness of the felicity concealed beneath their act of disobedience; as Adam said,

> full of doubt I stand,
> Whether I should repent me now of sin
> By mee done and occasion'd, or rejoice
> Much more, that much more good thereof shall spring . . .
>
> (XII. 473-76)

The "second Adam" would come to save mankind, and mankind would recognize Him just because of Adam's experience of sin: the long panorama of future history is not therefore C. S. Lewis's "undigested lump of futurity"[17] so much as an assurance to Adam and all men that individual salvation remains important, that human life is not

---

for further discussion of this point, see William Haller, *The Rise of Puritanism* (Columbia University Press, 1938), pp. 152-53.

[17] C. S. Lewis, *A Preface to Paradise Lost* (London, 1943), p. 125.

summed up in human defect; but that precisely from human defect springs an enhanced sense of moral choice and of the potentialities of salvation. That Milton deliberately aimed at this strongly optimistic lesson modern analysis of *Paradise Lost* makes clear.[18] As Adam is in each Christian, so is Christ; and in Christ lies the Christian's hope and his joy.

IN HIS self-appointed task as poet and moralist, the maker of a poem to teach a nation, Milton shared some of the problems of the creative Deity. As poet, the practitioner of a profession to which he felt himself called as surely as any convinced Christian to any activity, Milton recognized his own function as "maker" and his responsibility in the creation of a poetic and moral world. His Renaissance humanism honored the long Neoplatonic tradition of the poet as creator; his Christianity identified him irrevocably with Adam and thus with all mankind. Milton's preoccupation with the Creation in *Paradise Lost* is quite obvious;[19] from beginning to end the poem refers to creation, creativity, and re-creation. About the Creation he permitted himself the most unambiguous heterodoxy of the poem, the rejection of the orthodox notion of Creation *ex nihilo* and the postulation of a Creation *ex Deo* counter to the corpus of traditional belief.

In writing the poem, Milton shared with God an aspect of foreknowledge. He "foreknew," both by revelation and by the immutable authority of Scripture, the unchangeable course of the events of his poem. There was no changing

[18] Barker, "Structural Pattern," pp. 17-30; Prince, pp. 38-52; Lewalski, pp. 34-35; but see Martz, *The Paradise Within*, for a contrary view.

[19] W.B.C. Watkins, *An Anatomy of Milton's Verse* (Louisiana State University Press, 1955), pp. 43-44; Geoffrey H. Hartman, "Milton's Counterplot," *ELH*, xxv (1958), 1-12.

the facts of the Fall—after all, Milton wrote at a time when the failure of the Rule of Saints demonstrated to everyone the recurrence of human error—and there was no changing the ultimate end of the world and of the human race. To these data Milton's narrative had to conform: even more than in ancient tragedy, his plot assumed knowledge and foreknowledge on the part of his audience.

But he could also exercise his free will in the choice of poetic material, of ornament, of arrangement. Where matters of doctrine were not irrevocably laid down but were "indifferent,"[20] Milton was free to vary or to veil, even to invent; he was free to expand or explain as he chose, particularly about motivations—just why Satan fell, through what particular weaknesses he was able to seduce Adam and Eve, for what purposes Raphael and Michael were selected to instruct mankind. He was free to arrange his universe (ambiguously, as so many scholars have pointed out) to suit the imaginative needs of his poem; he could begin and end wherever he chose and could arrange the order of events in whatever way he considered most significant or most artful.

In this respect, his efforts to reconcile poetically the paradoxes involved in the concepts of eternity and time, of foreknowledge and free will, affected the structure and technique of his poem. Form and material both called for epic; Milton's brilliant dealings *in mediis rebus* have al-

[20] On Milton's heresies and doctrine see, *inter alia*, Lewis, p. 89; B. Rajan, *Paradise Lost and the Seventeenth Century Reader* (London, 1947), Chapter 2; Maurice Kelley, *This Great Argument* (Princeton University Press, 1941); George Newton Conklin, *Biblical Criticism and Heresy in Milton* (King's Crown Press, 1949); A.S.P. Woodhouse, "Notes on Milton's Views on the Creation: the Initial Phases," *PQ*, xxviii (1949), 211-36; Ruth Montgomery Kivette, "Milton on the Trinity," unpublished doctoral dissertation, Columbia University, 1960.

ready been discussed. The extraordinary balance of the poem, at beginning and end and at the points of stress throughout, could also have been achieved only by the most strategic use of material. Horace would have given full marks to Milton's order, with the first six books beginning and ending upon the same event, so entirely differently understood at the end of Book vi; with the second half of the poem beginning in the Creation and ending in continuing re-creation.

The books of Eden (iv, ix, x) fall at points of balance within the two halves of the epic; the climax of Book ix is both a contrast to the idyll of Book iv and a fulfillment of the foreknown in Book iii. The life of the devils in Book i and Book ii is contrasted and compared to the life of man in xi and xii; the irony that the Devil's act of destruction is God's act of re-creation solves, for poetic purposes at the very least, the problem of evil.

Milton's treatment of Creation may provide one kind of commentary upon his method of organization. We have seen how he used the act of Creation to contrast the immediacy of acts performed in eternity with the duration of acts accomplished in time, and how he connected the physical and metaphysical aspects of Creation with the moral problem of re-creation. He prepared for the narrative of the Six Days' Work in many ways, in constant reference or metaphor, in narrative, and in structure itself. Before Book vii, the hexaemeral book, we have heard of the Creation five times already—from Beelzebub and from Satan, who had heard earlier rumors of such a creation; from the "Anarch old" in his address to Satan in chaos; from Uriel, who describes it briefly and beautifully in the adequate language of supernatural beings; and from God, who tells, even more briefly, His Son about the Creation. Structurally, Milton prepared with the utmost care for his full account of the Creation: as far as Satan is concerned, God's ways toward him must be justified in full to Adam (and consequently to the readers) before man can understand the significance of the Creation. Raphael therefore clears away all doubts about the propriety of Satan's behavior which might have arisen in the first part of the poem. In his narrative in Book v, as well of course as in the whole tale from Book v to Book vii, Raphael unites the past and the future. He forewarns Adam by the example of Satan and forearms him by the example of Abdiel, and he explains to the audience the nature of the action they have already poetically witnessed.

This is not all. We meet created beings in an order that reinforces the ambiguities of a universe at once external and temporal. First we meet Satan and the devils fallen, then God and His Son, then Adam and Eve. The actual narrative of the Creation, broken at so many points, begins with the making of the last creature, Eve, who in Book iv tells Adam of her own sensations at the beginning of her conscious life. Milton is too subtle simply to work backward in the Creation from end to beginning; Raphael's story in Book vii gives the order of Genesis, much amplified, and is followed by Adam's polite countertale of his creation and his part in persuading God to create Eve.

After the tale of Creation is finished in Book viii, the story proceeds chronologically. Adam and Eve fall, are sentenced, and are brought to understand the parts they must play in the future of their race. The question of physical creation fuses with that of spiritual re-creation, symbolized particularly in the story of the Flood and confirmed in the revelation of the Messiah. At the poem's end, Adam and Eve learn something more of the relation of Creation to procreation, for Eve learns that she shall ultimately bear the seed flowering in the Messiah.

Milton had other techniques to cross the barriers of time and eternity. In his use of epic simile, for example, he often joins superhuman action to human by means of his own and his reader's sense of history. Galileo, whom he may have known personally, thrice enters the epic, once when Satan's shield is likened to the moon (i. 286ff.), once when Satan in the sun is likened to a sunspot (iii. 588-90), once when Raphael's flight among the heavenly bodies is likened to the mysterious revelations of the telescope (v. 261-63). In each case, the supernatural and almost unimaginable is made actual by so specific an analogy. Old Testament history is constantly evoked—the bondage of Israel (i. 305ff., 338ff.), the shameful idolatries which shall occur later in human history than the reference to them:

> Though of thir Names in heav'nly Records now
> Be no memorial, blotted out and ras'd
> By thir Rebellion, from the Books of Life,
> Nor had they yet among the Sons of *Eve*
> Got them new Names. . . .   (i. 361-65)

Milton describes the Paradise of Fools as Satan passes by it in terms of what it will become, not of what it then was. The dwellers in Babel, Empedocles, Cleombrotus, "Friars/ White, Black and Grey, with all thir trumpery" which he imagines are not at that moment in existence; only after the Fall shall the Paradise of Fools be

> to few unknown
> Long after, now unpeopl'd, and untrod.   (iii. 496-97)

By likening Satan to the "Soldan" and his wealth to that of Babylon, Egypt, Ormus, and India, Milton crosses the barriers of period to reassert the constancy of the battle between Christendom and paganism. He uses not only the geographical revelations of European expansion but the functions of men of that time as well: merchants and sailors with their specific experiences are called up (ii.

38ff.; iv. 159ff.; x. 290ff.) to remind readers of the reality of the experiences of supernatural beings. After the Fall, Adam and Eve cover their newly recognized nakedness, appearing as

> of late
> *Columbus* found *th' American* so girt
> With feather'd Cincture, naked else and wild
> Among the Trees on Isles and woody Shores.
> (ix. 1115-18)

Death comes upon the earth as Xerxes comes to Greece; death's hosts are like the Tartar hordes (x. 306; ix. 431-36). Jacob, Moses, Aaron, and Tobias are all the subjects of similes designed to connect the prelapsarian world with the later history of God's people and to remind readers that blessedness and virtue must ultimately triumph over the world's evils.

As the historical similes serve to keep simultaneously in the reader's mind great spans of history, so do the invocations serve to bridge time periods. The thematic and poetical importance of the great invocations at Books i, iii, vii, and ix, as well as of the momentary voice of the poet at the beginning of Book iv, is quite apparent, but their movement in time has, so far as I know, not yet been related to Milton's handling of time throughout the epic. In the Invocation to Book i, Milton ranges from the Creation through the Fall and the Mosaic inspiration to the coming of Christ: for him all those acts are related to his own creative act in "beginning" the poem. The Invocation to iii calls upon the great poets and seers, Orpheus, Thamyris, Homer, Tiresias, and Phineas, all concerned in actual or fabulous history and prophecy, and upon the Muse, who was "Before the Heavens." In iv, the brief reference to the Apocalypse recalls both John's act of foreseeing and the sight he foresaw, the end of the world and the ultimate destruction of Satan. In vii, the poet figures himself as returned from heaven to earth ("More safe I sing with mortal voice"), out of Bellerophon's dangers though subject still to the dangers besetting Orpheus. In ix, he rejects the standard heroic topic, drawn from the ancient past or from mediaeval Christendom, to turn to his "higher subject," the Fall, from which shall come "the better fortitude/ Of Patience and Heroic Martyrdom."

The invocations function as extra-narrative surveys of subject, theme, and symbol; they emphasize the poet's own particular and specific act of continuing creation, and they fuse different times in still another way with eternity. At the beginning of Book iv, with its picture of idyllic prelapsarian life in Eden, Milton wishes to cry with St. John the Divine, "Woe to the inhabitants on Earth!" in warning to Adam and Eve of their coming Fall. The reference to Revelations also makes all well: the Fall implies salvation. In the same way, in the Invocation to ix, the "foul distrust and breach/ Disloyal on the part of Man, revolt,/ And disobedience" implies at once its fulfillment in "the better fortitude/ Of Patience and Heroic Martyrdom." In i, iii, vii, and ix, Milton's own situation is dramatized into actuality—he is before his readers, a poet and a mortal fallen man; he is perhaps too old, born too late, or the inhabitant of too cold a climate to tell his great story as it deserves. In the Invocation to iii, he is not "rapt above the Pole," he says, but "More safe . . . on mortal soil." In Book vii, the reader experiences the Creation after he has experienced the created; he knows with Milton, like every other living man, of the long postlapsarian history of the created world; he knows poetically with Adam and Eve the prelapsarian condition. He learns with Adam and Eve from Raphael of the coming into being of the Creation itself. By presenting himself, an unmistakable seventeenth-century man, in the invocation to this book, Milton adds another dimension to the times he presents in the book and has added, psychologically and poetically, another phase of immediacy.

The epic ends on the same sort of fusion. Michael's last words are of the "New Heav'ns, new Earth, Ages of endless date"; the last words Adam speaks are about time and eternity:

> How soon hath thy prediction, Seer blest,
> Measur'd this transient World, the Race of time,
> Till Time stand fixt; beyond is all abyss,
> Eternity, whose end no eye can reach. (XII. 553-56)

As they pass into the historical time for which they have been prepared, the moral obligations and privileges of mankind (i.e., the exercise of free will upon the ground of time) are properly at the forefront of the minds of Adam and Eve. Behind and above their acceptance of their human condition lies their awareness of divine metaphysical truth (i.e., of God's foreknowledge and providence in and from eternity). In this sense one article of the doctrine Milton intended to teach his nation—the inextricable theological paradoxes of time and eternity, of free will and foreknowledge—is exemplified in the poem's action and demonstrated in its structure. The mysteries of religious truth are not explained in *Paradise Lost*, despite the occasional long dogmatic passages, for logic, even the logic of poetry, has no business explaining them. Those mysteries are by their nature contradictory, difficult, and yet inevitable—to be understood they must be, somehow or other, experienced. Through the incredible exercise of poetic tact and strategy, Milton presents these particular paradoxes so that their oppositions are at once fused and yet made clear. Understanding comes from the poem itself, from the experience of reading it, so that the paradoxes of time and eternity, of free will and foreknowledge, come to seem at the poem's end the natural, proper beginning and end of Christian experience.

6

Logos in The Temple

I am that I am, was his owne definition unto
Moses; and 'twas a short one, to confound mor-
talitie, that durst question God, or aske him what
hee was. . . .

Browne, *Religio Medici*, I. 11

THE POEMS of George Herbert, so transparent, so simple,
so direct, have the distinction of being among the hardest
poems in the English language to paraphrase. The more
one tries to say something intelligent in explication of these
poems, the more gibberish one tends to talk—about how
the poems in *The Temple* approach that mysterious literary apogee, "pure poetry," poetry that speaks for itself,
poetry that is self-sufficient and needs no interpreter. For
various reasons, statements like these are an inadequate
solution to the problems raised by verse in general and by
George Herbert's verse in particular: verse in general, as
we know from linguists and others, cannot speak for itself
any more than any other symbol system can, but takes its
meaning from its contexts, both those to which it specifically refers and those which it attempts to exclude from
the reader's attention.[1] As for Herbert's verse, clearly
there *are* great obscurities in what he says, some dependent
upon his subject matter, some upon the assumptions implicit in his references, images, and tone, some upon his

---

[1] E. H. Gombrich, *Art and Illusion*, pp. 110-11, 208-11; Winifred Nowottny, *The Language Poets Use* (London, 1962), p. 152.
For a discussion of the complexities of "plain" language, see that
sensible book by George Boas, *The Limits of Reason* (New York,
1961), Chapters 3, 4.

idiosyncratic vocabulary. Since these are the obscurities of
a poet that twentieth-century critics, both old and new,
delight to make plain, there have been some recent commentaries on Herbert's verse and poetic theory[2] that have
proved extremely useful in locating him in his proper
tradition.

But even iconology, the language of symbol and image,
has not proved sufficient to unlock the chest of Herbert's
treasure, helpful though it has been to know, at once and
without fail, that we can through iconological aids understand such poems as "The Sacrifice" and "The Bag," whose
central metaphors have seemed far-fetched and even, in the
case of "The Bag," grotesque to the point of silliness. With
a topographical map of Herbert's ground of reference,
though, we do not find his poetry easy to understand—
reading "The Reprisall" or "Vertue" is still something
like the experience of seeing a poem in, say, Swedish. One
knows that the arrangement of words forms a poem, recognizes just enough of the cognate words to suspect that
the poem is good, but in the end one is forced to recognize
the brute fact that one doesn't know the language. With
the Swedish poem, we can take comfort in the belief that,
if we only knew the tongue it was written in, the poem
would open up to us; with Herbert there is no such consolation, since we know that we already know the language he used. And though we can be helped by the traditional language of Christian worship, the language of
the Church alone is not enough to provide us with the
ground plan of his habitation.

That Herbert's habitation was, quite literally, the House

[2] Among them, Rosemond Tuve, *A Reading of George Herbert*
(London, 1952); Rosemary Freeman, *English Emblem Books* (London, 1948), Chapter 6; Louis L. Martz, *The Poetry of Meditation*,
Chapters 7, 8; Joseph H. Summers, *George Herbert, His Religion
and His Art* (London, 1954).

of God,[3] gives his poetry a peculiarity and propriety at a considerable remove from our notions of what to expect from a lyric poet, even from a sacred lyric poet. Common readers are no longer children (not even natural children) in God's House; common readers have to learn the appropriateness of Herbert's posture—quite literally, why he stood or sat or knelt—as if the House of God were the labyrinth of Minos. Herbert's own age, his country, and social position preserved him from such problems of religious unfamiliarity. He knew his own location in the Church which he—both conventionally and originally—selected as his major metaphor. Though, like all good Christians, he did not presume to know exactly *where* he stood in God's sight, like all good Christians, he knew that he always stood in God's sight and under His providence; he knew himself to be both child and servant in God's House.[4]

Part of what makes *The Temple* difficult for contemporary readers is that George Herbert, the Anglican priest, child of the upper gentry, was so natural a child of the Church that he rarely saw fit to explain anything relevant to that condition. For him, the worship of God, even the specific form of worship prescribed in Laud's England, was so securely immutable and timeless as to require neither comment nor explanation. Critical study of his works continues to show how completely he operated

[3] Cf. G.W.O. Addleshaw and Frederick Etchells, *The Architectural Setting of Anglican Worship* (London, 1948); George Boyd, "George Herbert: a Revaluation," unpublished doctoral dissertation, Columbia University, 1957, which gives a commentary on the structure of "temples"; and J. D. Walker, "The Architectonics of George Herbert's *The Temple*," *ELH*, xxix (1962), 289-305.

[4] Anne Davidson [Ferry], "Innocence Regained: Seventeenth-century Reinterpretations of the Fall of Man," particularly Chapter 2.

within a long tradition of Christian utterance—to understand his slant use of metaphor, we must know the *topoi*
of Christian worship, the regular phrases of Scripture and
the Book of Common Prayer, invoked Sunday after Sunday across England to recall to Christians the continuity
of their ritual and of the particular transcendent truth that
ritual commemorated.

As priest and poet, Herbert was thoroughly domesticated in God's House, so that the Word of God was his
natural preoccupation. His profession required proficiency
in the Word[5]—in his words and their relation to the
official Word of God in Holy Writ; and, more impor-
tantly still, in the Word that was from the beginning, that
was with God, and was God; the Word by whom everything was made that was made; the Word that was made
flesh. It is in the speculum of the great mystical self-
explanatory notion of the divine *logos*, I think, that Herbert's poetry may be most helpfully reflected. The difficulties involved in the doctrine of the *logos*, once understood in relation to Herbert's verse, may clarify some of
the content and method of that verse and serve as a model,
an emblem, for the difficulties inherent in both his subject
matter and his method.

The divine *logos*, the idea of God, God-the-Word, is
the ultimately self-sufficient idea, the idea of ideas which,
if understood, satisfies, suffices, fills, makes content. All
other ideas, all other words, can be separately dispensed
with, since all of them are implied, are folded into, and
can be explicated from, that ultimate Word for word that
was from the beginning, is now, and ever shall be.[6]

But the Gospel of John, like the *Timaeus*, assumes a
doubleness in the *logos* concept, a perfection of two differ-

[5] Cf. Summers, Chapter 5, "The Proper Language."
[6] See Introduction, n. 39.

ent modes, of Being and Becoming. The Word is self-sufficient: it is and remains forever, and is also the source of all (other) things, the creator of all things. The Word-made-flesh not only took part in the Creation as an aspect of the Triune God, but in His fleshly form entered history to make the Church, the authority for which was His own words. Here I shall merely attempt to examine the uses of the Word, intradeical and extradeical, in Herbert's verse, and to test the hypothesis that from his manipulation of the paradoxes inherent in the *logos* doctrine we can read the problems in his verse and his versing.

To start with the most obvious point, one cannot read ten pages into *The Temple* without noticing Herbert's constant reference to Scripture, the Book of God's Word. From the plainness of "The Church-porch" to the complexities of "The H. Scriptures,"[7] we can see his reliance upon the revealed Word of God.[8] More important still, in his work "verse" and "rhyme" are noticeably persistent metaphors for divine Creation, for bringing order from chaos, for fitting, for balancing, for satisfying, and for making content. Such a poetic vocabulary of self-reference is no novelty, though it is not so common in a religious as in a secular poet; but Herbert refines such reference to his own specialty, a concentration upon fitness, upon the matching of form to matter. In the crudest sense he

[7] George Herbert, "The H. Scriptures," *Works*, ed. F. E. Hutchinson, p. 58. All subsequent references to Herbert's poems are to this edition.

[8] Cf. "The Booke" in the poems "The Thanksgiving," "H. Baptisme (i)," "The Priesthood"; as well as other metaphors from Herbert's trade: "the lesson" in "The Church-porch"; "writing" in "The Church-porch," "The Sinner," "Good Friday," "Sepulchre," "H. Baptisme (ii)," "Sunday," "The British Church," to list only a few of the relevant poems. As for "inspiration," see "The Sacrifice," and "Church-monuments." For "words," see "Coloss. 3.3."

matches form and matter in "The Altar" and in the famous hourglass, angel wings, lark flight of "Easter-wings."
He matches in another way, still conceptually rather crude,
in "Trinitie Sunday," where the triple triads hammer
home the idea of three-in-one; in "Paradise," the "prun-
ing-poem" where the words are quite literally cut, letter
by letter, to fit the sense; in "A Wreath," where the
phrases repeated from one line to the next twine the
matter into a plaited crown. In "Sinnes Round," Herbert
again maintained circularity (the vicious circle of self-
generating sin); "Colossians 3:3," "Jesu," and "Lovejoy" are all arrangements of total poems around an emblematic central core, *in nuce* the meaning of each poem.

Anyone who puns as radically as Herbert in "Jesu," on
the Lord's name (at which every knee must bow), may be
suspected of having learned his holy levity at the knee of
another divine punster and old friend of the family, John
Donne. Certainly Herbert took something from Donne,
but he also rejected Donne's poetics by refusing the verbal
traditions for which Donne was so famous, in his own day
as he is now: indeed, Herbert was so cunning as to reject
"the Donne tradition" within its own terms. In "Jordan
(I)" and "(II)" and in "Love (I)" and "(II)" he osten-
tatiously abandoned the "fictions onely and false hair" of
the Petrarchan style, in both its Elizabethan and Jacobean
manifestations, and inveighed against the critical notion,
now called "metaphysical," that the meanings of poetry

> Must all be vail'd, while he that reades, divines,
> Catching the sense at two removes.

Like Sidney, Herbert learned to turn away from the af-
fectations of his art, from "quaint words, and trim invention," to look straight at love. But where Sidney, excellent

humanist that he was, had found sufficient truth in his own heart, Herbert took the divine love as his model:

Copie out onely that, and save expense.

In the "Love" sonnets, wit simplifies itself to true beauty, after blowing dust into the eyes of (mortal, dusty) man: at the resurrection, the dust raised by wit shall rise, as the whole man, to "praise him who did make and mend our eies."[9]

The pair of "H. Scriptures" poems, closely connected with the "Jordan" and "Love" pairs, sets up a counterpoint between the complex and the simple—appropriately enough, since Scripture itself, like these poems, is also dazzlingly intricate and blindingly clear. In the first poem, the Book is at once "a masse of strange delights" and a manuscript in which "heav'n lies flat." In the second, the Book "matches" whatever experiences a man may have, revealing, explicating the meaning of each man's individual life—

> This verse marks that, and both do make a motion
> Unto a third, that ten leaves off doth lie:
> Then as dispersed herbs do watch a potion,
> These three make up some Christians destinie. . . .
> (ll. 5-8)

Scripture opens upon a description and a prescription for every moral particular:

> Such are thy secrets, which my life makes good,
> And comments on thee: for in ev'ry thing
> Thy words do finde me out, & parallels bring,
> And in another make me understood.   (ll. 9-12)

Because the created world is the Book of God's Works and Scripture the Book of His Word, they must be parallel

---

[9] See also Martz, pp. 263-67, and Summers, pp. 179-80, on this point.

texts, simply two languages to express the same thing, which was God's providence. Scripture was in one sense more nearly immutable, closer to pure Being, than the obviously mutable world; man might be expected, then, to find texts in Scripture that brought order into mutability, explained and coded diverse human experience into a significant and recognizable pattern.

Upon the preacher, though, fell a heavy burden of responsibility for the proper reading of the two texts. The preacher was obliged to bring them into proper relation with each other for the spiritual benefit of his parishioners. Certainly, every Christian's obligation is to speak out in prayer or praise, whether he is cleric or layman; in the preacher's case, that speaking out is an obligation which can under no circumstances be shirked, can never be glossed over. For the sake of the sheep in his care, the pastor must speak the truth. And yet how can any man, however virtuous, really speak for the unspeakable God?

> Lord, how can man preach thy eternall word?
> He is a brittle crazie glass—

as Herbert said, in that preacher's poem, "The Windows." The best of men is, simply, incommensurate with the transcendent God, as later in the century Pascal was to warn his hubristic contemporaries; though created in God's image, by his original sin man inevitably distorts the truth in his reflections upon it. Moreover, even if a man could paraphrase the Word of God directly, what would be the good of that? The Word is self-sufficient and needs no human messenger. The preacher's dilemma is that, in spite of all these limitations, he is required by the spiritual structure of the Church to be the through-shine glass for light and the painted glass for pictures. And since he is merely a metaphysical window, that preacher is less secure, less fixed, than the church window, which had no responsibility for its text, and which was at least constant in its message. God's story in the windows is at least annealed in the glass, but for the preacher there is no such promise of security:

> speech alone
> Doth vanish like a flaring thing,
> And in the eare, not conscience ring.   (ll. 13-15)

Even if by chance his sermons should prove effective, the preacher can never know whether or not he has been a proper window, has let the white light of truth shine through upon his hearers.

Just as Herbert's situation as preacher presented problems to his poetry, so did his private, meditative situation. Heart and mind awry, he was often unable even to "write a verse or two" in modest praise of the God he served. In Herbert's symbolic system, in the domestic economy of his emotions and his art, "writing" became a sign of grace to the poet; his poems about writing poems avoid the trap of mere description, mere tautology, because the poems are altogether a metaphorical record of his Christian life. So in "Deniall," the untidiness of the poetic form matches the poet's spiritual disorder:

> When my devotions could not pierce
> Thy silent eares;
> Then was my heart broke, as was my verse:
> My breast was full of fears
> And disorder:
>
> My bent thoughts, like a brittle bow,
> Did flie asunder:
> Each took his way; some would to pleasures go,
> Some to the warres and thunder
> Of alarms.   (ll. 1-10)

In so completely neat a method as Herbert's was, the

dissonance of the nonrhyming last line inevitably strikes
very sharply on both eye and ear. The weight of the resolution in the last stanza is therefore the heavier—the technique hammers home the spiritual meaning of the poetic
movement, its final (and contradictory) "denial" of the
spiritual distress that gave rise to the poem:

> O cheer and tune my heartlesse breast,
> Deferre no time;
> That so thy favours granting my request,
> They and my minde may chime,
> And mend my ryme.
>
> (ll. 26-30)

One could say that George Herbert has implored his
God for a sign of active grace; and that the *logos* has
consented to his plea. Herbert has succeeded in making
his Creator show Himself (as He has always been in
Greek) a poet, a maker, has persuaded his Maker into
collaboration on this poem. On the poem's surface, its
emblematic matching of disorderly form to its disorderly
emotional state is perfectly clear: insofar as he was successful, Herbert achieved the tautology to which all poetry,
perhaps all likeness, aspires. But this poem does more than
repeat mood in form: it plucks the reader out of the poet's
lyrical preoccupation with spirit and letter, into a mystery
more enormous, more scarifying than even the deepest
secrets of the human heart. The last-minute solution, in
which order is restored to poet and poem, exhibits and recapitulates the abruptness of God's original act of creation.

For Herbert, the craft of poetry was a continual making,
a serial act of original creation—but poetry had no special
franchise. All human acts of creation were merely recreations, merely imitations of the creative act of God.
Again and again, his poems remind us of the nature of
language and the intent of metaphor. Like many a Renais-

sance poet, he glorified his trade because it was, in his view, impossible for any poet to be anything but a sacred poet, precisely because all acts of creation were imitations of God's model act.

The poem, "Home," turns the "Deniall" trick inside out: all the stanzas of "Home," save the last one, are regular and very simple (ababcc, the last couplet a refrain). The poem is, on its face, a lament for mortality—

> Nothing but drought and dearth, but bush and brake,
>   Which way so-e're I look, I see.
> Some may dream merrily, but when they wake,
>   They dresse themselves and come to thee.
>   O show thy self to me,
>   Or take me up to thee!   (ll. 49-54)
> . . . .
>
> What have I left, that I should stay and grone?
>   The most of me to heav'n is fled:
> My thoughts and joyes are all packt up and gone,
>   And for their old acquaintance plead   (ll. 67-70)

—until the last stanza, when mortality turns out to be merely the necessary preliminary to beatitude:

> Come dearest Lord, passe not this holy season,
>   My flesh and bones and joynts do pray:
> And ev'n my verse, when by my ryme and reason
>   The word is, *Stay*, sayes ever, *Come*.[10]
>   (ll. 73-76)

God has taken the poet's hand in His own and rewritten the poem; though His reason is good, His rhyme is false to the scheme. Not to the poem, however: on a second look, we see that the final word rhymes with the title, and forms an injunction, read with the title—"Come,"

---

[10] Cf. A. Alvarez, in *The School of Donne* (London, 1961), p. 76, who draws attention to this trick.

"Home." When God writes, He writes truer than we know.

Mr. Summers' fine analysis of "The Collar" demonstrates the abrupt conversion achieved by resolving an extraordinarily wild meter and rhyme-scheme into domestic peace, the reconciliation of a prodigal with his Father, and the prodigal's willing assumption of God's gentle yoke, the clerical collar. But there is even more to the poem than this: a reliance upon another aspect of the *logos* tradition. The infant Christ, the *in-fans*, the speechless one, the wordless Word,[11] presented an actual image, living paradox of being and becoming. Himself a tiny child, sufficient and all that is, He was nonetheless destined to speak out forever and ever, a baby carrying all the implications of the human life of God. In Herbert's poetry, the idea of that silent Word, the infant Christ, was not exploited as other poets had exploited it, but the idea of another *infans*, the poet as child, was certainly very important in Herbert's economy. The difficulty of paraphrase, mentioned above, encountered in dealing with Herbert's verse, is his aspect of the poetic "aspiration to muteness" of which Mrs. Nowottny speaks (p.156). The extraordinary simplicity, reduction, and translucency of Herbert's poems are often explicitly related to his images of childhood and innocence. In "H. Baptisme (II)" he looks back nostalgically to the purity of his own childhood, when he was baptized and others took responsibility for the errors of his ways ("Childhood is health"); in "Dialogue" his Saviour addresses the poet as "Child," and bids him trust in God as a child must trust in his earthly father; in "Longing," the poet laments his miseries, which he felt

<hr>

[11] R. L. Colie, "Constantijn Huygens and the Metaphysical Mode," *Germanic Review*, xxxiv (1959), 69.

were inappropriate to a true child of God ("yet am I stil'd/ Thy child").

"The Collar" makes explicit the equation of muteness with grace. The poet certainly lacks no words to rave against God, to deny the communion and reject submission to God's service, words noticeably pyrotechnic for a poet of Herbert's habitually low key. But all those words were useless, irrelevant to truth, since one word of God (which incidentally brings a disorderly poem into a proper resolution and order) was sufficient to demonstrate the uselessness and irrelevance of the poet's eloquent tirade—

> But as I rav'd and grew more fierce and wilde
> At every word,
> Me thoughts I heard one calling, *Child*!
> And I reply'd, *My Lord*.
> (ll. 33-36)

The child may legitimately be mute, since the grownup's words were bound to be so unsatisfactory;[12] and besides, in Herbert's confident poetics, God was always ready to take a hand in the versifying.

"A true Hymne" combines the Word of God with the poet's exercise of his own power to fit, to match words to matter. The first stanza is very plain:

> My joy, my life, my crown!
> My heart was meaning all the day,
> Somewhat it fain would say:
> And still it runneth mutt'ring up and down
> With onely this, *My joy, my life, my crown.*
> (ll. 1-5)

Obviously, this is deceptively plain talk, for a closer look at the poem shows that it too is a poem about a poem

---

[12] Compare here the "Sonnets" from Walton's *Life*, given in Herbert, *Works*, p. 206; and "Dulnesse," pp. 115-16.

(—indeed, about itself), and about the problems involved in writing any poem, including itself; it carries with it the risk of an infinite regress, in this case an infinite reflection in mirrors all returning the same images—"onely this, *My joy, my life, my crown*." Of course, there is a rightness and a fitness to this particular reiteration, since God, the crown of all joy and all life, *is* all that there is. Just the same, one is entitled to ask, how can a poem get away with that flat statement, however true it may be?

> Yet slight not these few words:
> If truly said, they may take part
> Among the best in art.
> The finenesse which a hymne or psalme affords,
> Is, when the soul unto the lines accords.   (ll. 6-10)

This is the overt statement of the poetics practiced so well in "The Collar" and in "Grief," the irregularity of whose lines accords exactly with the state of the poet's soul. Patness, though (a sin to which in his less successful verses the country parson was prone) is not fitness:

> He who craves all the minde,
> And all the soul, and strength, and time,
> If the words onely ryme,
> Justly complains, that somewhat is behinde
> To make his verse, or write a hymne in kinde.
> (ll. 11-15)

Intellect knows how far it falls short of truth; cleverness, even in poetry, is not enough, as all self-critical creators know, better than any of their critics. Herbert was working to express the insight religiously reached, that the human mind has no real control in solving professional dilemmas of expression. In such problems, as in all others, the mind can contribute at best only its own volition:

> Whereas if th' heart be moved,
> Although the verse be somewhat scant,

God doth supplie the want.
As when th' heart sayes (sighing to be approved)
O, could I love! and stops: God writeth, *Loved.*

(ll. 16-20)

As "Deniall" and "Home" demonstrated, whatever God
writes, turns out to be true, in this case both to the rhyme
and to the transcendent reason for which the rhyme stands.
Loving and being loved, the two aspects of love—the
only human emotion capable of reaching across finiteness
into infinity—each imply the other. The poem that began
with the threat of infinite regress has been turned inside
out into a progress toward infinite blessedness. The reversal of "Home," where leaving life suddenly becomes
an exit from prison, finds its parallel here in the meanings
folded into the word that God writes.

In these poems God demonstrates His metaphysical wit,
so often attributed to Him by one school of late-Renais-
sance literary criticism.[13] That wit of God's turns out, we
see, to be His saving grace: grace solves the problems of
art, as it does the problems of life. When the poet's heart,
on which is engraved the sacred name, *Jesu,* breaks, the
pieces fall out to spell a message from God: "I ease you";
the re-formation of the letters reconstructs the poet's heart.
Compared with those of Donne or of Marvell, Herbert's
open plays on words, his puns, are rare; but one sacred
pun he could not resist, in his poem on the double meaning of the homonyms *son* and *sun.*[14] It is a recommenda-
tion for the English tongue that God saw fit to incorporate
two such important notions in one of the English words
for the divine *logos.*

But even when God Himself does not lend a hand to

[13] J. A. Mazzeo, "A Seventeenth-Century Theory of Poetry,"
Renaissance and Seventeenth-Century Studies.

[14] "The Sonne," ll. 1-14.

the poet struggling for words for Word, that poet always
models himself on God in trying to be equal to His task.
It is by imitation of Christ that man may reach toward his
salvation; and in the priest and poet, called to His special
service, one obligation to imitate Christ is especially strong.
In "The Thanksgiving," Herbert wrote his greatest *imita-
tio Christi*: "O King of grief, . . . how shall I grieve for
thee?" he asked.

> Shall I weep bloud? why, thou hast wept such store
>   That all thy body was one doore.
> Shall I be scourged, flouted, boxed, sold?
>   'Tis but to tell the tale is told.   (ll. 1-8)

To suffer in his own body the sufferings endured by Christ
at His trial and crucifixion would be, in a mere man, both
an act of temerity and a work of supererogation. Sublima-
tion into poetry was for this particular man, the proper
imitation to which his calling ("Child!") directed him:

> Shall I then sing, skipping thy dolefull storie,
>   And side with thy triumphant glorie?
> Shall thy strokes be my stroking? thorns, my flower?
>   Thy rod, my posie? crosse, my bower?
> But how then shall I imitate thee, and
>   Copie thy fair, though bloudie hand?   (ll. 11-16)

One of many on the same theme, this poem is a contest
between the poet and his Lord—the poet will repay love
with more love, he will give his wealth away in alms, he
will predestine himself to build (three years hence) a
hospital for the afflicted. But God "prevents" him everywhere. Whatever the poet would do, God has always done
it already, and done it perfectly. Whenever the poet thinks
he has given *all* away, he meets the realization of God's
infinite resources of sacrifice and love. Even in verse, God
has "prevented" him—

If thou shalt give me wit, it shall appeare,
If thou hast giv'n it me, 'tis here.

(ll. 43-44)

In the published *Temple*, the next poem following, "The Reprisall," is in one manuscript entitled "The Second Thanksgiving." The theme of "The Thanksgiving" appears with extraordinary conciseness in "The Reprisall." God's "prevention" in this poem is the reprisal for the poet's temerity, as a fallen man, in entering into any sort of imitation of Him. The poem turns (turns literally) upon the Pauline paradox of the old and new Adam in each man. Though he loses his contest with God, the new man nonetheless makes a conquest of the old man, "Who once against thee fought." In the end, the reprisal is the gift of grace after all, a gift utterly incommensurate with man's highest deserts; in other words, the reprisal turns out to be, not a punishment but a reward, not a fine but a redemption, a recapture, a *reprise* of innocence; a rhetorical as well as a spiritual *reprise* of the theme with which the poem, as well as human history, began.

With these poems we move into an area of expression very difficult to discuss, since it is involved with problems at the limits of linguistic experience, or at the limits of discourse: tautology and paradox. Tautology, in the theoretically perfect definition, repeats itself; paradox (as well as antinomy and contradiction) makes an equation of two things manifestly unlike. In tautology, what is, is; in paradox, what is, is and is not. The *logos* theology, the *logos* idea, makes both statements; in Herbert's exploitation of the *logos*, he tries to achieve perfection in both its paradoxes and its tautology—and in both at once. In "Prayer (I)" he presents the supralogical nature both of the nature and experience of prayer, his syntax matching his passage beyond the conventional limits of feeling. The poem is an extended apposition of apparently haphazard metaphors, some original with the poet, others familiar *topoi*:

> Prayer the Churches banquet, Angels age,
>   Gods breath in man returning to his birth,
>   The soul in paraphrase, heart in pilgrimage,
> The Christian plummet sounding heav'n and earth;
> Engine against th' Almightie, sinners towre,
>   Reversed thunder, Christ-side-piercing spear,
>   The six-daies world transposing in an houre,
> A kinde of tune, which all things heare and fear;
> Softnesse, and peace, and joy, and love, and blisse,
>   Exalted Manna, gladnesse of the best,
>   Heaven in ordinarie, man well drest,
> The milkie way, the bird of Paradise,
>   Church-bels beyond the starres heard, the
>   souls bloud,
>   The land of spices; something understood.
>
>   (ll. 1-14)

For all the modulation of the tone, the juxtaposition of images is very taxing: though it is clear how prayer is an "Engine against th' Almightie," it is not so clear how it is the "sinners towre," or "Reversed thunder," or a "man well drest" (though the poem "Aaron" helps to explain the last puzzle). The whole poem is an attempt to bracket, to close in upon the *logos* without limiting its extent, to find some words to invoke the word for which no other words will do, the Word that is, in the end, simply "something understood."

The poem called "The Quidditie" in *The Temple* is, in the manuscript of Herbert's poems in Dr. Williams' Library, called "Poetry." In her fascinating essay,[15] Mrs. Stambler has pointed out Herbert's negative reliance upon the troubadour tradition in his resolute denial that verse

[15] Elizabeth Stambler, "The Unity of Herbert's 'Temple,'" *Cross Currents*, x (1960), pp. 251-66.

is any of the things secular poets say it is. It is not a crown, a point of honor, a gay suit, not a hawk, a banquet, or renown; it is neither a good sword nor a lute. It is not a lot of other things as well; this poem reverses the trick of "Prayer (I)." Instead of adding his metaphors until the poem approximates the inexpressible experience of "something understood," in "The Quidditie" Herbert subtracts. The poem relies upon the scholastic use of negative constructs, the elimination of everything about an essence by the definition of what it is not. Just as in "The Reprisall" to lose all (in that case, to lose one's self) was really to gain all (salvation), so in "The Quidditie" the major image is a game of hazard in which, as in Pascal's *pari*, everything is risked.

In the scholastic fashion, "The Quidditie" sets a riddle and never tells the answer, never tells what *what* is. The essence of a thing, its *quidditas*, can never be known, at best recognized only through the experience of paring away essentials, of discovery. In the case of quiddities, only the concept of *logos* subsumes the essences of separate things; and only the *logos* really knows what all things really are, because the *logos* is in all things, and only the *logos* knows itself. "The wayes of learning," as Herbert affirmed in "The Pearl," are of no fundamental use. Learning can never teach men the mysteries at the heart of things; scholars are betrayed to and by their books, are wrapped in their gowns as if in their shrouds. Cognition cannot tell the secrets of *logos*; the best that men can hope for is a kind of Platonic recognition, or "something understood."

Poetry is, then, once more displayed as an image for essential mystery—that is, for the hiddenness of all essences, as well as for the one mystery essential to (and necessary for) our salvation. The quiddity of the Word

is that it is, whether it be called *logos* or Jehovah or a
poem, for (as John had been at pains to incorporate into
the doctrine) from *logos* comes the whole conceivable and
actual world. The creating Word made the world and,
made flesh, knew the created world as all men may know
it. Poetry, words arrayed in an order expressive of God's
order, likewise attempts to describe and to create, to reconstruct the world and to move men to reconstruct themselves. In "Obedience" the poet managed (in a pun!) to
transform the metaphor of his poem into the substance of
that poem, which is the deed of conveyance between himself and God:

> My God, if writings may
> Convey a Lordship any way
> Whither the buyer and the seller please;
> Let it not thee displease,
> If this poore paper do as much as they.
>
> (ll. 1-5)

By the time the poem ("my speciall Deed") is done, so
is the transaction; metaphor has become content, the deed
so tightly drawn that the critic can no longer distinguish
between form and matter—*logos*.

In "Providence," Herbert dealt in one poem with all
the problems separately tackled before. He rejoices in the
neatness of the tightly packed, plenitudinous world—

> Thy creatures leap not, but expresse a feast,
> Where all the guests sit close, and nothing wants.
> Frogs marry fish and flesh; bats, birds and beast;
> Sponges, non-sense and sense; mines, th' earth and plants.
>
> (ll. 133-36)

"All the guests sit close, and nothing wants"—the world
is, in one of Herbert's major metaphors, a cabinet full-
stored with all the possible variety of created things. But
as critics observe about him, Herbert is as content, as full

of satisfaction, as the world he describes; his imagination
does not burst out of the world's confines into an infinite
space infinitely filled with an infinite variety of things, as
a little later in the century, in their different ways, Spinoza, Malebranche, and Traherne were all to do.[16] Herbert's metaphors are tidy, his fullness always fits, "nothing
wants" in his universe—not even the poet wants, with the
insatiable holy desires, for example, of Bruno or Traherne.
Just the same, he was not a poet of rigid limitation, afraid
of the implications of infinity, neat though his imagery of
closeness, rightness, fitness may be. The world for Herbert
was a box "where sweets compacted lie," but a metaphysical box, a box without dimensions. He never forgot that
the Creator's power was unlimited—however huge the
total universe, however tiny the least created thing, God
is always present in it.

> Thou art in small things great, not small in any:
> Thy even praise can neither rise, nor fall.
> Thou art in all things one, in each thing many:
> For thou art infinite in one and all.   (ll. 41-44)

Like the skeptically paradoxical Montaigne, or the scho-
lastically paradoxical Donne, Herbert recognized the inevitable paradoxes of the infinite and gloried in them as
images of God's inexpressible power. His immanent God
had the marvelous characteristic of making all things
greater than they were in themselves—indeed, through
God's good grace, the moral life of Christians exemplified
this miracle every day. So with this poem, full of the riddles of the wonderfully paradoxical Creator:

> Light without winde is glasse: warm without weight
> Is wooll and furre: cool without closenesse, shade:

[16] See Nicolson, *The Breaking of the Circle*, pp. 180-82.

> Speed without pains, a horse: tall, without height,
> A swift hawk: low without losse, a spade.
>
> (ll. 101-104)

And most wonderful of all, from one single thing many other things can be revealed as from the *logos* all meanings, all understanding, can be drawn:

> The Indian nut alone
> Is clothing, meat and trencher, drink and can,
> Boat, cable, sail and needle, all in one.   (ll. 126-28)

The coconut has never been so dignified as in this image for the providential God—the God, incidentally, Whose act of total foreknowledge, or providence, combines all things in one view, Whose providence is over all things forever—but, oddly enough, Herbert is merely deifying an ancient paradoxical trope, the praise of the nut.[17] Where Donne's rhetoric would somehow have pointed to his Sophist source in such a metaphor, Herbert always understates: he so mutes, so "evens" his references, fits them so closely into the pattern of his thought, that they appear completely natural, informally conceived and selected. The "fit" in Herbert's verse, we think, is exact.

Yet such a fit, surely, is an illusion: no fit is ever exact and all similitudes are rough likenesses. Over and over again Herbert reminds us (very quietly, it is true) of the failure of even the best poems truly to fit—of the paradoxes inherent in the quiddity of things, and therefore in the quiddity of poems, and particularly in poems dealing with the quiddity of poems. No fit need be exact, nor can be, since all things both are what they are and are more than that, by virtue of their creation by the divine Word. A poem partakes of the divine Creation in its own continuing creation.

[17] See Burgess, *Epideictic Literature*; Pease, "Things without Honour."

> O Sacred Providence, who from end to end
> Strongly and sweetly movest, shall I write,
> And not of thee, through whom my fingers bend
> To hold my quill?   (ll. 1-4)

The poem "Providence" tries to take the divine point of view, to review and re-create the Creation. Its message, in this case overtly the message of God, is designed to move the hearts of men and to re-create in men's minds a sense of the Creation's scope. So much is simple enough to grasp, but there is an implicit *num*, that pessimistic particle expecting the answer "no," in the very first stanza. It is in fact, as the poem "discovers," impossible for a poet to write "not of thee"; whether poets know it or not, all poems, Herbert finally comes to realize, are sacred poems. The quiddity of poetry, of making and creating, partakes of the original mysterious creating word, and is an imitation of the essence of *logos*.

We may think, Herbert says, that we praise God in our song, and that such praise of Him is our free offering. This is true, and it isn't—we can hardly help praising God, since all things by their existence praise Him all the time. God's "even praise can neither rise, nor fall" because it is always total, always perfect; whatever the poet does merely adds his consciousness to the poem of praise that all things continually raise. As he becomes aware of this mysterious fact of existence (for instance, in the very course of writing the poem "Providence"), the poet may founder, despairing of saying anything at all worthy of his God—

> But who hath praise enough? nay, who hath any?
> None can express thy works, but he that knows them . . .

And God's words cannot be known by mere human comprehension, neither in their specific essences nor in the range of their infinite variety:

> And none can know thy works, which are so many,
> And so complete, but onely he that owes them.
>
> (ll. 141-42)

Nevertheless, a poem must have its place in the total scheme, because

> All things that are, though they have sev'rall wayes,
> Yet in their being joyn with one advise
> To honour thee: and so I give thee praise
> In all my other hymnes, but in this twice.
>
> (ll. 145-48)

Twice, that is to say, once in the statement of the poem, which adds to the sum of all things that intrinsically testify to God's providence; and again, in the poet's conscious awareness that his poem is only a material copy, a copy in pen and ink and on paper, of the creating Word. For in the divine mind, all poems have always existed, "prevented" before poets could write them—

> If thou shalt give me wit, it shall appeare,
> If thou hast giv'n it me, 'tis here.
>
> (ll. 43-44)

How this is possible, how a poem can be in the mind of God before it is written from the mind of its specific poet, is a mystery and a riddle. Lest this gentle, essential mystery be unclear to any reader, Herbert rewrote his penultimate stanza in "Providence" in an ultimate variant, a riddling answer but a plain one:

> Each thing that is, although in use and name
> It go for one, hath many wayes in store
> To honour thee; and so each hymne thy fame
> Extolleth many wayes, but this one more.
>
> (ll. 149-52)

The poem ends, as its meanings do, upon a deliberate and

carefully limited ambiguity.[18] It ends, that is to say, on a double meaning, because only ambiguity and double meaning fit the subject, which is divine totality, necessarily involving ambiguity and multiple meaning. Specifically, the last line of "Providence" means that the poem adds another way to the many ways in which God's greatness is extolled; also that it adds more to the store of praise directed to God; and that by its own addition of "one more" voice to the choir of praise, it extends by one the infinite progression from man to his Creator. The paradox in the last line is a tautology, since it re-creates a simple fact about God—a fact that would be complex if it applied to any created thing (save perhaps creation itself), but is simple because it applies to God.

For Herbert, the poet's job is at once simple, like tautology, and impossible, like paradox: the only thing that can ease the poet's job at all, is his total devotion to the *logos*. Then inevitably he will be rewarded by his kindly Lord—

> And if I please him, I write fine and wittie . . . ;[19]

his poetry will shine, a reflection of holy wit. The rewards, indeed, are infinite, if the poet can learn to match his form to his matter; as Herbert said in the supremely contented meditation upon life, death, spiritual dryness, and creativity, "The Flower,"

> Thy word is all, if we could spell.[20]

The indefinable "something" of *logos* once understood, all

[18] For a brilliant discussion of the limits of ambiguity, see Nowottny, Chapter 7.

[19] "The Forerunners," l. 12.

[20] For another example of the poetic significance of spelling "right," see Constantijn Huygens' sonnet, "Sondag" (Colie, "Constantijn Huygens and the Metaphysical Mode," p. 66).

things become clear—the last shall be first, the small great, the least thing sufficient for total content:

> Let wits contest,
> And with their words and posies windows fill:
> *Lesse than the least*
> *Of all thy mercies,* is my posie still.
>
> This on my ring,
> This by my picture, in my book I write:
> Whether I sing,
> Or say, or dictate, this is my delight.
>
> Invention rest,
> Comparisons go play, wit use thy will:
> *Lesse than the least*
> *Of all Gods mercies,* is my posie still.[21]

In "Grief" Herbert had felt the whole world to be but "A narrow cupboard" for his "griefs and doubts," empty of provision (of nourishment and of providence) for his starving soul. Verses had seemed to him "too fine a thing, too wise/ For my rough sorrows"; he had then enjoined himself to "cease, be dumbe and mute," since words could neither match his misery nor shake him from his bitter discontent. But by the end of *The Temple* he had learned the full contents of his text—had taken both his provision and his contentment from the fullness of God's providential creation; so that in any created thing, whether infinitely large and complex or infinitesimally small and neat, he could read the paradoxes of totality and multiplicity implied in the notion of the divine *logos*.

[21] *The Posie,* ll. 1-12.

Part III
Ontological Paradoxes: Being and Becoming

7

"Nothing is but what is not":
Solutions to the Problem of Nothing

Nor need we feare this term annihilation. . . .
              Browne, *Religio Medici*, I. 50

THE TERM "nothing" presents logical problems as surely as does the term "infinity"—and presents as well much the same problem. At either end of the conceptual scale, "nothing" and "infinity" both bring man to the same impassable intellectual position, where he is himself by definition no longer the measure of all things, nor even the measure of anything at all. The problem of "nothing," beginning as a problem raised by negative affirmation, even in literature soon turned into a psychological as well as a logical and rhetorical problem. Not only is the logical problem raised, of affirming what is "not," but also, by the affirmation, "nothing" seems to be transformed exactly into "something," a positive entity.

For this reason, Parmenides warned his disciples against "the way of not-being," as his disciple the Sophist informs Theaetetus:

But the great Parmenides, my boy, from the time when we were children to the end of his life . . . constantly repeated in both prose and verse:

Never let this thought prevail, saith he, that
                    not-being is,
But keep your mind from this way of investigation.[1]

The dialogue from which this quotation comes, *The Soph-*

[1] Plato, *The Sophist*, ed. Harold North Fowler (Loeb Classical Library), pp. 336-39.

ist, illustrates the hopelessness of Parmenides' warning, since the dialogue at once proceeds to explore the problems of not-being inherent in all negative utterances. Ultimately the Sophist grants a kind of reality to statements about not-being, to untruths, falsehoods, and lies; though the "being" he grants such statements is a qualified one, even a paradoxical one. The being of not-being turns out to be the "truth" of falsehood, a truth appropriate to its untruth. Donne plays upon the notion in "Loves Deitie," at the poem's ending:

> Love might make me leave loving, or might trie
> A deeper plague, to make her love mee too,
> Which, since she loves before, I 'am loth to see;
> Falshood is worse then hate; and that must bee,
> If shee whom I love, should love mee. (ll. 24-28)

In the very falsehood of falsehood lies its peculiar truth: the statement, like the Liar paradox, is both tautology and paradox, since falsehoods must be false in order to be true.

In spite of Eleatic tendencies to paradox, Parmenides and Zeno drew the line at the kind of paradoxical speculation they could not control, such as paradoxes about "nothing." By being uttered, paradoxes of "nothing" had to grant to "nothing" a kind of being which Parmenides could not permit. Outside his Eleatic concept of being, "nothing" was not permitted to be conceived—the idea of nothing, then, threatened the ground of the Eleatic system. But not even Parmenides, as Plato's dialogue so ironically suggests, could legislate about speculative subjects: for minds of the dialectical habit, once "being" had been postulated, "not-being" and "nothing" inevitably came to attention.[2] In obedience to dialectical symmetry, "nothing," "not-being," the void, and the vacuum all had

[2] Martin Foss, *The Idea of Perfection* (Princeton University Press, 1946), p. 4, and passim.

to be considered as soon as "all," the cosmos, and the universe were conceived. All the same, the major philosophers of Greece were chary of "nothing," denying its validity as fact and as concept. Platonic plenism and Aristotelian *horror vacui* denied existence to "nothing"; Christian orthodoxy followed them in this respect, canonizing a single, divine *creatio ex nihilo* at which *nihil* was transformed, for good, by the blast of God's mouth into *omnis*, the cosmos, the universe, total being. After the Genesis with which Scripture began, Lear's dictum is self-evident, that "Nothing can come of nothing," as is Donne's hopeful view of his unhappy love:

> Yet nothing can to nothing fall,
> Nor any place be empty quite. . . .[3]

In spite of orthodox philosophical and theological rejection of "nothing," real and ideal, one persistent strain in Greek philosophy, never entirely repressed, concerned itself with the two related forbidden subjects, infinity (or limitlessness) and nothing (or the void).[4] The atomist tradition of Leucippus, Epicurus, and Democritus hypothesized an actual void in which, by chance alone, the flux of material atoms conjoined to form the physical types recognizable to human perception. In the Renaissance, that underground stream turned out to be the sacred river feeding the new physics, stimulating such men as Bacon, Galileo, Descartes, Gassendi, Boyle, Locke, Newton, and a host of lesser "naturalists" to new and increasingly persuasive descriptions of the physical universe. But draughts of that stream were dangerous to those baptized in Jordan: the Greek atomists, together with their spokesman Lucretius, were generally regarded as atheists, both because they

[3] "The Broken Heart," ll. 25-26, *The Poems of John Donne,* ed. Grierson.
[4] See below, Chapters 10, 15.

failed to postulate a regnant God in their universe and because, in the post-Aristotelian universe, acceptance of the idea of the void was *ipso facto* atheistic.[5]

Naturally enough, there was speculation into "nothing" during the Renaissance, usually undertaken in conjunction with notions of infinity. Nicholas of Cusa, as concerned with infinitesimals as with infinity, was never questioned on grounds of heresy, though his works are full of the metaphysics of "nothing." Copernicus too, safe so long as his hypothesis was in no danger of empirical ratification, laid the groundwork for speculation both about an infinite universe and an infinity of worlds within it. His notions were pleasing enough to Englishmen safe on their island, like Henry More and Thomas Traherne,[6] but transposed in the Italian mind of Giordano Bruno, they proved exceedingly dangerous to their defender.[7]

Even for logicians and rhetoricians, the twinned ideas of infinity and nothing are technically dangerous; since they are so wild, at the loose edge of conceptualization and of discourse, nullifying—literally—ideas of order and ordination, nullifying logical and rhetorical formulations. Certainly the two notions resist domestication within the mind: they are also psychologically destructive, threatening the familiar boundaries of human experience and of intellectual efforts to get the better of that recalcitrant experience. Within orthodoxy, the negative theology capitalized upon the attribution of transcendence to divinity—but the negative theology had to be carefully expressed, too, so as not to verge upon blasphemy. Even divinity should not be too roundly expressed in negative

[5] See below, Chapter 8, for a discussion of this point.

[6] See above, Chapter 4.

[7] For a general discussion of Bruno's cosmological views, see Alexandre Koyré, *From the Closed World to the Infinite Universe* (Johns Hopkins Press, 1957).

terms.[8] Of all the things that God was "not," not-being and nothing were chief. God, as it were, annihilated nothing by His Creation: "Mere vacuity, the first agent, God, the first instrument, will not admit. . . ."[9]

Because, as Donne said, formal paradoxes were self-cancellations and therefore "no things," they often took, as a subject to fit their own decorum, *nihil*, thus matching their matter to their form. In the Renaissance one can find many such paradoxes, appealing because of their impossible affirmations and opportunities for double negation. All affirmations about "nothing," it turned out, might be taken as analogues to God's original act of Creation, bringing "something" out of "nothing"—or, contradicted the truism of King Lear. The conciliation of opposites in paradox was already one kind of imitation of the divine Creation—*nihil* paradoxes aspire to the imitation of God's unique original act.

In precisely that imitation lay the danger: paradoxes about *omnis*, or "all" (such as Herbert's "Providence," discussed in the preceding chapter) might be regarded as pious imitations of God's plenist Creation, but *nihil* paradoxes were another matter altogether. They were engaged in an operation at once imitative and blasphemous, at once sacred and profane, since the formal paradox, conventionally regarded as low, parodied at the same time as it imitated the divine act of Creation. And yet, who can accuse

---

[8] Die zarte Gottheit ist ein Nichts und Übernichts:
   Wer nichts in allem sieht, Mensch, glaube, dieser sichts.
   (Angelus Silesius, *Cherubinischer Wandersmann*, 1.111, in
   Sämtliche Poetische Werke, ed. Hans Ludwig Held
   [München, 1949], III.17);

   Gott ist wahrhaftig nichts, und so er etwas ist,
   So ist ers nur in mir, wie er mich ihm erkiest.
        (*C.W.*, 1.200; *S.P.W.*, III.29)

[9] Donne, *Devotions*, p. 30.

the paradoxist of blasphemy, really? Since his subject *is*
nothing, he cannot be said to be impious in taking the
Creator's prerogative as his own—for nothing, as all men
know, can come of nothing. Nor indeed is he directing
men to dangerous speculation, since at the very most he
beguiles them into—nothing.[10] And, most important of
all points in the paradoxist's defense, the paradoxical *nihil*
imitates the truth of the Cretan's lie: if the paradoxist lies,
he does not lie, since he lies about nothing.

Furthermore, the temptation to play with the idea was
too great for men to pass up who wanted to try their
logical and rhetorical skill on difficult subjects, particularly
when the self-contradictions implicit in the subject granted
them immunity from the imputation of ungracious im-
piety. There were, thus, many *nihils* written in the Renaissance, of which the most famous was the Latin poem published by Jean Passerat, professor of rhetoric at Henry
III's Palace Academy in Paris. This poem was published,
republished, imitated, and annotated throughout the next
fifty years. Nothing, Passerat informs us, is richer than
precious stones and than gold; nothing is finer than ada-
mant, nothing nobler than the blood of kings; nothing is
sacred in wars; nothing is greater than Socrates' wisdom
—indeed, by his own affirmation, nothing *is* Socrates'
wisdom. "Nothing" is the subject of the speculations of the
great Zeno; nothing is higher than heaven; nothing is beyond the walls of the world; nothing is lower than hell, or
more glorious than virtue—and so on, and on, and on.[11]

[10] A. E. Malloch makes the point beautifully in his "The Techniques and Function of the Renaissance Paradox," cited above, Introduction, n. 1.

[11] Jean Passerat, "Nihil," to be found in many Renaissance an-
thologies, here cited from *Amphitheatrum sapientiae socraticae
joco-seriae*, ed. Dornavius, 1.736, where it is followed by its translations and adaptations.

The poem was translated into French (as "Rien," a word syntactically less maneuverable than "nihil"),[12] copied in another poem called "Aliquid," which was in turn translated as "Quelquechose," and in another called "Nemo," and finally answered in a fine poem called "Tout," which (naturally) summed up all the others:

> Du RIEN de Passerat QUELQUECHOSE n'asquit.
> Passerat pour un RIEN un bien grand los asquit.
> Et celuy qui d'un RIEN QUELQUECHOSE a fait naistre,
> N'a pas tiré sans los un estre d'un non estre.[13]

("Something has been added to Passerat's Nothing. Passerat acquired large praise for Nothing. And he who of Nothing made Something, has not taken without praise being from not-being").

Passerat's poem was a productive, originating "nothing," resulting in so many more paradoxes: as Donne warned in his letter, paradox begets paradox.

In an English poem, "On the Letter O," the ideas of perfection and totality connected with *omnis* and the image of the circle combine with the nihilisms of the idea of nothing. The letter "O," and the figure, is itself, the poet says, framed of nothing; the whole cosmos is a box of "O's." "0" (zero) is a cipher which, "deciphered,"—that is, understood and un-nothinged—makes "all." The last couplet plays upon the triviality, the "nothing" of the paradox itself:

[12] Passerat, *Le Bon-iour de R. de B. en reponce aux, Nihil, Nemo* . . . (Paris, 1599); see also William Cornwallis, *Essayes* (London, 1617), E₃-E₄; "The Prayse of Nothing," a poem attributed to Edward Dyer and to Edward Daunce, and a host of other "nothings" through the Renaissance and into the eighteenth century (Henry Knight Miller, "The Paradoxical Encomium with Special Reference to its Vogue in England, 1600-1800," gives the most efficient list of these).

[13] *Le Bon-iour*, p. 25.

But O enough, I have done my reader wrong,
Mine O was round, and I have made it long.[14]

From the "O" to the egg was an obvious step, since the
egg was the symbol of generation and creation; since, too,
it bore the shape of zero, contradictions of all and nothing
could be constructed on eggs, and were. The Dutch rhetorician, Erycius Puteanus, wrote a fine "Ovi encomium,"
in which the "everything" which comes from the egg is
likened to the "nothing" that is more beautiful and more
delicate than the egg.[15] The egg, of course, was a particularly creative nothing, since it contained within its smooth
zero-shape new fledglings, or new being. The last sentence
of the long praise of the egg reads, mock-solemnly:

Si recte expendimus, difficilius etiam dicas ovum, quam comedas.
Vestrum erit, Auditores, haec tanquam amoena, et simul tanquam seria amplecti. Qui jucundi estis, flores litterarum et
amoenitates, habetis; qui graves et severi, habetis fructuo. Ego
quidem de Ovo quia dixi, nec ab elegantia, nec a sapientia
recessisse videor: pulchrius nemo linguam, nemo ingenium
occupavit. Etenim quicquid natura benigne protulit, quicquid ars
industriaque in usum atque voluptatem humanam imitata est,
et excoluit, denique quicquid Orbis continet, in ovo est. Dixi.[16]

("If we weigh it rightly, you proclaim the egg with more
difficulty than you eat it. It will be your lot, my hearers, to be
filled with this [oration] both pleasant and serious. You who
are merry shall have the flowers and delights of letters; you
who are grave and severe shall have it for use. Since I speak
something of the egg, I shall be seen to have drawn neither

[14] *Facetiae* (London, 1817), II. 389-92.
[15] *Admiranda rerum admirabilium encomia* (Nijmegen, 1677),
pp. 1-56.
[16] See also *Pan Omnis*, by J. A. Brassicanus (Dornavius, 1.719),
and the many "omnis" paradoxes there following. The relation of
"all" and "nothing," the circle and zero, may bear some relation
to the translation of "l'oeuf," in tennis, into the English word "love."

from elegance nor from wisdom: no one has more beautifully taken possession of my tongue, my invention. And indeed whatever nature has kindly offered, whatever art and industry have imitated and cultivated for the use and pleasure of mankind, finally whatever the world contains, is in the egg. I have spoken.")

The frivolous spirit that brought forth paradoxical "no things" produced other forms of "nothing" as learned recreations. Donne's *Catalogus aulicorum*,[17] for instance, was one exercise on the model of Rabelais' Library of St. Victor, made up of nonexistent books, a library more miraculous and more admirable than the most recherché Renaissance collection.[18] Sir Thomas Browne had made another wonderful list with a good paradoxical title: his *Musaeum clausum, or, Bibliotheca abscondita*[19] was a collection, as he said, of "Some remarkable Books, Antiquities, Pictures and Rarities of several kinds, scarce or never seen by any Man now living"—in other words, a parody of the cabinets of the learned and the virtuosi, who displayed their connoisseurship (or that of their agents) to all visitors to their houses.[20] Browne's collection was composed of all kinds of learned jokes, resurrected books long lost, made-up books and pictures, and books pretended by false scholars to have been in existence. His "rarities" were largely made up, like the experiments in the Grand Academy of Lagado, of the "real" parts of recognized rarities—or, if his rarities were entirely made up, they bore inscriptions from Horace, Pliny, or another great writer, to authenticate them. In fact they were all made

[17] John Donne, *Library, or Catalogus librorum aulicorum . . .* , ed. Evelyn M. Simpson (London, 1930).

[18] See above, Chapter 1.

[19] Browne, *Works*, ed. Geoffrey Keynes (London and Oxford, 1964), III.109-19.

[20] See below, Chapter 10.

of thin air, sucked out of the thumb of Sir Thomas Browne: and though they were foolish, they displayed at once his learning and his wit.

The libraries Rabelais, Donne, and Browne made up were intended to cover "all" subjects, were a mock-encyclopedia of learning, "encircling" all learning by the selection of imaginary books. They formed a kind of empty circle, favorite emblem of both "all" and "nothing." In his long, elegant discourse upon "nothing," delivered before Goclenius at Wittenberg, Cornelius Gotz began with the ambiguous circle image, symbol at once of every-thing and nothing, of totality and (as Cusanus had made mystifyingly evident) of zero. Gotz diverted himself and his audience by asking perfectly reasonable questions about unreason: is it, he asked, something by sleight-of-hand, or is it nothing? does evil exist or does it not? is *place* (a point) nothing (emptiness, or empty space), or, as the Hebrew word *makom* has it, a substitute word for deity, and therefore a substitute word for absolute perfection and totality?[21] Even to the halting Latinist, Gotz's logical passages are very pretty, making distinctions very difficult in English structure:

Principium materiale mundi est non nihil: Enunciatum affirma-tum falsum est. Principium materiale mundi non est nihil. Enunciatum negatum verum est. Socrates dixit, hoc unum scio quod nihil scio; Enunciatio haec est exceptiva, sententio enim est, Nihil scio, praeter hoc, quod nihil scio.[22]

("The primary material of the world is not-nothing. Stated affirmatively it is false. The primary material of the world is-not nothing. Stated negatively it is true. Socrates said, I know only that I know nothing; this statement is excep-

[21] See Max Jammer, *Concepts of Space* (Harvard University Press, 1954), p. 26.

[22] Dornavius, 1.733.

tional, for the sentence is, I know nothing except that I know nothing.")

In return for such a fine display of (useless) learning, Goclenius paid his pupil a witty compliment, thereby robbing the joke of some of its point:

> Ex nihilo non ad nihil a Goetzee create,
> Non est de nihilo, de Nihilo quod agis.[23]

("Not from the nothing to the nothing made by Gotz, / It is not of nothing, that nothing with which you deal.")

There were many other *nihil* paradoxes, some entirely trivial, like the prose joke often attributed to Edward Dyer, Rochester's poetical encomium, and even Fielding's prose praise of nothing.[24] The most interesting mock-encomia of "nothing," however, are not the direct presentations of the subject, but those uses of nothing which relate the frightening concept of emptiness, of annihilation, to something else. Not at all surprisingly, love poetry often has recourse to the notion of "nothing," doubtless because the "totality" invokes its opposite, parallel to the recurrent dialectic of love and death in love situations: in the Sonnets, for instance, Shakespeare refers to himself as "nothing," both "nothing worth" and an actual "nothing" after his death and the death of his fame; throughout, his "nothing" image is used in contrast to the notion of his beloved's intrinsic worth and worthiness.[25] In Sonnet 136, one of the poems self-referring to "Will," he plays again upon his own value, and the value his lady sets on him:

> For nothing hold me, so it please thee hold
> That nothing me, a something sweet to thee. . . .

[23] Dornavius, 1.739.
[24] See Miller, "The Paradoxical Encomium," for a full list.
[25] Shakespeare, Sonnet 72. See below, p. 368.

That is, let her value him at nothing, for so long as that nothing is what she values, it is "something," a "nothing" brought into existence by the fact of her "holding" him at all.

Donne's love poetry is full of nothings and of annihilations, though that is far from his entire subject. "A Nocturnall upon St. Lucies Day"[26] is a highly serious poem, even if its ending is slightly less dark than its argument leads us to expect: and notions of annihilation are reversed on the divine analogy, into miraculous re-creation and resurrection.

The poet makes of himself, in short, an extraordinary nothing, like the egg, from whom new life comes. In the "Nocturnall" Donne describes "an ordinary nothing" as "shadow," the deceptive, illusory, elusive mark of darkness that a man makes between the earth and the sun. "Umbra," or shadow, was a popular paradoxist's subject; Janus Dousa had written a Latin poem called "Umbra" on the peculiar bodiless picturing-forth of body that the shadow is,[27] and the collections of paradoxes published many more. "A Lecture upon the Shadow" is a lecture upon the visibility, the sharpness, the depth, and the transiency of love itself: the shadow, an impalpable accidental record of human presence, is made the image of the nothingness of both love and the living, breathing lovers. With the high sun, as in the height of love, then "to brave clearnesse all things are reduc'd"; but unless love remains at its height, shadows overtake all the world:

> Except our loves at this noone stay,
> We shall new shadowes make the other way.

[26] See Frank Kermode, *John Donne* (British Council Pamphlet, London, 1957), pp. 21-23, and above, Chapter 3.

[27] Dousa, "Laus Umbrae," *Dissertationum ludicrarum et amœnitatum scriptores varii* (Leiden, 1638).

> As the first were made to blinde
> Others; these which come behinde
> Will worke upon our selves, and blind our eyes.
> If our loves faint, and westwardly decline;
> To me thou, falsly, thine,
> And I to thee mine actions shall disguise.
> The morning shadowes weare away,
> But these grow longer all the day,
> But oh, loves day is short, if love decay.[28]   (ll. 14-24)

With the lengthening shadows, "absence, darknesse, death; things which are not" overtake the intensity of love's life and reduce it, in its end, to nothingness.

Shadows are natural images for man's decay; for God's eyes, though, even light is a shadow. God, the Light of Light, is so brilliant that what human sense takes to be "light" is for Him merely shadow. All life, however light-filled, can thus be seen to be a valley of the shadow of death. As Montaigne said, all life is simply the learning to die well. "The first day of your birth doth as wel adresse you to die, as to live,"[29] he sternly informed his readers. Death can reduce a man to "nothing," but is far "lesse to be feared than nothing, if there were any thing lesse than nothing." After some exploitation of the psychological terrors inherent in the idea of existential nothing, Montaigne allays them, declaring death to be irrelevant to mortal speculation:

> Nor alive, nor dead, it doth concerne you nothing. Alive, because you are: Dead, because you are no more. Moreover, no man dies before his houre. The time you leave behinde was no more yours, than that which was before your birth, and concerneth you no more.   (1.xix.61)

---

[28] See below, Chapter 15, p. 477, for another significant shadow.
[29] Michel de Montaigne, *Essayes*, trans. John Florio, ed. J.I.M. Stewart (New York, Modern Library, 1933), 1.xix.59. All references are to this edition, and indicate Book, Essay, and page.

Montaigne's instructions for dying well involve coming to terms with not-being in general and privately, or intellectually and psychologically. His calmness in the face of death and its idea, rests on his having himself made his peace with his own ignorance, his own nescience. For him, the idea that matter must have existed before the Creation was simply another example of human provincialism: "This law thou aleagest is but a municipall law, and thou knowest not what the universall is . . ." (ii.xii.469). Since God's "nothing," whatever it is, cannot be evil and may not be nothing, man has, then, nothing to fear. Browne repeats the *topos* in an epigram: at their deaths, men pass from the sunlight into light ineffable—on earth, "*Lux est umbra Dei.*"[30] By the indomitable logic of contradiction, the notion of nothing, in the atomist philosophy the "proof" of atheism, becomes another way of figuring forth God and of measuring, by negative affirmation, His everlasting totality and light.

As Professor Jorgenson has pointed out, in the sixteenth century the word "nothing" had so many applications to so many important matters that there was bound to be much ado about it—part of the fun of that grim comedy, *Much Ado about Nothing*, is in the sexual reference of the word "nothing," now fairly submerged, which spoke at once to the Elizabethan ear.[31] In the same sense, Shakespeare managed, in *Hamlet*, to make "nothing" refer to a great deal more than the female genitalia, though that fundamental vulgarity lay at the base of much said about "nothing," as well as at the base of much of the play's

---

[30] Browne, *Religio Medici*, ed. L. C. Martin (Oxford, 1964), p. 10.

[31] Paul A. Jorgenson, "Much Ado about *Nothing*," *SQ*, v (1954), 287-95.

action.[32] In Shakespeare's tragedies, there are remarkable uses of nothing, the "nothing" of the bawdy play, exploited in comic situations, the metaphysical "nothing" of the rhetorical paradoxists, and the psychological sense of not-being with which Montaigne was concerned.

As a literary form, tragedy particularly deals with a man's moral and psychological being, with a man's measure and with man's measure, with the implications for other human beings of any human action. Tragedy is, also, the literary form most dependent upon the "paradox of the fortunate fall," translated from divine into human terms.[33] Thematically, tragedy relies upon this paradox for its meaning. Since the hero falls and is expected to reach his end not by accident but by some moral logic, making his end credible and fitting, he must conventionally be involved in his own destruction, his own undoing. One of the possible "fortunate" aspects of his fall is that he may "know" as a result of his undoing far more than he knew while he wittingly or unwittingly connived at it. All this is so deeply traditional in tragedy that, outside of the classroom, we take it all for granted as the necessary thematic rule of a fairly strict form. Within the form, however, a writer has license to exploit more or less verbal, rhetorical, religious, metaphysical, or moral paradoxes as he chooses; and Shakespeare chose. The idea of nothing is remarkably powerful in several of his tragedies.

Macbeth, that extraordinarily brief Shakespearean play, concentrates with peculiar intensity on not-being, and therefore on nothing. Certainly Macbeth destroys Macbeth, by design, on purpose, scrupulously, and completely. The play is about Macbeth's undoing, which is also, in a

---

[32] Thomas Pyles, "Ophelia's Nothing," *MLN*, XLIV (1949), 322-23.

[33] See Herbert Weisinger, *Tragedy and the Paradox of the Fortunate Fall*, for a study of this problem.

verbal and moral paradox, entirely Macbeth's doing: it is about his substantial suicide. Furthermore, Macbeth is always aware of the hazard of his enterprise, and he has bet on his own victory. His bets accumulate: as he seems to win, he hazards his accumulated winnings— "Glamis, Cawdor, Scotland, all"—in a wager ever larger, against ever longer odds, upon himself. As the tension builds, within the play and in the audience, Macbeth himself, whoever "he" may be or have become, ever more clearly is the prize itself. There can be no substitute, either way, for Macbeth's life.

In this play, "absence, darknesse, death; things which are not" dominate from the beginning, are given external form in the Weird Sisters, in Hecate, and in the apparitions. The world of not-being, attractive to Macbeth from the beginning, finally becomes his total reality, as he himself says in the paradox that can serve as epigraph to the whole play: "Nothing is/ But what is not" (i.iii.141-42).

After all the doing—the murdering, the suffering, the tyranny, the rebellion—"nothing" is literally what Macbeth gets. His kingdom is no kingdom, every subject is his enemy, his wife dwindles away before his eyes and beyond the range of his attention, consumed by the same guilt which he knows he has, but also knows he cannot feel. Furthermore, he cannot "feel" the fact of her death. As Macbeth and Banquo variously learn, there is a sense in which the devil can speak true: the Macbeth who was, as his wife once feared, "too full o' the milk of human kindness," altogether lost his "kindness," his humanity naturally sucked in with mother's milk; by his own choice he forfeited his human soul and sensibilities. Macbeth has indeed been "unman'd," as Lady Macbeth taunted him, but not in the sense she meant. He loses his humanity to become, in his own superb irony, "the servant to defect."

The word "defect" is crucial, implying a condition unfinished or ill-made, a physical, psychological, or moral lack. In Christian morality, which assimilated from classical *paideia* both the notions of self-control and of moral improvement, man was assumed, by inheritance of original sin, to be "lacking," to require grace and salvation in order to be properly finished—and, as Christian moralists tediously explicated, usually assumed to be unable by his own power to fill in his defects. At best, man has in him a kind of moral vacuum not necessarily bad, but dangerous until it is filled with virtue, or with love of God. A major tradition of morality, canonized by Augustine, generalized the problem of evil into "defect," into "privation," emptiness, or lack, of God. So the devil, in Augustine's scheme, is not, has no being; or, put another way, the devil's being is absence of being, is not-being: the devil is a moral vacuum. According to that view, to be "servant to defect" is, inevitably, to be not good, and even not to "be."

Macbeth speaks more truly than he knows, then, when he says, fearing Banquo's insight into his mind, "To be thus is nothing"—according to the Augustinian morality, to be "bad," or wicked, is exactly to be "nothing." But Macbeth means by "To be thus," to be king: and therefore desires "To be safely thus"—only to discover that one can never be "thus" safely. Light can only thicken for Macbeth; the rooky wood comes to surround him at last. As he says,

> I have a strange infirmity, which is nothing
> To those that know me.   (III. iv. 86-87)

—a description of his condition which is, once more, far truer than he knows or intends it to be. Finally coming to understand his own defect, Macbeth learns the being of not-being. Macbeth's heroism and extraordinary power are demonstrated by the very fact that he can analyze him-

self and his whole situation at the exact point at which
that situation is most terrible. What man can really bear
the genuine discovery that his life, perhaps all life, "is a
tale/ Told by an idiot, full of sound and fury,/ Signifying
nothing" (v.v.26-28)?

The discovery comes to Macbeth at the moment when
he realizes just what death is. After all his murders, it has
taken the death of someone who had loved him and whom
he had loved, the person who had collaborated with him
in his (and her) undoing, to bring the idea of death forward to reality. And yet Macbeth cannot fully realize *her*
death: compared to his own, as he notes in his detailed
consideration of himself, her death means nothing to him.
As clearly as he senses the imminence of his own death, his
own life still means much to him. His prospective death
means defeat, disgrace, inaction, conditions he regards as
worse than the horrible life he knows himself to be leading, but he still cannot let life go. The irony lies in the fact
that at exactly the instant he realizes the existential nothingness of death, Macbeth's life, "all" he has and wants,
is robbed of its meaning too. "All" life is, is a mere
accumulation of points of time, indistinguishable one from
the other. His wife has passed from the expectation of
"tomorrow," but he still "is," still has some expectation
of the tomorrows before him:

> Tomorrow, and tomorrow, and tomorrow,
> Creeps in this petty pace from day to day
> To the last syllable of recorded time. . . .
>
> (v.v.19-21)

The whole conceivable future is spread before his imagination—and what is it? Merely the repetition of petty and
insignificant units of time.[34] Nor is the past more dignified,
more exciting, more heroic, more significant:

[34] Compare the wonderful passage from Augustine's *Confessions*
(trans. William Watts), p. 18, addressed to God: "But Thou art the

> And all our yesterdays have lighted fools
> The way to dusty death.   (v.v.22-23)

For Macbeth, who has broken tradition, broken off traditional lives, "life" leads only to the extinction of life: for him, no tradition holds together the succession of human lives in some meaning. From the single point between all the tomorrows and all the yesterdays, Macbeth compresses his total awareness of existence and what he is; he sees all time, future and past, time in prospect and in retrospect, take on the nothingness he defines as his own life.

The horror lies far deeper than the sound and the fury of conventional violence, the murders of Duncan and the grooms, of Banquo, Lady Macduff and her children; nor does it lie in Macbeth's initially wayward choice of not-being over Being. The horror is no more, and no less, than Macbeth's awareness that his active, violent life was not lived, that he has been crushed out of "being" by the pressures of the moral void. He has become the embodiment of his paradox, that nothing is but what is not: the most terrible thing about that whole tragedy is that he knows it absolutely.

Hamlet is another, and a quite different, tragedy of knowing. In this play, "nothing" also turns out to be real —from the beginning, it is clear that the ghost is a true ghost—but the "nothing" of *Hamlet* is not the existential not-being of Macbeth so much as the paradoxical nothing

---

same still; and all *To Morrowes* and so forward, and all *Yesterdaies* and so backward, thou shalt make present in this day of Thine: yea and hast made present. what concernes it me? If any understand not this, let him rejoyce notwithstanding; saying *What is this mystery?* Let him so also rejoyce, and rather love to finde in not findeing out, then by findeing it, not to find thee with it."

of the rhetoricians, the kind of "nothing" that points toward truth, being, and "all." Though Hamlet tests the ghost by way of "probation" in the mouse-trap, all along he has known that the ghost of his father spoke the truth, and that the test was really not of the ghost but of his stepfather. In *Macbeth*, the Weird Sisters' world of values invaded the whole action of the play: Banquo exists to demonstrate that those values need not have been accepted. But Macbeth, not fully "perfect," accepts the apparitional values and therefore brings the whole world of reality to apparition. *Hamlet* is the self-conscious play supreme of *Sein und Schein*; the lesson its well-educated hero must learn is that, contrary to university teaching, appearances are often true. *Hamlet* is the adolescent's nightmare of the classic guilt fantasies young men experience. Under common conditions, such guilts turn out to be ephemeral: in Hamlet's case they all turn out to be true. The role-playing Hamlet discovers the realness of roles and uses them for himself: the melancholy romantic role in which he had cast himself becomes first a defensive and then an offensive weapon against realities which, in a "normal" world, would have turned back into fantasies, appearances, or dreams.

A player himself, Hamlet uses the play, playing, roles, appearances, imitations, falsehoods, and falseness, to find out the truth: by indirections he too finds directions out. Somehow, in the course of the play, Hamlet's acting turns into action; he forsakes the actor's tears for something more like Fortinbras' pursuit of his proper aims. In more than one way, Hamlet is a man of action, quick to draw and strike when he must; a man of action, too, in his intellectual life. Quite unlike Macbeth, who fears the eternal silence, the eternal nullity of death, Hamlet fears that death will *not* put a stop to his mind's activity:

> to die—to sleep.
> To sleep—perchance to dream: ay, there's the rub!
> For in that sleep of death what dreams may come
> When we have shuffled off this mortal coil,
> Must give us pause.   (III.i.64-68)

The scholastic Hamlet can practice with the idea of nothing without self-harm. Though the sexual *double-entendre* in his exchange with Ophelia served one of his purposes well enough, his use of the word "nothing" points to his industrious reduction of all his relations to nothing. In some strange way, Hamlet always plays fair, even when he plays brutally: in wild words, he warns Claudius that he has lost his paralyzing impotence, to which the King replies, "I have nothing with this answer, Hamlet; These words are not mine" (III.ii.93-94). And Hamlet, having given his warning, and therefore not obligated to repeat it, rejoins, "No, nor mine now." He has ceased his conversation with Claudius: in all senses of the word, there is nothing between them any longer.

As for Ophelia, he is coarser, in both senses; needing to kill someone else, he wounds her:

> Hamlet: Lady, shall I lie in your lap?
> Ophelia: No, my lord.
> Hamlet: I mean, my head upon your lap?
> Ophelia: Ay, my lord.
> Hamlet: Do you think I meant country matters?
> Ophelia: I think nothing, my lord.
> Hamlet: That's a fair thought to lie between maid's legs.
> Ophelia: What is, my lord?
> Hamlet: Nothing.   (III.ii.119-28)

Later, Ophelia returns the compliment to Hamlet, when he will not explain the mouse-trap play to her: "You are naught, you are naught. I'll mark the play"—meaning the production, not Hamlet's plays upon words.

In the play, much is made of suicide,[35] both direct self-destruction and indirect: Hamlet, who can consider both death and bringing himself to death, finds a kind of relief in speculation about suicide and "nothing." He uses "nothing," as did the rhetoricians under whom presumably he studied, as a balance against the fullness of the world, of life, or human existence. For Hamlet the world itself offers no recreation, no relief for *his* perturbed spirit; for him, it only becomes more and more oppressively "real." To think of "nothing" is one metaphor for escaping the responsibilities of a world far too actual. Though his responsibilities are more than mortal man can bear, Hamlet has his ways of enduring their contradictions. Even in the worst of moments, Hamlet's mind operates with ease—and he can take some pleasure in that operation —between the extremes of the world's total significance and death's total oblivion. Where Macbeth discovers that death is oblivion, Hamlet discovers that it is not. Macbeth discovers that, when death is oblivion, life is insignificant; Hamlet discovers that when one does not fear death, life with all its painful responsibilities can be borne and even borne nobly. In the end, Hamlet knows for himself the relation between "to be" and "not to be" by which even his own death can affirm life.

In *Othello*, there are no such obvious verbal plays upon "nothing," no such verbal references to not-being as there are in *Macbeth* and *Hamlet*, but as much as they, *Othello* is a play about the moral vacuum and "defect." In many ways, *Much Ado about Nothing* was the comic rehearsal for this tragedy about "nothing": in *Othello*, not only is a great man brought low by the "nothing" of his sexuality, but also Iago represents, acts out, the kind of moral

---

[35] See below, Chapter 16, for a fuller discussion of this matter.

privation that Augustine attributed to the devil.[36] The
plot is contrived, in the fullest sense, out of words in a
false man's mouth, a handkerchief, and human defects.
Except for *Hamlet*, *Othello* is the most epistemological
of Shakespeare's tragedies, an examination of the relation
between truth and expressing the truth. For the handkerchief is real enough—that is, there *was* certainly a handkerchief; but it becomes much more than a piece of cloth,
becomes the "web" that Othello calls it, to catch the innocent. Othello thinks that the handkerchief is magic, but
of course no real handkerchief has the witchcraft Othello
attributes to it. Nor need it have such attributes, as Iago
cynically observes:

> Trifles light as air
> Are to the jealous confirmations strong
> As proofs of holy writ. . . .   (III.iii.322-24)

The handkerchief is, really, a "nothing" on which Iago
manufactures his rational-seeming plot.

As for human defect, Desdemona and Othello both have
their share, though their "defects" are very different from
Macbeth's. For a woman of such mettle, who undertook
to dispose of herself without her father's knowledge and,
as she knew, against his will, who requested the Duke of
Venice to let her accompany her husband to the wars
precisely for the reason that she had married him in the
first place, Desdemona's innocence is remarkable. Evidently she does not know guilt in herself, as her conversation with Emilia demonstrates; never having known it,
she could not recognize it in another. Wiser though she
was in the world's ways than her mistress, Emilia is as
ignorant as Desdemona of the domestic locus of evil, as

---

[36] See Bernard Spivack, *Shakespeare and the Allegory of Evil*
(Columbia University Press, 1958), first and final chapters.

resistant, to the end, as Desdemona to the notion that one's own husband might intend evil. Like Desdemona, Cassio had managed to live a magnanimous life, protected from evil; like Emilia, Roderigo knows that evil exists and, like Iago, he is willing to sanction its practice. But as Desdemona and Emilia are unable to think evil of husbands, Cassio and Roderigo are unable to think evil of friends. Iago therefore undoes them as he undoes their betters, by exploiting their inexperience, their ignorance, and the defects in their characters springing therefrom.

It is precisely Othello's defect, his lack, which makes him vulnerable to undoing—not, really, his pride, though that was sympathetically great; not his birth, of which he was naturally proud; nor his color, for he had achieved in both love and war far greater success than any Venetian: but his guilelessness, his innocence, his ignorance, and his inexperience of the world. For such as Othello and Desdemona, it is difficult to find descriptive phrases, for the wine they drink *is* made of grapes. They are not disembodied spirits; on the contrary, their bodies are fully alive. Their greatness of soul and character is ordinary human greatness raised to a higher power than is customary. Othello's attempts to express his happiness with Desdemona are fully human: he is brought by them to the very edge of experience, to the abyss into which all words tumble every which way, which all lovers know and all poets attempt to cross by the swaying suspension bridge of vocabulary and syntax. Othello tries to express the contentment, the fullness, the sufficiency of his life with Desdemona:

> It gives me wonder great as my content
> To see you here before me. O my soul's joy!
> If after every tempest come such calms,
> May the winds blow till they have waken'd death!

> And let the labouring bark climb hills of seas
> Olympus-high, and duck again as low
> As hell's from heaven! If it were now to die,
> 'Twere now to be most happy; for I fear
> My soul hath her content so absolute
> That not another comfort like to this
> Succeeds in unknown fate.   (II.i.185-94)

As in Donne's love poems, the *frisson* comes at the moment of greatest fullness: Othello's profound consciousness of love conjures up the idea of death, a contrast reinforced by the high-low, heaven-hell imagery of his speech. "As hell's from heaven," inevitably, so is death from love, and the death of love from love's fullness.

The "fullness" of Othello and Desdemona and the "fullness" of their love are threatened by their very innocence; Iago, another "servant to defect," stands in relief opposite to them. For its balance as well as for its plot, the play depends upon Iago. We come to understand Othello and Desdemona better because of him, and him because of them. That is, each side is defined, given limitation, by what it is not; in the extremely organized dialectic of this play, being is understood by not-being, not-being by being.

The warnings sound at once and repeatedly, a bell telling the true time. Iago's "I am not what I am" means in fact all the audience fears it to mean—he is not what he seems to the persons on the stage. The truth is even deeper than this, and in his paradoxical sentence Iago lies and does not lie; for he *is* in fact what he is not, since he is, and proves himself by the action of the tragedy to be, not really a man, a member of human kind. As he says of himself, in an ultimate deceit, telling the truth out of context:

> Men should be what they seem,
> Or those that be not, would they might seem none!
>   (III.iii.27-28)

Warnings sound in Othello's speech as well—what sort
of man dares speak of his "perfect soul"? If perfection is
total, then nothing can threaten it. It can only be, therefore, "nothing" that threatens Othello, both the lack
within him of worldly strength and the "nothings," the
paradoxes and the lies invented by Iago.

Iago's paradoxes, like most, fit Donne's functional description of the mode; Iago's "nothings" multiply and
generate, until they seem to provide sufficient reason for
the destruction of "all." Iago's statement, "I am not what
I am," tells us that Iago is never totally definable, limited,
or enclosed. His paradoxes are always more than they seem
—not just, as Desdemona called them, "old fond paradoxes to make fools laugh i' th' alehouse." His praise is
dispraise, his dispraise, awkwardly, praise; but like Satan
he recognizes the truth of defect, the weakness, the corrup-
tibility, in all the men and women of his company.

There is much to be said for the argument that Iago's
role in the play is that of the necessary antagonist in a
psychomachia, that he is the expression, simply, of Othello's baser nature. Again and again, Iago's nondirectional
comment pushes Othello deeper into the abyss of himself
—and, each time, Iago is technically innocent of falsehood.
He is the perfect equivocator,[37] the figure of evil so feared
by the straight-seeming English: sometimes he repeats
Othello's final words (as in III.iii.103ff.); sometimes he
muses as if irrelevantly on incidental facts ("She did
deceive her father, marrying you"). Certainly Iago's expressed opinions about Desdemona turn into Othello's
opinion of her; and that transformation could not have

[37] For material on equivocation, see Frank L. Huntley, "*Macbeth*
and the Background of Jesuitical Equivocation," *PMLA*, LXXXIX
(1964), 390-400; A. E. Malloch, "John Donne and the Casuists,"
SEL, II (1962), 57-76.

taken place had Othello not been ready for those thoughts.

But Iago is by no means only a projection of Othello's mind: he is not, as he tells us, Othello—

> It is as sure as you are Roderigo,
> Were I the Moor, I would not be Iago.
>
> (1.i.56-57)

Though he is not what he is, nonetheless he is himself: or, Iago is both what he is and what he is not.

In terms of the clichés of Renaissance society, Iago is a self-made man, with all that tautology implies. Everyone else in the play has his recognized station—Brabantio is, as Iago insultingly states, a Senator; Michael Cassio is an arithmetician, a young tactician (and, with a name like that, clearly a gentleman); Othello is a stranger in Venice, to be sure, which causes him crucial pain, but his strange birth is high and his worth recognized, by himself and by others. Everyone has some recognized origin, except Iago, who obviously has hoped to "make" himself, to make a place in the world, through promotion into the officer class. In terms more familiar in Elizabethan literature than to us, Iago is a "nobody," a nobody trying to be "somebody." The first literary "nobody" was Odysseus, who was always somebody even though often disguised; in his encounter with Polyphemus, Odysseus lies about his station, his nature, and his existence as a man in order to pass uneaten through the Cyclops' hands. In the sixteenth century, notice had to be taken of the apparent disruption in social orders, the arrival into every class and social group of "new men," mushroom upstarts shouldering out the true-born: in common with European expression in general, Englishmen picked up and exploited both the literary and the pictorial conventions of the "nobody"[38] to comment upon social aspiration and pretension.

[38] See Gerta Calman, "The Picture of Nobody," pp. 60-104, and

In this context, Iago is a real nobody: though, as the paradoxes of "nobody" all imply, all "nobodies" also somehow exist, somehow are "real." In the pictorial tradition, Nobody has a particular household function. He breaks everything, shatters the pots and pans, cracks the mirrors and windowpanes, lets the domestic animals run away or starve at home, in general displaying notable irresponsibility toward his master. Bruegel, Holbein, and lesser draftsmen all record the domestic chaos caused by "Nobody" who looks after the house while the master is away: in part a commentary on the "new" irresponsibility of servants in the period, the paradox also points directly to the master's irresponsibility on his own behalf. As one critic put it, the householder who blames Nobody is himself responsible for the collapse of his household.[39]

Such a householder is Othello, as at the play's end he recognizes: by not looking, not seeing, he has permitted "nobody" to destroy his household—not just the pots and pans, the windowpanes and the chickens, but the household itself, the personalities who make it up. "Nobody" destroys Desdemona and Othello; and in each case, as Desdemona says in her last words, nobody is "I myself."

Bruegel's "Nobody" drawing carries the motto, "Niemand en erkent hy selven": that is, nobody knows or recognizes himself in the mirror; no one can accurately assess himself.[40] Othello, the master who allows "nobody" to wreck his household, does not recognize himself in the mirror: that is, he represents the straight truth of the statement, "Niemand en erkent hy selven." But Iago represents its other truth; he is the Nobody who *does* recog-

---

below, Chapter 9.

[39] Calman, pp. 61-64.

[40] See below, Chapter 12.

nize himself in the mirror. He knows what he is, and what he is not—"'Tis in ourselves that we are thus and other." He knows too what he is doing, and why he does it:

> Let's see:
> After some time to abuse Othello's ear. . . ,
>
> (I.ii.400-401)

and to engender "monstrous births" of "Hell and night." A "nobody" on the scale of secure Venetian social values, Iago was also nobody as the Augustinian devil is, a "real" negative quality, a negative quality that *does* exist to affect the world of moral being. Iago knows what he wants to do, and he does it: that is, he knows how to do what he wants, how to manipulate to his own advantage. What is so interesting is that he operates in vacancies, in moral vacua: he works on the negative virtues, the innocence, ignorance, inexperience of his victims. Like the Nobody of sixteenth-century social criticism, Iago knows how to destroy households—by doing nothing.

Like *Hamlet*, *Othello* also deals in the extremes of all and nothing, this time through the metaphor and action of human love. Inherently, love is the trickiest of emotions; its contradictory elements promise a multitude of paradoxes, anomalies, puzzles. Othello had been a great and self-respecting man before he met the good Desdemona, and as he testifies, his love for her deepened his sense of his own completeness. Of his wife he says:

> Excellent wretch! Perdition catch my soul
> But I do love thee! and when I love thee not,
> Chaos is come again.
>
> (III.iii.90-92)

The apocalyptic language carries its irony: for when in fact he loves her not, perdition does catch his soul, chaos does come again. With the appearance of minor disorders in his household, order altogether disappears until truly "Othello's occupation's gone" and his perfect soul destroyed. As he thrice says within fifteen lines, Othello can deny Desdemona nothing (III.iii.83); in the end, it is nothing that he gives her.

It is, really, "nothing" that Iago does to Othello: he creates the semblance of honesty in the most natural way, by telling the truth:

> (As I confess it is my nature's plague
> To spy into abuses, and oft my jealousy
> Shapes faults that are not) . . . .
>
> (III.iii.146-48)

His double bluff works: how can anyone suspect so blunt a soldier, so honest a man? Iago is the dramatic figure acting out the duplicity of the Liar paradox, for he lies in speaking the truth. The fault he "shaped" was not, but the ostentatious nothing he made of it began at once to work in Othello's brain, to corrupt his innocence and to destroy him:

> I had been happy if the general camp,
> Pioners and all, had tasted her sweet body,
> So I had nothing known.
>
> (III.iii.345-47)

Just after, Othello bethinks him that Iago may not be right, and in his righteous manhood cries out:

> If thou dost slander her and torture me,
> Never pray more; abandon all remorse;
> On horror's head horrors accumulate;
> Do deeds to make heaven weep, all earth amaz'd;
> For nothing canst thou to damnation add
> Greater than that.   (III.iii.368-73)

With the irony that tragedy requires, Othello passes judgment on the moral action of the play, and speaks, conditionally in his own mind, the absolute truth about what Iago is doing.

Iago's task is quite clear. By being brought to accept Iago's "truth," Othello is unmanned, reduced to nothing. In that process of reduction, Iago taunts his victim with his design:

> O grace! O heaven forgive me!
> Are you a man? Have you a soul or sense?
> (III.iii.373-74)

Iago continues, an effective *eiron*, speaking the perfect truth in a context where Othello can only perceive it as falsehood:

> God b' wi' you! take mine office. O wretched fool,
> That liv'st to make thine honesty a vice!
> O monstrous world! Take note, take note, O world,
> To be direct and honest is not safe.
> (III.iii.375-78)

Later, after Othello's fit, Iago mocks him again—"Good sir, be a man"; and,

> Marry patience!
> Or I shall say you are all in all in spleen,
> And nothing of a man.   (IV.i.88-90)

In Houyhnhnm language, Iago says "the thing which is not," even when he says the thing which is. He is false to what is, as he describes it: he is fundamentally false to being, the bearer of the contagious disease which Augustine had defined as evil, spread by him among those in whose midst he lives. Iago is the carrier of not-being, and not-being invades the being of being to destroy it. His falsehoods, even when descriptively accurate, turn what is into what is not: in plain English, Iago cannot help lying. After a scene in which the vulgar pun on "lie" is exploited in reference to Cassio and Desdemona (iii.iv.34-44). Iago picks up the play on "lie" in a double meaning so clear that it is incredible that Othello does not hear it. But Othello, concentrating on the magnitude of the lying in bed, cannot hear Iago's lie any more than Desdemona recognizes the purport of Iago's sexual paradoxes.

By the end of the play, Othello recognizes that he is undone, unmanned: "That's he that was Othello: here I am." The destroyer of goodness and good men, Iago survives Othello's wound to give cogency to Othello's fear that he is indeed the devil. Iago remains a creature of no being; Othello, recognizing his defect and sin, asserts his own not-being to show his moral understanding of the magnitude of the tragedy. "That's he that was Othello"—because Othello's occupation, which was to "be" Othello, has been destroyed by his denial of his own nature and his own being. The punishment, all the same, he can endure: "here I am," a man again, even if not the identical hero with whom the play began.

As for Desdemona, her integrity was qualified by her charity. She may indeed have "like a liar gone to burning hell," as her husband furiously says, since she died acting out either a lie or a paradox of love. The Desdemona who could not lie and would not deceive learned at last to lie and to deceive, attempting at the end to protect her husband against the disgrace she knew he could not endure. She lied, because Othello *had* killed her; she did not lie, since by not looking to her household, she had permitted "Nobody" to undo it and her. Desdemona lied, but in her charity turns lies to truth. Her essence was certainly honor: as Iago had said, intending irony, but for once stating the truth, "Her honour is an essence that's not seen." No essence is; and even if it were visible, love is a blind god.[41] Morality's universe is a plenum: "nothing" and "nobody" may not exist, but their nonexistence destroys all order and reduces constructions to chaos.

[41] *Wits Recreations* produces a crude parallel to this point:

> Who can define, this all things, nothing love,
> Which hath so much of every thing in it?
> Which watry, with the planets oft doth move,
> And with the zoane it hath a fiery fit;
> Oft seizes men, like massy stupid earth,
> And with the aire, it filleth every place;
> Which had no midwife, nor I think no birth,
> No shrine, no arrowes, but a womans face.
> A god he is not, for he is unjust;
> A boy he is not, for he hath more power;
> A fiction 'tis not, all will yeeld I trust;
> What is it then, that is so sweetly sowre?
> No law so nice, that can his absence prove?
> But (ah) I know there is a thing call'd love.
>
> (*Facetiae*, II.323)

8

Le pari: All or Nothing

Now, the necessary Mansions of our restored selves
are those two contrary and incompatible places wee
call Heaven and Hell. . . .

Browne, *Religio Medici*, 1. 49

IN THE idiosyncratic work of Blaise Pascal two traditions
of "nothing" combined with peculiar force, the moral problems involved in existential and psychological nothing,
and the moral-intellectual problems involved in the vacuum, or the physical nothing. Of the two "nothings,"
western thinkers had found it easier to deal with the first,
a nothing "merely metaphysical," than with a "nothing"
hypothesized or scientifically established as a part of the
universe. Crucially, Pascal expropriated from the discoveries of the new science lessons for morality. He who of
all men was entitled to authority in speaking of the newly
established vacuum, who had, as it were, demonstrated
the being of not-being, was not content to leave the discovery to professional men of science, but popularized
that scientific fact in terms of everyman's Christian life.
An Augustinian in other ways, Pascal was quick to extend
the range of Augustine's moral instruction in not-being.

Both the Platonic and the Aristotelian physics postulated
a plenist universe; both assumed the truth of *horror vacui*.
The long train of interpretations of the *Timaeus* elaborated the notion of a full scale of creation, spiritually and
physically occupying the total universe, leaving, as Traherne had said, "No empty space."[1] The "principle of
plenitude," in Mr. Lovejoy's happy phrase, accounted for

[1] See above, Chapter 4, p. 160.

an orderly and hieratic creation, in theory at least: if there seemed to be gaps in the chain, or scale, of being, then those gaps were interpreted rather as an epistemological or experiential failure on man's part than as a lapse of the Creator's power or attention. In an infinite universe, however, the principle of plenitude cannot be counted on as sufficient, nor can it be trusted to impose order within such limitlessness, since an infinite plenitude, though often intellectually satisfying, is a difficult conception to actualize.[2]

As physical investigation proceeded in the Renaissance, a vacuum came to be "needed"—that is, a vacuum hypothesis was useful in physical speculation. As early as 1612, Galileo was convinced of the possibility of a vacuum, and in the Netherlands a little later, Isaac Beeckman clearly recognized the likelihood of the hypothesis. Beeckman corresponded with Mersenne on the subject, who in turn had connections with the group of Roman scientists around Torricelli. Evidently inspired by Galileo, the Torricellian group—Berti, Magiotti, and the ubiquitous polymath Athanasius Kircher—worked on experiments of the vacuum between 1639 and 1644, when the report of Torricelli's successful experiment was published. Probably fearful of ecclesiastical opposition, the Roman group did not pursue their researches into the subject, but in Paris, Mersenne, who had been in touch with the Roman developments, encouraged Pascal to further experimentation, which produced decisive confirmation of the existence of a vacuum. "Nothing" thus became unmistakably "something," to be reckoned with and to be counted on.[3]

[2] A. O. Lovejoy, *The Great Chain of Being*, Chapter 4; Koyré, *From Closed World to Infinite Universe*; "Le vide et l'espace infini au XIVe siècle," *Etudes d'histoire de la pensée philosophique* (*Cahier des Annales*, vol. xix, Paris, 1961).

[3] W. E. Knowles Middleton, "The Place of Torricelli in the

By temperament Blaise Pascal was eminently suited to experimentation on so paradoxical a subject as *le vide*. His scientific and mathematical interests ran to the paradoxical, the improbable, and the ambiguous: his work on infinitesimals and infinite series and on permutations and combinations led to his remarkable contributions, in a correspondence with Fermat over the hazards of gambling, to probability theory. He was concerned not simply with unsolved problems at the outskirts of mathematical knowledge, but with the kind of unsolved problem which is fundamentally irrational, and denies altogether the formulation of conceptual limits. His interest in the vacuum is of a piece with his attraction to such problems as those of infinite series and of probability theory. He knew that the vacuum was by definition an "impossible" subject, that the establishment of its actual existence implied not only a revolution in physical thought but a revolution in moral and ontological thought as well.

The first stage of Pascal's barometric experiment was performed at Rouen, with Pierre Petit, in 1646; in 1647 Etienne Périer, Pascal's brother-in-law, carried out the second stage, following Pascal's directions, at Puy-de-Dôme in Auvergne, atop the pinnacle on which the town is improbably set. Pascal's subsequent publications on the matter, *Expériences nouvelles touchant le vide*,[4] the letters to his Jesuit opponent, Père Noël, and to Le Pailleur, all made plain the incontrovertibility in fact of a vacuum. Naturally enough, there was a considerable polemic against the idea and against him, of which Noël's work is the most interesting. Noël engaged to defend both the plenism of

History of the Barometer," *Isis*, LIV (1963), 11-28; see also his definitive *The History of the Barometer* (Johns Hopkins Press, 1964), Part I.

    [4] (Paris, 1647).

his brilliant pupil René Descartes and the sovereignty of
God over all things—i.e., that a vacuum could not exist,
in the sense that God pervaded everything and prevented
the vacuum from coming into being. Pascal had strong and
"modern" support, however, from his family, from Père
Mersenne, who had first propounded the "Torricellian
hypothesis" in France, and members of his circle. Scientific
"progress" vindicated Pascal, of course: the spectacular
and ponderous Magdeburg experiment of Otto von
Guericke, in which eight horses failed to sunder two brass
hemispheres hermetically sealed together, served to convince doubting Thomases among the vulgar. Guericke's
and Boyle's more delicate experiments with the air pump
satisfied the learned as fully as the eight horses had satisfied grosser intelligences. The vacuum could be perceived
to be a "real" part of natural totality, a part therefore
which somehow had to be domesticated into men's thought.

In a book with a paradoxical title,[5] Père Noël at once
attacked both the validity of Pascal's experiment and
Pascal himself, urging Pascal to call the controversial area
induced in his pipette, not "the void," but simply "empty
space," a linguistic device designed to protect both the
Aristotelian physical hypothesis and the Christian God.
Jesuitically, perhaps, Noël did not deny the existence of
the space in the pipette so much as question the name
Pascal unequivocally assigned to it:

Mais ce vuide ne seroit il point l'intervalle de ces anciens
philosophes qu'Aristote a tasché de refuter, ou bien l'espace
immaginaire de quelques moderns, ou bien l'immensité de
Dieu qu'on ne peut nier, puisque Dieu est partout? A la verité,
si ce vuide veritable n'est autre chose que l'immensité de Dieu,
je ne puis nier son existance; mais aussy ne peut on pas dire
que cet immensité n'estant autre chose que Dieu mesme, esprit

---

[5] Père Etienne Noël, *Le plein du vuide* (Paris, 1648).

tres simple, ayt des parties les unes hors des autres, qui est la définition que je donne aux corps, et non pas celle que vous dites estre de mes auteurs, prise de la composition de matiere et de forme.[6]

(But is this void not the "interval" of those ancient philosophers that Aristotle attempted to refute, or rather the imaginary space of certain moderns, or rather the immensity of God that cannot be denied, since God is everywhere? In truth, if this true vacuum is nothing other than the immensity of God, I cannot deny its existence; but likewise one cannot say that this immensity, being nothing but God Himself, a very simple spirit, has parts one separate from the other, which is the definition I give to body, and not that you attribute to my authors, taken from the composition of matter and form.)

In a letter to M. le Pailleur, Pascal laid out in detail his answer to Noël's physical objections, but refused to discuss the theological implications of his finding:

Les mystères qui concernent la Divinité sont trop saints pour les profaner par nos disputes; nous devons en faire l'objet de nos adorations, et non pas le sujet de nos entretiens: si bien que, sans en discourir en aucune sorte, je me soumets entièrement à ce qu'on decideront ceux qui ont droit de la faire.[7]

(Mysteries concerning the Deity are too holy to be profaned by our disputes; we ought to make them the object of our adoration, not the subjects of our discussions: so much so that, without discussing them at all, I submit entirely to whatever those persons shall decide who have the right to do so.)

Père Noël was obviously trying to call Pascal's motives into question by referring to "those ancient philosophers

[6] "Seconde lettre du P. Noël à Pascal," in Pascal, *Oeuvres*, ed. Léon Brunschvicq et Pierre Boutroux (Paris, 1908), ii. 108-09.

[7] *Oeuvres*, ii. 110-11; Pascal to Le Pailleur, in Pascal, *Oeuvres complètes*, ed. Jacques Chevalier (Paris, 1954), p. 282. Unless otherwise indicated, all references to Pascal's works are to this edition.

who had postulated a nothing," the atheistic atomist philosophers. And equally obviously, Pascal, who was to become the gadfly of the Jesuits, knew enough to avoid entering into a debate with a Jesuit upon the nature of deity. Other men noticed, however, the association between Pascal's discovery and the ancient belief in a "nothing": in 1647 Pierre Guiffart, a professor at Rouen, wrote of Pascal's experiment:

Quoy que les experiences de M.ʳ Pascal nous paroissent nouvelles, il y a de l'apparence qu'elles ont esté autres fois pratiquées, et que plusieurs anciens [*en marge*: Democrite, Leucippe, Diodore, Epicure, Lucrèce] on prins de la sujet de maintenir qu'il pouvoit avoir du Vuide en la Nature. . . .[8]

(Although M. Pascal's experiments appear new to us, they are like some earlier ones, which several ancients [in the margin: Democritus, Leucippus, Diodorus, Epicurus, Lucretius] have taken up to maintain that there could have been a Void in Nature. . . .)

After Pascal's experiments, men began to accept the vacuum they had hitherto believed nature to have abhorred, began to come to terms anew with the words designating it—*le vide, le néant, l'espace vide*. Not immediately—such shifts in point of view always take a while to be fully accomplished—but quite naturally, considering the antiquity and strength of the antipathy to the idea. Pascal himself provided a clue to dealing with the problem, by entitling his description of the Puy-de-Dôme experiment, *Réçit de la Grande Expérience de l'Equilibre des Liqueurs*.[9] By emphasizing the idea of balance, *équilibre*, Pascal gave his experiment a positive rather than a negative stress, and shifted attention away from the idea of the void.

[8] *Oeuvres*, ed. Brunschvicq-Boutroux, II. 9.
[9] (Paris, 1648).

Though he stressed equilibrium in his physical theory, accommodating the vacuum naturally into the physical scheme of being, Pascal prepared to lay his moral stress not upon balance, or equilibrium, but upon extremity, to exploit the distance between moral and psychological extremes. In other words, though he rather played it down in his physics, in his moral philosophy Pascal exploited the idea of the void with an intense *horror vacui.*

For theologians before Pascal, the existence of a void space had seemed to threaten notions of providence, divine creativity, and benevolence. For Pascal, such a view was ludicrous: "C'est une chose admirable que jamais auteur canonique ne s'est servi de la nature pour prouver Dieu. Tous tendent à le faire croire. David, Salomon, etc., jamais n'ont dit, 'Il n'y a point de vide, donc il y a un Dieu.' "[10] For Pascal, the opposite could be seen to be true: there was a *vide*, and God unquestionably existed.

That God existed Pascal had always known. Like Traherne, Pascal had from childhood sensed the existence of some "nothing":

Parce, dit-on, que vous avez cru dès l'enfance qu'un coffre était vide lorsque vous n'y voyez rien, vous avez cru le vide possible. C'est une illusion de vos sens, fortifiée par la coutume, qu'il faut que la science corrige.

That is, even when officially there was no such thing as a vacuum, the child who had "experienced" it had to be retrained to arrive at the "right" opinion. But

[10] *Pensée* 6, *Oeuvres complètes*, p. 1090; *Pensées*, trans. W. F. Trotter (New York, Modern Library edn., 1941), No. 243, p. 87: "It is an astounding fact that no canonical writer has ever made use of nature to prove God. They all strive to make us believe in Him. David, Solomon, etc., have never said, 'There is no void, therefore there is a God.' "

les autres disent: "Parce qu'on vous a dit dans l'école qu'il
n'y a point de vide, on a corrompu votre sens commun, qui le
comprenait si nettement avant cette mauvaise impression, qu'il
faut corriger en recourant à votre première nature." Qui a donc
trompé? le sens ou l'instruction?[11]

The conclusion he intended to be drawn from the observation was the correct one: common sense *was* superior to
rationalized "instruction." With this, another conclusion
also emerges—that for common sense, the vacuum always
was—as even children know.

On that common sense Pascal constructed the terrifying
argument *du vide* which was his major persuasive to faith.
Le vide, interpreted in various ways, was simply one extreme of the physical, psychological, and intellectual oppositions he set up, between which each compromised
human being had to reach some balance and, therewith,
some self-knowledge. Pascal's man, too, under the idea of
God, had in some measure to make himself up between
the contrarieties of his nature and his situation:

Contrariétés.—L'homme est naturellement crédule, incréd-
ule, timide, téméraire.
Description de l'homme: dépendance, désir d'indépendance,
besoin.[12]

[11] *Pensée* 104, *OC*, p. 1119; Modern Library edn., No. 82, p.
34: " 'Because,' say some, 'you have believed from childhood that a
box was empty when you saw nothing in it, you have believed in
the possibility of a vacuum. This is an illusion of your senses,
strengthened by custom, which science must correct.' 'Because,' say
others, 'you have been taught at school that there is no vacuum, you
have perverted your common sense which clearly comprehended it,
and you must correct this by returning to your first state.' Which
has deceived you, your senses or your education?"
[12] *Pensées* 159, 160, *OC*, p. 1130; Mod. Lib. edn., Nos. 125,
126, p. 46: "*Contraries.*—Man is naturally credulous and incredu-
lous, timid and rash." "Description of man: dependency, desire of
independence, need."

Condition de l'homme: inconstance, ennui, inquiétude.[13]

Contradiction: mépris de notre être, mourir pour rien, haine de notre être.[14]

In dealing with cases of human morality, Pascal's method of moral medicine was to prescribe the Galenic antidote, to restore balance by opposing extremes to one another:

> S'il se vante, je l'abaisse; s'il s'abaisse, je le vante: et le contredis toujours, jusqu'à ce qu'il comprenne qu'il est un monstre incompréhensible.[15]

According to his own testimony, the method worked for his own problems:

> Toutes ces contrariétés, qui semblaient le plus m'esloigner de la connaissance, d'une religion, est ce qu'il m'a le plus tôt conduit à la véritable.[16]

As he said, "à la fin de chaque vérité, il faut ajouter qu'on se souvient de la vérité opposée."[17] And further, "Le croire est si important! Cent contradictions seraient vraies."[18]

---

[13] *Pensée* 199, *OC*, p. 1137; Mod. Lib. edn., No. 127, p. 46: "Condition of man: inconstancy, weariness, unrest."

[14] *Pensée* 156, *OC*, p. 1129; Mod. Lib. edn., No. 157, p. 57: "Contradiction: contempt for our existence, to die for nothing, hatred of our existence."

[15] *Pensée* 330, *OC*, p. 1170; Mod. Lib. edn., No. 420, p. 132: "If he exalt himself, I humble him; if he humble himself, I exalt him; and I always contradict him, till he understands that he is an incomprehensible monster."

[16] *Pensée* 437, *OC*, p. 1204; Mod. Lib. edn., No. 424, p. 133: "All these contradictions, which seem most to keep me from the knowledge of true religion, have led me most quickly to the true one."

[17] *Pensée* 791, *OC*, p. 1331; Mod. Lib. edn., No. 566, p. 185: ". . . and we must even add at the end of each truth that the opposite truth is to be remembered."

[18] *Pensée* 249, *OC*, p. 1154; Mod. Lib. edn., No. 260, p. 91: "Belief is so important! A hundred contradictions might be true."

For Pascal, as for Cusanus, all oppositions must unite in transcendent deity; contradiction was as much an emotional as a dialectical device for reaching some comprehension of the divine. Accustomed to the either/or of ordinary experience, human beings distrust contradiction, are used to eliminate one of two contradictory elements in order to arrive at "truth." But Pascal's relativity denies that method of elimination and choice: his truth embraces many contradictions:

Contradiction est une mauvaise marque de vérité: plusieurs choses certaines sont contredites; plusieurs fausses passent sans contradiction. Ni la contradiction n'est marque de fausseté, ni l'incontradiction n'est marque de vérité.[19]

But though contradictions may not in fact be decisive, extremes are. Extremes exist in fact and spiritually; and, in Pascal's moral economy, make their demands on every human being, suspended willy-nilly between them.

In *Pensée* 84, his great discussion of human nature, Pascal dealt with the tiny holdfast man has on his life. Macbeth had seen himself, suddenly and with utter clarity, alienated from everything, detached from everything, between all the yesterdays and all the tomorrows of conceivable time; Pascal's man is in an equally precarious position, located in an undefended open space between two vast deserts, variously called "all" and "nothing," "infinitude" and "emptiness," "infinity" and the "infinitesimally small," between total time and the absence of time.

Tout ce monde visible n'est qu'un trait imperceptible dans l'ample sein de la nature. Nulle idée n'en approche. Nous avons

[19] *Pensée* 250, *OC*, p. 1154; Mod. Lib. edn., No. 384, p. 124: "Contradiction is a bad sign of truth; several things which are certain are contradicted; several things which are false pass without contradiction. Contradiction is not a sign of falsity, nor the want of contradiction a sign of truth."

beau enfler nos conceptions, au delà des espaces imaginables, nous n'enfantons que des atomes, au prix de la réalité des choses. . . .

Mais pour lui présenter un autre prodige aussi étonnant, qu'il recherche dans ce qu'il connait les choses les plus délicates. Qu'un ciron lui offre dans la petitesse de son corps, des parties incomparablement plus petites, des jambes avec des jointures, des veines dans ses jambes, du sang dans ces veines, des humeurs dans ce sang, des gouttes dans ces humeurs, des vapeurs dans ces gouttes; que, divisant encore ces dernières choses, il épuise ses forces en ces conceptions, et que le dernier objet où il peut arriver soit maintenant celui de notre discours; il pensera peut-être que c'est là l'extrême petitesse de la nature. Je veux lui faire voir là-dedans un abîme nouveau. Je veux lui peindre non seulement l'univers visible, mais l'immensité qu'on peut concevoir de la nature, dans l'enceinte de ce raccourci d'atome.

Just as one thinks that Pascal must annihilate this man, crush him between hostile extremes, he invokes the idea of balance, of equilibrium, to establish man as a being of relative strengths and weaknesses, relative magnitude, relative value:

. . . qui n'admirera que notre corps, qui tantôt n'était pas perceptible dans l'univers, imperceptible lui-même dans le sein du tout, soit à présent un colosse, un monde, ou plutôt un tout, à l'égard du néant où l'on ne peut arriver?

Horror vacui is real enough, but it is made relevant to the human condition, a reasonable experience of sensible terror at the enormous silence of infinite space, at the colossal indifference of the natural world to any individual man.

Car, enfin, qu'est-ce que l'homme dans la nature? Un néant à l'égard de l'infini, un tout à l'égard du néant, un milieu entre rien et tout. Infiniment éloigné de comprendre les extrêmes, la fin des choses et leur principes sont pour lui invinciblement cachés dans un secret impénétrable, également incapable de voir le néant d'où il est tiré, et l'infini où il est en-glouti.[20]

Man, "un milieu entre rien et tout," with both "noth-ing" and "all" beyond his comprehension. If a man cannot find a balance between these (rightly) terrifying extremes, then he becomes "nothing": for within him, as the Preacher everlastingly says, is vanity, emptiness. Pride, curiosity, presumption, all are vanity:

La vanité est si ancrée dans le coeur de l'homme, qu'un soldat, un goujat, un cuisinier, un crocheteur se vante et veut

[20] *Pensée* 84, *OC*, pp. 1105-09; Mod. Lib. edn., No. 72, pp. 21-28: "The whole visible world is only an imperceptible atom in the ample bosom of nature. No idea approaches it. We may enlarge our conceptions beyond all imaginable space; we only produce atoms in comparison with the reality of things. . . . But to show him another prodigy equally astonishing, let him examine the most delicate things he knows. Let a mite be given him, with its minute body and parts incomparably more minute, limbs with their joints, veins in the limbs, blood in the veins, humours in the blood, drops in the humours, vapours in the drops. Dividing these last things again, let him exhaust his powers of conception, and let the last object at which he can arrive be now that of our discourse. Perhaps he will think that here is the smallest point in nature. I will let him see therein a new abyss. I will paint for him not only the visible uni-verse, but all he can conceive of nature's immensity in the womb of this abridged atom."

. . . "For who will not be astounded at the fact that our body, which a little while ago was imperceptible in the universe, itself imperceptible in the bosom of the whole, is now a colossus, a world, or rather a whole, in respect of the nothingness which we cannot reach? . . .

"For in fact what is man in nature? A Nothing in comparison with the Infinite, an All in comparison with Nothing, a mean be-tween nothing and everything. Since he is infinitely removed from comprehending the extremes, the end of things and their beginning are hopelessly hidden from him in an impenetrable secret; he is equally incapable of seeing the Nothing from which he was made, and the Infinite in which he is swallowed up."

avoir ses admirateurs; et les philosophes mêmes en veulent; et ceux qui écrivent contre veulent la gloire d'avoir bien écrit; et ceux qui lisent veulent avoir la gloire de l'avoir lu; et moi, qui écris ceci, ai peut-être cette envie; et peut-être ceux qui le liront. . . .[21]

Because vanity—pride, curiosity, vainglory, or whatever form it takes—is a moral condition resulting from undue preoccupation with "nothings," with the transient, inconsequent values of the world, that vanity is enlarged until it becomes simply the man: a skin arranged around emptiness, around nothing. The terms of Pascal's strictures are all perfectly traditional. What he adds to the Christian *memento mori* is the force of his authority as the man who established the *fact* of the vacuum, and therefore as a particular connoisseur of vanity, emptiness, and *le néant*. "Nothing" can no longer be dismissed as a mere intellectual construct, a mere metaphor: "nothing" is something to which a man may be palpably reduced.

The "everything" that man's psychology affirms that he is—"Chacun est un tout à soi-même, car, lui mort, le tout est mort pour soi"[22]—is an illusion. When one thinks, and as Pascal made clear, man's sole hope for himself was his capacity to think, one must realize, like Macbeth, the insignificance of one's life—of "la petite durée de ma vie, absorbée dans l'éternité précédente et suivante, le petit espace que je remplis, et même que je vois, abîmé dans

[21] *Pensée* 153, *OC*, p. 1129; Mod. Lib. edn., No. 150, p. 56: "Vanity is so anchored in the heart of man that a soldier, a soldier's servant, a cook, a porter brags, and wishes to have his admirers. Even philosophers wish for them. Those who write against it want to have the glory of having written well; and those who read it desire the glory of having read it. I who write this have perhaps this desire, and perhaps those who will read it. . . ."

[22] *Pensée* 139, *OC*, p. 1127; Mod. Lib. edn., No. 457, p. 151: "Each one is all to himself, for he being dead, all is dead to him."

l'infinie immensité des espaces que j'ignore et qui m'ignore."[23] Over and over again, Pascal drives home the
lesson of man's incommensurability against the infinite
stretches of time and of space. In a witty self-reference,
Pascal pictures his own "néant":

> En écrivant ma pensée, elle m'échappe quelque-fois; mais cela
> me fait souvenir de ma faiblesse, que j'oublie à toute heure;
> ce qui m'instruit autant que ma pensée oubliée, car je ne tends
> qu'à connaître mon néant.[24]

The remedy is to know one's self; if one is all "vanity,"
all nothing, one can, after Pascal's experiments, know that
without paradox at last, since the void "really" exists. One
must know, inevitably, what one does *not* know: that is,
one must recognize one's limitations—

> Connaissons donc notre portée: nous sommes quelque chose,
> et ne sommes pas tout; ce que nous avons d'être nous dérobe la
> connaissance des premiers principes, qui naissent du néant;
> et le peu que nous avons d'être nous cache la vue de l'infini.[25]

Man must come to terms with his own frontier, know the
limits of his substance and endurance:

[23] *Pensée* 88, *OC*, pp. 1112-13; Mod. Lib. edn., No. 205, p. 75:
"When I consider the short duration of my life, swallowed up in
the eternity before and after, the little space which I fill, engulfed
in the infinite immensity of spaces of which I am ignorant, and
which know me not. . . ."
[24] *Pensée* 100, *OC*, p. 1115; Mod. Lib. edn., No. 372, p. 121:
"In writing down my thought, it sometimes escapes me; but this
makes me remember my weakness, that I constantly forget. This is
as instructive to me as my forgotten thought; for I strive only to
know my nothingness."
[25] *Pensée* 84, *OC*, p. 1108; Mod. Lib. edn., No. 72, pp. 24-25:
"Let us then take our compass; we are something, and we are not
everything. The nature of our existence hides from us the knowledge
of first beginnings which are born of Nothing; and the littleness of
our being conceals from us the sight of the Infinite."

. . . trop de bruit nous assourdit, trop de lumière éblouit, trop de distance et trop de proximité empêche la rue, trop de longueur et trop de brièveté de discours l'obscurcit, trop de vérité nous étonne (j'en sais qui ne peuvent comprendre que, qui de zéro ôte 4, reste zéro) . . . .[26]

The symbol "zero" is, paradoxically, a remarkably useful, active, and constructive principle in arithmetic. Pascal translated the zero principle, as he had the void, into moral terms, playing back and forth with the concept of zero, the metaphysical "nothing" for which it stands, and the physical vacuum so newly received. Man is an integer and a unit but that very integrity may prove to be nothing. Pascal's operation, practiced with the accomplished charlatanry of a man accustomed to deal in several variables at once, is Montaigne's trick in the "Apologie," only here intensified. Like Montaigne, Pascal builds man up only to dismantle him again: like Montaigne, he threatens man with utter annihilation before the incomprehensible grandeur of the infinite—but unlike Montaigne, Pascal seems to confirm the operation by the modern method of quantification.

L'unité jointe à l'infini ne l'augmente de rien, non plus qu'un pied à une mesure infinie. Le fini s'anéantit en présence de l'infini, et devient un pur néant. Ainsi notre esprit devant Dieu; ainsi notre justice devant la justice divine. Il n'y a pas si grande disproportion entre notre justice et celle de Dieu, qu'entre l'unité et l'infini. . . .

Nous connaissons qu'il y a un infini, et ignorons sa nature; comme nous savons qu'il est faux que les nombres soient finis,

[26] *Pensée* 84, *OC*, pp. 1108-09; Mod. Lib. edn., No. 72, p. 25: "Too much sound deafens us; too much light dazzles us; too great distance or proximity hinders our view. Too great length and too great brevity of discourse tends to obscurity; too much truth is paralyzing (I know someone who cannot understand that to take four from nothing leaves nothing)."

donc il est vrai qu'il y a un infini en nombre; mais nous ne
savons ce qu'il est: il est faux qu'il soit pair, il est faux qu'il
soit impair; car, en ajoutant l'unité, il ne change point de
nature; cependant c'est un nombre, et tout nombre est pair
ou impair . . . Ainsi on peut bien connaître qu'il y a un Dieu
sans savoir ce qu'il est.[27]

The method is *not* in fact quantification, however much it
may appear to be, since "nothing" and "the infinite" are
not numbers but denotations of numerical concepts designed to transcend the limitation of numbers. Pascal plays,
quite consciously, a numbers game, by sleight-of-hand, to
"prove" his spiritual hypothesis. By his professional association of the mysteries of mathematics with the mysteries
of God, he makes the metaphysical *frisson* seem a mere
schoolroom draught: he stresses precisely the fear of moral
death, of personal annihilation, to bring men to an awareness of the nescience and impotence he regarded as conditions of human life. Man does not know how he came
into the world, nor what the world is, nor what he shall
become when he leaves the world, nor what is when he is
not:

Je vois ces effroyables espaces de l'univers qui m'enferment,
et je me trouve attaché à un coin de cette vaste étendue, sans

[27] *Pensée* 145, *OC*, p. 1212; Mod. Lib. edn., No. 233, pp. 79-
80: "Unity joined to unity adds nothing to it, no more than one
foot to an infinite measure. The finite is annihilated in the presence
of the infinite, and becomes a pure nothing. So our spirit before
God, so our justice before divine justice. There is not so great a
disproportion between our justice and that of God, as between
unity and infinity."
    "We know that there is an infinite, and are ignorant of its nature.
As we know it to be false that numbers are finite, it is therefore
true that there is an infinity in number. But we do not know what
it is. It is false that it is even, it is false that it is odd. . . . So we
may well know that there is a God without knowing what He is."

que je sache pourquoi je suis plutôt placé en ce lieu qu'en un autre, ni pourquoi ce peu de temps qui m'est donné à vivre m'est assigné à ce point plutôt qu'en un autre de tout l'éternité qui m'a précédé et de toute celle qui me suit. Je ne vois que des infinités de toutes parts, qui m'enferment comme un atome et comme une ombre qui ne dure qu'un instant sans retour. Tout ce que je connais est que je dois bientôt mourir, mais ce que j'ignore le plus est cette mort même que je ne saurais éviter.

Comme je ne sais d'où je viens, aussi je ne sais où je vais; et je sais seulement qu'en sortant de ce monde je tombe pour jamais ou dans le néant, ou dans les mains d'un Dieu irrité, sans savoir à laquelle de ces deux conditions je dois être éternellement en partage. Voilà mon état, plein de faiblesse et d'incertitude. . . .[28]

Combien de royaumes nous ignorent!
Le silence éternel de ces espaces infinis m'effraie.[29]

Pascal's God, like Spinoza's, has no anthropomorphic affection for man or mankind—in Pascal's system, loving

---

[28] *Pensée* 335, *OC*, p. 1175; Mod. Lib. edn., No. 194, p. 68: "I see those frightful spaces of the universe which surround me, and I find myself tied to one corner of this vast expanse, without knowing why I am put in this place rather than in another, nor why the short time which is given me to live is assigned to me at this point rather than at another of the whole eternity which was before me or which shall come after me. I see nothing but infinites on all sides, which surround me as an atom, and as a shadow which endures only for an instant and returns no more. All I know is that I must soon die, but what I know least is this very death which I cannot escape.

"As I know not whence I came, so I know not whither I go. I know only that, in leaving this world, I fall for ever either into annihilation or into the hands of an angry God, without knowing to which of these two states I shall be for ever assigned. Such is my state, full of weakness and uncertainty."

[29] *Pensées* 90, 91, *OC*, p. 1113; Mod. Lib. edn., No. 207, p. 75: "How many kingdoms know us not?" No. 206, p. 75: "The eternal silence of these infinite spaces frightens me."

is left to the Second Person of the Trinity—for Pascal's is a terrible God, *Deus absconditus*, *le Dieu caché*, hidden at the Fall from man's experience and from his speculation. In a universe without divine animation, in a universe hostile or, at best, neutral to human pathos, how might a man measure himself, still less aspire to salvation? The extremes stretching infinitely beyond man on every side *are* infinite and therefore provide no relevant measuring rod for man's knowledge of his own frontiers and his own action.

Not for nothing was Pascal a comfort to gamesters, however. His formulation of the laws of chance gave to gamblers some insight into their precarious future, reduced to some order the infinite choice evidently facing them. Pascal provided gamesters and desperate men at the extremity of their being the same chance to win. Furthermore, recognizing the universal uncertainty of life, he exhorted them all to bet. In an extreme situation, betting is no more absurd than any other human act:

—Examinons donc ce point, et disons: "Dieu est, ou il n'est pas." Mais de quel coté pencherons-nous? La raison n'y peut rien déterminer: il y a un chaos infini qui nous sépare. Il se joue un jeu, à l'extrémité de cette distance infinie, où il arrivera croix ou pile. Que gagerez-vous?

As the man hesitates, Pascal sketches the chances:

—Voyons. Puisqu'il y a pareil hasard de gain et de perte, si vous n'aviez qu'à gagner deux vies pour une, vous pourriez encore gagner; mais s'il y en avait trois à gagner, il faudroit jouer . . . et vous seriez imprudent, lorsque vous êtes forcé à jouer, de ne pas hasarder votre vie pour en gagner trois, à un jeu où il y a un pareil hasard de perte et de gain.

He introduces at this point a new rule of the game: as the man hesitates and withdraws from choice, Pascal insists

that a man *must* bet. No one can remain neutral to the
wager, because in fact, whether he knows it or not, a man
does wager, does choose sides. And in any case, why not,
when the extremes are so great?

Mais il y a une éternité de vie et de bonheur; et cela étant,
quand il y aurait une infinité de hasards dont un seul serait pour
vous, vous auriez encore raison de gager un pour avoir deux; et
vous agirez de mauvais sens, en étant obligé à jouer, de re-
fuser de jouer une vie infiniment heureuse à gagner. Mais il y
a ici une infinité de vie infiniment heureuse à gagner, un hasard
de gain contre un nombre fini de hasards de perte, et ce que
vous jouez est fini. Cela ôte tout parti: partout ou est l'infini,
et ou il n'y a point infinité de hasards de perte contre celui de
gain, il n'y a point à balancer, il faut tout donner. Et ainsi,
quand on est forcé à jouer, il faut renoncer à la raison pour
garder la vie, plutôt que de la hasarder pour le gain infini aussi
prêt à arriver que la perte du néant.

Finally, he matches the uncertainty against the certainty:

Il n'y a pas infinité de distance entre cette certitude de ce qu'on
expose et l'incertitude du gain; cela est faux. Il y a à la vérité,
infinité entre la certitude de gagner et la certitude de perdre.
Mais l'incertitude de gagner est proportionée à la certitude de
ce qu'on hasarde, selon la proportion des hasards de gain et de
perte; et de là vient que, s'il y a autant de hasards d'un coté
que de l'autre, le parti est à jouer égal contre égal; et alors la
certitude de ce qu'on expose est égale à l'incertitude du gain:
tant s'en faut qu'elle en soit infiniment distante. Et ainsi, notre
proposition est dans une force infinie, quand il y a le fini à
hasarder à un jeu où il y a pareils hasards de gain que de perte,
et l'infini à gagner.[30]

[30] *Pensée* 451, *OC*, pp. 1213-14; Mod. Lib. edn., No. 233, pp.
81-2: "Let us then examine this point, and say, 'God is, or He is
not.' But to which side shall we incline? Reason can decide nothing
here. There is an infinite chaos which separates us. A game is

In this particular throw, the chances are not equal, for in the end, only the chance of winning is recognized, with its paradoxical reward, "la perte du néant," the loss of nothing. Nothing is lost, and one need not fear the idea of nothing. If there is no God, the man who bets on Him

---

being played at the extremity of this infinite distance where heads or tails will turn up. What will you wager?"

"Let us see. Since there is an equal risk of gain and of loss, if you had only to gain two lives, instead of one, you might still wager. But if there were three lives to gain, you would have to play . . . and you would be imprudent, when you are forced to play, not to chance your life to gain three at a game where there is an equal risk of loss and gain."

"But there is an eternity of life and happiness. And this being so, if there were an infinity of chances, of which one only would be for you, you would still be right in wagering one to win two, and you would act stupidly, being obliged to play, by refusing to stake one life against three at a game in which out of an infinity of chances there is one for you, if there were an infinity of an infinitely happy life to gain. But there is an infinity of an infinitely happy life to gain, a chance of gain against a finite number of chances of loss, and what you stake is finite. It is all divided; wherever the infinite is and there is not an infinity of chances of loss against that of gain, there is no time to hesitate, you must give all. And thus, when one is forced to play, he must renounce reason to preserve his life, rather than risk it for infinite gain, as likely to happen as the loss of nothingness." "There is not an infinite distance between the certainty staked and the uncertainty of the gain; that is untrue. In truth, there is an infinity between the certainty of gain and the certainty of loss. But the uncertainty of the gain is proportioned to the certainty of the stake according to the proportion of the chances of gain and loss. Hence it comes that, if there are as many risks on one side as on the other, the course is to play even; and then the certainty of the stake is equal to the uncertainty of the gain, so far is it from fact that there is an infinite distance between them. And so our proposition is of infinite force, when there is the finite to stake in a game where there are equal risks of gain and of loss, and the infinite to gain."

loses all, and is annihilated; but so does he also, if he bets against God and wins. The only way to win is to bet on God, a bet which, according to Pascal, is a sure thing. By Pascal's manipulation of the chances, betting becomes safe; quite clearly, Pascal considers that the existence of nothing no more threatens God than the existence of any other defined thing. The vacuum exists, moral annihilation exists, as they have always done; but God has always known them, even if man did not, for God permitted them their equivocal being. "Nothing" is far less terrible to Pascal than to the orthodox physicists who denied its existence: after all, like God, Pascal was able to produce his own "nothing" at will. Since nothing was, it must serve God's purposes, like everything else in God's mysterious creation. As part of His original plan, nothing is a *datum*, a given, to be taken—literally—*for granted* like any other gift of God. In less complicated systems than Pascal's (that of the abacus, for example), "nothing" was simply a notation of absence. In Pascal's view of the world, where all things were wonders and mysteries, and "nature" simply the signature of the mysterious Creator, "nothing" ceases to be more wonderful than anything else and becomes a natural part of the sum of creation and of human experience. By a proper knowledge of nothing, a reverent contemplation of the mysteries of its paradoxical extremities, man was bound to achieve something—even, with some courage, to achieve all.

9

Still Life: Paradoxes of Being

> I hold there is a generall beauty in the works of
> God, and therefore no deformity in any kind or
> species of creature whatsoever . . . To speake yet
> more narrowly, there was never any thing ugly, or
> mis-shapen, but the Chaos. . . .
>
> Browne, *Religio Medici*, I. 16

A picture by Sebastian Stoskopff in the Strasburg
Museum[1] shows a partly consumed pâté resting on an
opened letter, beside a wicker basket holding several delicate wine glasses. The basket is very thin, with many
empty spaces; the glasses are extraordinarily delicate, so
that one can see straight through them, as if they were
not wholly there. The representation is a *tour-de-force* of
the still-life painter's particular skill, whereby he shows us
things of such delicacy that they seem only barely there,
only barely real. The illusionism that all still-life painters
strive to achieve brings to a focus the illusion of all painting and all art. Just as Cleopatra's reference to the boy-
actor, possible only because the playwright's grasp upon
his craft was tight enough to permit the risk of breaking
the illusion, or the self-references of Erasmus or Robert
Boyle, alluded to elsewhere,[2] break through conventional
illusionism by pointing to palpable, living men and women,
so the illusionism involved in the still life risks the painter's art by drawing attention to the artifice.

[1] Charles Sterling, *Still Life Painting from Antiquity to the Present Time* (New York and Paris, 1959), Plate 43. See also Max J.
Friedländer, *Landscape, Portrait, Still-Life* (New York, 1963),
pp. 272-84.

[2] See above, Introduction; and below, Chapter 10.

The Stoskopff picture brings into focus even more than relativities of illusionism customarily do: the way in which the beholder is invited to look through the basket and the glasses leads him to "see through" the art as well as the subject of the painting, to the ontological truth residing beyond the painted objects, beyond the painting itself. For Stoskopff deliberately drew our attention to the "emptiness" of his painting—the "vanity," the "nothing," of which the Preacher spoke. He was, as it were, painting as specific subject the theme of his *genre*: painting, according to the rigorist view, was a vanity, an emptiness, a frivolity, a meaningless thing, an illusion: painting was, in short, false. A painting of the things of this world was, traditionally, called *Vanitas*; paradoxically, pictures of riches heaped up—such as Dutch and Flemish painters loved to paint and clients, apparently, to buy in the late sixteenth and seventeenth centuries—were called *vanitates*, since they pointed, with such remarkable mastery of illusionistic technique, to the precise worldly values which misled so many men from their proper spiritual goals, devotion to God and the cultivation of spiritual strengths.

Professor Gombrich has pointed to an important descriptive *coincidentia oppositorum* when he extended the *vanitas* concept from the still-life type to all painting: "Any painted still life," he said, is "*ipso facto* also a *vanitas*," is a moral criticism directed to the deceit of the senses. "For every painted still life has the *vanitas* motif 'built in' as it were, for those who want to look for it. The pleasures it stimulates are not real, they are mere illusion. Try and grasp the luscious fruit or the tempting beaker and you will hit against a hard cold panel. The more cunning the illusion the more impressive, in a way, is this sermon on semblance and reality."[8] To extend Gombrich's conceit, it

[8] E. H. Gombrich, "Tradition and Expression in Western Still Life," *Meditations on a Hobby Horse* (London, 1963), p. 104.

is possible to regard any picture as both a still life and a *vanitas*: for any picture is in some measure a representation of the transient, a *memento mori*, a metaphysical comment upon semblance and reality. The problems of painting and poetry evidently seemed more alike to Horace than they do to us: many poets have found Horace's *ut pictura poesis*[4] an indecisive guide. From one perspective, the specific genres of still life and paradox can be seen to be very like, since both, in spite of their concern for precision and exactness in both delineation and expression, rise from such specific details into larger figures of thought, to preach lessons which provoke speculation and contemplation.

This emphasis upon *techne* in both forms invites comparison, from which it is plain that the technical problems in the two arts are quite different. The limits of painting and poetry, as arts, are not the same, a fact which makes for difficulty in imitation of the one by the other. Most simply, the poet's chief illusion is the achievement of stasis;[5] no matter how he does it, the poet must arrange his words in a linear order involving action on his and on his readers' parts. It takes time, even for the most experienced reader, to read a poem, and the time it has taken, no matter how short, involves action and movement: the supreme illusion for the poet is to seem to have checked the movement, to have reached stasis, balance, a moment eternal in its implications of perfect totality. The painter's illusion is exactly opposite: he attempts to imitate action, motion, life. His medium binds him to stillness, to

[4] Rensselaer W. Lee, *"Ut Pictura Poesis*: the Humanistic Theory of Painting," *Art Bulletin*, xxi (1940), 197-269; Jean H. Hagstrum, *The Sister Arts* (Chicago, 1958), especially Chapters 1 and 2.

[5] See above, Chapter 3; E. H. Gombrich, "Moment and Movement in Art," *JWCI*, xxvii (1964), 293-306; and Murray Krieger's forthcoming study on the ecphrastic principle in art.

arrest; his art challenges him to transcend that stillness.

The still life seeks to transcend its medium in a curious way: by drawing attention to its craft, it flaunts its illusionism, its technical trickery. In this action, still life is an overt commentary on the art of painting, a kind of self-reference. Involved in both trickery and self-reference is paradox, to which the various names of the genre draw attention too. In Greek, what we call still life was first called by the word used to describe one aspect of the paradoxist's operation, rhopography, the "depiction of insignificant objects, of odds and ends."[6] Its analogies to the subjects of the rhetorical paradox, "things without honor," are evident: furthermore, these paradoxical verbal and visual genres had a contemporaneous vogue in late antiquity. As Dr. Sterling tells us, the genre "was mockingly baptized rhypography (i.e., painting of the sordid),"[7] in recognition that the genre deliberately flaunted high classical ideals of art. The painter Piraikos (the "Pyreicus" to whom Rabelais likened himself) was the most famous painter of this sort; his art had its obvious analogies to the paradoxical encomia of the Sophists. In spite of its subversion of artistic ideals, the art of rhypography was authoritatively recorded; classical critics and reporters provide records of successful *trompe l'œil*. The story of Zeuxis and Parrhasios, the first of whom painted grapes so lifelike that the birds pecked at them, the other a curtain so real that his fellow-painter tried to draw it aside to see the picture beneath, is the *locus classicus* for *trompe l'œil*. Though, as Gombrich remarks, the brilliant experiments of the zoologist Niko Tinbergen with the herring-gull suggest that it takes little technical skill to deceive birds,[8]

---

[6] Sterling, p. 11.   [7] *Ibid.*

[8] Niko Tinbergen, *The Study of Instinct* (Clarendon Press, 1952), pp. 28-31.

and we know how readily men are deceived by their own
expectations from any given situation,[9] the story is all the
same archetypal for the painter's attempt to rival, if not
God, then at least Nature. *Trompe l'oeil* is always part of
the painter's bag of tricks; or, every painting is a still life
that tries at once to be and to surpass life itself.

Modern terms for the genre are also oxymoronic—
nature morte, nature, whose very quality is life, now dead;
still life, evidently originally meaning no more than "a
motionless model"[10] in the Dutch phrase. But even so, it
is still an oxymoron, since (even in Holland) life is never
quite still. The terms themselves, Greek and modern, point
directly to the technical problem facing the painters, a
problem perceived as part of the doctrine of imitation. In
this respect, the still life coincides with the rhetorical
paradox, this time not in its subject matter only, but in its
preoccupation with itself, with its own technique, its own
activity. The still life, like the paradox, deals in subject
matter less than heroic, less than tragic, subject matter
commonplace, trivial, and familiar. Everyone knew about
scraps of food, about flowers, fruit, skulls, and candles,
just as every adult knew about lice, fleas, baldness, the
infidelity of women, and folly in general—all the more
skill, then, required to make these commonplaces seem
rare, interesting, and attractive, to endow them with the
qualities of recognition that art usually reserves to grander
subjects.

The "things without honor" that were the subjects of
both paradoxical encomium and still life received the most
intent scrutiny from the rhetorician and the painter, who

[9] E. H. Gombrich, *Art and Illusion*, pp. 101-02.
[10] Ingvar Bergström, *Dutch Still-Life Painting in the Seventeenth
Century*, trans. Christina Hedstrom and Gerald Taylor (New York,
1956), pp. 3-4; Sterling, pp. 43-44.

concentrated upon reproducing the thing itself, the thing in its very essence. So Sophist orations on baldness, tyranny, imprisonment, and the rest, described in the most graphic detail, in the utmost roundness and fullness, the state or condition being praised: no wonder that Gorgias' praise of Helen, originally classified as a paradox because Helen was so obviously "bad," soon became a traditional encomium of the perfectly beautiful woman, and entirely lost its paradoxical nature. Gorgias had been too persuasive —he described his subject too well. The paradoxical encomium, with its concentration upon something regarded as without merit, separated and distinguished that thing from all others, endowed it with a kind of merit, simply by treating it, in a parody of the traditional encomium, with the same care and attention that, for example, Thucydides attributed to Pericles in his oration on the Athenian war-dead. Helen, or tyranny, or imprisonment, or a goose, or a nut, or folly was delineated in its every aspect and detail, for its own sake. So too with the subject of the classical and modern still life: it was presented so exactly, so "really" that its very existence takes on significance and importance. Pascal's clear sight took him at once to the heart of the problem: "Quelle vanité que la peinture qui attire l'admiration par la ressemblance de choses dont on n'admire point les originaux!"[11]

One might say that the paradox and still life abstracted their subject from its conventional context, discussed it, or painted it, separately, precisely, and for itself alone. A millennium after the Hellenistic rhopographers were busy at their art, Francis Bacon called for the exact examination of "things without honor"—the examination of things normally regarded as vile; though not for themselves

---

[11] Blaise Pascal, *Oeuvres complètes*, ed. Jacques Chevalier (Paris: Bibliothèque de la Pléiade, 1954), *Pensée* 116, p. 857.

alone, as we assume the rhopographers to have done, but
for the advancement of learning and the use and benefit
of mankind.[12]

Sterling has suggested that the vogue for illusionism in
painting was related to relativist strands in Greek thought,
Heraclitan ideas of flux and Gorgias' Sophist aesthetics,
based on illusion and even on deceit. He associated the still
life also with the philosophy of Epicurus and other sensa-
tionalists:

The writings of the period, from Theocritus to Lucretius, bear
witness to an almost impressionistic sensitivity to color, to the
integument of things, to the changing face of nature in the
variable light of day. When in the first half of the third century A.D. Philostratus wrote: "Everything has a color of its
own, clothes, weapons, houses and apartments, woods, mountains, springs and *the air that envelops all things*," he was
summing up the ocular experience and the pictorial consciousness of many generations of artists.[13]

Stress upon *quidditas*, upon the individuation of each
thing, challenged the painter to "reproduce" it as accurately, that is, as illusionistically, as he could: one of the
most famous of such pictures, surely an example of rhypography rather than of rhopography, is the famous mosaic,
"The Unswept Room," of Sosos of Pergamon,[14] the floor
of a banqueting hall with all sorts of table scraps, nut-

[12] Francis Bacon, *Novum organum*, Book I, Aphorism cxx: "And
things that are mean and even filthy—things which (as Pliny says)
must be introduced with an apology,—such things, no less than the
most splendid and costly, must be admitted to natural history. . . .
For whatsoever deserves to exist deserves also to be known, for
knowledge is the image of existence, and things mean and splendid
exist alike." *Selected Writings*, ed. Hugh G. Dick (Modern Library, 1955), p. 530.

[13] Sterling, p. 11.

[14] Sterling, Plate 4.

shells, snailshells, a bird claw, bits of fruit and crusts of bread; at one nut, with the meat still in it, crouches a little mouse, like many a real visitor to an unswept dining room. This mosaic is a *trompe l'oeil* and an extension of reality: like the Hall of Mirrors at Versailles, it artfully enlarges the reality of which it is a functional part.

The paradox, the still life, even the Hellenistic floor, reflect upon their own art. Both paradox and still life have close connections with the mirror,[15] that smooth portrayal of impermanent realities. Though mirrors have always made their contributions to art, there is a sense in which they have always terrorized the painter, since their reflection is always so much more "exact" than his representation. Mirrors have been part of the painter's tool chest; in the general improvement of illusionistic technique, the mirror has given impressive lessons. Indeed, "instruments and helps,"[16] as Bacon called them, have always been at the service of the painter's search after the truth of illusion. Mirrors helped to align an artist's view, and later the still-life and naturalistic painter was greatly helped by the microscope.[17] When the *camera obscura* came into use, Sir Henry Wotton recognized at once its relevance to the painter's art, but disapproved of it—"To make landscapes by it were illiberal, though surely no painter can do them so precisely."[18] When he visited Cornelis Dreb-

[15] See below, Chapter 12; and G. F. Hurtlaub, *Zauber des Spiegels. Geschichte und Bedeutung des Spiegels in der Kunst* (München, 1951).

[16] Bacon, *Selected Writings*, p. 461.   [17] Bergström, pp. 40-41.

[18] *The Life and Letters of Henry Wotton*, ed. Logan Pearsall Smith (Clarendon Press, 1901), II. 206; see *De Jeugd van Constantijn Huygens, door Hemzelf Beschreven* (Rotterdam and Antwerp, 1946), pp. 87-88 for a story about the use by the painter Torrentius of a *camera obscura*; and Ludwig Goldscheider, *Jan Vermeer* (London and New York, 1958), pp. 26-27, 34-36, for Vermeer's use of mirrors, frames, and perhaps also the camera.

bel's English laboratory in 1621, Constantijn Huygens was particularly interested in the implications for painting of both the camera and the magic lantern. He wrote to his parents:

J'ay chez moy l'autre instrument de Drebbel, qui certes fait des effets admirables en peinture de reflexion dans une chambre obscure; il ne m'est possible de vous en déclarer la beauté en paroles; toute peinture est morte au prix, car c'est icy la vie mesme, ou quelque chose de plus relevé, si la parole n'y man-quoit. Car et la figure et le contour et les mouvements s'y rencontrent naturellement et d'une façon grandement plai-sante. Les Degheyns s'y plaisent merveilleusement, mais nostre cousin Carel s'y enragera.[19]

(I have at home Drebbel's other instrument, which certainly makes admirable effects in painting by reflection in a *camera obscura*; I cannot do justice to its beauty in words; compared to it, all painting is dead, for this is life itself, or something raised to an even higher power, if words do not fail me. For figure, shape, and movement fuse naturally and in a highly pleasing manner. The De Gheyns will enjoy it greatly, but our cousin Carel will be enraged at it.)

In the remarkable work of Hoefnagel, Flegel, and the De Gheyns, father and son, increased scientific naturalism is evident;[20] one may postulate that, in the case of the later painters at the very least, both magnifying lenses and microscopes served them in their art.

Of optical "helps," mirrors were the most important,

[19] Constantijn Huygens, *Briefwisseling*, ed. J. A. Worp (The Hague, 1911-1918), I. 94; Huygens was related through his mother to the painter Joris (Georg) Hoefnagel, and was closely connected with the De Gheyns. He himself painted a still-life with a fly, of which he was very proud and the De Gheyns approved (*De Jeugd*, pp. 13, 68).

[20] For Flegel, see Georg Flegel, *Sechs Acquarelle*, ed. Friedrich Winkler (Berlin, 1954).

though magnifying glasses came to rival them in their usefulness to artists. One famous mirror, Jan van Eyck's in the Arnolfini portrait, demonstrates both the skill of the painter and his witty self-reference: as Panofsky has shown, the painter had a function within the scene he painted, as witness to the secular troth-plighting. Solely as a virtuoso display of technique, that mirror is impressive; the precise, reduced reflection in the convex mirror holds, it seems, all the implications of the meaningful room. In the mirror, the beholder can "see" the painter and the door behind him; the illusion extends the illusion. Marvell's poem, "On a Drop of Dew," offers an analogue to the mirror and the illusionism, for like Van Eyck's mirror, the drop of dew is in little the world of which it is a part. Both its shape and its mirroring quality make it entirely self-contained:

> For the clear Region where 'twas born
>   Round in its self incloses:
>   And in its little Globes Extent,
> Frames as it can its native Element.   (ll. 5-8)

The drop of dew diminishes, as the mirror diminishes, the world it reflects; and since it "reflects" that world, it speculates upon it too, and invites such speculation in the beholder:

> And, recollecting its own Light,
> Does, in its pure and circling thoughts, express
> The greater Heaven in an Heaven less.   (ll. 24-26)

The drop of dew is both real and "metaphysical," itself its own reflection, itself "its pure and circling thoughts." The mirror image is taken as both thinking (reflection, speculation), and the instrument to stimulate thinking: in this poem, as in much still-life painting, image and theme become one.

The "diminution" of the mirror reflection is an important element in illusionistic painting: the precision of Van Eyck's convex mirror reflection distorts as it reduces, just as the reflection in the drop of dew distorts the reflection of the whole world around it. Marvell plays with images of reduction in other places as well, for example, in his description of the haymakers at Nunappleton:

> They seem within the polisht Grass
> A Landskip drawen in Looking-Glass.
> And shrunk in the huge Pasture show
> As Spots, so shap'd, on Faces do.   (stanza LVIII)

Such reduction imagery (as in "Such Fleas, ere they approach the Eye,/ In Multiplying Glasses lye") in Marvell's work is related to his complicated personal view of the nature and functions of mind.[21] Whenever he creates a world upside down, or reversed, he does so very carefully, very intellectually, as in his reference to the local salmon fishermen, who "like *Antipodes* in shoes,/ Have shod their *Heads* in their *Canoos*"; or the men like grasshoppers in "that unfathomable Grass"; or the rails massacred by the "whistling Sithe"[22]; or the reduced, orderly, fragrant, decorative warfare of the Nunappleton gardens. For Marvell, the proper image for mind was

> that Ocean where each kind
> Does streight its own resemblance find,[23]

because each kind is mirrored, neatly, precisely, in the microcosmic mind.[24] The Mower's mind could "see its Hopes as in a Glass" until Juliana distorted the scenery

[21] See also the forthcoming paper by Geoffrey H. Hartman on "The Nymph complaining for the Death of her Faun."

[22] "Upon Appleton House," stanzas LXXXXVI, XLVII, L.

[23] "The Garden," stanza VI.

[24] I hope soon to prepare a paper amplifying this point.

within and without that mind until it could no longer truly reflect. So also the poet's mind was easily imaged as a gallery of pictures of Clora in different moods, because it was actually a hall of mirrors in which she was reflected and reflected upon.[25]

Marvell internalized the function of optical instruments as the functions of the human mind. Certainly epistemology traditionally tends to express itself in terms of ocular experience—vision, revelation, insight, illumination, enlightenment, and so forth; an external experience is both absorbed into an internal experience and made to stand for that experience. The Renaissance still life, similarly, exploited and celebrated ocular experience—but very rarely for itself alone. The sight directs appeals to the other senses and to the mind as well. Sixteenth- and seventeenth-century still life, with its emphasis on the differences among specific things and the separateness, variety, and variation in the plenitudinous things of this world, are virtuoso displays of technique, rendering all the particular qualities of particular things in as exact an imitation as the painter's skill could achieve. In the North, still life derived part of its strength and much of its subject matter from the realistic strain so noticeable in fifteenth-century painting, where light[26] is exploited to delineate uniquely all kinds of remarkable objects, tactilely as well as visually —brass chandeliers, convex mirrors, jeweled crowns, cut velvet and damask cloth, carafes, towels, candlesticks, mousetraps, oranges, and shaggy dogs, to name some of the most famous, as well as live canons, donors, and chancellors, specific individuated saints, the Virgin, and the only

---

[25] Marvell, "The Mower's Song," "The Gallery."

[26] Millard Meiss, "Light as Form and Symbol in Some Fifteenth-Century Paintings," *Art Bulletin*, xxvii (1945), 175-81; and E. H. Gombrich, "Light, Form, and Texture in XVth Century Painting," *Journal of the Royal Society of Arts* (October 1964), pp. 826-49.

Son of God. Some of the obvious interests in the "skin" of things demonstrated in these paintings, as well as in later still-life arrangements, may be related to the stimulus of scientific inquiry.[27] Certainly the work of Hoefnagel, Flegel, and the De Gheyns, all highly talented illustrators of the new taxonomy, suggests a close connection between their style and the new science. Illustrations for scientific books necessarily delineate, separate, and mark off one object from all others (whether for the new science or the old, one might note: technical accuracy may have increased, but old herbalists showed their subjects as separately as new botanists did); so, from its beginnings, does the traditional still life. In the "breakfast pieces" of Nicolaes Gillis and Clara Peeters, one sees the same kind of distinctness and separateness in the articles on the table that one sees in Hoefnagel's moths and butterflies, or Flegel's strawberries and ladybugs. Clarity and distinctness were by no means the inventions of Descartes:[28] two generations before the *Discourse on Method*, still life painters pointed toward "Cartesianism." Cartesianism too relied upon already formulated concepts of definition, delimitation, and determination; the same scientific formulations, from Uccello's *dolce prospettiva* to the clarifying *camera obscura*, help to define both the Cartesian method and the painter's craft.

Sterling has suggested a connection between the antique still life and the philosophy of Epicurus; that is, a connection between two such different kinds of preoccupation

[27] James Ackerman, "Science and Visual Art," *Seventeenth-Century Science and the Arts* (Princeton, 1962), pp. 74-78.

[28] See Jurgis Baltrušaitis, *Anamorphoses* (Paris [1955]), where the connection is made clear between Cartesian analytic rationalism and the exploitation of anamorphic deformation. For "clarity," see also Wilfrid Blunt, *The Art of Botanical Illustration* (London, 1950), pp. 193-94.

with material things. The connection holds, I think, for the
Renaissance as well, though still life is by no means associated only with the materialist philosophy. Nonetheless,
concentration upon techniques of representation certainly
resulted in extraordinary canvasses crowded with *things*—
the breakfast and fruit pieces, the kitchens from Pieter
Aertsen to Heda and Stoskopff (whose kitchenmaids, as
if cut from cardboard, spoil the illusion of reality in his
still-life paintings), the fishmarkets of Van Beyeren and
Emmanuel de Witte, the flower-pieces of Bosschaert and
Savery, the game-pieces of Van Aelst and Weenix. These
pictures of *things* were precisely those called *vanitates*,
vanities, emptinesses, reminders of the transience of mortality. For some imaginations, the contradiction between
things and "nothing" was carried further: ordinary additive accumulation of objects was an insufficient challenge
to the painter's technique, and the usual clutter was complicated by a kind of visual punning, as in Arcimboldo's
paintings of grotesque gods and goddesses composed entirely of flowers, fruits, and vegetables.[29]

The body-landscape into which Panurge is metaphorically transformed[30] is a verbal example of the same trick;
Marvell's fawn also "becomes" its landscape:

> Among the beds of Lillyes, I
> Have sought it oft, where it should lye;
> Yet could not, till it self would rise,
> Find it, although before mine Eyes—

its cryptic coloration the result of its having turned the
landscape (the roses and the lilies) into itself, until it was
almost

[29] See Benno L. Geiger, *I dipinti ghiribizzosi di Giuseppe Arcimboldi* (Firenze, 1954); Francine-Claire Legrand and Felix
Sluys, *Giuseppe Arcimboldo et les archimboldesques* (Aalter, Bel-
gium, 1955).

[30] See above, Chapter I.

Lillies without, Roses within.[31]

In "Upon Appleton House," the poet anamorphizes himself into a piece of the landscape he describes. "Retiring from the Flood" he "imbarks" himself into a tree. Later in the same poem, the leaves and insects cover him so that he is indistinguishable from the wood—

> The Oak-leaves me embroyder all,
> Between which Caterpillars crawl;
> And Ivy, with familiar trails,
> Me licks, and clasps, and curles, and hales.
>
> (stanza LXXIV)

The poet is minutely, exactly depicted, like the still life, even down to the familiar still-life insect, the caterpillar, crawling "between" the leaves. Finally, he pleads to be imprisoned, as a landscape element, in that natural place, thus combining the classical Ovidian metamorphosis with Christian imagery (briars, nails) to sanctify the classical *numen*:

> Bind me ye *Woodbines* in your twines,
> Curle me about ye gadding *Vines*,
> And Oh so close your Circles lace,
> That I may never leave this Place:
> But, lest your Fetters prove too weak,
> Ere I your Silken Bondage break,
> Do you, *O Brambles*, chain me too,
> And courteous *Briars* nail me through.
>
> (stanza LXXVII)

There was classical precedent in painting for such *double-entendre*. Zeuxis' and Parrhasios' miracle-paintings, in the antique report, "changed completely according as seen from close at hand or from a distance,"[32] as did Arcim-

---

[31] Marvell, "The Nymph complaining for the Death of her Faun," ll. 77-80, l. 92.

[32] Sterling, p. 10, and n. 9.

boldo's seasonal allegories, in which the reclining deity is far clearer from across the gallery, and the specific fruits, flowers, and vegetables, dim from a distance, obscure the larger pattern of the human figure from near at hand. Sometimes a painting could be "read" in two directions, so to speak—one way up, a bowl of vegetables for the kitchen, the other way, a grotesque head formed of turnips, carrots, and so forth, with the bowl now serving as hat. Another *double-entendre* was to be seen in Daniele da Volterra's painting of the crucifixion, which was painted to accommodate two visual perspectives: looked at first from the right, then from the left, it seemed to "shift" toward the beholder.[33] The development of perspective and of optics increased both the geometrical illusionism in painting and the possibility of "anamorphosis," or scientific deformation—

> perspectives, which when rightly gaz'd upon
> Show nothing but confusion, ey'd awry,
> Distinguish form. . . .[34]

Anamorphosis is particularly interesting, since its deformations depend upon the rationalized principles of optics—the skull in Holbein's "Ambassadors" is not the result of Holbein's observation of actual skulls, but is his application to a skull of the principles of projection in plane geometry. Furthermore, anamorphoses exploit increased knowledge to insist upon relativity: the skull in Holbein's picture is disturbing because it can be brought into focus only if the beholder squints at it from the side of the whole painting. To bring the skull into focus, the beholder must forego his sight of the four-square ambassadors, so dignified amongst their vanities. There is no way to see everything

[33] Jean-François Nicéron, *Thaumaturgus opticus, seu admiranda optices, catoptrices, dioptrices* (Paris, 1646), p. 189.
[34] *Richard II*, ii.ii.ll. 18-20.

in that picture "right" from a single point of view—this is, perhaps, Holbein's comment on the function of the ambassador in general, a man sent, as one of them wrote, "to lie abroad for his country."

Anamorphic pictures served another purpose: they could act out graphically the miracle of creativity, as exemplified, for instance, in the rather obvious work of the fifteenth-century German artist Erhard Schoen. There the lines, rightly gazed upon, are utterly chaotic; looked at awry, they become a scene from the Bible[35]—the death of Saul, or Jonah cast up on the shore, the Creation itself. Chaos is brought into order: the great act of God at the Creation is graphically demonstrated by the artist's skill and wit.

No genre ever stays put, and still life was no exception. Pieter Aertsen's Butcher-shop[36] is a picture filled with the ordinary wares of the butcher's trade, and shows the apprentice himself, just outside, and a steer hanging in another shed. But through another opening in the shop, we look out upon quite a different scene, a man leading an ass on which a woman sits—the Flight into Egypt. Butchery is appropriate: the Holy Family fled from the butchery of the sons of Israel. Two more paintings by Aertsen, and one by Beuckelaer[37] show in the foreground breakfast-pieces and a kitchen-piece: but past the still life we see, in each case, Christ in the House of Mary and Martha. Once more, the sacred subject is set in its appropriate profane environment. In Beuckelaer's "Christ Shown to the People"[38] the foreground is a fishmarket scene, the fish being the symbol specifically of Christ, the early Christian demonstration of faith. In these pictures, apparently the symbolic substance has run away with the painting, has become

[35] Baltrušaitis, Plate II.
[36] Sterling, Plate 15.
[37] Bergström, pp. 20-21.
[38] Bergström, p. 21, Plate 19.

the center of attention—but for busy men, in a busy and materialist society, the double meaning was clear. As the housewife bustled about the market on her daily or weekly errands, she could say her prayers as well as at home: seeing the actual meat, the actual fish, she was to think first of the symbol and then of the spiritual substance for which the symbol stood.

To carry this notion one step further, the atmosphere of the still life comes to invade depictions even of life itself. In Emmanuel de Witte's beautiful picture in Rotterdam, with the lady turned away, the chandelier gleaming in the sidelong light, a mirror, a door, and the afternoon sun slanting into the rooms beyond, ever more distant from the observer, life is more metaphysical than real. Vermeer's "Sleeping Girl" in the Metropolitan Museum is like the sleeping beauty, spared waking into a coarse and robust local life. Though the models were certainly believable, solid women, there is an air of eternal arrest—*vie coite, nature reposée*[39]—in Vermeer's ladies reading letters, weighing pearls, pouring milk, that reminds us willy-nilly sooner of eternity than of the daily tasks in which they are engaged. Terborch's lady at the viol will never turn around, and no sun can fade or split the perfect silk and satin of her clothes; Saenredam's buildings have the same perfect remoteness. If a human being should walk through the Alkmaar church door—where in fact human beings crowded every Sunday—we would be as shocked as if Hoefnagel's lizards, like Escher's, were to crawl out of the picture and off the page; or if Fabritius' goldfinch were to blink its black eyes and chirp. These pictures, with all their emphasis on things-in-themselves, on the separate and autonomous identity of everything depicted there, are at the same time *natures mortes* from the peaceable king-

[39] Sterling, p. 43; Friedländer, pp. 193-94.

dom of perfect forms, platonic ideas rather than the clut-
tered, busy, disorderly changing samples of *becoming*
which sat for them. Whole towns could sit for the painter
in the same way—Delft is posed forever, not just on a
showery day when Jan Vermeer decided to memorialize
his own town, but a monument to eternity of that changed
and changing commercial city.

These pictures exploit the arrested motion by which the
painter is bound, catching something mutable into an
eternal immutability; this sort of picture turns technical
limitation into extraordinary strength. Still life can serve
eternity in a more overt way than this, too: sometimes the
very materiality of a depiction serves, not to celebrate an
Epicurean life full of delicious sensations, but to remind
mortal men of the worthlessness of the world's best worth.
Baugin's "Five Senses" in the Louvre,[40] appeals to each of
the five in one or another image, each immaculately separate from the others, to demonstrate the transience of
them all. Things point to the meaninglessness of their
own materiality *sub specie aeternitatis*; being alive is in
itself a *memento mori*.

Transient things particularly demonstrate transience in
general;[41] flowers woven into a garland surround little
William of Orange in De Heem's picture,[42] and were
selected to remind both of mortality and immortality.
Literary parallels are not far to seek: Marvell's "Picture
of Little T. C. in a Prospect of Flowers"[43] and Browne's
Garden of Cyrus[44] teach the same message. Little T. C. is
a young and fresh girl, Browne's treatise is about seeds

[40] Sterling, Plate 23.
[41] Bergström, p. 155.
[42] Bergström, p. 207.
[43] Marvell, *Poems*, I. 38-39.
[44] Sir Thomas Browne, *The Garden of Cyrus*, in *Religio Medici and Other Writings*, ed. L. C. Martin.

and growing, about generation and resurrection: but both of them, as much as Browne's *Urn-Buriall*, turn out to be meditations also upon death.

In "The Coronet" Marvell displays the snake in the grass in each garden from Eden on. In "Upon Appleton House," even "young Maria" Fairfax, that model maiden, was not exempt from meditations upon death; comment upon her very modesty called up to Marvell the image of an old worldly woman aging toward her death:

> Yet your own Face at you shall grin,
> Thorough the Black-bag of your skin. . . .
>
> (stanza LXXXXII)

Iconographically, the *vanitas* motif seems to derive from elements associated with St. Jerome. The objects he kept on his desk to remind him of his own mortality and to spur him to his task of translation of the eternal word—a skull, an hourglass, books, papers, a candle or a lamp—were detached from the presence of that holy man and given a career of their own as types of *memento mori*. Skulls, timepieces (clocks, pocket watches, hourglasses), candlesticks, lamps, soap bubbles, flowers, and fruit spoke directly to the transience of human life and human pleasure; any and all of the riches of this world spoke indirectly to self-indulgent men of the futility of their lives. Eternity waited for the candle to gutter and burn out; death left the wine glass half-empty, the song half-heard, the hand of cards half-played, the pâté unfinished, the letter unread or unanswered. "Vanity of vanities, saith the Preacher": and the painters, Pieter Claeszoon, David Bailly, De Heem, Heda, and a host of others, repeated the text. Stoskopff's frail basket of brittle glasses looks like a painting of emptiness because it is just that: a domestic *vanitas*, an eternal reminder of the emptiness of things.

In still-life painting, because the objects are so important, one is always conscious of the space *not* filled by
them: the objects themselves insist that the space surround-
ing them come into consideration. Leonardo da Vinci,
interested in all problems of metaphysics, physics, and
craft, was much interested in problems of emptiness, vacuum, and space. A speculator in the free market of ideas,
Leonardo played with the notion of nothing, both a metaphysical nothing and an actual absence of substance:

Among the great things which are found among us the
existence of Nothing is the greatest. This dwells in time, and
stretches its limits into the past and the future, and with these
takes to itself all works that are past and those that are to
come, both of nature and the animals, and possesses nothing
of the indivisible present. It does not however extend to the
essence of anything.[45]

Sometimes Leonardo denied the existence of anything
positively classified as nothing, except in the speculative
realm of nonbeing; sometimes he gave to "nothingness"
the capacity of distinguishing among things:

Nothingness has a surface in common with a thing and the
thing has a surface in common with nothingness, and the surface of a thing is not part of this thing. It follows that the
surface of nothingness is not part of this nothingness; it must
need be therefore that a mere surface is the common boundary
of two things that are in contact; thus the surface of water
does not form part of the water nor consequently does it
form part of the atmosphere, nor are any other bodies interposed between them. What is it therefore that divides the atmosphere from the water? It is necessary that there should
be a common boundary which is neither air nor water but is
without substance, because a body interposed between two

[45] Leonardo da Vinci, *The Notebooks*, trans. and ed. Edward
Macurdy (London, 1954), p. 61.

bodies prevents their contact, and this does not happen in water with air because they are in contact without the interposition of any medium.

Therefore they are joined together and you cannot raise up or move the air without the water, nor will you be able to raise up the flat thing from the other without drawing it back through the air. Therefore a surface is the common boundary of two bodies which are not continuous, and does not form part of either one or the other for if the surface formed part of it it would have divisible bulk, whereas however it is not divisible and nothingness divides these bodies the one from the other.[46]

According to this interpretation, "nothing" is in fact a real thing, however indeterminate, whose function is to separate objects one from another. Things are, in Leonardo's view, separated by a nonphysical, ideal boundary just outside the limit of their own extension, to which he assigned the name of nothing. An artist, dealing in line, an arbitrary and conventional method of demarcation without a physical correlative in nature, he was able to assign to line, the creation of the craftsman, the same reality that "nothing" assumed in his discussion. For line, without representation in actual nature but essential to the life of both artist and art, is a real "nothing," an indispensable item in the artist's subsistence economy.

Empty space can be a very crude method of demarcation or a very subtle one, and sometimes it is both. The naturalism of Hoefnagel's drawings is belied—as we know from modern field guides to birds, ferns, mammals, and so forth—by the artist's absolute ignoring of habitat, of context, in this case naturalistic background naturalistically portrayed. In such pictures, the separate thing is of paramount importance; there is no effort to understand the in-

[46] *Ibid.*, pp. 73-74.

terrelation, the ecology of things. These artists are delineators, the enemies of camouflage and the illustrators of a world conceived with Cartesian clarity and singularity. The aim of such artists is taxonomic, to identify once and for all the disparate elements of a various and confusing creation.

In the Renaissance, a period of taxonomic as well as more famous reforms, collectors made a great display of curiosities of nature, gathered from everywhere in the wide, and widening, world. From the Emperor Rudolph II to gentlemen like Constantijn Huygens[47] or John Tradescant, men domesticated the natural world, displayed the range of nature in their studies. Sometimes a cabinet displayed the orderliness of God's providential creation, sometimes it displayed the unclassifiable wonders of the world, *lusus naturae* collected from all quarters of the earth. The great Wrangel-Schrank of Augsburg (1566)[48] illustrates that preoccupation with chaos which was one current, flowing through caverns measureless to man, beneath the ordered and ordering enclosures of the Renaissance landscape of ideas. This elaborate intarsia chest (captured and carried off to Sweden during the Thirty Years' War) displayed a turbulent chaos of things in random juxtaposition, objects of all kinds, creatures living and fantastic, all of them in and out of perspective and proportion. Neither eye nor spirit is allowed to rest at any point on this piece of furniture: it opens in a maze of ever more

[47] Constantijn Huygens, "Daghwerck," *Gedichten*, ed. J. A. Worp (Groningen, 1893), III. 48-108; see Colie, "*Some Thankfulnesse to Constantine*" (The Hague, 1956), Chapters 6 and 7; Julius von Schlosser, *Kunst- und Wunderkämmern der Spätrenaissance* (Leipzig, 1908); Gustav Klemm, *Zur Geschichte der Sammlungen für Wissenschaft und Kunst in Deutschland* (Zerbst, 1837).

[48] Liselotte Möller, *Der Wrangelschrank und die verwandten süddeutschen Intarsienmöbel des 16. Jahrhunderts* (Berlin, 1956).

interiors, to display further scenes of disorder, of battles, storms, shipwrecks, horrors, as far inside as one can penetrate. The Augsburg chest is a monument to the idea of a disorderly world; its lesson is that not even art has a secure holdfast on a hazardous life.

The still life in this case teaches not a lesson of quietism or pietism, but a lesson of a far more unsettling kind, a lesson that life is never "still." The Augsburg chest derives from the same tradition as Holbein's "Ambassadors," where the artist demonstrates the simultaneous existence of more than one point of view of things. In the sixteenth century another type of picture, again a type connected with paradoxical expression, existed to express the same vision of a disparate world. This tradition illustrated the ubiquitous "Nobody," a skimpy creature, surrounded by fragments of things unrelated to each other and to everything else.[49] The "Nobody" of these pictures—Holbein's table top, Joerg Schan's broadsheet, Schoen's engravings, the various illustrations to Ulrich von Hutten's *Niemand* paradox—is usually taken as the "nobody" responsible for the deterioration of ordinary household economy, illustrative of domestic proverbs deriving from a disorderly social world in which no man's position is fixed. The "nobody" paradoxes are connected in many ways with the picaresque novel, another form reflecting social disruption and indefinite identity; like such picaresque narratives as *Lazarillo de Tormes* and *Simplicissimus*, themselves types of "nobody," the "nobody" paradoxes and pictures illustrate also a hazardous universe of chance, in which fragments of experience haphazardly combine to produce a "plot" in which the picaro's life is the only measuring rod of a world otherwise quite without meaning or pattern. Such a uni-

[49] Gerta Calman, "The Picture of Nobody," *op.cit.*, pp. 60-104; see particularly Plates 9, 10, 11, and 12.

verse is the modern version of the fragmented, vacuist cosmography of the ancient atomists, of Democritus, Epicurus, and Lucretius, in which whatever happens, happens by chance, and no one is responsible for events predetermined by an unknown, undiscoverable mechanist fate, in which all human values are relative and readily reduced to random insignificance.[50]

In Democritus' universe "nothing" is the context for "everything"—the atoms exist in a sea of nothing, as it were; their combinations occur to form temporary and mutable material things, precisely because they exist within no fixed boundaries or limitations, and have no pattern. Pictures of "nobody," in which the complete things, the whole objects so scrupulously depicted in the conventional still life are reduced to fragments and atoms, are a secular critique of the intimations of immortality implied in all still life. They depict objects constant only in their disorder and consequently always mutable, always in motion, always altogether denying the concept of "still" life.

One drawing in this tradition, Bruegel's "Elck," or Everyman, bears the motto, "Niemand en erkent hy selven"—No one knows [or recognizes] himself.[51] The phrase repeats the materialist criticism of all idealist introspection and may echo as well something of Augustinian psychological nescience. Certainly it is true, in grammar at least, that "nobody" can know himself, especially if he has no context within his disrupted and fragmentary environment. Nobody himself does not exist, in an environment existing only to change. Even if a man might recognize himself in a true mirror, he never can in a false one:

[50] This paragraph is painfully compressed: I hope to explore some of its implications in a further study centered on Robert Burton. See below, Chapter 15.

[51] Calman, p. 87 and Plate 11; see above, Chapter 7.

if he himself is false, even a true mirror will not reflect a true man. In every sense, a universe of chance is hazardous for a man in search of himself amid a broken, meaningless composition, decomposition, and recomposition of meaningless fragments. In such a universe he can find Nobody—he must read himself out of his context to become, like the figure in Holbein's picture, merely Nobody. Searches for identity of this kind too often lead to despair, for which the iconography of melancholy offers an example and an explanation.[52] For Dürer's heroic figure, as for the crouching Nobody on Holbein's table top, disparate things impinge too forcefully upon the thinker struggling to orient himself and his thoughts, struggling to find his bearings among the fragments of the insistently material world. "Melencolia I" belongs in a nobler tradition than Holbein's Nobody: she may, with God's grace, shake off her paralysis by the act of understanding and stand up free to use her wisdom about the paralyzing world.[53] For her, everything is too much; for Nobody, nothing is enough. Both pictures drive home Gombrich's nail to truth, that all pictures are, somehow, *vanitates*; all pictures demonstrate, not just the weakness and deceits of our senses, but also the relative meaninglessness of things. By the Christian paradox which the *vanitas* illustrates, the more ruinous and hazardous the world we are born to, the greater the consolations offered by the contemplation of heaven. When the best things the world can offer are seen as separate, unitary, additive fragments, even when they are whole, men are invited to contemn the world precisely at the moment they are tempted to love it most. All living things are thereby *memento mori*, all the full world simply a sign of the world's essential vanity, its essential emptiness:

[52] Erwin Panofsky and Fritz Saxl, *Dürers Melencolia I, Studien der Bibliothek Warburg* (Leipzig, 1923).

[53] See below, Chapter 15.

like the flower that fades, the bubble that breaks, the candle that burns itself out, everything comes to nothing in the end. As so often with the paradoxical formulation, however, the reverse is also possible: "nothing" in its turn can yield, to the man who can read its meaning under the aspect of infinity, everything that he requires or desires. All things are intimations both of mortality and immortality, everything and nothing are sufficient for salvation: as Folly says, ". . . what outwardly seemed death, yet lokyng within we shoulde fynde it lyfe: and on the other side what semed life, to be death. . . ."[54]

[54] Erasmus, *The Praise of Folly*, Eiij.

10

Being and Becoming: Paradoxes in the Language of Things

> Now nature is not at variance with art, nor art
> with nature; they being both the servants of his
> providence: Art is the perfection of Nature: Were
> the world now as it was the sixt day, there were
> yet a Chaos: Nature hath made one world, and
> Art another. In briefe, all things are artificiall, for
> nature is the Art of God.
>
> Browne, *Religio Medici*, I. 16

WE ARE used to thinking of the "scientific revolution"
of the sixteenth and seventeenth centuries as a rational
dependence upon the linear progress of cause and effect, or
on the linear progress of thought: "science," we think,
above all things, surely put an end to paradox. So it did,
but the battle for clarity in cause-and-effect progression
was not easily won, and for a long time the "miraculous"
and the "wonderful" held its old sway, even in the domain
of natural philosophy. Faustus and Bacon—the Lord
Chancellor, not the Friar—both took all knowledge to be
their province, but neither could defend their claim; the
flags they set up over their provinces flapped in the breeze
unnoticed for many years. God's omniscience defeated
Faustus, but science herself defeated Bacon; for the realm
of science proved too great for him; his sensible and economical method proved too difficult even for Bacon himself to follow.

Both Faustus and Bacon were concerned, not for knowledge only, but for the power that both were convinced

resided in pure knowledge: power to do good or evil, or simply to do one's will, to bend nature to some service which she did not "naturally" perform for mankind. For Faustus, quite simply, to master nature was to obtain supernatural power: for Bacon, to master nature was to make the supernatural customary, and natural; but for both of them, it was not enough simply to know the ways of nature and to understand natural laws; they needed rather to control and to direct nature, to re-create natural effects, to modify the Creation of God.

To modify, perhaps even to rival, the Creation of God— for the line between natural and black magic was not easy to draw. Even Bacon, with his commonsense attack upon the natural world, said of his *Sylva Sylvarum*,

For this *Writing* of our *Sylva Sylvarum*, is (to speake properly) not a *Naturall History*, but a high kinde of *Naturall Magicke*. For it is not a Description only of Nature, but a Breaking of Nature, into great and strange *Workes*.[1]

Like the "natural magic" of Giovanni Battista Porta, Bacon's art was one by which "we overcome those things in Art, wherein Nature doth overcome us."[2] The scientists of Salomon's House were involved in overcoming in art precisely those things in nature which remained mysterious to them: they began by imitating the phenomena of the natural world. They reproduced meteorological conditions (including "Generations of Bodies in Aire; as Froggs,

[1] Francis Bacon, *Sylva Sylvarum: Or, A Naturall Historie* (London, 1627), p. 29.

[2] Giovanni Battista Porta, *Natural Magick* (London, 1658), p. 2; cf. Francis Bacon, *The Twoo Bookes of the Proficience and Advancement of Learning* (London, 1605), II. 5: ". . . . from the Wonders of Nature, is the neerest Intelligence and passage towardes the Wonders of Arte: For it is no more, but by following, and as it were, hounding Nature in her wandrings, to bee able to leade her afterwardes to the same place againe."

Flies, and divers others");[3] they made models of the heavens; they experimented on the size of animals and plants; they had perception chambers where they studied human sense reactions.[4] They also "feigned," or created delusions, just as the mountebank magician or Faustus did: in the "Perspective Houses" the scientists presented

All Delusions and Deceits of the Sight, in Figures, Magnitudes, Motions, Colours: All Demonstrations of Shadowes. Wee finde also diverse Meanes yet unknowne to you, of Producing of Light, originally, from diverse Bodies. We procure meanes of Seeing Objects a-farr off; As in the Heaven, and Remote Places; And representing things Neare as A-farr off; And things A-farr off as Neare; Making Faigned Distances.[5]

Similar imitations and deceptions were practiced in the Sound-Houses and Perfume-Houses; in the Houses of Deceits of the Senses, the scientists could "represent all manner of Feats of Jugling, False Apparitions, Impostures, and Illusions; And their Fallaces," their explications, so that any man might see for himself the way the tricks were done. For Bacon recognized that the line between imitation and creation was very fine indeed, and, though he knew that the progress of natural philosophy carried with it the temptation to delude an ignorant mankind, he wanted mankind informed of whatever was known, and of whatever could be done. Hence the rules laid down for the wise men of the New Atlantis:

wee doe hate all Impostures, and Lies: Insomuch as wee have severely forbidden it to all our Fellowes, under paine of Ignominy and Fines, that they doe not shew any Naturall worke or thing, Adorned or Swelling; but only Pure as it is, and without all Affectation of Strangeness.[6]

[3] Francis Bacon, *The New Atlantis*, in *Sylva Sylvarum*, p. 34.
[4] *Ibid.*, pp. 39, 35, 40, 41-42.
[5] *Ibid.*, p. 40.   [6] *Ibid.*, p. 43.

In line with this intention, the *Sylva Sylvarum*, though its contents differ so little from the late medieval and Renaissance compendia of amusing "scientific" wonders, was intended as something more important than just a register of the marvels of nature; as Bacon's editor, the devoted William Rawley, wrote in the "Preface to the Reader":

the Difference betweene this *Naturall History*, and others. For those *Naturall Histories*, which are Extant, being Gathered for Delight and Use, are full of pleasant Descriptions and Pictures; and affect and seek after Admiration, Rarities, and Secrets. But contrariwise, the Scope which his Lordship intendeth, is to write such a *Naturall History*, as may be Fundamentall to the Erecting and Building of a true Philosophy. . . .[7]

Bacon's hope was to make everything "clear," and to make causal connections so evident that cheating in natural philosophy would forever be impossible: his scientists stood, very self-consciously, at the self-elected point of redefinition and reconstruction in their subject, and desired above all things clarity and truth in its reformation. Bacon's great works all are, in one way or another, a call to the truthful, the exact, the definite restatement of *things*. To this end he urged the rejection of muddling verbal structures, which had, he thought, distorted truth on what he regarded as rhetorical and logical beds of Procrustes; he rejected language on the grounds that its tautologies were insufficient and its paradoxes simply lies.

For Bacon's God was a classical Creator, who created in an orderly and rational way: Bacon did not adopt the notion of Cardanus and others that God had played a kind of game with the world, creating not according to a preconceived plan but according to His lucid whim. By that

[7] *Ibid.*, "Preface to the Reader," in *Sylva Sylvarum*.

non-Baconian interpretation, God was an Heraclitan inventor of a world "compounded of Contraries and Agree-
ments of Discords";[8] the world was then a *discordia concors*, a composition to which oxymoron was the most
appropriate figure of rhetoric. For minds given to this
metaphor, the scientist's task was, like the poet's, to re-
create, to make an exact model of the world in all its complexity, its ambiguity, and its contradiction.

It took a long time before Bacon's clear-sighted view of
the natural world triumphed over the empirical fact that
even scientific definition could not utterly clarify the world,
could not eradicate the ambiguities of creation: men loved
nature's discords as much as, and often more than, her
regular displays. In the *Wunderkammern* and *Kunst-
schraenke*, the cabinets of princes and virtuosi, nature was
not displayed "most plain and pure," but rather "*Nature
Erring*, or *Varying*," or "*Nature Altered* or wrought,"[9]
the oddities, rarities, wonders, and puzzles of the natural
world. The virtuosi loved, collected, and paid sizable
sums of money for such things as fossils of unknown creatures, stones in the shape of feet, vegetables shaped like
human heads, double-headed calves, wonder-working
stones and other such talismans.[10] The great collections
had, too, their quota of ingenious machines and mecha-
nisms, the products of an increasingly learned technology,

[8] Baltasar Gracian, *The Critick*, trans. Paul Rycaut (London,
1681), pp. 33-34. For a general theory of play in Western civilization, see Johan Huizinga, *Homo ludens*.

[9] Bacon, *Advancement of Learning*, II. 8.

[10] See Julius von Schlosser, *Die Kunst- und Wunderkammern der
Spätrenaissance*; Gustav Klemm, *Zur Geschichte der Sammlungen
für Wissenschaft und Kunst in Deutschland*. For the tricks of perspective played in the cabinets themselves, see Lieselotte Möller,
*Der Wrangelschrank und die verwandten süddeutschen Intarsien-
möbel des 16. Jahrhunderts*.

the *joco-seriae* and paradoxes of the language of things.[11]

Not all men could afford to collect for cabinets and private museums: for them such books as Cardanus' *De subtilitate* and *De rerum varietate*,[12] Scaliger's corrective to Cardanus, *Exotericarum exercitationum liber*,[13] and a mass of similar compendia provided a substitute survey of the wonders and marvels of nature, at which men were intended to gaze in stupefaction, just as they were to be reduced to wondering stupefaction by the rhetorico-logical mystifications of paradox.[14]

The most important of such compendia were the work of the great Jesuits, Mario Bettini, Gaspar Schott, and Athanasius Kircher, famous not for their paradoxical science alone but for their considerable contributions to the history of serious science. Bettini's beautiful book was the first of the major encyclopedias of the light and the grave in science: *Apiaria universae philosophiae mathematicae* obligingly yields the desired parallel in its subtitle, *In quibus paradoxa, et nova pleraque machinamenta ad usus*

[11] One of the most famous of these collections was that of Athanasius Kircher, often referred to by Schott; in the eighteenth century a catalogue was printed of his collection of antique art, but not of scientific collections (*Musei Kircheriani in Romano Societatis Jesu Collegio aerea*, Rome, 1763). There are many printed books recording like collections, the names of which Schlosser gives; I have managed to see only two for careful study: *Museum Wormianum, seu historia rerum rariorum* (Leiden, 1655), and M. B. Valentini, *Museum museorum* (Frankfurt-am-Main, 1714, 2 vols.).

[12] Cardanus, *De subtilitate* (Nürnberg, 1550); *De rerum varietate* (Basel, 1557).

[13] (Paris, 1557).

[14] Cardanus, *De subtilitate*, pp. 342-43: "Nam ludunt, pugnant, venantur, saltant, tuba canunt, coquinarium exercent artem, atque haec omnia ut mirabilia sunt, ita nullius ut dixi utilitatis, et cum resciveris rationem qua oculos fallunt, ea autem duobus constat, instrumentis variis ad hoc paratis, manuumque agilitate, nec si te docere velint precario digneris discere."

eximios traducta.[15] The "paradoxes" Bettini offers are of
many different kinds—scientific ideas contrary to received
opinion, logical and mathematical paradoxes, geometrical
problems still resistant to solution, curious machines and
engines, illusions, games, and tricks. He tackled the
"learned hallucinations" constellated about the quadrature
problem, and about asymptotic lines which "go *de infinito
in finito*," as well as those that result from deformations
of the rules of perspective. Archimedes' screw (which
raised by lowering itself), wedges, levers (to lift the world,
as usual), all appear, magnificently illustrated, in his
book. However little Bacon's scientists would have ap-
preciated the fact, paradox had become the normal mode
of Bettini's physical world.

The titles Gaspar Schott chose for his big books again
spring from the attitude of wonder informing paradox—
Magia universalis naturae et artis;[16] *Physica curiosa, sive
mirabilia naturae et artis*;[17] *Technica curiosa*;[18] and *Joco-
seriorum naturae et artis, sive magiae naturalis centuriae
tres.*[19] Schott was the disciple and colleague of Athanasius
Kircher, and his books drew heavily on Kircher's idiosyncratic genius, presenting many notions and schemes Kircher
had published in his own works or had discussed with his
colleague. Schott made no secret of his admiration for
Kircher, and of his own dependence on the master's work,
stressing in his long introduction the playfulness with
which Kircher, emulating a playful nature, tackled the
problems of natural philosophy:

> Hic curiositate Theatrum panditur,
>   In quo *Ars* et *Natura* ludunt:
>   Sed dum ludunt doctis; indoctis illudunt.[20]

[15] (2 vols., Bologna, 1642).
[16] (Nürnberg, 1657).   [17] (Nürnberg, 1662).
[18] (Nürnberg, 1664).   [19] (Würzburg, 1677).
[20] Schott, *Magia universalis*, "Prologus encomiasticus ad lectorem."

(Here the theater where art and nature play is exposed to curiosity: but while they play for the learned, they deceive the ignorant.)

From Kircher's tricks, games, and illusions, Schott came to understand the fundamental mystery of metamorphosis,[21] which may be practiced upon nature by art, so that their collusion, their playing together, may result in protean formations and deformations, may result in *serio ludere*. The marvelous anamorphic pictures and landscapes developed and exploited by Kircher and Schott not only exhibited man's technical art but imitated in their orderly copiousness the work of "God Himself, the author of Nature, who plays on the earth."[22] Illusion and game are, of course, not the only products of these men's admiration for nature (and of their jealousy of her power); many of their inventions and notions were by no means "paradoxical" or ambiguous or joco-serious. But the ambiguous, the paradoxical, the joco-serious played an essential part in their considerations of God, of nature, and of themselves, and gave tone to the wonder and admiration they paid to God's universe.

Paradox played its part in serious scientific undertaking, too, naturally enough, given the nature of scientific inves-

[21] The subject of metamorphosis has been extensively studied in relation to concepts of the baroque, but, curiously enough, Ovid has had little attention paid him in this connection. The Ovidian resources of a nonbaroque poet, Edmund Spenser, are touched on below, Chapter 11. For discussion, to another end, of the rhetoric and aesthetics of the "metaphysical" style, see the suggestive chapters by J. A. Mazzeo, *Renaissance and Seventeenth-Century Studies*, pp. 29-59.

[22] Schott, *Magia naturalis*, p. 170; *Joco-seriorum*, pp. 1-2. I do not wish to imply that such games were peculiar to the seventeenth century—Giuseppe Arcimboldo, as well as Erhard Schön, Holbein himself, and many others, practiced such *trompes l'oeil* and tricks of double vision in the preceding century.

tigation. Paradox operates across limits, across beginnings, ends, and the boundaries man sets to his knowledge; scientific investigation, naturally enough, operated at the edge of knowing, thus making relative what man knows and relative the limits of his discourse. In his *Philosophia libera*, Nathanael Carpenter suggests the relativity of the term in its scientific usage, asserting that his view had been taken by some as paradoxes, suggestions contrary to received opinion, and by others as paradoxes in which they had faith.[23]

As in the phrase, "Copernican paradox," the paradox was the scientific term for a new hypothesis, a new suggestion making old truths untrue, an undoing of an old understanding.[24] Carpenter's book makes fascinating use of mathematical and logical paradoxes to control the physical world and also to delineate theological truth. In 1661, when Robert Boyle published his *Skeptical Chymist*, he gave it a fine subtitle: *Or Chymico-Physical Doubts and Paradoxes, Touching the Spagyrists' Principles Commonly call'd Hypostatical, As they are wont to be Propos'd and Defended by the Generality of Alchymists.*[25] Carneades, the hero of the dialogue, was selected because he was "so conversant with nature and with Furnaces, and so unconfin'd to vulgar Opinions, that he would probably by some ingenious Paradox or other, give our minds at least a pleasing Exercise, and perhaps enrich them with some solid instruction."[26] That is just what Carneades did: in the traditional debate with his fellow virtuosi, he laid out his own views with great grace and decorum, of course winning over his friends to his own point of view. At one point

[23] Carpenter, *Philosophia libera* (Oxford, 1622), "Praefatio ad lectorem."

[24] See above, Introduction.

[25] (London, 1661).

[26] Boyle, *Skeptical Chymist*, p. 3.

in his instruction, Carneades performed a major trick of the artful paradoxist—he introduces the composer into the work he is composing:[27]

And, if I could here shew You what Mr. *Boyle* has Observ'd, touching the Various Chymicall Distinction of Salts, you would quickly discern, not only that Chymists do give themselves a Strange Liberty to call Concretes Salts. . . .[28]

This is an unexpected turn from an author so little playful as Boyle, the generality of whose work has an austerity and even a ponderousness that made it easy prey for the young Swift in his paradoxical parody, "A Meditation upon a Broomstick." In this passage, though, Boyle reminds his readers at once by this device of the levels of reality out of which any creative thought is constructed; his intention is to jar his reader into some reflection on this epistemological point.

In *Hydrostatical Paradoxes*, Boyle gives his reason for using the term in his title, a reason involved with concepts of creative wit and the *mirabilia naturae*:

For (first) the Hydrostaticks is a part of Philosophy, which I confess I look upon as one of the ingeniousest Doctrines that belong to it. Theorems and Problems of this Art, being most of them pure and handsome productions of Reason duly exercis'd on attentively consider'd Subjects, and making in them such Discoveries as are not only pleasing, but divers of them surprising, and such as would make men wonder by what kind of Ratiocination men came to attain the knowledg of such unobvious Truths.

In his view, hydrostatics should be rescued from its subservient position to geometry and established as a legitimate subject of its own:

[27] See above, Introduction, and below, Chapter 12 on self-reference.

[28] *Skeptical Chymist*, p. 252.

. . . I hop'd I might doe something, both towards the illus-
trating and towards the rescue of so valuable a Discipline, by
Publishing the ensuing Tract; where I endeavour to disprove
the receiv'd errors, by establishing Paradoxes contrary to them,
and to make the Truths the better understood and receiv'd. . . .[29]

The term "paradox" remained in legitimate chemical
employment. Both Jean-Baptiste van Helmont and his
son, Franciscus Mercurius, used the word *paradox* in all
sorts of connections, theological, physical, and chemical,[30]
so that Boyle came upon it naturally enough as a term of
his art. He dealt at considerable length with another
problem, in its own nature a physical paradox, that of the
vacuum.[31] In Schott's *Technica curiosa* there is a fine illustration of the "wonderful" Magdeburg experiment, in
which eight horses proved too weak to pull apart the two
halves of a vacuum-sealed copper ball. Guericke's and Torricelli's experiments on the vacuum were for their contemporaries exercises in the problem of *nothing*, that *nihil*
existing before the Creation miraculously transformed it
into all matter. Torricelli's experiment dealt with mercury
in a glass tube, and engaged good men in its explanation
—Helmont, Gassendi, Kircher, Schott, Charleton, Hobbes,
Pascal, Maignan, Fabri, Linus, and Boyle, as well as
Henry More and Sir Matthew Hale, all with a vested
interest in the existence or nonexistence of the vacuum.[32]
The "corpuscularians," among them Boyle, Gassendi, and

[29] Boyle, *Hydrostatical Paradoxes* (Oxford, 1666), "Preface."

[30] J. B. van Helmont, *Works* (London, 1664), pp. 284ff., 690,
693ff.; F. M. van Helmont, *The Paradoxical Discourses Concerning the Macrocosm and the Microcosm* (London, 1685); J. B. van
Helmont, *A Ternary of Paradoxes*, trans. and ed. Walter Charleton
(London, 1650).

[31] See above, Chapter 8.

[32] See Dornavius, I. 730-38, where eight paradoxes on *nihil* are
given: another interesting *De nihilo* (Groningen, 1661), is by the
mathematician Martinus Schoock; see Henry More, *Enchiridion*

Charleton, all held for the existence of a vacuum against the "plenists," and were industrious in their defense of its existence.[33] For men on both sides, however, the problem was a paradox in the plain sense, as well as a problem involving paradox in both words and things, the possible illustration of the impossible "nothing."

Illusion of any kind may involve paradox, particularly the paradoxes of relativity, in the sense that one thinks that something is "real" when in fact it is not. Though they are not identical, illusion and paradox are close kin and often in alliance. "My mother: father and mother is man and wife; man and wife is one flesh, and so my mother"—an illicit logic to express an illicit conjunction. In Bacon's chambers of experiment and illusion there are paradoxes enough, but paradoxes of a rather different kind from Boyle's. Late Renaissance scientific analysis proceeded with incredible speed and yielded some unexpected results. In the first instance, it resulted in the Baconian proposal to manipulate natural laws to some immediate and practical effect, preferably an effect beneficial to mankind but in any case an effect well within the context of society; in the second, it resulted in "re-creation," in both senses of that word.

Recreation can mean relaxation, often "marvelous" or tricky, as well as rebuilding, repreparing for action. It can also be the remaking, imitating, the "making and counter-faiting" of Puttenham's phrase.[34] When nature is reassembled after analysis, as in the perspective and sound-houses

---

metaphysicum (London, 1671); Matthew Hale, *Difficiles nugae* (London, 1674); Henry More, *Remarks upon Two Late Ingenious Discourses* (London, 1676); Matthew Hale, *Observations Touching the Principles of Natural Motions* (London, 1677).

[33] See *An Essay Concerning a Vacuum* (London, 1697), for the anti-plenist view; for a standard expression of plenism, see Porta, *Naturall Magick*, pp. 303-04.

[34] George Puttenham, *The Arte of English Poesie*, p. 1.

of the New Atlantis, she may appear "as she is" or she may appear deformed and grotesque. In the grotesque recreations paradox lurks, a concealed threat to the accuracy of perception and thus a threat to knowledge itself. Deceits of the senses that are two things at once, two-or-more-in-one, are the parallel in natural philosophy of the verbal paradox of contradiction, since they raise and illustrate the same puzzles about the nature of perceived reality.

Such deceits were widespread in Europe in the late Renaissance, cultivated in circles of the greatest intellectual concentration upon "reason"—in the Cartesian group around Mersenne at Paris and among the Jesuits, both in Rome and Germany gathered about the polymath Athanasius Kircher. Baltrušaitis has shown the extraordinary relationship between Cartesian rationalism and the fantastic world of optical illusion created by Cartesian workers in the vineyard, who put their new knowledge of optics to work to undo the normal rules of vision. Their deformations are not, when one comes to reflect upon them, in such odd relationship to "truth," since in the paradoxical tradition technical mastery of any subject often turns against the subject. When it does, a kind of paradox occurs, that of self-denial, as when logic turns back upon itself in circular reasoning or infinite regression, or when rhetoric produces paradoxes that transcend and deform the rules of rhetoric. The outburst of anamorphosis in the late Renaissance illustrates the forms such deformation took—pictures which when observed frontally look like nothing at all, or like chaos, but when looked at from the side resolve into genuine pictures of recognizable things, persons, and scenes.[35]

[35] Jurgis Baltrušaitis, *Anamorphoses, ou perspectives curieuses*; I have borrowed heavily from this fascinating book for the section in this chapter on optics. See also the important discussion in Gombrich, *Art and Illusion*, pp. 242-87.

Or a painting might be made so that when seen from two different vantage points it presented two different pictures. Such a painting was the "Descent from the Cross" by Daniele da Volterra, now lost, a copy of which was formerly in Mersenne's Franciscan Church in the Place Royale (now Place des Vosges). Jean-François Nicéron, the pupil and friend of Mersenne, described it as follows:

Christum velut primariam tabulae figuram adumbravit tanto artificio ut spectatus e latere sinistro, tabulae plano velut transversè incumbere videatur et ad eandem partem pes illius dexter prosilire; at in dextra parte constitutis totum corpus quasi erectum in tabula, atque idem pes qui prius versus sinistram, iam ad dexteram protensus appereat; quod hic etiam agnoscat qui volet attentè contemplari ectypum illius tabulae quod Ecclesiae Nostrae Parisiensis Hippodromum Regium, altare maius exornat.[36]

(He portrayed Christ as the principal figure of the picture with such skill that, seen from the left, He seems to incline transversely to the picture-plane, His right foot seeming to stretch out in that direction; but . . . seen from the right, the whole body seems erect, and that same foot which at first stretched out to the left, now appears stretched out to the right; which anyone will acknowledge who looks closely at the engraved version of the picture which adorns the high altar of our church in the Place Royale in Paris.)

In this picture, the same lines and brush strokes, looked at from two different angles, produced two different effects—like the double effect produced by the Liar paradox

[36] Jean-François Nicéron, *Thaumaturgus opticus*, p. 189. See also Robert Burton, *Anatomy of Melancholy* (Everyman edn.), 1. 115; *re* the contradictory characteristics of men, ". . . they are like these double or turning pictures; stand before which, you see a fair maid on one side, an ape on the other, an owl; look upon them at the first sight, all is well; but further examine, you shall find them wise on the one side, and fools on the other. . . ."

in logic. There were lesser ways to produce double pictures: Nicéron described pictures layered on the same surface "par petites bandes," looked at one way producing one image, another way, quite a different one.[37]

Nicéron described other sorts of optical illusions, such as the pictures (of St. Francis receiving the Stigmata, or of St. John on Patmos) drawn on the wall by a projection device that threw properly foreshortened images on the surface to be covered. Catoptrics, or the science of mirrors, was able to produce still more remarkable effects, though its practitioners often met with accusations of sorcery. With concave and convex glasses, concave and convex cylindrical mirrors, all sorts of deformations were possible, as in modern fun-fairs. By arranging several mirrors in different ways, a figure might be made to seem to walk on the ceiling, or even to fly, and a single figure multiplied to seem an army of men.[38]

Faceted crystals could be cut to produce various images which could be made to fuse into one. That "one" might be the basis of all the transforming pictures, as in Cornelis Drebbel's magic lantern, when he himself seemed to turn into one after another quite different member of society;[39]

---

[37] Jean-François Nicéron, *La Perspective curieuse ou magie artificiele des effets merveilleux* (Paris, 1638), pp. 50-51: "On fait certaines images, lesquelles, suivant la diversité de leur aspect, representent deux ou trois choses toutes differentes, de sorte qu'estant veuës de front, elles representeront une face humaine; de costé droict une teste de mort, et du gauche quelque autre chose encore differente; et à la vérité des images dans la nouveauté ont eu assez de cours, encore qu'il n'y ait pas grand artifice à les dresser. . . ."

[38] Nicéron, *Perspective curieuse*, pp. 74, 76, 79.

[39] See Drebbel's description of this instrument (The Hague, Royal Library, Kon. Akad., Ms. Huygens XLVII, fol. 207, cited in my *"Some Thankfulnesse to Constantine,"* The Hague, 1956, pp. 97-98); and also Porta, *Naturall Magick*, p. 356, for a description of the operation of the machine.

or it might be the unification of many different pictures. Nicéron's examples were of the second sort, witty in subject as well as in execution—thirteen Ottoman Turks who turned into His Most Christian Majesty, or a series of great popes who fused into Urban VIII.[40] Optics produced a sensible solution to the metaphysical problem of the One and the Many.

That such enterprises were regarded as paradoxical the

---

[40] Nicéron gives a little poem, extraordinarily bad, about the Turks who turned into His Most Christian Majesty:

> Que va representer cette plate peinture?
> Tu le veois curieux, et ne le cognois pas;
> Tu veois des Ottomans, et sous leur pourtraicture
> Un visage est caché, qui ne se montre pas;
> Si tu veux cognoistre, met l'oeil à l'ouverture
> De ce petit canal, et tu recognoistras
> Du Monarque François la naifue peinture,
> Qui doit des Ottomans l'empire mettre à bas;
> Qui fera des Croissans de la race infidelle
> De ces Mahometans, surgir les Fleurs de Lis
> De nos Roys Tres-Chrestiens, que la France fidelle
> A tousiours recogneu du ciel les favoris.

(*Perspective curieuse*, p. 116). Cf. Burton, *Anatomy of Melancholy*, I. 427: ". . . 'tis ordinary to see strange uncouth sights by catoptrics; who knows not that if in a dark room the light be admitted at one only little hole, and a paper or glass put upon it, the sun shining will represent on the opposite wall all such objects as are illuminated by his rays? With concave and cylinder glasses, we may reflect any shape of men, devils, antics, (as magicians most part do, to gull a silly spectator in a dark room), we will ourselves, and that hanging in the air, when 'tis nothing but such an horrible image as Agrippa demonstrates, placed in another room." And II. 96: "But especially to do strange miracles by glasses, of which Proclus and Bacon writ of old, burning-glasses, multiplying glasses, perspectives, *ut unus homo appareat exercitus*, to see afar off, to represent solid bodies by cylinders and concaves, to walk in the air . . . , which glasses are much perfected of late by Baptista Porta and Galileo, and much more is promised by Maginus and Midorgius, to be performed in this kind."

title of Giulio Troili's book on optics suggests: *Paradossi per Pratticare la Prospettiva senza saperla,*[41] in which "perspective machines" as developed from Dürer through the seventeenth century were described and depicted. Troili's is one of the finest such handbooks of scientific paradoxes deriving from the new technology, but there were many other such books, all depending upon the double meaning in the word "recreation." Re-creations of nature involved "counterfaiting" nature's creatures in automata, another preoccupation of the Renaissance. The French engineers Isaac and Salomon de Caus could counterfeit "The Voices of smal Birds by means of Water and Aire,"[42] to deceive the hearer who could not see the machine making the sounds; they also made complicated fountains in which, for instance, Galatea was drawn by dolphins or Neptune encircled by moving tritons and horses.[43]

Mathematics was both an important science and a recreation: there were many mathematical paradoxes, puzzles, and "impossibilities," to which great mathematicians from antiq-

[41] (Bologna, 1683).

[42] Isaac de Caus, *New and Rare Inventions of Water-Works,* trans. John Leak (London, 1659), pp. 20, 26, 27, 28; Salomon de Caus, *Les Raisons des forces mouvantes* (Frankfurt-am-Main, 1615), passim. See also A. Chapuis and E. Droz, *Les Automates* (Paris [1949]), for a full discussion of enterprises of this sort. John Wilkins, *Mathematical Magick* (London, 1647) is an important compendium of experiment; see also Burton, *Anatomy of Melancholy,* I. 427-28: "They can counterfeit the voices of all birds and brute beasts almost, all tones and tunes of men, and speak within their throats, as if they spoke afar off, that they make their auditors believe they hear spirits, and are thence much astonished and affrighted with it."

[43] Burton, *Anatomy of Melancholy,* I. 38, for "impossibles." See Cornelis Drebbel, *Kort Tractaet van de Natuere der Elementen* (Haerlem, 1621); Thomas Tymme, *A Dialogue Philosophicall* (London, 1612); and Bettini, *Apiaria,* I, Book IV, p. 12, for perpetual motion schemes.

uity on had contributed. Many such paradoxes are "fixed," that is, are either insoluble by present mathematical tools or are verbal or numerical tricks with but one ingenious answer. Zeno's query, or the query attributed to him, about which grain makes the noise when a bushel of wheat is poured from its basket (Is it the first?—No. The second then?—No; etc.) turns up again and again in the volumes of mathematical recreations published through the seventeenth century. One of these, Jean Leurechon's *Recréations mathématiques*, appeared in 1627 and subsequently went into several editions, often with the additions and improvements of the eminent mathematician Claude Mydorge, another collaborator of Mersenne and Nicéron. That book, along with Mydorge's *Sections coniques* (the sort of optical study that made anamorphosis possible) was published in English under the auspices of William Oughtred, whose importance as a serious mathematician did not in the least prevent him from taking recreation from his subject.[44]

Many problems in the books of recreation involve the "impossible," a negative word difficult to conceive and difficult to use. Mathematics is the science of relations (ambiguously called "ratio" by mathematicians), and therefore the problems its language presents and represents are often paradoxes apparently susceptible of no solution but actually soluble outside the "set" of the problems, from another point of view. Like anamorphoses, such problems, without any solution, seem to be "nothings" or seem chaotic when viewed head on but are quite orderly when one finds the proper point of vision. Elaborate number games, in which a man guesses what number another man is thinking of, or guesses which knuckle on a possible

[44] Jean Leurechon [ps., Hendrick van Etten], *Les Recréations mathématiques* (Lyon, 1629); trans. William Oughtred, *Mathematical Recreations* (London, 1633), reprinted in 1653 and 1674.

ten fingers a man has set his ring on, deal in a science with a paradoxical name—the laws of chance.[45] Other problems, less strictly mathematical, can be cast into mathematical language. For example, directions are given to weigh the blow of a fist, of a hammer, or of an axe; to weigh the smoke of a combustible body, or its flame; to balance three knives, or a millstone, on the point of a pin.[46] Some such exercises are trivial in the extreme, such as the directions for breaking an apple into equal parts without breaking the skin (with a needle and thread), for making a cheating scale hang true when empty which can also weigh uneven weights as if they were even, and for weighing a bowl falsely, so that it runs amusingly awry.[47] Others are not amusing at all, though rather marvelous and certainly recreations in another sense, such as the earphone for the deaf and the spy-mirror reflecting activities in another room.[48]

Still other problems were, as Mydorge put it, "purely metaphysical," such as the receipt for dropping a perfect sphere from a great height into a glass of water without breaking the glass, or the arrangement of all the angels and all the men in the world so that they could pull upon a spider's string without breaking it, or the construction of a stone bridge, or ring, around the world so that it will hang without support and never fall.[49] Some are logical beauties about the center of the earth and the poles, riddles asked every teen-aged child by one more sophisticated in school. To one of these, "Comment est-ce qu'un homme peut avoir en mesme temps la teste en haut, et les pieds en

[45] Leurechon, *Les Recréations mathématiques*, fifth edition (Paris, 1661), pp. 28, 44, 49, 56, 57.
[46] *Ibid.*, pp. 13, 41, 42, 40, 38.
[47] *Ibid.*, pp. 49, 119, 4-8.
[48] *Ibid.*, pp. 138-39, 333-34.
[49] *Ibid.*, pp. 109-10, 106.

haut, encore qu'il ne soit qu'en une place?" Leurechon's answer was "at the center of the earth"; but Mydorge remarked with Swiftian matter-of-factness that a man could fulfill the conditions just as easily in his own bed, by lying on it and raising both feet and head, and went on to give a less decent version of his own.[50]

Numbers of course bring their own paradoxes, which scientists and logicians love, and so does geometry. Where there are circles there are inevitably paradoxes—indeed, the circle is the emblem for the great paradox of eternity, as well as of the equally impossible notion of infinity.[51] The area of the circle, also, is technically immeasurable, however small it may be; efforts to arrive at the correct area of the circle have resulted only in infinite approximation. Therefore the area of the circle cannot be equated to the area of any other geometrical figure with flat sides, though the effort to square the circle, or to equate it with any other polygon, has gone on from antiquity. There is of course an absolute area of a circle to which one can conceive a square of equal area; but until recently the solution to that problem was, in Mydorge's phrase, purely metaphysical, the analytical proof absent. Which is cleverer, asked Leurechon, he who draws a circle freehand, or he who finds the center of a circle already given? On the authority of Aristotle and St. Augustine, he responded that the more difficult task was to find the center of a circle already drawn, the single center of a line of infinite points.[52]

Squaring the circle was an antique recreation at which great mathematicians since had tried their wits. Friendly

[50] *Ibid.*, pp. 58-60.

[51] For this idea, see Bolzano, *Paradoxes of the Infinite*, and Martin Foss, *The Idea of Perfection in the Western World*, esp. pp. 13-26.

[52] Leurechon, pp. 133-34.

enemies gladly demonstrated the futility of their friends' attempts or lent themselves to the same futile task. Medieval scholars left the record of their attempts to square the circle, and Renaissance mathematicians pursued the same will-o-the-wisp, in love and in hate. Porta, Cataldo, Rheticus, Clavius, and Vieta, to name but a handful of the best known, all quadrated; in the seventeenth century there were first-class quadrature rows, stemming chiefly from the "solution" of Longomontanus, who stimulated directly and indirectly John Pell, Descartes, Mersenne, Roberval, Golius, Cavendish, Hobbes, and Wallis to tackle the job. Over and over again, one is struck by the bitterness of this controversy. Although quadrature was officially a "game" and so accepted by mathematicians, it was a game with the most serious intellectual stakes. For one thing, to render the impossible possible is to conquer the problem of knowledge at one of its bastions, in this case to advance the cause of mathematics both as a language and as an instrument, so that it could both do and say—and thus be—more than it could do, or say, or had been, before. In the second place, methods of quadrature derived from geometrical systems which were in hazard at precisely the point of the problem and which, however lightly their inventors undertook to square, were most serious and seriously defended intellectual constructs. So the tone of the quarrel between Hobbes and Wallis, both of them superb polemicists, became particularly virulent over Hobbes' "solution" to the quadrature and to other classical mathematical problems.[53]

[53] A useful bibliography (though in the nature of the work incomplete) can be collected from De Morgan's *A Budget of Paradoxes*, particularly from the edition made by David Eugene Smith (2 vols., London and Chicago, 1915). See also Ferdinand Rudio, "Das Problem von der Quadratur des Zirkels," *Vierteljahrsschrift der Naturforschenden Gesellschaft in Zürich* (1890), pp. 1-51. For a bibliography of the Hobbes-Wallis battle, see Hugh Mac-

Circle-squaring is a particular teaser not just because it is "impossible." To make the circle square is the logical operation, in this case illustrated in geometry, of breaching categories and uniting forms; to square the circle is to advance man's control over the intellectually possible, but it is to endanger geometrical category, which depends upon the differences between shapes. If the proof that the circle "equals" or "is the same as" the square is a true proof, the Eleatic view of the universe is confirmed, which implies the annihilation of the very barriers, definitions, and limitations by which geometry exists. In connection with the quadrature problem, Schott remarked that if Zeno were right, then it is both possible *and* impossible to square the circle, possible because the circle is a finite unity, impossible because the implications of the circle are that it is always in motion, always spinning.[54] The fact that Snel van Rooijen, Huygens, Pascal, and a host of other talented mathematicians all had their say about circle-squaring suggests the seriousness of the game: the impossible is better handled *sub specie ludi* in case it doesn't work—or, in case it does.

Circle-squaring is "useless," by Baconian standards, and in English became the standard trope for time-wasting intellectual activity. Still another mathematico-logical paradox, though, had its social and economic uses and was, also, the object of hard-headed formulation by first-class minds: the study of the laws of chance. The phrase has become so familiar to us that its initial yoking of opposites is almost inaudible to us, but when Cardanus wrote his *De ludo aleae*, he directed it to a moral end, the analysis of deceit, as well as to a scientific end, the study of probabil-

---

donald and J. M. Hargreaves, *Thomas Hobbes. A Bibliography* (London, 1952), pp. 41-58, 63.

[54] Schott, *Technica curiosa*, p. 607.

ity.[55] Arbuthnot's introduction to his adaptation of Christiaan Huygens' *De ratiociniis in ludo aleae*[56] makes quite clear that man has little insight into the distributions of chance or fortune, however much he may say about them:

Every man's Success in any Affair is proportional to his Conduct and Fortune. Fortune (in the sense of most People) signifies an Event which depends on Chance, agreeing with my Wish; and Misfortune suggests such an Event contrary to my Wish: an Event depending on Chance, signifies such an one, whose immediate Causes I don't know, and consequently can neither foretel nor produce it. . . .[57]

Since gaming had become so common a profession that every man ran some danger of ending, like Hogarth's Rake, in Bedlam and penury, any system that could be descried in the operations of chance might serve, thought Arbuthnot, to keep a man's shillings in his pocket. The laws of probability were applicable to more than gaming, too: "It is," for instance, "but 1 to 18 if you meet a *Parson* in the Street, that he proves to be a *Non-Juror*, because there is but 1 of 36 that are such [*sic* (!)]. It is hardly 1 to 10, that a *Woman* of Twenty Years old has her Maidenhead, and almost the same Wager, that a *Town-Spark* of that Age has not been clap'd." Arbuthnot played on the moral applications of the statistical techniques developed by

[55] See the English translation by Sydney Henry Gould, in Oystein Ore, *Cardano, the Gambling Scholar* (Princeton University Press, 1953).

[56] Christiaan Huygens, *De ratiociniis in ludo aleae*, in Franciscus van Schooten, *Exercitationum mathematicarum libri quinque* (Leiden, 1657); for remarks on the gambling habits of the late sixteenth and early seventeenth centuries, see Lawrence Stone, *The Crisis of the Aristocracy, 1558-1641* (Clarendon Press, 1965), pp. 567-72.

[57] John Arbuthnot, *Of the Laws of Chance, Or, a Method of Calculation of the Hazards of Game* (London, 1692), Preface.

Petty and Graunt, as did Swift in the *Modest Proposal*. Like all scientists of the period after Huygens and Newton (but quite unlike Swift), Arbuthnot believed that numerology had to give way, and give way for good, to mathematics:

The Reader may here observe the Force of Numbers, which can be successively applied, even to those things, which one would imagine are subject to no Rules. There are very few things which we know, which are not capable of being reduc'd to a Mathematical Reasoning, and when they cannot, tis a sign our Knowledg of them is very small and confus'd; and where a mathematical reason can be had, it's as great folly to make use of any other, as to grope for a thing in the dark when you have a Candle standing by you.

The mathematical analysis to which Arbuthnot gave his allegiance is the original mathematics of quantitative analysis, the mathematics of "one answer," untroubled by the paradoxes of either numbers or logic, and to some extent Arbuthnot's sensible statement marks a temporary end to conscious paradoxology, even in mathematics. For him, the laws of chance did not seem a phrase uniting opposites so much as a limited but direct statement of one aspect of the unknown. Arbuthnot's gamester, following the injunctions of Salomon's House, will not do tricks: he will at any point reveal his special knowledge to anyone else. In fact, Arbuthnot's aim is egalitarian, to reduce to order one aspect of the unknown so that any man may, if he must, gamble with some safety. The gamester in question is concerned only with practical life: the rest is not his business, its mysteries are not his concern.

Arbuthnot's practicality coincides with the decline of paradoxology: the paradoxes, deceits, and tricks of mathematics and science tend to lose their playfulness, their "wonder" in the course of the seventeenth century, as knowledge ever increasingly was set to good uses. Teleology puts a check on wonder, for wonder is a tremendous time-waster. Ends that are aims replace the paradoxical ends which are always beginnings. Though he understood, for example, perspective deformation thoroughly, Grégoire Huret did not enjoy anamorphosis as Nicéron, Mersenne, Schott and Kircher had enjoyed it. For him, its "déprava-tions" were monstrous and inartistic; they were

visions de songe lugubres, ou des sabats de sorciers, seulement capable de donner de la tristesse et frayeur, et mesme faire avorter ou dépraver le fruit des femmes enceintes. . . .[58]

(. . . gloomy night-mare visions or witches' sabbaths, capable only of inducing sorrow and fear, capable even of aborting or misforming the fruit of women pregnant. . . .)

As far as Huret was concerned, *trompe l'oeil* was useful only to disguise the shape of an improperly balanced room, and neither wonderful nor amusing; figures should be represented as they are, or as we see them, not as deformations of actuality. Since we see in perspective, the rules of perspective were to be observed in painting not to deform but to achieve correctness, as in the work, he said, of Rubens and "Raimbram Holandois."[59]

Another scientist of the late seventeenth century, Jacques Ozanam, opened his *Mathematical Recreations* with the same direct analytical intention:

Ignorance keeps the World in perpetual Admiration, and in a Diffidence, which ever produces an invisible Inclination to blame and to persecute those that know any Thing above the Vulgar; who, being unaccustom'd to raise their Thoughts beyond Things sensible, and unable to imagin that Nature implyeth Agents that are invisible and impalpable, ascribe most

[58] Grégoire Huret, *Optique de portraiture et peinture* (Paris, 1670), pp. 64-65.
[59] Huret, p. 11.

an end to Sorceries and Demons, all Effects where they know not the Cause. To remedy these Inconveniences is the Design of these Mathematicall Recreations, and to teach all to perform those Sorceries. . . .[60]

Ozanam did not underestimate the power and the pleasure of "Pastimes of the Mind, and Entertainments equally fitted to excite Pleasure, and to give Enlargement of Understanding," nor did he deny the close proximity of games and speculation; he did, though, always emphasize the reasonableness of such recreations over their wonder, and he believed in their invariable surrender to rational examination.

This kind of solution, the Baconian demonstration of the "Fallace" of the scientific paradox or illusion, is one way of disposing of nature's *discordia concors*. Analysis and explanation—"The End of our Foundation is the Knowledge of Causes"—puts a check upon the kind of stupefaction that paradox for its life must induce. To the verbal magic of rhetorical and logical paradox another kind of solution increasingly offered itself, the discounting of such paradox by the simple indication of its self-denial, its absence, in two senses of the word, of end. This method was Bacon's, Ozanam's, and Arbuthnot's.

There was another kind of attack on this sort of paradox, reserved to the exceptionally talented, the satirical method of proposing one's own made-up paradoxes to undo the whole paradoxical method. This was the way of Jonathan Swift, who knew all the conventional ways of paradox very well indeed. He himself had raised the paradoxical encomium to its highest level of irony in the nonpareil *Modest Proposal*. His anti-rationalism epitomized the ra-

[60] Jacques Ozanam, *Recreations Mathematical and Physical; laying down, and solving Many Profitable and Delightful Problems* (London, 1708), "The Author's Preface."

tionalist attack upon rationalism. He was past-master of the tricks relativity plays, and could play them himself whenever he chose. Swift's terrifying relativities did not preach a rigid absolutism, as lesser satirists so often find themselves driven to do when dealing in the trickeries of relativity and relativism; Swift's relativities plead eloquently for other relativities, those of common sense and of ordinary civilized social life. In the "Voyage to Laputa" Swift made up his own brilliant paradoxes out of the authentic reports of scientific investigations he found in that staid and serious periodical, the *Philosophical Transactions of the Royal Society*. Swift's method has been demonstrated past doubt—how he combined the real experiments on vegetables, dyes, insects, dogs, and meteorology in the lunatic activities carried on in the Grand Academy of Lagado.[61] His experiments follow two traditions, the amusing one of the marvels of natural science, by which readers are supposed to be entertained and titillated,[62] and the satiric tradition, in which he makes a new kind of fun of what was originally fun in a simpler sense. He rings the changes that are the knell of the old projectors, with their wonders and marvels: the attempts in Lagado are the same old ones, really, that stuffed the Renaissance scientific compendia. Caus, Stevin, Kircher, Schott, and the other hydraulic engineers all found ingenious methods to raise water uphill, so that it might flow out in a fair fountain, to cleanse a city, to turn mills on hills. The blind man who could tell colors apart was a stock marvel for those secre-

[61] See Marjorie H. Nicolson and Nora Mohler, "The Scientific Background of Swift's 'Voyage to Laputa,' " *Annals of Science*, II (1937), 299-334; "Swift's 'Flying Island,' in the 'Voyage to Laputa,' " *Annals of Science*, II (1937), 405-30.

[62] See Miss Nicolson's suggestion in *Mountain Gloom and Mountain Glory* (Cornell University Press, 1959), p. 170, n. 28.

taries of nature: he existed as an experimental case long
before Boyle, Molyneux, and Locke sent him on his travels
through the rationalist literature of the eighteenth century.
Experiments to "improve" vegetables, to make animals
larger, to make better weather indicators and gnomons fill
the pages of Porta, Wecker, Bacon, Bettini, and Schott.
Their machines to reduce probability to some order need
only Swift's application to the production of imaginative
literature to be entirely ludicrous; the frame from which
all natural knowledge was to be extracted was simply a
thing made to seem ridiculous by our having taken a long
hard look at it.

Swift's sort of experiment was very economical; he
merely exaggerated some small aspect of "reality." Both
the joke and the seriousness of such mechanical ingenuity
are increased, the joke is made funnier so that the underlying seriousness may gain moral context. Swift uses, in
short, one paradoxical rhetoric, the joco-serious expression
in the language of *things* to assert the superiority of an
older rhetoric, that of human experience and understanding. The great "Bundle of *things* upon his Back" that the
ordinary Laputan Academician must carry about in order
to have any conversation with his fellows is the Baconian
burden carried to the nth power, or *ad absurdum*: Swift
cuts off the bundle with his two-edged sword of rhetorical
paradox. In this book of *Gulliver* all the traditions of paradox meet—in Swift's insistence on the value of realities as
opposed to appearances, in his re-creation of things into a
new world, in his rhetorical persuasions at the limits of
rhetoric, his joco-serious reconsideration of man's whole
intellectual and moral activity.

Man's intellectual pride is put into its place. Though
men might attempt to contrive "a new Method for building Houses, by beginning at the Roof, and working down

wards to the Foundation,"[63] only God can do that trick:

> The proceeding of this Soveraign Architect in the Frame of this great Building of the Universe, not being like to the Architecture of men, who begin at the bottom; but he began at the Roof, and Builded downwards, and in that process, suspended the inferior parts of the World upon the superior.[64]

God's world was the only world legitimately, truly paradoxical: the greatest paradoxes are divine, inimitable by mere human ingenuity. Lagado's attempts to imitate the inimitable are doomed to fail, as even Gulliver and the dullest reader can perceive at once; because they are not only foolish in themselves, but are also the emblems of man's idiotic human pride. Lagado is, happily, utopia, or nowhere: we are relieved at that, since they are such fools in that country. But Lagado is, unmistakably, also eighteenth-century England and, nowadays, everywhere. Swift has not attempted to build his house down from the roof: he has managed a more daring emulation of the divine paradoxology, has created out of nonbeing, out of nothing, out of nowhere, a major lesson of being.

[63] Jonathan Swift, *Travels into Several Remote Nations of the World* (London, 1747), p. 173.

[64] Hale, *Difficiles Nugae,* p. 57.

11

Being and Becoming in
The Faerie Queene

. . . herein is Divinity conformant unto Philosophy,
and generation not onely founded on contrarieties,
but also creation. . . .
Browne, Religio Medici, I. 35

IN THE hierarchy of forms classically presented in the
Timaeus and elaborated for scholars in Professor Lovejoy's *The Great Chain of Being*, the static order is presented of a dualistic world imitating the ideal world in
material form. The world of change, mutability, of Becoming, is by its materiality imperfect, and as it "aspires,"
or mounts in the chain from grosser materiality through
more refined until it passes into the world of spirit and
spirits, it more closely imitates the world of Being, of the
pure idea, the good, or God.[1] Obviously, something had
happened to the idea of this great chain between Plato and
Pope, for what Pope called "the Great Chain of Being"
was precisely the world of created forms, the material
world formed in imitation of God's originating idea, that
Plato would not dignify with the word "being" but called
rather "becoming."[2] The word for becoming, *genesis*, is
(like all words: but more than most) obviously ambiguous; it implies both that the sensible world is a world
that *has happened* and that it is a world that *is constantly
happening*; or, it implies that the world is fixed and that it
is in flux. Pre-Socratic philosophers favored physical hypotheses of flux, but both Plato and Aristotle left their

[1] A. O. Lovejoy, *The Great Chain of Being*, passim.
[2] F. M. Cornford, *Plato's Cosmology* (New York, 1952), p. 24.

steadying hands upon the normative physics of the western world, through antiquity and the middle ages, and their efforts had been to organize the flux into concepts of minimal mutability, into the doctrine of ideas and the doctrine of forms.

To abbreviate scandalously, Renaissance philosophy and physics somehow came to upset the notions that Being and Becoming were inevitably different in kind, and that the world of Becoming, or the world beneath the changeable moon, was by definition "less" than the world of Being, of ineffable and unchanged essence, of *logos*. One means by which the physics of the period could be reread and reinterpreted was by the revival of atomist philosophy,[3] from which Bacon, Gassendi, Boyle, Locke, and Newton drew so much strength; another means was the reanimation of Plotinian Neoplatonism, or adaptation of Ptolemaic or concentric metaphysical arrangement, in which Becoming is an emanation and a dilation of Being, to which it constantly returns. One Renaissance philosopher was able to marry the Platonic and Democritan worlds, in language at least, to achieve a fusion of Being and Becoming in which the concepts were mutually inextricable. Bruno presents the puzzling portrait of a philosopher and a poet who was at once a pantheist—for which, among other things, he was terribly burned—and an atomist, a man who quite deliberately attempted the fusion of these utterly different traditions, with their utterly different concepts of the value of materiality. Relying on the Brunonian concept of fusion, Henry More entitled his poem in a paradoxical phrase even more suited to Bruno than to More, *Democritus Platonissans*: the phrase is perfect, really, for Bruno's enthusiastic acceptance of the transcendence of the material world. In Bruno's work, particularly *De l'infinito*

[3] See above, Chapter 7; below, Chapter 14.

*universo e mondi, De monade numero et figuro, De rerum
principiis elementis et causis,* and *De immenso, innumera-
bilibus et infigurabilibus,*[4] the unitary autonomy of each
material thing is honored with the same transcendence
he attributes to idea, and to his odd deity: for Bruno,
Becoming was as essential to reality as Being, the two in-
termingled, if not fused. In the work of Edmund Spenser,
more accessible than the work of Bruno, I should like to
examine the process by which the "ideal" ceased to be the
only "reality," as it had been for Plato and the medieval
realists; and, second, by which our modern use of the word
"real," applied to actuality material and factual, came into
being. Put the other way, Spenser is a writer whose work
beautifully illustrates the point of crossing at which Being
and Becoming became one. Though Spenser was no phys-
icist, his attitude toward the physical world had much in
common with that of Francis Bacon, or Boyle, or even
Newton: for Spenser, the physical world was not to be
contemned, for it was, both in the Platonic and the modern
sense, good and real.

In the *Fowre Hymnes*, Spenser presented a view of
being and becoming, of metaphysics and physics, predominantly Platonic, a view which has been demonstrated to
derive from Ficino's commentaries on the Platonic dialogues, in particular the *Symposium* and the *Timaeus*.[5] In

[4] The works of Bruno can best be consulted in *Opere Italiane*,
eds. B. Croce, G. Gentile, and V. Spampanato (Bari, 1923-1927),
3 vols.; and in the so-called National Edition, *Jordani Bruni Nolani
opera latina conscripta*, eds. T. F. Fiorentino *et al.* (Florence, 1879-
1891). See also Frances A. Yates, *Giordano Bruno and the Hermetic
Tradition* (London, 1964).

[5] For commentary on Spenser's sources for the *Fowre Hymnes*,
see particularly Josephine W. Bennett, "The Theme of Spenser's
Fowre Hymnes," *SP*, xxviii (1931), 18-57; *SP*, xxxii (1935),
131-57; F. M. Padelford, "Spenser's 'Fowre Hymnes,'" *JEGP*,
xxiii (1914), 418-33; and *SP*, xxix (1932), 207-32; and William

"An Hymne in Honour of Love,"[6] love, the power described in the *Symposium*, is the actual organizer of the
moral and physical world, corresponding to the Demiurgos
of the *Timaeus*. Love is the prime mover among the quar-
reling elements of primordial chaos; love sets them in
their proper places:

> He then them tooke, and tempering goodly well
> Their contrary dislikes with loved means,
> Did place them all in order, and compell
> To keepe them selves within their sundrie raines,
> Together linkt with Adamantine chaines;
> Yet so, as that in every living wight
> They mixe themselves, and shew their kindly might.
>
> (ll. 85-91)

The pattern for the world, and the form into which the
created world falls, is beauty, and beauty is both the creation and proper object of love. In "An Hymne in Honour
of Beautie," Spenser touches on the relation of form to
matter:

> What time this worlds great workmaister did cast,
> To make all things, such as we now behold,
> It seemes that he before his eyes had plast
> A goodly Paterne, to whose perfect mould
> He fashiond them as comely as he could;
> That now so faire and seemely they appeare,
> As nought may be amended any wheare.   (ll. 29-35)

This "wondrous Paterne wheresoere it bee,/ Whether in
earth layd up in secret store,/ Or else in heaven, that no
man may it see," is "perfect Beautie which all men adore."

Nelson, *The Poetry of Edmund Spenser* (Columbia University
Press, 1963), pp. 97-115.
    [6] Spenser, *The Poetical Works*, eds. J. C. Smith and E. de Selin-
court (London, 1937). All references to Spenser's poetry are to this
edition.

And this is in fact not material, but spirit. In a couplet managing neatly to combine Platonic notions with Aristotelian terms, he put it thus:

> For of the soule the bodie forme doth take:
> For soule is forme, and doth the bodie make.

(ll. 132-33)

The Platonic doctrine is clear: from the fixed soul, or being, the body, or becoming, is made. Moreover, in the *Hymnes*, Spenser maintained the notion of three hypostases, three stages of existence, as postulated in the *Timaeus*: the absolute realm of Being, in which all forms, and all ideas are fused into one pure Being or *logos*; the realm of ideas in which the Demiurgos resides and from which he takes his patterns for the creation of the becoming world; and finally the "becoming" sensible world itself. In "An Hymne of Heavenly Love," using an image more dependent on Plotinus than on Plato, Spenser looks through the heavens to the intermediate world of ideas:

> For farre above these heavens which here we see,
> Be others farre exceeding these in light,
> Not bounded, not corrupt, as these same bee,
> But infinite in largeness and in hight,
> Unmoving, uncorrupt, and spotlesse bright,
> That need no Sunne t'illuminate their spheres,
> But their owne native light farre passing theirs.

(ll. 64-70)

None of the visible heavens, though, is quite absolute:

> And as these heavens still by degrees arise,
> Untill they come to their first Movers bound,
> That in his mightie compasse doth comprize,
> And carrie all the rest with him around,
> So likewise doe by degrees redound,
> And rise more faire, till they at last arive
> To the most faire, whereto they all do strive.

(ll. 71-77)

Beyond all the created heavens is a heaven most fair: Spenser assumes in these poems a ladder of cosmic creation, in which each lower stage depends by imitation on the stage above.

> Faire is the heaven, where happy soules have place,
> In full enjoyment of felicitie,
> Whence they doe still behold the glorious face
> Of the divine eternall Maiestie;
> More faire is that, where those *Idees* on hie,
> Enraunged be, which *Plato* so admyred,
> And pure *Intelligences* from God inspyred.
>
> Yet fairer is that heaven, in which doe raine
> The soveraine *Powres* and mightie *Potentates*. . . .
>
> (ll. 78-86)
>
> And fairer yet, whereas the royall Seates
> And heavenly *Dominations* are set. . . .   (ll. 89-90)

And so on, through the heavenly hierarchies of the Christian religion, until

> These thus in faire each other farre excelling,
> As to the Highest they approch more neare,
> Yet is that Highest farre beyond all telling,
> Fairer then all the rest which there appeare,
> Though all their beauties ioynd together were:
> How then can mortall tongue hope to expresse,
> The image of such endlesse perfectnesse.
>
> (ll. 98-103)

Like Ficino, Spenser has Christianized the presentation in the *Timaeus* of metaphysical perfection and the Plotinian hypostases: his cosmos is a reflection, an image, seen by the light of the sun, which in itself is another kind of image of ultimate essential truth, an image of God. In the *Fowre Hymnes*, Spenser's cosmology is the traditional hieratic, patterned one, thoroughly in the tradition of metaphysical scale, by which man may climb to ultimate and essential truth.

In Book III of the *Faerie Queene*, the Legend of Brito-martis, or Chastitie, a different kind of cosmos, or a different kind of nature, is provided us in the Garden of Adonis, a picture of nature at variance with that of the *Fowre Hymnes* and with Lovejoy's schema of hieratic creation.[7] In the story of the Garden of Adonis, there is no clear-cut hieratic organization rising from physics to metaphysics, through nature, sense, and intelligence, to a realm of unity where all things are at one with their ideas and their being, where the contemplator knows them, their ideas, and their being, and is in his own right at one with his knowledge and what he knows. In the Garden of Adonis, Spenser does not deal in the three realms of the *Timaeus*—the purest realm of Being, the Original One, is neither mentioned nor implied. His whole concern, in this episode, is with the other two realms, the Realm of Forms or Ideas, and the Realm of Created Matter, or the natural world; and to present them in an arrangement strikingly different from that of the *Fowre Hymnes*.

The Garden of Adonis is not specifically located—

> Whether in *Paphos*, or *Cytheron* hill
> Or in *Gnidus* be, I wote not well,

[7] This passage has been extensively commented upon: see, e.g., Nelson, 207-24; J. W. Bennett, "Spenser's Garden of Adonis," *PMLA*, XLVII (1932), 46-78; E. A. Greenlaw, "Spenser and Lucretius," *SP*, XVII (1920), 439-64; Brents Stirling, "The Philosophy of Spenser's Garden of Adonis," *PMLA*, XLIX (1934), 193-204; E. C. Knowlton, "Spenser and Nature," *JEGP*, XXXIV (1935), 366-76; Harry Berger, Jr., "Spenser's Garden of Adonis: Force and Form in the Renaissance Imagination," *UTQ*, XXX (1961), 128-49; Rosemond Tuve, "Spenser and the Zodiake of Life," *JEGP*, XXXIV (1935), 1-19; and Thomas P. Roche, Jr., *The Kindly Flame* (Princeton University Press, 1964), pp. 117-33.

he says, and it does not particularly matter, either; what
matters is

> that this same,
> All other pleasant places doth excell,
> And called is by her lost lovers name,
> The Garden of Adonis, farre renowned by fame.
>
> (*FQ*, III. vi. 29)

Certainly the place is an earthly, not a heavenly paradise:
to describe it Spenser relied on all sorts of traditions, from
Hesiod, from Ovid, from Lucretius, from Genesis, from
medieval natural philosophy, and even from Chaucer, to
make clear that this is the earthly paradise, a perfection and
combination of earthly qualities:

> There is continuall spring, and harvest there
> Continuall, both meeting at one time:
> For both the boughes doe laughing blossomes beare,
> And with fresh colours decke the wanton Prime,
> And eke attonce the heavy trees they clime,
> Which seeme to labour under their fruits lode:
> The whiles the joyous birdes make their pastime
> Amongst the shadie leaves, their sweet abode,
> And their true loves without suspition tell abrode.
>
> (*FQ*, III. vi. 42)

Our mutable and seasonal life teaches us that such earthly
perfections cannot coexist; the Garden is the material imitation of the divinely paradoxical realm, where all things,
however different, are one; but the Garden is, proudly and
assertively, an imitation manifestly in the realm of becoming.

The problem posed in the Garden of Adonis is the relation of things to their forms, of Becoming to Being. The
garden is a garden of love, of procreation, of physical and
sexual generation and genesis, as its name tells us. One
cannot, after all, regard Aphrodite's relation to Adonis as

purely in the realm of ideas; and the lightly disguised to-
pography of the garden unmistakably refers to the female
anatomy (*FQ*, III. vi. 43).[8] Spenser indicates again and
again that he is talking about actual procreation as well as
about the idea of it. The garden is "the first seminarie/
Of all thinges, that are borne to live and die,/ According
to their kindes,"—its multiplicity and variety are beyond
the reach of human imagination and the human tongue:

> Long worke it were,
> Here to account the endlesse progenie
> Of all the weedes, that bud and blossome there;
> But so much as doth need, must needs be counted here.
>
> (*FQ*, III. vi. 30)

But though there are too many specific things for the human mind to take in, the pattern is distinguishable. The
garden has two gates, "The one of yron, the other of
bright gold," guarded by a porter, "Old Genius, the which
a double nature has."

> He letteth in, he letteth out to wend,
> All that to come into the world desire;
> A thousand thousand naked babes attend
> About him day and night, which doe require,
> That he with fleshly weedes would them attire:
> Such as him list, such as eternall fate
> Ordained hath, he clothes with sinfull mire,
> And sending forth to live in mortall state,
> Till they againe returne backe by the hinder gate.
>
> (*FQ*, III. vi. 32)

As in the "Hymne to Heavenly Love," the essences of
things, their forms, or their ideas, are presented as *amorini*,
the results of Venus' activity and her proper accompani-

---

[8] The anamorphic landscape of this passage seems obvious, especially when considered in relation to Chaucer, *Parliament of Fowls*,
ll. 253-66. See Nelson, pp. 207-09.

ment. The flesh, however pleasant it may have seemed to
Spenser in his sonnets, the *Epithalamion,* and the first
two *Hymnes,* is nonetheless here "sinfull mire"; the
ordinary mortal state is not so agreeable, we are given to
understand, as the condition prevailing in the garden. But
what is unmistakably true of the mortal state in this myth is
that it *is*: it is no imitation, no shadowy copy of real life,
but a condition of existence that must be accounted for and
cannot be ignored. It is a state, a station, a stage, a condition, a part; something fixed in the flux of individual life
and death; and for this paradoxical idea Spenser sought to
provide an image in the Garden of Adonis. The garden
plot itself remains fixed, though the units that make it up
are in continual flux there as they are on earth. The garden
is the point at which the cycle of creativity is renewed. In
the garden there is a patterned irregularity—old Genius

> letteth in, he letteth out to wend,
> All that to come into the world desire . . .

After that they againe returned beene,
>   They in that Gardin planted be again;
>   And grow afresh, as if they had never seene
>   Fleshly corruption, nor mortall paine.
>   Some thousand yeares or soe doen they remaine;
>   And then of him are clad with other hew,
>   Or sent into the chaungefull world againe,
>   Till thither they returne, where first they grew:
So like a wheele around they runne from old to new.

Infinite shapes of creatures there are bred,
>   And uncouth formes, which none yet ever knew,
>   And every sort is in a sundry bed
>   Set by it selfe, and ranckt in comely rew:
>   Some fit for reasonable soules t'indew,
>   Some made for beasts, some made for birds to weare,

> And all the fruitfull spawne of fishes hew
> In endlesse rancks along enraunged were,
> That seem'd the Ocean could not containe them there.

> Daily they grow, and daily forth are sent
> Into the world, it to replenish more;
> Yet is the stocke not lessened, nor spent,
> But still remaines in everlasting store,
> As it at first created was of yore.
> For in the wide wombe of the world there lyes,
> In hatefull darkenesse and in deepe horrore,
> An huge eternall *Chaos*, which supplyes
> The substances of natures fruitfull progenyes.

(FQ, III. vi. 23, 33, 35-36)

These are the passages that have led commentators to suggest that Spenser borrowed from Lucretius, or at least from Ovid, sources regarded as dangerous both to his Neoplatonism and to his orthodoxy.[9] Certainly there is much Ovid and some Lucretius in *The Faerie Queene*. In this passage, as elsewhere, Spenser was arbitrary and eclectic in the service of his own idea; he did not need to rely upon a single source, not even Ovid's *Metamorphoses*. In the Garden of Adonis, Spenser set out to connect the world of being with the world of becoming in a fusion more thorough than he had been able to by the scheme adopted in the *Fowre Hymnes*.

His notion of materiality is calm, but nonetheless his chaos is still unbeautiful by classical standards—it dwells

[9] See E. A. Greenlaw, "Spenser and Lucretius"; W. P. Cumming, "Ovid as a Source for Spenser. . . ," *MLN*, LXV (1930), 166-68; C. W. Lemmi, "Monster-spawning Nile Mud in Spenser," *MLN*, XLI (1926), 234-38; J. W. Bennett, "Spenser's Venus and the Goddess Nature in the Cantos of Mutabilitie," *SP*, XXX (1933), 160-92; Lyle Glazier, "Nature and Grace in Spenser's Imagery," *MLQ*, XVI (1955), 300-310.

in "the wide wombe of the world," "in hateful darkenesse
and in deepe horrore," as formless, and therefore as ugly,
as in Greek philosophy or aesthetics. But the Spenserian
chaos does not dwell *outside* the world; formlessness exists
directly in the world. In the metaphor given, it is the
natural product, the child, of the world. Formlessness is
not dangerous, however, for it is the substance from which
forms must emerge:

> All things from thence doe their first being fetch,
>   And borrow matter, whereof they are made,
>   Which when as forme and feature it does ketch,
>   Becomes a bodie, and doth then invade
>   The state of life, out of the griesly shade.
>   That substance is eterne, and bideth so,
>   Ne when the life decayes, and forme does fade,
>   Doth it consume, and into nothing go,
> But chaunged is, and often altred to and fro.
>   (*FQ*, iii. vi. 37)

As in the atomist philosophy, substance is eternal. Since
its being is eternal, it has a kind of virtue and properly
receives the gift of forms.

> The substance is not changed, nor altered,
>   But th' only forme and outward fashion;
>   For every substance is conditioned
>   To change her hew, and sundry formes to don,
>   Meet for her temper and complexion:
>   For formes are variable and decay,
>   By course of kind, and by occasion;
>   And that faire flowre of beautie fades away,
> As doth the lilly fresh before the sunny ray.
>   (*FQ*, iii. vi. 38)

There has been an exchange of values in this stanza—in
the garden, forms are eternal and changeless, save in respect to the substance they take on; in the world, substance

is eternal and changeless, save in respect to the forms they embody. Each has its separate immutability; each is mutable in the other's world. Both are in one sense changeless and in another sense in flux. Substance changes with respect to forms, and the garden changes with respect to its complement of individual forms. Both have the paradoxical qualities of changelessness and change; both are in fact being and becoming, in such a way as to be mutually dependent—which makes Spenser's observation at once physical and metaphysical. In explaining the nature of nature, of physics, of the sensible world, he has made an ontological statement too, about the essence of things and the essence of being. His paradoxical reformation of the relation of being to becoming is the poetic parallel to the systematic revaluation of the natural world effected by Renaissance physics.

But Spenser did not leave matters tucked away in the mythical Garden of Adonis. In the "Two Cantos of Mutabilitie," he set his problem in a far grander allegorical scene and on a far larger scale. The *Mutabilitie Cantos* are not set in a mythical paradise, but in the whole recognizable cosmos. "Wicked Time," the "Great enimy" in the Garden of Adonis, is enlarged into its metaphysical condition, mutability, which is, for purposes of the poem, conceived of as a Titaness aspiring to become a Goddess.[10]

[10] The literature on Spenser's *Mutabilitie Cantos* is overwhelming. Some of it was valuable to me, in particular Nelson, pp. 297-314; Greenlaw, "Spenser's 'Mutabilitie,'" *PMLA*, XLV (1930), 684-703; W. P. Cumming, "The Influence of Ovid's *Metamorphoses* on Spenser's *Mutabilitie Cantos*," *SP*, XXVIII (1931), 241-56; Brents Stirling, "The Concluding Stanzas of Mutabilitie," *SP*, XXX (1933), 193-204, and "Two Notes on the Philosophy of Mutabilitie," *MLN*, L (1935), 154-55; George Williamson, "Mutability, Decay, and Seventeenth-century Melancholy," *ELH*, II (1935), 121-50; A.S.P. Woodhouse, "Nature and Grace in *The*

On the face of it, Mutabilitie's enterprise is hubristic aspiration which ought to come to grief, and we might expect Spenser to bring her down like Archimago or the Giant Orgoglio. But he does not. Mutabilitie is a violent girl, but her intention to overthrow natural order is not made to seem either blasphemous or ludicrous. She lurches a bit as she attacks the spheres of heaven traditionally regarded as beyond her prerogative, but Spenser's picture of the gods quaking before the threat of mutability suggests that *Götterdämmerung* is what such weak gods deserve. Finally, though Jove intended to crush Mutabilitie for her temerity, her beauty forced him to modify his justice and his judgment. Not surprising, after all, since it is precisely the beauty and variety and mutability of the natural world which is—and always was, for artists—the chief glory of the natural world.

Mutabilitie's reign is described in terms of both morality and physics, and certainly the Lucretian (or Ovidian) condition Spenser presents he does not admire:

Faerie Queene," *ELH*, xvi (1949), 194-228; "Nature and Grace: a Rejoinder," *RES*, n.s. vi (1955), 284-88; Milton Miller, "Nature and *The Faerie Queene*," *ELH*, xviii (1951), 191-200; E. M. Albright, "Spenser's Cosmic Philosophy and his Religion," *PMLA*, xliv (1929), 715-59; "Spenser's Reasons for Rejecting the Cantos of Mutabilitie," *SP*, xxv (1928), 93-127; J. W. Bennett, "Spenser's Venus and the Goddess Nature in the Cantos of Mutabilitie," *op.cit.*; Judah L. Stampfer, *"The Cantos of Mutabilitie*: Spenser's Last Testament of Faith," *UTQ*, xxi (1952), 140-56; Kathleen Williams, " 'Eterne in Mutabilitie': The Unified World of *The Faerie Queene*," *ELH*, xix (1952), 115-30; Theodor Gang, "Nature and Grace in *The Faerie Queene*: the Problem Reviewed," *ELH*, xxvi (1959), 1-22; Millar MacLure, "Nature and Art in *The Faerie Queene*," *ELH*, xxvii (1961), 1-20; and Sherman Hawkins, "Mutabilitie and the Cycle of the Months," *Form and Convention in the Poetry of Edmund Spenser*, ed. William Nelson (Columbia University Press, 1961).

As for her tenants; that is, man and beasts,
>   The beasts we daily see massacred dy,
>   As thralls and vassalls unto mens beheasts:
>   And men themselves doe change continually,
>   From youth to eld, from wealth to poverty,
>   From good to bad, from bad to worst of all.
>   Ne doe their bodies only flit and fly:
>   But eeke their minds (which they immortall call)
> Still change and vary thoughts, as new occasions fall.
>   (*FQ*, vii. vii. 19)

Water, earth, air, fire: all things change their forms, their
states, their conditions; nor do they change in a regular
progress but as if entirely arbitrarily. Not quite, though:
for since the physical elements are all part of each other,
too, unlike Lucretius' atoms, they can change into each
other naturally and properly.

>   Yet are they chang'd (by other wondrous slights)
>   Into themselves, and lose their native mights;
>   The Fire to Aire, and th'Ayre to Water sheere,
>   And Water into Earth: yet Water fights
>   With Fire, and Aire with Earth approaching neere:
> Yet all are in one body, and as one appeare.
>   (*FQ*, vii. vii. 25)

Spenser here subsumes teleology to ontology: what is important to him is not the end-product of a process—rather,
it is the relationships among aspects of Being. That one
kind of matter can in fact partake of another, even change
into another, is an assertion of the physical and moral importance, an argument, from the mundane world, that
ultimate abstract Being is also one, the collection and rec-
ollection of all separate material beings.

"Wicked Time," the "Great enimy," parades a pageant
of the Old Style, seasons, months, days, and nights, all
different yet all the same; all differently clad, with differ-

ent attributes, and tending to different results, but all in
fact subsumed under one name, and under one form, Time.
Mutabilitie argues for the various aspects of time:

> For, who sees not, that *Time* on all doth pray?
> But *Times* do change and move continually.
> So nothing here long standeth in one stay:
> Wherefore, this lower world who can deny
> But to be subject still to *Mutabilitie*?   (*FQ*, VII. vii. 47)

Jove answers ontologically: Time itself is a form of
change and rules regularly, with predictable seasons—
therefore the gods control time. Time is not merely an
aspect of things, and the cause or measure of things changing in themselves, but is an idea, a form, and as such has
structure which men can ultimately read.

The judgment is rendered between Mutabilitie and the
gods by Nature, who considers the arguments in relation
to the world of which she is genius. This Nature is not
unambiguous either—just as Mutabilitie could not be categorized as an enemy or Jove as the automatic protagonist,
so Nature cannot be simply defined:

> Yet certes by her face and physnomy,
> Whether she man or woman inly were,
> That could not any creature well descry:
> For, with a veile that wimpled every where,
> Her head and face was hid, that mote to none appeare.
>
> That some doe say was so by skill devized,
>> To hide the terror of her uncouth hew,
>> From mortall eyes that should be sore agrized;
>> For that her face did like a Lion shew,
>> That eye of wight could not indure to view:
>> But others tell that it so beautious was,
>> And round about such beames of splendor threw,
>> That it the Sunne a thousand times did pass,
> Ne could be seene, but like an image in a glass.
>
>   (*FQ*, VII. vii. 5-6)

One notices at once that the nature of nature, the being of nature, is described in terms traditionally associated with the divinity: God himself cannot be looked on, cannot be described, cannot be defined; in the same way truth, time's daughter, can be only progressively, never wholly, revealed to mortal man.[11] Her essence, like that of divinity, was too great to be carried merely by sense or merely by words —and now Nature partakes of a like being, indescribable, not to be understood, not to be imitated or approximated, never fully known to any man in his mortal state.

The judgment Nature renders is a paradox like the paradoxes traditionally associated with the realm of pure being, or the divine. What is relevant to that realm goes so far beyond human categories and classifications that it can be expressed only in physical, emotional, logical, or rhetorical paradoxes. Nature finally says,

I well consider all that ye have sayd,
> And find that all things stedfastnes doe hate
> And changed be: yet being rightly wayd
> They are not changed from their first estate;
> But by their change their being doe dilate;
> And turning to themselves at length againe,
> Doe worke their owne perfection so by fate:
> Then over them Change doth not rule and raigne;
But they raigne over change, and doe their states maintaine.

(*FQ*, VII. vii. 58)

The solution Nature presents is the paradox uniting Being and Becoming: one must note here that she expresses herself in syntactical paradox so fitting to her matter that it is a decorous tautology. "Dilate" is Plotinus' word. The Fifth Ennead discusses the relation between forms and

[11] See Fritz Saxl, "Veritas Filia Temporis," *Philosophy and History, Essays presented to Ernst Cassirer*, eds. Raymond Klibansky and H. J. Paton (Harper Torchbook, 1963), 197-222.

things, in which forms enlarge their being to include matter and to infuse it and its being with their essences, so that all that is, always partakes of its form, whatever specific form that may be. And that form is itself a "dilation" of the Form of Forms, or the *logos*. So in Plotinus' solution, the dilated things of this world, their essences, and the forms of the ideal world all circle about the *logos* at the center of all dilated being, about, in short, the Being of Being. Spenser certainly approaches the Plotinian solution, eclectically, poetically—he never abandons his Platonic ideas and the vocabulary traditionally bearing those ideas, but he weds them to a Lucretian pleasure in the things of this world, a delight in variety and change; he writes to unite two world views, as Henry More, calling himself Democritus Platonissans, was later to do in one of his most Spenserian poems.

But Spenser arbitrarily draws a line, even in the *Mutabilitie Cantos*: though he identifies the flux of Being and Becoming so that we are free to use either word or both about the process of which both are a part, he remains determinedly Christian in his ultimate metaphysics. Just as in the "Hymne to Heavenly Beautie" there was a heaven beyond all the conceivable heavens of space, a heaven in which both space and qualities were infinite—like the metaphysical playgrounds of Plotinus and Ficino—so in the *Mutabilitie Cantos* there is a state in which

> all shall changed bee,
> And from henceforth, none no more change shall see.
>   (*FQ*, vii. vii. 59)

Spenser by no means abandons the old pure Being of the Platonists, as Lucretius had done; nor does he make the total fusion between Being and Becoming adopted by Bruno. He still drew an absolute terminal line between this world and the next, but he drew it *above* the realm of

ideas, rather than below it, between that multifarious metaphysical world which he had united with the sensible
world, and the Christian-Platonic state of blessedness, of
perfect Being.

> Then gin I thinke on that which Nature sayd,
>> Of that same time when no more *Change* shall be,
>> But stedfast rest of all things firmely stayd
>> Upon the pillours of Eternity,
>> That is contrayr to *Mutabilitie*:
>> For, all that moveth, doth in *Change* delight:
>> But thence-forth all shall rest eternally
>> With Him that is the God of Sabbaoth hight:
> O that great Sabbaoth God, graunt me that Sabaoths sight.
>> > > > > > > > > (*FQ*, VIII. 2)

This is the second and last stanza of "the VIII. Canto,
unperfite" of Mutabilitie. Spenser could not go on, one
assumes. He reached the dilemma of all poets and all
philosophers, who say in as many words as they can muster
that there are no words for ultimate Being. He had displayed the fundamental paradox of all verbal expression,
whether in thought or in poetry: that there are no words
for anything, and yet of our words we make things all the
same. We can even get our words to get us somewhere,
"up" to ultimate truth, if it is at the top of a ladder or
chain, "in" to ultimate truth if it resides in Being. In the
two worlds in which human beings habitually move, Spenser's solution is a proper paradox, for he united categories
traditionally separate. Flux and form in the Spenserian
philosophy cannot exist without each other, because they
are each other, they endow each other with being. But in
the world of perfect Being, this language, however paradoxical, is inadequate, and one can only pray, like Spenser,
to be granted a sight of that other world in which being
and knowing are one, and need no human utterance to
reinforce themselves.

There are literary implications in Spenser's solution to the problem of being and becoming which may cast some light on his own method of composition. It is not entirely an analogy to say that Spenser himself was a bit like the Genius of the Garden of Adonis, who "letteth in and letteth out to wend." In the first place, he wrote continually about the things of this world; he of all writers most gracefully and most profoundly evoked the right words for all the varieties of things, experiences, and emotions that men may know in the mixed and darkling wood of human life, and yet he has always a moral and spiritual lesson to which all the beauties of ordinary life are subordinated. Indeed, though obviously his style and his preoccupation with things demonstrate his love for things and his appreciation of their beauty, his stories on the whole end on a metaphysical moral to which narrative and experience seem irrelevant. For instance, the Redcrosse Knight is purified to the extent that he is permitted a sight of the New Jerusalem at the end of the first book; but the New Jerusalem itself is denied him in this life. He is sent back to Cleopolis, to the service of the Faerie Queene, and expected to obey moral rules there which are imperfect, and which can only impair his efforts at perfection. At the end of the second book Sir Guyon, having experienced all the spiritual and physical temptations that flesh is heir to, is as dependent upon God's grace as he was before he underwent his wearing series of tests: he is no more sure of salvation at the end than at the beginning.[12] We may be a bit surer for him, but only because we have been let in

---

[12] Kathleen Williams, " 'Eterne in Mutabilitie,' " takes a similar view of the poem; for a fuller development of this idea, see Nelson, pp. 140-46 and passim. I am much indebted to Professor Nelson for years of conversation about Spenser: I have, as he will recognize, pirated much from him; he is not, however, responsible for the conclusions drawn in this chapter.

upon the poet's—and thus presumably upon God's—moral preferences, and we know that a good God usually grants grace to a man so sorely tried as Guyon. There is a great rift between human life and the life after death that runs through the whole *Faerie Queene*—we are nowhere assured of the relevance of what happens on earth to what will happen in heaven.

The Faerie Queene is not a linear narrative: we are not taken from one point to another, progressively, farther along. A lot happens, of course, and there are descriptions of the most incredible richness; but as his critics have commented again and again, in various degrees of exasperation, Spenser is incredibly inconsistent in plot, in character, and in all manner of detail. He drops out of the poem altogether characters for a time evidently important; he introduces new knights with great freedom, ladies with abandon; characteristics change (Sir Claribell is sometimes good and sometimes "lewd," for instance); and characters run together, as Arthur with Artegal. We have many things in the poem, and the things run together, change their forms and metamorphose, sometimes because the poet seems to want them to, and sometimes because he doesn't care whether they do or not. Spenser's preoccupation with ontology has its analogue in his method of composition: he is not really interested in teleology, in getting somewhere, either in life or in poetical narrative. Getting somewhere is just what the characters do not do: rather they *discover* themselves and others; precisely because Spenser is so interested in essence does he deal so constantly in veils, disguises, and in the difference between appearance and reality, between substantial and metaphysical being. Normally even experienced and good men cannot tell the difference between appearance and reality—so Redcrosse believes his sight of Una sleeping with another knight to be real, and is deceived by Duessa, but true being remains absolute in spite of Redcrosse's muddle. Una is Una, and Duessa is false: this is what he comes to know. In the incident of Hellenore and Malbecco, for example, a story really quite irrelevant to the main plot of the book, what we are left with is not an event, not a plot, but a revelation of moral being: Hellenore is a lustful woman whom only a troop of satyrs can satisfy, and Malbecco is *so* jealous that he himself becomes jealousy.

The more we study *The Faerie Queene,* the more its plan reveals itself among all the changes and variations and vicissitudes of the poet's verisimilar and monstrous world. Things continually metamorphose, but not really into different things—they metamorphose more and more into themselves most visible and evident, into their essence. They become their being. Like the Garden of Adonis, *The Faerie Queene* has a plan, a form, which looks arbitrary in all its aspects, seems so fluctuating as often to be meaningless; but the more we look at specific details, evidently so atomistic and so fragmentary, the more we perceive that they support each other—as Britomart supports on the one hand Florimell and on the other Amoret, until we are ready to see in all these girls aspects of one womanhood, until their individualities all flow into one form, one idea. This sort of notion is ontological, not teleological; and we deny the method when we try to read Spenser's poem as if it were written in a linear or forward progression.

We deny it, too, if we try to read it as a presentation of ordered and hieratic creation—what Spenser tells us is that we are not to conceive of nature, either external or human, as a chain or a line, but rather as a circular seine, where the threads all cross and form a web that cannot be divided. *The Faerie Queene* has no place in Mr. Tillyard's "Elizabethan world picture,"[13] because the notions of hierarchy

---

[13] Tillyard, *The Elizabethan World-picture.*

with which Tillyard dealt were too simple for Spenser, who knew that aspects of existence had greater complexity and interpenetration—greater "spissitude," in Henry More's word—than Sir John Davies permitted in his patterned *Orchestra*, for example. The overthrow of kings, for instance, did not seem particularly tragic to Spenser, since for him the value of each king lay in his value as a man. Though he deplored unfilial behavior, he did not regard it as a threat to cosmic order, which had its own arrangements for immutability.

Spenser was willing to suspend judgment about specific connection because he saw a more active, more fundamental fusion in being than Mr. Tillyard's, or even Mr. Lovejoy's, schema allowed for. He wanted to present his schema of the universe, too, of course: and because his universe was ordered more arbitrarily, in a less patterned way, than the usual Neoplatonic universe of the Renaissance writers (if indeed there is such a thing), he was both more arbitrary and less patterned—or less conventionally patterned—in the construction of his poem. We look in vain really in Spenser for application of the principle of universal analogy by which each hierarchy is constructed in exact parallel: all things in Spenser may be seen to be like all other things, not like a specific correspondent; the distinction of specific things is that each is also itself, and not something else. All the girls are Belphoebe, or are Elizabeth, and can be related to her; but they are themselves too, separate and related to each other and to other people. In *The Faerie Queene*, analogy is universal, but it is patterned every which way. The poem can be better understood, not by elaborate maps of levels of meaning and layers of analogy and allegory, which may (and may not) all fit together at the end; but by reading into each incident, each name, each character to perceive its being, then by examining each incident, name, and character to see the degree to which it fuses with, "becomes," the next. This sounds like a tedious tautology: to understand *The Faerie Queene* is to understand *The Faerie Queene*; but the obvious remark can be defended. Tautology in this case is appropriate to Spenser's needs—first, because he thought of the world, the physical, moral, and metaphysical world, as made up of a set of tautologies, all ultimately dilations of ultimate truth and ultimate being. Second, because he was engaged as an artist upon a description naturally tautologous: the imitation in his variegated poem of the world he understood, a world in which every single thing referred finally to *one* thing, *one* form, *one* idea, and *one* Being: a world in which Becoming led to Being both because it was with Being, and because it *was* Being.

Part IV
Epistemological Paradoxes

12

"I am that I am": Problems of Self-reference

> . . . wee carry with us the wonders, we seeke with-
> out us: There is all *Africa*, and her prodigies in
> us. . . .
>
> Browne, *Religio Medici*, I. 15

MAN's relations with himself are inevitably paradoxical. The most casual, the most neutral self-reference is inevitably in part descriptive. Therefore, like all descriptions, it attempts to achieve the perfect fit, or to achieve tautology: for the better any description, either of something "other" or of the self, the more it is a work of supererogation. The reflexive self-reference is, as the term suggests, a mirror image; as in mirror images, self-reference begins an endless oscillation between the thing itself and the thing reflected, begins an infinite regress. One of my acquaintance obviously thinks very successfully and constructively when he is shaving; much of his own original perception theory is illustrated by examples from this morning contemplation. But he is a naturally paradoxical man, who can make of what may in fact be tautology also an observation about "objective reality." The mirror holds no terrors for him. For my niece, it was otherwise: washing her hands in a bathroom entirely walled by mirrors and seeing her pink self endlessly reflected wherever she looked, she began to cry. The psychological effect of mirrors is that they both confirm and question individual identity—confirm by splitting the mirrored viewer into observer and observed, giving him the opportunity to view himself objectively, as other people do; question, by repeating him as if he were simply an object, not "himself," as he so surely "knows" himself to be, by repeating himself as if he were not (as his inmost self insists that he is) unique.[1] The mirror is the most obvious sort of self-reference: self-reference by words generally confirms, or re-creates, the self; but, either in words or by mirror, re-creation is not a thing that most selves are prepared to endure for long. The re-created self, the separated and objectified self, may turn out, one fears, to do instead of one's self, may replace the original and originating self. The re-created self is a threat to the self.

For artists of various kinds, who "look" all the time in the service of their art, mirror reflection has its particular uses against the death of the particular artist. In his art, the created self-image, made by means of the mirror, gives the artist double assurance of worldly life after death: it is, in the painter's or the sculptor's hands, a *monumentum aere perennius* designed to stand for him and demonstrating both himself and his art, showing himself by means of his art, long after he has gone down to the night of endless sleep. For painters and sculptors, the mirror is the means by which they can treat themselves as their own models, can study themselves as keenly as they would any other physical personality sitting for them. The mirror shows them as the sitter sees them, too: so much is this a truism of painting that the intentness of a man's gaze has been adopted, rather dubiously, as a criterion for identifying "self-portraits"—dubiously, since obviously we do not know what a painter otherwise unrecorded looked like and therefore cannot be sure that the man gazing with peculiar penetration back at us is in fact the painter whose style we think we recognize in the picture.[2] Such a method is sus-

[1] The phenomenon is much commented on in the literature of psychoanalysis; the problem of narcissism is a splitting of the self into lover and beloved.

[2] See Erwin Panofsky's comments on Jan van Eyck's Portrait of a

pect because it is self-confirming—but the assumption is a natural one, since the painter painting himself is also involved in a self-confirming (and therefore suspect) operation. As for the self-portrait, is it of the painter? Would his apprentice recognize "him," or would his wife? Has he painted himself in his best clothes? Is he handsomer than usual? Or more melancholy? Who can trust the picture of a man painted by himself?

Leaving all this aside, there is another habit of identification resorted to by critics of pictures: "self-portraits" of painters are often so called because of the trick of half-representation. That is, a face peering through a split in the door, or around a corner at the extreme edge of a picture, or a man asleep, or with his back to the beholder (as Vermeer seems to have painted an artist, in exploitation of this pseudo-tradition), will be conceived of as the painter who wittily draws attention to himself, much as Hitchcock intrudes inessentially into the pictures he directs. In other words, a half-figure, a half-concealed figure, or a commonplace figure in a crowd is deemed to be the painter who introduces himself into his own work in order to comment on the "reality" of imitation by recording himself with the same objectivity as the rest of the scene. This sort of assumption relies upon the limited self-revelations and self-concealments of the paradoxist, upon the paradoxical character of self-reference: by this method, the paradox—paradoxically and quite illegitimately—gives authority to the identification of a man unidentified and unidentifiable.

This sort of identification is, like the method of identification-by-intent-gaze, unverifiable (and unfalsifiable as well); also, it leaves out of account the commonplace fact that artists, always short of models, continually use them-

---

Man in a Red Turban: *Early Netherlandish Painting* (Harvard University Press, 1953), 1.198.

selves, or parts of themselves, as models, "know" their
faces (from shaving and so forth) better than they know
most other faces, and therefore use themselves as models
for all sorts of "other" people in self-references that are,
and were intended to be, submerged into their subject
matter. In a way, "The Artist in his Atelier," in Vienna,
is a spoof on what we are "supposed" to think about self-
portraits: Vermeer has painted a picture of an artist painting a picture (—in which the painted painter begins his
picture at the most improbable point on the canvas, with
the wreath on the girl's head) of the allegory of fame; or,
Vermeer has painted a painter painting his own fame, or of
a painter imitating what, in fact, Vermeer was doing when
he painted the picture. But really we have no license to
assume that the man sitting with his stockings down and
his back to the beholder *is* Vermeer. The fact that there is
a man in the same costume in "The Procuress" in Dresden,
is no conformation of anything, after all; and *that* identification also depends upon the beholder's fondness for the
self-reference trope, by which it would be mildly witty for
the painter to have painted himself into the procuress'
transaction.[3]

Sometimes there are self-portraits, or slant self-portraits,
that insist upon "speculation": painted in mirrors, indicating the mirrors in which they were painted, they force the
beholder into thinking about what reality "really" is. One
such picture—a picture arrogant in more than the pose
of the self-confident painter—is Velasquez' "Las Meniñas,"
in which the largest object is the easel, seen from the back,
on which the painter paints. At first glance, from the pose
of the familiar doll-form of the Infanta, the beholder assumes that the painter is painting her, since, the beholder
knows, he had so often painted her in like poses. The

[3] See Ludwig Goldscheider, *Jan Vermeer* (London, 1958), Plates
13, 56.

theatrical disposition of the ladies-in-waiting, the little boy, the dwarf, and the benevolent mastiff, all grouped so pointedly about the little girl, imply a display being readied for the painter's formal display-portrait of the child. The courtier standing in the lighted doorway at stage-left rear and the mirrored King and Queen, quite recognizably Velasquez' "pictures," seem to be checking on an official undertaking. But the presence of the painter, obviously posed as involved in painting, actually confuses the picture: if he were actually painting the child, his subject would have to be posed where the viewer is (or where the audience is, in the tableau staged in the painting); from stage-right rear he could not paint the Infanta head on. The pictured reality offers a solution to the confusion—the painter is painting the King and Queen, who think the Infanta would make a nicer picture. The painter paints the Infanta—his original picture, as it were, is turned inside out. Instead of painting her directly, he paints the whole scene reflected in a mirror, in which all the figures, courtiers, ladies-in-waiting, princess, dwarf, and dog, can control and organize their appearances. Since he must needs paint in a mirror, he is reflected in the mirrored scene and thus "faithfully" paints himself in. But what a way to paint a picture of people! The likelihood is that Velasquez did not paint the whole scene from its mirror reflection, but painted the Infanta and her retinue straight, as usual; then he painted himself in, of course from a mirror, as is usual for that kind of portrait. But the inclusion of two points of view cannot have been accidental: Velasquez comments in the picture not only on different levels of reality, but also on his own power, at the heart of the Hapsburg court, to manipulate that reality, to present the royal family as it "should" be presented.

In literature, the problem is as tricky. As far as lyric poetry is concerned, the poet always enters into his creation, detaches a part of himself, a limited and artificial self, "about" whom he writes his verse. Sometimes the poet professes far more, presents more "sincerely" the inward life which is the subject of his lyrical expression.[4] However privately Sidney looked in his heart and wrote, though, the lyric "I" is Astrophel rather than P. Sidney, Kt., son and son-in-law of great men and heir to broad estates. No one nowadays takes biography seriously as the sole, or even the major, clue to literary imagination: the poet writing lyric verse has license to present himself however he will, to distort his own personality and feelings however he wishes to make his poetic point. For, even supposing the poet were totally "sincere," his sincerity is, to other men, unverifiable.

The Liar paradox is the classical paradox of self-reference, as well as the classical paradox of infinite regress. It cannot be verified internally, since there is no measuring rod for its accuracy; it cannot be confirmed externally, since it refers only to itself.[5] So is it also with self-portraits: the more faithful the likeness, the greater the falsity of the picture, the greater its isolation from any reference point outside of the creating, re-creating self. Escher's print of the hand drawing the hand,[6] or, better yet, Steinberg's marvelous drawing of the same subject,[7] expresses the impossibility exactly. A man cannot make himself.

But, as in Steinberg's drawing and Escher's print, some Renaissance men had a kind of belief that man could make

---

[4] See Henri Peyre, *Literature and Sincerity*, Chapter 1.

[5] The best study of the Liar paradox is Alexandre Koyré's *Epiménide le menteur; Actualités scientifiques et industrielles* (Paris, 1946); for problems of consistency and verification, see Ernest Nagel and James R. Newman, *Gödel's Proof* (New York University Press, 1958).

[6] M. C. Escher, *Graphic Work* (London, 1961), p. 47.

[7] Steinberg, *The Passport* (New York, 1954), n.p.

himself, and believed furthermore that to make himself was a lifetime job to which he owed most of his attention. Castiglione's *Courtier* is in this sense a fundamental paradox, since it is a handbook to self-making—and as befits such a book, it has many paradoxes within it.[8] There are other versions of the same idea: free-will theology suggested, too, that man had a greater part in the formation of his particular character than was granted in predestinarianism.[9] In general, Renaissance discussions of man were attempts to define the class to which all men belonged, and only sometimes did they exploit tricks of self-reference either simple or elaborate, so dear to official paradoxists. Comments on human nature, however, which came to grips with problems of epistemology were—or "contained"—very subtle sorts of self-reference. For this there was classical precedent, as for example, Plato's manipulations in presenting Socrates in the dialogues, as well as the example of Epimenides already referred to. Socrates often takes himself as an example of a psychological, moral, or philosophical point, both discursively and dramatically. The self-conscious introduction, or the self-critical examination by an author of his own mind or his own work, or the arch introduction of an author into his own work of art is paradoxical in its infinitely regressive reference. It is also paradoxical in that it introduces at once a second level of "reality" into the imaginative invention, conventional fictive reality together with the representation of actual, fleshly, sensible reality. Like the para-

---

[8] See above, Introduction. *The Courtier* presents several paradoxes besides the beautiful example of self-making.

[9] E.g., one of Ralph Venning's orthodox paradoxes: "He believes and knowes that without Christ he can do nothing; and that it is God worketh in him both to will and to doe, of his own good pleasure: and yet he believes that 'tis his own fault, if he will not and do not that which is good." Venning, *Orthodox Paradoxes*, p. 6.

doxical form itself, self-reference forces consideration of relativity. Self-reference draws attention to the artist's techniques, and usually to his mastery of technique: Jan van Eyck's tiny picture of himself in the convex mirror hanging behind the troth-plighting couple is not only a useful record of his presence at the ceremony but also a comment on the skill with which he could paint, even the distorted "reality" of the convex mirror. That his picture was a legal testimony as well as a conventional encomium of marriage manages to combine both the "real" and the "ideal" worlds into an economical unity.

When Shakespeare allows Cleopatra to say,

> and I shall see
> Some squeaking Cleopatra boy my greatness
> I' th' posture of a whore,   (*Antony*, v.ii.219-21)

he dares remind the audience, deeply involved in the "fate" of the Egyptian queen (who was, after all, a whore), that "she" is not there at all, but only an English boy "squeaking" her lines; that is, Shakespeare permits the actor playing Cleopatra to break into his own illusion with a self-reference to what he is then and there doing, as if the acting reality were an imitation of the imaginative reality depicted by the actors—which is precisely what it is. Prospero's great speech is a cliché for Shakespeare's view of art: like Cleopatra's remark above, it has an immediate reference within the play itself—in this case, to the masque of Hymen that has just "appropriately" taken place in honor of Miranda's betrothal to Ferdinand. But its larger reference is unmistakable too, to the entire illusory world of stage plays, of acting, of imagination, and of life itself:

> Our revels now are ended. These our actors,
> As I foretold you, were all spirits, and
> Are melted into air, into thin air:
> And, like the baseless fabric of this vision,

> The cloud-capp'd towers, the gorgeous palaces,
> The solemn temples, the great globe itself,
> Yea, all which it inherit, shall dissolve,
> And, like this insubstantial pageant faded,
> Leave not a wrack behind. We are such stuff
> As dreams are made on; and our little life
> Is rounded with a sleep.   (*Temp.*, iv.i.148-59)

The comparison itself is a *topos*, of the world to a play.[10] What is particularly ingenious is that the comparison is made within a play, a mirror reference to what is going on in the act, and a reminder of the technical and official illusion which audiences have agreed to accept.

Prospero's speech, like Hamlet's on the players, comments on the mirror action of all artistic imitation. It also acts as a mirror to the play of which it is a part, as Hamlet's play-within-the-play reflects awkwardly, crudely, in little and in dumbshow, the problem of the greater play. The chinese box effect serves to remind us of the illusion involved in all imitation, of the tautology and identity involved in perfect matching. Paradoxes exploit the same critical relativism: it is from one great arch-paradox, Erasmus' *Praise of Folly*, that the classic self-reference comes. In the first place, there is something silly in the "real" situation, that the man officially regarded as the most learned man in Christendom should write an encomium of folly, foolishness, and play. The figure of Folly exceeds the foolishness of all sophists, who praise worthless things, since she not only praises a low thing—namely, Folly—but, in praising that low thing, she praises herself. The praise of folly can only be folly, a reinforcement and a proof of the fundamental folly of folly. Folly "is her own *trumpet*," and exhibits the un-Christian qualities of pride and self-love (the second of which is one of

[10] Ernst Robert Curtius, *European Literature and the Latin Middle Ages*, pp. 138-54.

her natural handmaids). All the world, and the gods, too, turn out to be foolish and self-regarding: Philautia, then, turns out to be the fundamental weakness of the foolish world. Folly is both like the world ("on all sydes I dooe resemble my selfe") and also she governs the world, though she makes no particular effort toward sovereignty. Simply, Folly is the natural state of human life, and from her self-love and vain-glory all human enterprises take their start. She knows this, since she knows herself better than anyone else knows her: as she says, her honest self-praise is surely better than the suborned praise of some purchasable poet or orator. At the end, Folly casts doubt upon her whole discourse, so that even the irony of the cutting distinction drawn between folly and wisdom becomes equivocal. All kinds of self-reference are exploited in Erasmus' extraordinary paradox. Every wisdom that Folly utters must be considered in relation to everything else she says, and to her authority for saying what she says.

The kind of self-reference Erasmus played with, citing himself scornfully in the course of Folly's disquisition,[11] is one that many other writers have used in their paradoxes —Rabelais introduces himself, as Alcofribas, into his heroic narrative; Burton, in a particularly poignant way, introduced himself, without quite naming his name, into his *Anatomy*; and Boyle, from whom one would scarcely expect such playfulness, played up to the paradox in his most serious works. In poetry, one expects the writer to provide something of his own lyric subject, and to be his own lyric hero. In this respect, Petrarca, who does not refer to himself by name, although he refers to his own situation in a deliberately recognizable way, set the tune to which Renaissance poets thenceforth sang. Like Erasmus, John

[11] See above, Introduction, pp. 18-19.

Donne famously played upon his proper and well-known name in his verse, introducing his very self into the action described by the poems. One such poem, a verse-letter "To Sr Henry Wotton," then departing on a voyage, ends with the poet's signature, itself a useful pun. The pun and the signature are both appropriate, since the poem makes an identification between writer and receiver of the letter:

> But, Sir, I advise not you, I rather doe
> Say o'er those lessons, which I learn'd of you:
> Whom, free from German schismes, and lightnesse
> Of France, and faire Italies faithlessnesse,
> Having from these suck'd all they had of worth,
> And brought home that faith, which you have carried forth,
> I throughly love.   (ll. 63-69)

The lessons Wotton had set, Donne paraphrased in his poem; they all dealt with the fullness of the self:

> Be thou thine owne home, and in thy selfe dwell;
> Inne any where, continuance maketh hell.
> And seeing the snaile, which every where doth rome,
> Carrying his owne house still, still is at home,
> Follow (for he is easie pac'd) this snaile,
> Bee thine owne Palace, or the world's thy gaile.
>   (ll. 47-52)

He can paraphrase them because he has been learning them for himself, with the result that he is ever more thoroughly Wotton's servant:

> But if my selfe, I' have wonne
>
> To know my rules, I have, and you have
>   DONNE.
>   (ll. 69-70)

Wotton was the model, but Donne developed himself upon the example until the work of identification was accomplished.

In "A Hymne to God the Father," the poet plays upon his name in his relation to a greater patron than Wotton, God Himself. The question with which the poem begins— "Wilt thou forgive that sinne where I begunne,/ Which is my sin, though it were done before?"—establishes the common use of "done," in relation to the moral convention. God's patience is invoked, for even if He can forgive original sin, the poet has compounded his primal fault by his own peculiar errors:

> Wilt thou forgive those sinnes through which I runne,
> And doe them still: though still I doe deplore?
> When thou hast done, thou hast not done,
> For, I have more.   (ll. 1-6)

While there is life, there is sin: no sooner has God forgiven than He is entreated to forgive again, so long as a man lives. The poem, like a man's life, must end, however, and does:

> I have a sinne of feare, that when I have spunne
> My last thred, I shall perish on the shore;
> Sweare by thy selfe, that at my death thy Sunne
> Shall shine as it shines now, and heretofore;
> And, having done that, thou hast done,
> I have no more.   (ll. 13-18)

By a poetic pun the poet comes to the miracle of grace. The Son will shine upon the poet's death as the sun-star shines at the moment of writing, and by that assurance, the poet will cease to sin long enough to die in faith.

According to the ordinary Platonic pattern for friendship, Wotton's morality had provided a mirror for Donne's: the poet had looked upon his friend and become more and more like him as he gazed. In Shakespeare's *Sonnets*, the looking-glass motif is exploited still more fully in relation both to the poet and his beloved and to the metaphorical quality of their connection.[12] The poetry properly exhibits a preoccupation with the "likenesses," not just of lover to beloved, but of writer to his subject, and of the poems to their subject. In the courteous manner of the Renaissance lover, schooled directly and indirectly to follow the Platonic model, the writer makes the fundamental assumption that whatever in his verse is beautiful is the reflection of the beloved's perfection; whatever is awkward or "natural" is the reflection of the author's inadequacy. In Sonnet 32, "If thou survive my well-contented day," the poem ends on the notion that after his death, his poems will remain dear to the beloved because of their matter, in spite of their manner, which demonstrates inadequacy in poetic talent:

> O, then vouchsafe me but this loving thought:
> Had my friend's muse grown with this growing age,
> A dearer birth than this his love had brought,
> To march in ranks of better equipage;
> > But since he died, and poets better prove,
> > Theirs for their style I'll read, his for his love.

In Sonnet 55, "Not marble nor the gilded monuments of time," written in the traditional metaphor of poet's pride in his craft, the death of the lover is kept from the poems:

> 'Gainst death and all-oblivious enmity
> Shall you pace forth

in the meter of the poems themselves:

> So, till the judgment that yourself arise,
> You live in this, and dwell in lovers' eyes.

[12] See, chiefly, Murray Krieger, *A Window to Criticism, Shakespeare's Sonnets and Modern Poetics* (Princeton University Press, 1964). I have shamelessly appropriated from Mr. Krieger in too many places for me to footnote.

Because of their literary merits, lovers will read the sonnets and thus re-create the perfections of the beloved; further, the poems shall become the container of what was beautiful and memorable, the real tomb of the beloved: "You live *in this*." In another sonnet on the Horatian theme, 65, "Since brass, nor stone, nor earth, nor boundless sea," the couplet faces the fact of total oblivion, physical and literary. The honest poet is thrown back upon his own resources in answer to the question, "What strong hand can hold time's swift foot back?" The answer is straightforward enough:

> O none, unless this miracle have might,
> That in black ink my love may still shine bright.

There is one chance to check mortality's march, and a slim chance at that, dependent upon the fragile purchase of paper and ink. The poet's craft as well as the paradox is "miracle," to be wondered at: the poet's imagination is ephemeral foundation for eternity, but it is sufficient. Often enough the poet regarded his own imagination an inadequate mirror of the beloved's extraordinary qualities, though conversely a proper record of the poet's own lack of virtue and of art. In Sonnet 72, the poet welcomes the notion that his name will die with his body:

> For I am sham'd by that which I bring forth,
> And so should you, to love things nothing worth.

More commonly, in this sequence, poetry is assumed to be the instrument of identification of poet with beloved, since though the poet "makes" the verse, the verse is about—therefore "is"—the unnamed qualities of the beloved. By the conventional identity of lovers, the poet "is" the beloved: to love the beloved is to love one's self and therefore, perhaps, to be guilty of *philautia*. Preoccupation with poetry is merely the proof and the example of the poet's self-love, since the verse deals only with his love for his beloved. Sonnet 62 plays upon the narcissism of that identity:

> Sin of self-love possesseth all mine eye,
> And all my soul, and all my every part;
> And for this sin there is no remedy,
> It is so grounded inward in my heart.

The next quatrain demonstrates, as the mirror demonstrates, himself as the object of his attentions:

> Methinks no face so gracious is as mine,
> No shape so true, no truth of such account,
> And for myself mine own worth do define
> As I all other in all worths surmount.

But an objective glance at the mirror changes that blind, unseeing self-admiration into something else:

> But when my glass shows me myself indeed,
> Beaten and chopt with tann'd antiquity,
> Mine own self-love quite contrary I read;
> Self so self-loving were iniquity.

In the first quatrain, there was "no remedy" for the poet's preoccupation with himself. By the third quatrain, his level glance has restored him to a proper Platonic condition of love, so that it is not himself but his love for and in the beloved, that he really loves; therefore, Christianlike, he loves not himself really, but another:

> 'Tis thee, my self, that for myself I praise,
> Painting my age with beauty of thy days.

It is not, then, merely his unbeautiful appearance, "Beaten and chopt with tann'd antiquity," that the poet laments, but himself, his own character, qualities, and personality— all "nothing worth," as he expressed it in Sonnet 72. Identification with the beloved does the poet honor and restores his beauty and his worth, though in the sequence that problem is never happily resolved for long. In Sonnet 39, the poet moves away from narcissism to a sense of unity even in separation from the beloved:

> O how thy worth with manners may I sing,
> When thou art all the better part of me?
> What can mine own praise to mine own self bring?
> And what is't but mine own, when I praise thee?

In the end, the poetry is a tautology: the subject itself is enough; his encomia of the beloved are simply the encomia of those qualities in the beloved which he has incorporated into himself, until at last the beloved can truly be said to be the better part of the poet. The unity, however forced, permits the poet to contemplate and tolerate the physical separation of lover and beloved, and to direct the poetry to an objective rather than a purely reflexive subject. This conceit avoids the pool of narcissism into which Neoplatonic imagery plunges poets, but it carries other problems of its own.

Since the poetry reflects and "is" both poet and beloved, it must vary in value, depending upon the poet's state of mind. Sometimes it is "nothing worth," as in Sonnet 72, sometimes "this miracle," as in Sonnet 65. In 76, the relation of the poet's mind to his verse is explored:

> Why is my verse so barren of new pride?
> So far from variation or quick change?
> Why, with the time, do I not glance aside
> To new-found methods, and to compounds strange?
> Why write I still all one, ever the same,
> And keep invention in a noted weed,
> That every word doth almost tell my name,
> Showing their birth, and where they did proceed?

The poem is a remarkable commentary on the moving boundaries of a style, as well as upon the notion that, for better and for worse, for richer and for poorer, a style really *is* the man. Not only are Shakespeare's lines clothed in "a noted weed," "dressed" in his manner, but they also bear his signature—"every word doth almost tell my name."[13] The poet's subject, he says, also marks him, since he merely repeats himself again and again in praise of his single subject, "you and love." The style must be repetitious, since the poet is, in so many ways, self-consciously dedicated to the tautologies of self-repetition.

In Sonnet 116, "Let me not to the marriage of true minds," the poet actually hazards all verse, his own and that of all other men, in defense of his principle: though rosy lips and cheeks must be destroyed by time, love is nonetheless unalterable—in spite of a long history of evidence to the contrary, so much of which is bitterly recorded elsewhere in this very sequence. In spite of all that, in spite of his better knowledge, the poet stakes his whole accomplishment and the immortality granted to poets upon the correctness of his (indefensible) position:

> If this be error, and upon me prov'd,
> I never writ, nor no man ever loved.

He *has* written, because he has loved; and other men have loved, unmistakably. The sequence itself exists to "prove" how right the poet is—and how wrong. The very illusion that this poem sets out to create, that love can be immutable, is contradicted by the illusion of reality created by the whole sequence, in which a living, breathing man attempts, in the curious cramped formulations demanded by sonnets, to deal with the racking contradictions of human love.

In the usual arrangement of the sonnets, both Platonic

[13] This particular statement carries the social contradiction that decorum demanded: the anonymous circulation of such verse, always officially unsigned. Of course cognoscenti, then as now, knew who was responsible for what work, unsigned or no.

and human realities are thenceforward maintained in the sequence, in a precarious realist-idealist balance that double-tongued, two-faced poetry accommodates so remarkably. "I am that I am," the poet asserts, whatever others may say and think. He settles for his human love, who treads upon the ground, and in whom he believes though he knows she lies. This is of course outdoing the Petrarchan praise of love, and is also a praise of the art that can make of frankly imperfect love for an obviously imperfect human being something so transcendent and so reliant. In Sonnets 135, 136, and 143, the poet plays upon his own name and nature—since, by the luck awarded to poets, his proper name bears a significant other meaning. In these sonnets, he introduces himself, not in the descriptive psychological examination of Sonnet 29, "When in disgrace with fortune and men's eyes"; or of Sonnet 110, "Alas, 'tis true I have gone here and there/ And made myself a motley to the view"—but as a double-faced counter in the commerce between him and his love, its duplicity matched in the poetic language by which he pursues his aims:

> Whoever hath her wish, thou hast thy Will,
> And Will to boot, and Will in over-plus—

in those lines, he mocks both himself and her, "burdened" by the intensity of his love.

> More than enough I am that vex thee still,
> To thy sweet will making addition thus,
> Wilt thou, whose will is large and spacious,
> Not once vouchsafe to hide my will in thine?

He is his will—that is, Will is so concentrated on getting his will, or her submission to his love, that he has become that will; this is, as often in sonnet sequences, after Petrarca's model, a Christian concept translated into the language of secular love. "I am that I am": but behind the

"Will" play, lies a whole continent of accidental reference which must be adduced to gloss the poems. Her will can enlarge to include his, to fuse with his will and thus with him, to "hide" therefore his will in her own—

> The sea, all water, yet receives rain still,
> And in abundance addeth to his store;
> So thou, being rich in Will, add to thy Will
> One will of mine, to make thy large Will more. . . .

The capital "W" 's might be redistributed without much disturbing the meaning, since man, desire, and the object of that desire are so identified in "Will" or "will." Simply, the lady must become him, or must allow her will to be identified with his:

> Let no unkind, no fair beseechers kill;
> Think all but one, and me in that one Will.

In the next sonnet, 136, the poet not only persists in pressing his will, but identifies himself with the "nothing" which can content her (and which, in quite a different way, he had used in the earlier sonnets comparing his insufficiency with the enormous treasure of his beloved's worth). This time the "nothing" recalls the sexual reference of *Much Ado* or *Hamlet*, as it unfolds the meanings hidden within the poet's name:

> If thy soul check thee that I come so near,
> Swear to thy blind soul that I was thy Will,
> And will, thy soul knows, is admitted there;
> Thus far for love my love-suit, sweet, fulfil.
> Will will fulfil the treasure of thy love,
> Ay, fill it full with wills, and my will one.
> In things of great receipt with ease we prove
> Among a number one is reckon'd none.
> Then in the number let me pass untold,
> Though in thy store's account I one must be;

> For nothing hold me, so it please thee hold
> That nothing me, a something sweet to thee;
>   Make but my name thy love, and love that still,
>   And then thou lov'st me, for my name is Will.

This lady is, evidently, distinguished for her willfulness toward him; he wills, by his particular qualifications, to fill her with Will. In a vulgar play, the more willful she is, the better. "I am that I am," and I am Will. The sequence commemorates the shifting will of the poet himself, the risings and fallings of his emotion and his art. After the magniloquence of the great sonnets, it may seem trivial to arrange the sequence so that these punning poems come so near to the end; but they have their place as a signature; they "almost tell" the poet's name.

The most famous of all self-references in the Renaissance is also a self-examination, a psychological casebook, a record of a well-read, considerate, and sensitive man, a theoretical and practical behavior book, a documentary source for the life of a cultivated *politique* petty nobleman during the French Religious Wars—Montaigne's *Essayes*.[14] The title alone indicates the mark of the empirical attitude: Montaigne constantly weighed his subject, in the beautiful hanging scale of the Renaissance that was his *impresa*, a scale always slightly in motion, always adjusting its balance to the barely perceptible changes in its pans. For Montaigne, the essay was not merely a weighing process, but a metaphor for experience and experiment: "To conclude, all this galiemafry which I huddle-up here, is but a register of my lives-Essayes."[15] Montaigne set himself the original

[14] The quotations are all from the *Essayes*, in Florio's translation, ed. J.I.M. Stewart, Modern Library edition (New York, 1933). In the citations which follow, the Book and Essay numbers will be given, as well as the page in that edition.

[15] *Essayes*, III.xii.976. For an interesting discussion of the development of Montaigne's thought, see Donald M. Frame, *Mon-*

task of reporting "himself," as faithfully as he could, without the varnish or traditional organization of a man presenting himself officially to the public.[16] His evident frankness and sincerity, contrasting so strikingly with other men's references to themselves, helped to make his strange book an immediate success; because it seemed to describe one man "as he really was," the book spoke to the unexpressed private personalities of many other men, who read themselves, with relief and comfort, in his self-display.

"I studie my selfe more than any other subject," he wrote calmly. "It is my supernaturall Metaphysike, it is my naturall Philosophy."[17] Montaigne's calm presentation of the man he claimed to be "himself" provided a comfortable model to men and women laboring alone under the difficult burden of their natural selfishness—"I live from hand to mouth, and with reverence be it spoken, I live but to my selfe: there end all my designes."[18] For Montaigne, the preoccupation of his age with Man rather than with individual men seemed simply foolish: he set himself, empirically, to such human considerations as he might be expected to conclude:

Every man lookes before himselfe, I looke within my selfe: I have no busines but with my selfe. I uncessantly consider, controle, and taste my selfe . . . as for me, I roule me into my selfe. (II.xvii.596)

"I roule me into my selfe": Montaigne acted out the epistemological paradox, that when one reaches a terminus of

taigne's Discovery of Man (Columbia University Press, 1955). See also Erich Auerbach, *Mimesis*, pp. 219-73; and Imbrie Buffum, *Studies in the Baroque from Montaigne to Rotrou* (Yale University Press, 1957), pp. 1-76.

[16] See Peyre, pp. 36-42.
[17] *Essayes*, III.xiii.970.
[18] III.iii.746.

thought, one turns back to examine the process of thinking by which one arrived at the impasse. Though Montaigne's ultimate preoccupation was epistemological, certainly, epistemology was only his covert, his incidental subject: ostensibly, he merely weighed himself. The operation of rolling one's self back into one's subjective self can be stated as a reversible proposition. What Montaigne studied (himself) he referred to himself; he made objective his subjective self, and subjectively reabsorbed the objectified self he studied. He externalized himself to internalize himself again, and always "more" so, or cumulatively. He continually confirmed himself:

Many yeares are past since I have no other aime, whereto my thoughts bend, but my selfe, and that I controule and study nothing but my selfe. And if I study any thing else, it is immediately to place it upon, or to say better, in my selfe.

(ii.vi.333)

Referring to the Renaissance commonplace of "forming" men by means of moral teaching, Montaigne asserted the conscious tautology of his own endeavor: "Others fashion man, I repeat him; and represent a particular one, but ill made; and whom were I to forme a new, he should be far other then he is; but he is now made."[19] Since change is, for Montaigne, the nursery and residence of all that is, and Montaigne registered a man living in the world, his *Essayes* naturally demonstrated the changes in their own subject, and therefore were, in their unfixed form, a reflection themselves of that changeableness. As Montaigne so famously—and so radically—said, "I describe not the essence, but the passage; not a passage from age to age, or as people reckon, from seaven yeares to seaven, but from day to day, from minute to minute. My history must be fitted to the present."[20] The present indeed: Montaigne is

[19] iii.ii.725.   [20] iii.ii.725-26.

one of the earliest writers to force the illusion of immediacy on his readers; but it fitted also to the future, as he noted to "My Lady of Duras":

For, al I seek to reape by my writings, is, they will naturally represent and to the life, pourtray me to your remembrance. The very same conditions and faculties, it pleased your Ladyship to frequent and receive, with much more honour and curtesie, then they in any way deserve, I will place and reduce (but without alteration and change) into a solide body, which may happily continue some dayes and yeares after mee. . . .
(II.xxxviii.703)

Though he was dedicated to the "hard" Stoical doctrine of Seneca and Plutarch, whom he proclaimed again and again to be his favorite authors,[21] Montaigne spent most of his time observing, condoning, and relishing the very quality in himself that those moralists most deplored, mutability.[22] With an ease extreme even for Skeptics, Montaigne took it for granted that man is a creature of change; without *frisson*, though he roused many a shudder in his readers, Montaigne contemplated physical and emotional mutability as the ordinary data of human life. As a result, his essays are mutable too, full of contradiction and inconsistency, a contradiction and inconsistency fitting the decorum of the mutable human psychology he postulated and accommodated to the persistence of some personal identity. The present to which Montaigne thought "history must be fitted" was a moving series of points of perception:

I may soone change, not onely fortune, but intention. It is a counter-roule of divers and variable accidents, and irresolute imaginations, and sometimes contrary: whether it be that my selfe am other, or that I apprehend subjects, by other circum-

[21] "A Defence of *Seneca* and *Plutarke*," *Essayes*, II.xxiii.647-52.
[22] For Montaigne's Skepticism and eclecticism, see below, Chapter 13.

stances and considerations. Howsoever, I may perhaps gaine-
say myself, but truth (as *Demades* said) I never gaine-say:
were my mind setled, I would not essay, but resolve my selfe.
                                                    (III.ii.726)

Even his misrepresentation has its kind of truth—which
is, that men tend to misrepresent themselves; but when
the fundamental truth of human existence is that *"Diversity is the most universall quality,"*[23] then he must necessarily contradict himself again and again, quite without
deliberate misrepresentation—or any misrepresentation at
all. Montaigne's writings, therefore, to "fit" properly, express the paradoxes of contradiction and self-contradiction.
Most characteristically, Montaigne played his Stoicism
against his Skepticism in essay after essay;[24] he also devoted an essay to the commonplace contrast of Heraclitus,
the Weeping Philosopher, with Democritus, the Laugher;[25]
his opinions were, frankly, as unstable as his moods.

To put it another way, Castiglione's courtier was
thoroughly up-to-date, but Montaigne was modern. The
courtier's conviction that a man could make himself derived from the Platonic belief in educational reformation;
Montaigne's conviction was at once simpler and more complicated. Like Folly, he believed that a man *was* himself,
for better and for worse, and, no matter what the man
himself may have thought, he acted as if he was, for himself, the measure of all things. Without question for Montaigne, however weak and vacillating his own personality
may have been, it was an arbitrary sovereign over the dispositions of his world. In an utterly matter-of-fact way,
Montaigne accepted the fact that his own perception of
himself was the center of his world, and that his world

[23] II.xxxvii.705.
[24] I.xii.34-36; xix.48-63; xxii.76-88; xxxviii.188-89.
[25] I.i.260-63.

was "made up" of his own ideas, his own values, combined, recombined, sorted through again and again, exactly as his whimsical preference dictated.

A world of change, or of flux, is by definition made up of contraries and contradictions; Montaigne's was a more circumscribed world than those postulated by Pico, Nicholas of Cusa, or Giordano Bruno, but like theirs, his world was made up of contradictory materials and ideas. In orthodoxy, only God could compose the contrarieties of which material existence is made. For Montaigne, as later for Robert Burton, accommodation of contradictions was the job of every thinking, feeling, and acting man, a man who was himself the point of coincidence of all the contradictions he could perceive. Though the notion owes something to Pico's confident assertion of man's intellectual ability to resolve all contraries, Montaigne was entirely unpretentious in the same assumption of human dignity. For him, the natural condition of man is to make his way among enigmas, puzzles, antinomies, and contradictions, and to work through the paradoxes, physical, intellectual, and spiritual, that life invariably presents.

Such consistency as Montaigne attempted to achieve and to portray, is a consistency of method rather than of character. Indeed, he took particular pleasure in listing his qualities of variability, indecisiveness, inattention, absentmindedness, and inconsequence. Idleness, the creative idleness discovered by Renaissance artists,[26] writes his register of himself; Idleness

begets in me so many extravagant *Chimeraes*, and fantasticall monsters, so orderlesse, and without any reason, one hudling upon an other, that at leasure to view the foolishnesse and monstrous strangenesse of them, I have begun to keep a regis-

[26] See Rudolf and Margot Wittkower, *Born under Saturn* (London, 1963), pp. 59-63.

ter of them, hoping, if I live, one day to make [idleness] ashamed, and blush at himselfe. (i.viii.24)

He admits to no memory whatever, so that what he may have said one day he has forgotten by the next. Two juxtaposed essays, expressing diametrically opposed opinions, may therefore nonetheless be equally true records of his thought—or, by extension from Montaigne himself, the thoughts of every man.

Montaigne's calm in the face of psychological inconsistency, his confidence in the ultimate balance reached by the shifting personality, permitted him an intellectual prodigality few men were confident enough to risk. His novel decorum defied the masterly stylists and thinkers of the Renaissance by informality, illogicality, repetitiousness, and general disorder. The essays were left half-finished, or rewritten and revised, or not rewritten or revised, simply as his inclination dictated:

This hudling up of so much trash, or packing of so many several pieces, is done so strangely, as I never lay hands on it, but when an over lazie idlenesse urgeth me: and no where, but in mine owne house. So have it beene compact at sundry pauses, and contrived at severall intervalls, as occasions have sometime for many months together, here and there in other places, detained me. Besides, I never correct my first imaginations by the second, it may happen, I now and then alter some word, rather to diversifie, then to take any thing away. My purpose is, to represent the progresse of my humours, that every part be seene or member distinguished, as it was produced. I would to God I had begunne sooner, and knew the tracke of my changes, and course of my variations . . . I am growne elder by seaven or eight yeares since I beganne them; nor hath it beene without some new purchase. (ii.xxxvii.680)

Though "he would to God" he had begun keeping the register before he actually did, Montaigne nevertheless suffered with equanimity the loss of parts of his work to a light-fingered copyist. He was in no doubt of his creative power to make more essays, or of those essays' power to make readers: he could lose a few, without any threat to himself. The essay in which he tells about the copyist's theft, is one about Montaigne's aging health, the stone, and other infirmities the years had brought him. The greater part of the essay is devoted to his physical condition, his ailments, their cures, illnesses in general and their treatment. But its title is "Of the Resemblances betweene Children and Fathers," the matter of cynical discussion by worldlings. It is Montaigne's ill-health which provides the title—"The Antipathie, which is betweene me and [the physician's] arte, is to me hereditarie. My father lived three score and fourteene yeares: My grandfather three score and nine; my great grandfather very neare fourescore, and never tasted or tooke any kinde of Physicke."[27] The four men had compacted to "prove" an hypothesis: "It is now two hundred yeares; wanting but eighteene, that this Essay continueth with us: For, the first was borne in the yeare of our Lord one thousand foure hundred and two." Montaigne, alas, broke the strain and the experiment, seized as he was from his forty-eighth year with sundry ailments. The son of giants of health, in his frailty he had ceased to resemble his forebears. His own "children," though, do resemble him, as he stressed through the essays' collective length. The essays that are the register of his thoughts are "like" him, in his bad days and good, now defective, now well-written; however imperfect in accuracy and style, they are indisputably the record of someone, specifically, of a man with a certain recognizable habit of internal discourse. By their variety, Montaigne's essays are his true children—a paradox itself. They are,

[27] *Essayes*, ii.xxvii.685.

too, more than his children: they are both his original creation and his imitation of himself, both his children and himself. In another place, he wrote, "Here my booke and my selfe march together, and keepe one pace. Else-where one may commend or condemne the worke, without the workeman; heere not: who toucheth one toucheth the other."[28]

However much the style is the man, in one respect Montaigne spoke false. His book and he could never exactly "keepe one pace." In the process of living, the man is always ahead of the author, even though one may well suspect that, for Montaigne, the man ahead of the author did not feel himself entirely alive. To have full "possession"—Florio translated that word "holdfast"—of himself, Montaigne had to make his observation, to write the essay relevant to the life just lived through.[29] The man's sense of his own identity seems to have depended upon the process of assaying; even though by his own admission no such identity was ever possible—"never were there two opinions in the world, no more than two haires, or two graines."[30]

Obviously there was a sense in which Montaigne's register was all-important to him. But there was also a sense in which it was not. The *Essayes* weighed the man himself, for himself; their possible significance to others was, he asserted, irrelevant to him: "And if it happen no man read me, have I lost my time, to have entertained my selfe so many idle houres, about so pleasing and profitable thoughts?"[31] His self-regard is always evident. We know that he, quite literally, satisfied himself in the contempla-

[28] III.ii.726.
[29] This point is beautifully made by Georges Poulet in *Studies in Human Time* (New York: Harper Torchbook, 1956), pp. 43-46.
[30] *Essayes*, II.xxxvii.705.
[31] II.xvii.602.

tion of himself. The interest he took in himself as his own subject, describing and discovering parts of himself hitherto invisible to himself and certainly to the perceptions of others, is plain enough. Montaigne flaunted his natural *philautia* for all who cared to look. He indulged in the traditionally more involuted paradoxical self-reference as well. In a phrase worthy of the Erasmus of the *Encomion*, he said, "Were I a composer of books, I would keepe a register"—not of himself, but "of divers deaths, which in teaching men to die, should after teach them how to live."[32] The paradox is not just in the play on life and death: it is in the self-reference. Montaigne *is* a composer of books, and his book *does* teach men to live, and therefore how to die.

But for all his disclaimers, Montaigne's book was, and was intended to be, like its indolent and diffident author, a doer in the world, designed to effect moral ends and to correct moral defect. In a letter "To My Lady of Duras," he wrote of his hopes for himself and the book:

I make no account of goods, which I could not employ to the use of my life. Such as I am, so would I be elsewhere then in Paper. Mine art and industry have been employed to make myselfe of some worth. My study and endeavour to doe, and not to write. I have applied all my skill and devoire to frame my life. Lo-heere mine occupation and my worke. I am a lesse maker of bookes, then of any thing else . . . Good Lord (Madame) how I would hate such a commendation, to be a sufficient man in writing, and a foolish-shallow-headed braine or coxcombe in all things else. . . .   (II.xxxviii.703-04)

Certainly, Montaigne's concern is with man's living and doing within his regulated though hazardous society; but his major concern is with a man's relations to himself, his ordering of his own mind and emotions to his principles,

[32] I.xix.57.

and of his principles to the reach and capacity of his nature. Sometimes Montaigne's stress on habit, custom, and behavior becomes paradoxical, too, strongly stoical that it is: the essay "To Philosophize, is to Learne how to Die," is, in spite of its title, an essay not on death but on life and the conduct of life. The idea of death is a hazardous and untrustworthy idea, an idea that must be ordered so that a man in his lifetime shall not be unmanned by it. "[T]he premeditation of death," as Montaigne wrote, "is a forethinking of libertie. . . . To know how to die, doth free us from all subjection and constraint."[33] By means of paradoxical self-reference, he continued to draw attention to the paradoxicality central to this tenet of his doctrine: "Were I a composer of books, I would keep a register . . . which in teaching men to die, should after teach them to live." No man was surer of the pleasures of life than Montaigne, though also no man was less sure of life's values: and yet, remarkably, he seemed quite untroubled by the fact of his own extinction. That, too, he could contemplate in calm, as the title to another essay indicates, "That we Should not Judge of our Happinesse, untill after our Death," when, under normal conditions, a man is not the judge of his own happiness.[34]

For all the intensity of life, it is inevitably surrounded by death:

All the time you live, you steale it from death: it is at her charge. The continuall worke of your life, is to contrive death; you are in death, during the time you continue in life: for, you are after death, when you are no longer living. Or if you had rather have it so, you are dead after life: but during life, you are still dying: and death doth more rudely touch the dying, than the dead, and more lively and essentially.

(I.xix.59-60)

[33] I.xix.53.   [34] I.xviii.45-48.

For the living man, though, it is life, not death, that is felt. Even virtuous men, unafraid of death, feel their lives to be "all": "As our birth brought us the birth of all things, so shall our death the end of all things."[35] Man is his own world: but Montaigne was aware of the withering of that world with increased age. Age had weakened and diminished him: "What hereafter I shall be, will be but halfe a being, I shall be no more my selfe. I daily escape, and steale my selfe from my selfe."[36]

But though he himself tried by means of his essays to double the significance of the lived moments of his life,[37] Montaigne refused to waste a moment of life fearing the inevitable death. "[D]eath is a part of your selves: you flie from your selves,"[38] he said to men who feared death unduly. Again, he positively recommended the therapy of an occasional flight from the self:

. . . it is not enough, for a man to have sequestred himselfe from the concourse of people: it is not sufficient to shift place, a man must also sever himselfe from the popular conditions, that are in us. A man must sequester and recover himselfe from himselfe. (i.xxxviii.190)

Particularly must he do so when he fears—though the fearful self is a difficult self to escape successfully. "Our evill is rooted in our minde: and it cannot escape from it selfe." "We carry our fetters with us: it is not an absolute libertie"[39] which we enjoy. Part of the evil is fear of life, and fear of the end of life: part of it is in the very enchantment of living, the habit of reaction and sensation which fetters us to the comforts of our worldly lodging.

---

[35] i.xix.59.   [36] ii.xvii.581.

[37] ii.xvii.596: "Those have assured me of my hold-fast of them, and have given both the enjoying and possession thereof more absolute and more cleare."

[38] i.xix.59.   [39] i.xxxviii.190, 191.

But "Since God gives us leasure to dispose of our dislodging [, l]et us prepare our selves unto it, packe wee up our baggage. . . . Shake we off these violent hold-fasts, which else-where engage us, and estrange us from our selves."[40]

But however deep the penetration into the self's infinite labyrinth, the center is still the problematical self: the self reflected and reflected upon, the self self-regarded. Self-regard undid Narcissus, from man to flower; self-regard toppled Lucifer from heaven and drove Adam and Eve from paradise, with all men trooping subsequently into sin. With respect to pride and selfishness, clearly, Montaigne operated in the terms he so loved, of infinite regress: he steadily undermined the basis of humanist optimism about human nature. The ordinary record of his own qualities leaves little room for genuine greatness, genuine heroism in human affairs. Montaigne confutes Pico, so to speak, not by a public argument, but by empirical demonstration.

If Montaigne does not seem proud, that is his art: for he was extremely proud—of his originality in the sedulous pursuit of himself, of the fidelity of his observations. More than this, as is hardly necessary to say, Montaigne was self-absorbed in ways that no priest and few humanists could approve. As he did not scruple to report (disarmingly, in a moral double bluff), he easily fell into the traps set by *philautia*: "I continually tricke up my selfe; for I uncessantly describe my selfe."[41] Worse than this, self-love led him to pose, to paint himself as other—as better—than he really was:

In framing this pourtraite by my selfe, I have so often beene faine to frizle and trimme me, that so I might the better extract my selfe, that the patterne is thereby confirmed, and some sort formed. (II.xviii.602)

[40] I.xxxviii.192-93.
[41] II.vi.333-34.

In short, Montaigne presents here the puzzle left unsolved in Plato's theory of imitation: each constructed imitation is also a separate creation—in Montaigne's case, the confirmation of himself has also, as it should not actually have done, "made" something new, something different from the original. Montaigne has created, not just the mirror image, but a separate, limited, limiting, interpreting portrait. "Drawing my selfe for others, I have drawne my selfe with purer and better colours, then were my first."[42] Even so, the narcissistic self-regard that led him to do this, has its own kind of truth. To have done so, and to have recorded having done so, is to register the truth too. A self-regarding man has self-regard: he might be expected to "frizle and trimme" a little.

Infinite regress, in this case, the effort to make "A booke consubstantiall to his Author,"[43] is an endless re-creation, a re-creation that turns out to be creation, which in turn must be registered. Only with his death is Montaigne's occupation gone. So long as he lives, "with all his might, and with all his credit he engageth himselfe in a register of continuance."[44]

A fact of *continuance* is that it has no particular end, or, that such end as it has is accidental. The further one goes into one's self, the further one finds to go. The tighter one's holdfast upon one's self, the tighter one wants it to be. And yet not the world only, but this sort of intensive self-analysis has its estrangements. One is the subjective-objective split, inevitable in any operation of self-regarding or self-portraying. Montaigne often considered his own duplicities, both in the moral and the psychological sense: the deceptions of the self by the self, which mislead a man from the truth of his own being, the doubleness, at least, of every relational man pursuing his various duties and

[42] ii.xviii.602. [43] *Ibid.* [44] *Ibid.*, ii.xvii.602.

functions. "The Maior of *Bourdeaux*, and *Michael* Lord of *Montaigne*, have ever been two, by an evident separation,"[45] a separation which decreed the different interests, occupations, and preoccupations of the two aspects of one personality. Hence the problem of coming to terms with the elusive self, or selves, that one is, of forcing the divisive personality into a single integrity. "I engage my selfe with difficulty," Montaigne wrote; and yet, in the next sentence, "As much as I can, I employ my selfe wholly to my selfe."[46]

But even that reflexive operation gives no assurance that Montaigne could keep his judgment clear:[47] again and again he records having seduced himself into folly, a particular kind of folly that he has come to recognize as his own: "I am not bound to utter no follies, so I be not deceived to know them: And wittingly to erre, is so ordinarie in me, that I erre not much otherwise; and seldome erre casually."[48]

That is, his errors, if initially unconscious, are brought irrevocably to his consciousness by the recording of them —and that consciousness in turn can lead to further manifestations of folly. "How often and peradventure foolishly, have I enlarged my Booke to speake of himselfe?"[49] he asked. The answer was,

I had rather understand my selfe well in my selfe, then in *Cicero*. Out of the experience I have of my selfe, I find sufficient ground to make my selfe wise, were I but a proficient scholler.   (III.xiii.971)

Certainly there was much that Montaigne learned about himself. He was a diligent if not a proficient scholar of that

[45] III.x.916.   [46] III.x.909.

[47] II.xvii.591: here Montaigne gives an account of his absent-mindedness and unhandiness.

[48] II.xvii.592.   [49] III.xiii.967.

subject, and his references to his waverings, his debates with himself, his frank presentation of his weakness and defects, testify to his increased self-knowledge, but they also led him to the conclusion, so familiar by now, that "A man must learne, that he is but a foole."[50] The paradoxical recognition is necessarily the end of knowledge, since the more one knows about one's self, the less one knows that one knows. And yet a man is a labyrinthine subject of regard, continually "rouled" into himself:

My selfe, who professe nothing else, finde [in my selfe] so bottomlesse a depth, and infinite variety, that my apprentisage hath no other fruit, than to make me perceive how much more there remaineth for me to learne. (III.xiii.972)

That "much more" inevitably confirms the doctrine of learned ignorance: *"Wisdome hath hir excesses, and no lesse need of moderation, then follie."*[51] Wisdom about one's self particularly leads to the conviction of folly:

When by others reason, I finde my selfe convicted of a false opinion, I learne not so much, what a new thing hee hath told me; and this particular ignorance; which were but a small purchase, as in generall I learne mine owne imbecility and weakenesse, and the treason of my understanding. . . . A man must learne, that he is but a foole: A much more ample and important instruction. (III.xiii.971)

That lesson is driven home again and again, chiefly in Montaigne's longest and most important essay, "An Apologie of Raymond Sebond," one of the most learned arguments in the literature—for nescience. The "Apologie" is a complicated piece of paradoxy: it denies its expressed aim, since it does not defend but destroys the position Sebond held; it calls into question, for good and all, the Renaissance praise of man, of human dignity, and of human rea-

---

[50] III.xiii.971.   [51] III.v.756.

son, thus running strikingly counter to "received opinion."
Most of all, throughout its length, the "Apologie" operates by a contradictory method, most learnedly adducing
all the evidence, from the world of learning as well as
from the world of experience, to demonstrate the ignorance
of mankind. Montaigne brings in evidence for his position
all the contradictory opinions about life, truth, and the
sources of truth that the philosophers of antiquity had
stressed. He detaches human experience not only from
reason but also from faith; in the end, he expresses his
tautological view of the autonomy and incommunicability
of each individual man's thought and perception. As for
perception in general, it is entirely untrustworthy: he adduces difference in sensations relative to health (as in the
case of wine, tasting sweet when the drinker is healthy,
bitter when he is ill), as well as the misleading effects of
water-refraction ("an Oare crooked in the water, and
streight to them that see it above water"); and the peculiar
sensation of touching a bullet with the tips of two crossed
fingers ("To roule a bullet under the fore-finger, the
midlemost being put over it, a man must very much en-
force himselfe, to affirme there is but one, so assuredly
doth our sense present us two").[52] As the senses normally
mislead, so does custom, endorsing in one place what is
criminal in another. The process of thought itself is no
less duplicitous: the Skeptics, whose model in this very
essay Montaigne follows, mislead by their inquiries into
subjects:

They put forth their propositions, but to contend with those,
they imagine wee hold in our conceipt. If you take theirs, then
they will undertake to maintaine the contrary: all is one to
them, nor will they give a penny to chuse. If you propose that
snow is blacke, they wil argue on the other side, that it is

[52] II.xii.529, 536.

white. If you say that it is neither one nor other, they will maintaine it to be both. If by a certaine judgement, you say that you cannot tell, they will maintaine that you can tell. Nay, if by an affirmative axiome, you sweare that you stand in some doubt, they will dispute, that you doubt not of it, or that you cannot judge, or maintaine, that you are in doubt.

(II.xii.449)

Whosoever shall imagine a perpetuall confession of ignorance, and a judgement upright and without staggering, to what occasion soever may chance; That man conceives the true Phyrronisme [*sic*]. (II.xii.451)

"A perpetuall confession of ignorance, and a judgement upright and without staggering" is a difficult posture for any man to maintain—far more difficult, really, than to maintain an upright judgment while trusting in man's knowledge or one's own wisdom. In many ways, Montaigne serves warning on the High Renaissance in this essay, has marshaled the evidence against man's belief in himself, has reduced man to a being by his very nature— and also, by the nature of things, according to reason and the evidence—fundamentally uncertain, outside all comforts but a delusive self-deception. Montaigne has fulfilled in this essay the difficult dictates of the *docta ignorantia topos*, by a scrupulous display of his command of knowledge and information refuting all claims to all and any knowledge or information; and he has called his own alleged intention into question as well. Reason cannot be trusted to make any affirmation—the very structure of language "lies," resulting in the end in the Liar paradox;[53] but reason and language can be trusted, to the extent that

[53] II.xii.472: "If you say, it is faire weather, and in so saying, say true; it is faire weather then. Is not this a certaine forme of speech? Yet it will deceive us: That it is so; Let us follow the example: If you say, I lye, and that you should say true, you lye then."

they cancel themselves out, to leave the only alternative clear to a mankind reduced to absurdity. That alternative is faith, rational choice in an irrational universe: faith in an immutable, consistent, omnipotent, and entirely hidden God. Citing familiar sources, Augustine, Plato, Cicero, and Paul, Montaigne returned again and again to the theme of a learned (and happy, as in Traherne's assertion) ignorance.

> The simple and the ignorant (saith S. *Paul*) raise themselves up to heaven, and take possession of it; whereas we withall the knowledge we have, plunge our selves down to the pit of hell.   (II.xii.443)

In the end, Montaigne managed to sweep everything away, in a virtuoso display of the "ablative method"; all the securities the world offers are reduced to vanity, to nothing, to emptiness, and man is left alone and undefended to face his unalterable alienation in a void. Naturally he chooses faith in a transcendent deity: to know one's self comes in the end to the fact that one cannot know one's self, because one has no instruments to plumb the depths of that ever-changing creature, and because, really, one has not the means to know anything at all, not even, or especially not, one's self. In the "Apologie" Montaigne carried the method to extremes, denied everything, even the validity of his method designed to "repeat," or reproduce, himself. As he says,

> My profession is not to know the truth, nor to attaine it. I rather open than discover things. *The wisest man that ever was being demanded what he knew, answered, he knew that he knew nothing.* He verified what some say, that the greatest part of what we know, is the least part of what we know not: that is, that that which we thinke to know, is but a parcel, yea and a small particle of our ignorance.   (II.xii.447)

Insofar as this conclusion is accepted, then of course Montaigne's effort to "repeat" himself is doubly doomed: he can never uncover "all"—even of the most shallow character, and his own character, as it turned out, was far from shallow. A mirror reflection, furthermore, is itself deceptive, since it gives back to the viewer the reflection only of what is turned toward the mirror. In self-portraits of artists painting, the left hand (the right hand in fact) is usually somehow concealed, huddled out of the way, since except in a paradoxical drawing, with no body, or nobody, attached to it, no man can draw his drawing hand while he is drawing it. In the same way, the weighing, the assaying, of the self, is always short: one cannot catch up on one's self to weigh it "all," not and register its weight at the same time. The author's book is not so much the essays themselves, which necessarily give short weight, but the record of the assaying. The man is the instrument of his own measurement. The man must be, however humble or unimportant in fact, vaster and more labyrinthine than any collection of essays. "To conclude, all this galiemafry which I huddle-up here, is but a register of my lives' Essayes"—the record of the record-taking, the self-conscious recapturing of the meaning, the lack of meaning, and the meaning in lack of meaning in the life of one ordinary man "moyen sensuel." But the essays have their miraculous aspect: fruits of Montaigne's idleness that they were, the essays were created, like God's original Creation, out of emptiness, and were created, as God had created the world, in idleness; like God's Creation, they were of universal importance, and they were, however defective, the animate substance of their creator, "consubstantiall" with the author.

Hee hath past his life in idlenesse, say we; alas I have done nothing this day. What? Have you not lived? It is not onely the fundamentall, but the noblest of your occupation.

(III.xiii.1005)

Life is unstable, dreamlike, insecure, but it is an occupation for a man, after all: the opportunity offered (the only opportunity offered) for a man to know himself. Montaigne's occupation was that "booke consubstantiall with" himself: he was his subject and object, he was reader and critic of the book; he measured and considered his shifting weight, and found that multifold occupation entirely sufficient.

And, if it happen that no man read me, have I lost my time, to have entertained my selfe so many idle houres, about so pleasing and profitable thoughts? . . . Have I mis-spent my time, to have taken an account of my selfe so continually and so curiously?

(II.xviii.602)

If no one were to read him and the book lie useless, shall he have misspent his life after all, in the delusion that he was sufficient reward to himself? And shall his self-analysis, so unguarded and so undefensive, prove in the end merely folly? Might Montaigne have lived more gloriously had Montaigne been more willing to "frizle and trimme" his portrait? Nothing, in fact, was to be gained by further misrepresentation: "Who so falsifieth the [Word], betraieth publick society." But for a man who is his own subject, object, amusement, recreation, critic, teacher, to falsify his word is to falsify himself not merely to the public, but to himself as well: and thus to strike fatally at his own integrity. Lying is the destruction of a man in his honor— "Is there any more manifest, than for a man to eate and deny his owne Word?"[54]

[54] II.xviii.603.

Given human nature, given the nature Montaigne has sketched out as his own, no self-reference can be "true." The truest record is false, just as the greatest or the most accurate knowledge is also false: and self-reference focuses all the "normal" fallacies of life to one center. As the Liar paradox is simply grammar turning on itself, logic turning on itself, so is self-reference simply assertion turning on itself. In self-reference any assertion, however "true," must also be a denial: self-assertion is equally self-denial. Self-reference is a contradiction in terms of its self—not just the spectacular "Apologie," but Montaigne's whole book is therefore paradoxical by nature. The "Apologie" is the most paradoxical, the most focused, the most extreme example of the whole enterprise; but the enterprise itself, the public display of a man engaged in the most intimate self-regard, is paradox. Like Erasmus' *Encomion*, where Folly calls her own discourse into question at the end, and the reader is left wondering, like Pilate, about the nature of truth, so Montaigne, another wise fool, intransigently followed his Skeptical logic to question the questionable enterprise to which he had devoted most intensely the most selfless energies of his noticeably selfish life.

13

The Rhetoric of Transcendent Knowledge

... the first day of our Jubilee is death ...
Browne, *Religio Medici*, I. 44

I. TRADITIONS OF PARADOX IN
RENAISSANCE VERSE-EPISTEMOLOGIES

THE period in European thought from 1550 to 1650, just before the great schematic reformulations of the Enlightenment, displayed a prodigal enthusiasm for speculation into the nature of things. The nature of man, the nature of God and of His Son, the nature of nature itself —all were primary subjects for investigation during that century. Montaigne is properly the secular patron of the investigation, with his catholic interests, his intelligent if transient commitment to a variety of philosophical positions, his talent for combination, for paradox and surprise, as well as his remarkable concern both for himself and for his society. The work of the generation after Montaigne bore his stamp (and in England, Florio's)[1] not only upon the subject and style of its speculations, but in the lack of prescribed system, the flexibility, the toleration, and the nonchalance with which Montaigne faced the implications of the philosophical materials he assayed. Most of all, the generation after Montaigne followed his lead in self-conscious speculation about the processes of the mind, about, in short, human understanding.

[1] See particularly Frances A. Yates, *John Florio* (Cambridge University Press, 1933). I am indebted to conversations with John B. Jarzavek for a realization of the range and depth of Montaigne's influence upon English literature in the seventeenth century.

In his inconstancy and his eclecticism, Montaigne conveniently reflects both the philosophical openness of the period (that amateurishness of which more traditional logicians complained so bitterly) and the practice of the Christian tradition itself. In spite of a reputation for doctrinal intolerance, Christianity has throughout its history proved remarkably adaptable to different philosophical systems, or parts of them; in many ways, distorted though they have been within Christianity, western philosophies have been preserved within Christian orthodoxy. Platonism, Neoplatonism, Aristotelianism, Stoicism, and Skepticism all found their way into the Christian tradition. Once the great Renaissance shift away from orthodoxy had taken place, in religion, in political theory and practice, in geography and cosmology, in economics, there was opportunity for intellectual recombination, deliberate and random: Montaigne's stout corpus of essays is not only the record of one man's inner life but also a convex mirror reflection of the intellectual universe in which he lived. No stock adjective can characterize the speculative activity of Montaigne, or of the Renaissance: no scheme reduces to a single formulation their irregular, independent, and arbitrary activities.

For various reasons, the kinds of speculation current in the Renaissance resulted in a rich variety of formally stated paradoxes—paradoxes in faith and doctrine, in philosophy, in the natural sciences, and in the literary and visual arts. This chapter describes the natural coincidence of several traditions of paradox in epistemological thought. It attempts to show how the "epistemological paradox" became one of the poetic themes of the late Renaissance, as well as how, once that paradox entered poetry, poetry by its own operation enriched the traditional paradoxes of content by an appropriate rhetoric.

The epistemological speculations of antiquity bequeathed

a rich legacy of paradoxy: Parmenides and his pupil Zeno contributed to their followers, the Stoics, the paradoxical dialectic designed to persuade that, despite all appearances to the contrary, the many are in fact one.[2] In the hands of the Sophists, enemies of monism, the paradox became a standard rhetorical category, an argument contrary to common opinion and expectation, often contrary to truth, designed to display the power of argument.

Though the Sophists contributed to the Skeptical tradition, they cannot be counted as serious Skeptics, since they did not so much doubt truth as dismiss truth altogether. The Sophist had, like Prufrock, "known them all already, known them all," until all "truths" came to seem to him merely the commodities of relative and expediential value. The Skeptic, on the other hand, was more philosophical: he attempted the exhausting intellectual task of doubting his way through all the hypotheses presented to him. Skepticism is not for the insecure man, for radical doubt does not lead to certain conclusions: it is, like the Sophists' *techne*, more a method than a system of philosophy.

To make his relativist point, the Skeptic exploits the appearances of truth, develops the inconsistencies, contradictions, and problems of philosophical systems, whether singly or together, and thus naturally expresses himself in paradox. When Skeptical doubt and Stoical monism collide or coincide, as they habitually did in Renaissance speculation, the paradox involved is often double and triple—double, because both Stoic and Skeptical methods employed formal and rhetorical paradoxes, often very traditional ones; triple, because there was inevitable "paradox," or contradiction, in the coincidence of attitudes so strikingly opposed.

[2] For Renaissance readers the most readily available Stoical paradoxes, edited by Erasmus, were Cicero's *Paradoxa Stoicorum*.

The elements of the two systems concurred very often. Montaigne himself, that constant reader of Plutarch and Seneca, with whose maxims he decorated his study, took the Pyrrhonist part in his greatest and most sustained essay, "The Apologie of Raymond Sebond." Among his other tortures, Hamlet was stretched on the rack of a Stoicism appropriate to the son of Denmark's king and the Horatian Skepticism of modernist Wittenberg. For all sorts of reasons, Stoicism and Skepticism provided methods for dealing with the excitements, confusions, and disruptions of late Renaissance thought. The first offered against a too pressing world the traditional bulwark of ethical single-mindedness; the second permitted indefinite postponement of commitment to any idea or set of ideas. Montaigne and Hamlet, like many a lesser man, balanced the two philosophies against each other.[3]

Stoicism and Skepticism not only concurred, they also conjoined with Christianity. With its assertion of a single truth absolute against a bewildering confusion of accidentals, of a single natural law, of a philanthropic morality nonetheless capable of detachment from ordinary mortal concerns, Stoicism was an obvious support to Christianity, as the list of Renaissance Christian Stoics shows.[4]

[3] For the literary background of Renaissance Stoicism, see Robert Hoopes, *Right Reason in the English Renaissance* (Harvard University Press, 1962); for Skepticism, see Richard Popkin, *A History of Skepticism from Erasmus to Descartes* (Assen, Holland, 1960). Victor Harris' *All Coherence Gone* (University of Chicago Press, 1949) provides an account of naturalistic pessimism in the seventeenth century.

[4] It includes the flower of Roman and Protestant orthodoxy: Erasmus, Calvin, Lipsius, the Scaligers, Agrippa, Du Plessis Mornay, La Primaudaye, Montaigne, Sidney, Greville, Spenser, Donne, and Milton, to name only some of the legitimate children of the titled line. Cadet branches are more difficult to number and bastards impossible.

The Stoic's chief duty, like the Christian's, was to know himself. Detachment from the world, for which the Stoic had at hand instruction in a hundred books of morality and a thousand ready maxims, necessarily involved him in detaching himself also from the sciences that interpreted the world. All the same, the Stoic could not take hasty refuge in a blank anti-intellectualism; he was obliged to understand those sciences. For the Stoic, to know himself meant to know the world of which he was a part. To know what he was, he had to know exactly what he was giving up, what he was subtracting himself from—or, he had to know what he was not.

This is, of course, a paradox, one result of which is, for example, the spectacle of an extraordinarily learned man, Erasmus, learnedly doubting in *The Praise of Folly* (perhaps even denying) all that he had come to know, as well as the methods by which he had come to know what he knew. Another result is the sight of another learned man, Henry Cornelius Agrippa, rejecting the supernatural learning he had been at such pains to gather. After he had written his huge defense and compendium of occult philosophy, Agrippa denied out of hand the worth of that study, and published a systematic derogation of all the arts and sciences of the learned world. His *Vanity of Arts and Sciences* owed its being, though, to his thirst for knowledge; his invention sprang from his own passions:

. . . the name of Cornelius in his vanity of Learning was famous, not only among the *Germanes*, but also other Nations; for Momus himself carpeth at all amongst the gods; amongst the Heroes, *Hercules* hunteth after Monsters; amongst the divels *Pluto* the King of hell is angry with all the ghosts; amongst the Philosophers *Democritus* laugheth at all things, on the contrary, *Heraclitus* weepeth at all things; *Pirrhias* is ignorant of all things; *Aristotle* thinketh he knoweth all things; *Diogenes* contemneth all things; this *Agrippa* spareth none, he contemneth, knows, is ignorant, weeps, laughs, is angry, pursueth, carps at all things, being himself a Philosopher, a Demon, an Heroes [*sic*], a god, and all things.[5]

He "knows, is ignorant, weeps, laughs": the tone of Agrippa's work tells us that it denies itself. The critic dare not assign Agrippa the role he seems to demand, for in demanding to be believed, he presents us also with the evidence for disbelieving him. Even his retractations do not leave Agrippa's ultimate view of knowledge very clear.[6]

Most Stoical writing is less ticklish than Agrippa's, or Erasmus'—less Skeptical, one might say; Stoical writing is habitually plain to the point of boredom. Three very influential Stoical works, however, were far from boring, and were thus widely read and calmly plundered: Philippe du Plessis Mornay's two books, one on religion, the other on self-knowledge,[7] and Pierre de la Primaudaye's compendium of all knowledge, *The French Academie*.[8] For both authors, a strong Christian Stoicism dominates their doctrine and their view of the world. Both were men of the real world and knew that knowledge of one's self involved above all things knowledge of the world, as well

[5] Henry Cornelius Agrippa, *Three Books of Occult Philosophy*, trans. J. F. (London, 1651), "Life."

[6] Agrippa's *Occult Philosophy* (*De occulta philosophia libri tres*, Cologne, 1533) contains his retractation of his earlier *Vanity of Arts and Sciences* (*De incertitudine et vanitate scientiarum, et artium*, Cologne, 1530). See also his *Apologia adversus calumnias propter declamationem de vanitate scientiarum* ([Cologne], 1533).

[7] Philippe du Plessis Mornay, *De la vérité de la religion Chrestienne* (Antwerp, 1581); I cite from the English translation by Sir Philip Sidney and Arthur Golding, *A Woorke concerning the Trewnesse of the Christian Religion* (London, 1587); and *The True Knowledge of a Mans owne Selfe*, trans. A[nthony] M[unday] (London, 1602).

[8] Pierre de la Primaudaye, *Academie françoise* (Paris, 1577); trans. Thomas Bowes[?] (London, 1618).

as sufficient judgment to reject the world and a will ready to receive true revelation. With Erasmus, Agrippa, and the Stoic moralist Du Vair,[9] Du Plessis Mornay and La Primaudaye counsel ultimate attention to spiritual matters, through the gradual mastery and rejection of the things of this world.

Like the Skeptics, the Stoics recognized the importance of the senses in transmitting, however inadequately, information about the external world to the human mind. Inviolable right reason dwelt, for them, among the extremely transitory data of human lives. So Du Vair could say, "Silence is the father of discourse and the fountaine of reason,"[10] an axiom which could be explicated into sense (called reason) only after considerable reflection. The Stoic system of ethics was full of such ambiguities, dependent for their formulation upon the inward life of a reflective man. After all, when the world is reduced to a "thing indifferent," when a man's senses and reason must measure the whole world, when values are turned into value judgments, paradoxes like Du Vair's are inevitable. The world becomes a set of indeterminate circumstances, as Stoical meditation attests. In spite of natural law, each Stoic makes his own interpretations of the world, invests the world with the qualities he judges it to have. As Du Vair said,

For by this meanes wee shall come to know, that griefe and pleasure are drawne both of them out of the same well, if a man have but the skill to turne his bucket when he would fill

[9] Guillaume du Vair, *De la constance et consolation des calamitez publiques* (Rouen, 1604), trans. as *A Buckler against Adversitie; or a Treatise of Constancie,* by Andrew Court (London, 1622); Du Vair, *The Moral Philosophie of the Stoicks,* trans. Thomas James (London, 1598).

[10] Du Vair, *Moral Philosophie,* p. 188.

it with either: for the use is all in a thing, and every thing as it is used is good or bad.[11]

When even Stoics view the external world so subjectively, paradoxes can be counted upon to appear.

One fundamental tenet of Stoicism, however, tended to counteract the subjectivism to which the system sometimes led: the belief in an external, objective natural law, by which all things from the beginning had been providentially organized by the deity. Belief in natural law runs parallel to belief in innate right reason, with which every man is endowed; and exploits the notion that all knowledge, however partial or partially apprehended, ultimately derives, both externally by natural law and internally by right reason, from the word and work of God. The theory implies, though it does not insist, that all knowledge is good. The natural law theory was extremely useful in Renaissance thought, since it provided a ready-made justification for the study of external nature. God had created an orderly nature, both in the world and in the mind of man; one way to know Him was to know His works, including one's self.

Since one knows by the senses before one can know by right reason, the Stoic was not lightly anti-sensationalist. Du Plessis Mornay included among atheists not only those whose wit denied God, but also those whose senses denied Him, those who refused to read God's word from "natural law," from the "book" of His steady and orderly creation.[12] Morally, too, the senses held the balance of salvation, for only by the proper regulation on earth of his senses might a man's reason bring him into the salvation promised by faith.

By the same theory, another way to know God was to

[11] *Ibid.*, pp. 106-07.
[12] Du Plessis Mornay, *Trewnesse*, "Epistle Dedicatorie."

know the workings of one's own mind.[13] For the antique Stoic and his Christian descendant, epistemology was a problem in morality, that of the relation of the reason to the soul, or of the intelligence to the will. In Stoic philosophy and free-will Christianity, that relation is crucial, since his choosing reason relates a man's multiple behavior to the single truth of God. Though Christian Stoics were committed to the orthodox view that ultimate truth is beyond the reach both of reason and the senses, they put their faith in common human reason to lead man to the point where faith takes on the burden of truth and makes revelation credible. As Du Plessis Mornay put it,

so farre off is Reason from abasing fayth, to make us attaine thereto, that contrariwise shee lifteth us up as it were upon her shoulders, to make us to see it, and to take it for our guide, as the only thing that can bring us to God; and the onely schoolemistresse of whom we ought to learn our salvation.[14]

Neo-Stoic defenders of religious truth insisted on the value of knowledge in general, on the value of sense evidence derived from a world created good, and on the conviction that knowledge is possible and the attainment of knowledge part of man's obligation.[15] The Skeptic punctured such conventional securities. Montaigne's "Que scay-je?" provoked, not a resolute justification of things as they had been considered to be, but a relativist consideration of man's variability, fragility, and waywardness in a world fluid, variable, and broken.[16] Like the Stoics on whom he

[13] See, *inter alia*, Du Plessis Mornay, *True Knowledge*, "The Epistle Dedicatorie," and *Trewnesse*, "Epistle Dedicatorie."

[14] Du Plessis Mornay, *Trewnesse*, "Epistle to the Reader."

[15] See Howard Schulz, *Milton and Forbidden Knowledge* (New York, 1955), for a discussion of the ethics of knowledge going far beyond the limits suggested in the book's title.

[16] Montaigne, "Apologie," *Essayes*, ii.xii.385-547; see above, Chapter 12.

modeled so much of his style of life and letters, Montaigne was forced back into himself for his intellectual and moral definitions. Unlike the Stoics, though, Montaigne could never fully acquiesce either in the idea of a right reason common to all mankind or in the idea of a universal law of nature. His "Apologie" is the classic Renaissance statement of the dilemmas of knowledge, with all their intricate interrelatedness. Montaigne's disciple, Pierre Charron, affords by his simplicity more economical Skeptical truisms than his master does. (Like John Donne's work, Montaigne's is excerpted at the critic's peril. Charron is less complex.) Charron began with the classical and Christian maxim, to know one's self; and he knew from Montaigne the difficulty of this riddling and lifelong task. Unlike Montaigne, who moved in and out of paradox without warning and without preparation, Charron codified the antinomies, contradictions, and paradoxes of Skepticism in his handbook. At the end of Charron's *Of Wisdome*, the reader finds real difficulty in distinguishing his message from the Stoical one, for, like Du Plessis Mornay, like La Primaudaye, Charron laid his command ultimately upon the human will, to choose well among the bewildering data presented to the human mind.[17] The greater part of his teaching simply counsels the proper control and direction of the passions. In an ultimate anomaly, then, the teachings of the two schools of thought traditionally opposed, Stoicism and Skepticism, turn out to be identical.

The connection of Stoicism and Skepticism in Renaissance thought is not simply complementary. Renaissance thinkers did not typically go through a Skeptical, then a Stoical phase,[18] or *vice versa*; it is that their subject matter

[17] Pierre Charron, *De la sagesse* (Bordeaux, 1601); trans. as *Of Wisdome*, by Samson Lennard (London, 1608), pp. 336, 467-68.
[18] Louis I. Bredvold, "The Religious Thought of Donne in Relation to Medieval and Later Traditions," *University of Michigan*

was fundamentally similar, no matter how different their message. If one were to attempt excision of either his Stoicism or his Skepticism from Erasmus' works, for instance, or from Montaigne's, or from the utterances of Hamlet, there would be little left, for the ideas were interrelated and inseparable. Erasmus, Montaigne, and Hamlet, together with the host of Stoic writers concerned with knowing themselves, were engaged in something other than the moral self-examination required by religious tradition and exemplified in manuals of devotional meditation, but in something more cutting, the self-conscious effort to understand understanding, their own and that of mankind. In late Renaissance England, this enterprise became the subject of poetry, in such works as Sir John Davies' *Nosce teipsum*,[19] Fulke Greville's *Treatie of Humane Learning*,[20] John Davies of Hereford's *Mirum in modum, Summa totalis*, and *Witte's Pilgrimage*,[21] and John Donne's Anniversary Poems. These strongly Christian poems are all in the Stoical tradition and owe a debt to their Skeptical inheritance; their poets were engaged in fulfilling their Christian-humanist obligation to know themselves, and to know how they knew what they knew.[22]

Sir John Davies' poem, published in 1599, begins with the traditional antithesis between principle and practice, between form and appearance:

Publications in Language and Literature, 1 (1925), 193-232; "The Intellectual Milieu of John Dryden," *University of Michigan Publications in Language and Literature*, XII (1934).

[19] (London, 1599).

[20] Fulke Greville, *A Treatie of Humane Learning*, in *Poems and Dramas*, ed. Geoffrey Bullough (London, 1945), I. 154-91. All references are to this edition.

[21] John Davies of Hereford, *The Complete Works*, ed. Alexander B. Grosart (2 vols., London, 1878).

[22] See Louis I. Bredvold, "The Sources Used by Davies in *Nosce Teipsum*," *PMLA*, XXXVIII (1923), 745-69.

> Why did my parents send me to the schooles,
>> That I with Knowledge might enrich my mind?
>> Since the *desire to know* first made men fooles
>> And did corrupt the root of all mankind?[23]

Flawed by that first tricky "desire to know," "What can we know? or what can we discern?" Can man hope to know more than "the wisest of all Morall men," who said of himself that *"he knew nought, but that he nought did know"*? (p. 4) One after another, Davies dismisses the vanities of learning, to return ultimately to the proper study of mankind:

> My self am *Center* of my circling thought,
> Onely *my selfe* I studie, learne, and know. (p. 8)

For Davies, as for Montaigne, Charron, Scaliger, and the other memorialists of human limitation, human existence was made up of contrarieties:

> I know my Bodi's of so fraile a kinde
>> As force without, feavers within can kill;
>> I know the heavenly nature of my minde,
>> But tis corrupted both in *wit* and *will*:
>
> I know my *Soule* hath power to know all things,
>> Yet is she blind and ignorant in all;
>> I know I am one of *Natures* litle kings,
>> Yet to the least and vilest things am thrall.
>
> I know my life's a paine, and but a span,
>> I know my *Sense* is mockt with every thing;
>> And to conclude, I know my selfe a *Man*,
>> Which is a *proud*, and yet a *wretched* thing. (p. 8)

External nature provided for Davies a less sure guide to truth than the natural law had provided the antique

---

[23] *Nosce teipsum* (London, 1599), p. 1. All further references to Sir John Davies' poem are to this edition.

Stoics. Furthermore, the sixteenth-century world, under-
going its geographical and cosmographical reconstruction,
inevitably delivered such contradictory data to the senses
and the judgment that a man had slight chance at arriving
at a just assessment of the physical and intellectual world.
The soul, however, has deeper perceptions than the mind
and is capable of reaching fundamental truths: the soul
can know substances, not merely skins of things: can know
the nature of, say, a tree, not just the look of a particular
bark or leaf; can recognize true concords, not just the
heterogeneous noises of natural things. The senses have
their inadequate uses (Davies followed Du Plessis Mornay
in regarding as "senseless" those Epicurean advocates of
sense experience alone), but only the soul can transcend
human contradictions. The soul is both substantial and
spiritual, active and passive, reflective and creative; only
the soul possesses the nobly paradoxical qualities and functions that Davies defends with all his wit and will:

> When without hands she thus doth Castels build,
>> Sees without eyes, and without feete doth runne,
>> When she digests the World, yet is not fild,
>> By her owne power these miracles are done. (p. 14)

Under the exercise of the soul's power, material limitations disappear, and with them, definitions also disappear.
As the image of God in man, the soul contains everything
in its proper place. It travels with all imaginable speed;
like the deity, is at once here and there; combines the
separate empires of wit and will into the single search for
the true wisdom of God:

> Now God the *Truth* and *first of causes* is,
>> God is the last *goodend*, which lasteth still,
>> Being *Alpha* and *omega* nam'd for this,
>> *Alpha* to wit, *omega* to the will.   (p. 59)

The puns indicate Davies' need for a rhetoric to transcend ordinary descriptive, even metaphorical, statements, and to express the transcendence which is his subject. "The last goodend" and "alpha to wit" begin and end, without setting limits to, the idea of God's perfect knowledge of Himself and all His works.

In spite of occasional syntactical tricks, though, Davies' basic lesson is as direct and unparadoxical as he could make it. Since his subject, the soul, is by traditional definition ultimately unknowable, the poet must rely upon both the general epistemological tradition of paradox and its special development in the paradoxes of the negative theology.[24] Because of its Platonic likeness to the deity, the One in Whom the many are subsumed, the soul and all its operations could also be expressed in the paradoxes of the negative theology.

Like his courtly namesake, John Davies of Hereford was a deeply religious man deeply concerned in the organization of knowledge under God. Though he too believed that "The 'externall *Sences* serve the common *Sence*," and that Reason "useth every *Sences* facultie,"[25] the deficiencies of sense were perfectly evident to him:

But yet in cases of our constant faith
Wee *Faith* beleeve, and give our Sence the lie,
Nay, whatsoe're our humane reason saith,
If it our faith gainesay, we it deny:
On highest heights Faith hir foundation laith,
Which never can be seene of mortall eye.
　　For if *Faith*, say, a *Maid* may be a *Mother*,
　　Though *Sence* gainesay it, wee beleeve the other.
If *Faith* affirme, that God a man may bee,
(A mortall man and live, and die with paine)
We it believe, though how, we cannot see,

---

[24] See above, Chapters 3 and 4.
[25] Davies of Hereford, *Mirum in Modum*, *Works*, I. 9.

For heere strong *Faith* doth headstrong *Reas'n* restraine:
And with the truth compells hir to agree,
Lest she should over-runne hir selfe in vaine:
So, if *Faith* say one's three, and three is one,
Though *Sence* say no, we *Faith* believe alone.[26]

Only God, the *summa totalis* of a later poem by the same
man, could finally compose the contradictions all men invariably experience in their sublunary lives. Didactic poetry, this is: even less than Sir John Davies does Davies
of Hereford show the transcendence of truth.

In 1633 Greville's *Treatie of Humane Learning*, which
deals with the same problems as those raised by the other
poets, was finally published. Stoic, Platonist, and Christian
determinist, Greville knew and set down at once the difficulties of his task:

The Mind of Man, is this worlds true dimension;
And *Knowledge* is the measure of the minde:
And as the minde, in her vast comprehension,
Containes more worlds than all the world can finde:
So *Knowledge* doth it selfe farre more extend,
Than all the minds of Men can comprehend.[27]

Unknowable knowledge demands the paradoxical expression to which Sir John Davies had had to turn earlier:

A climbing height it is without a head,
Depth without bottome, Way without an end,
A Circle with no line environed;
Not comprehended, all it comprehends;
  Worth infinitude, yet satisfies no minde,
  Till it that infinite of the God-head finde. (1. 154)

After such a beginning, an encomium of knowledge and
of the human mind, Greville then proceeds—by rhetorical
rather than syntactical paradox—to argue against the per-

[26] *Ibid.*, 1. 12.   [27] Greville, *Poems and Dramas*, 1. 154.

fections of the human mind and to present, not its marvelous transcendent wholeness, but its defects in all its parts. He too exposes the vanity of all the arts and sciences, as well as the vanity of the creature who, in his temerity, thinks that he comprehends them. In failing to clarify precisely, the human understanding may positively mislead:

> Againe, we see the best Complexions vaine,
> And in the worst more nimble subtilty;
> From whence *Wit, a distemper of the braine*;
> The Schooles conclude, and our capacity;
> > How much more sharper, the more it apprehends,
> > Still to distract, and lesse truth comprehends. (I. 159)

No man has ever been able to prove a single thing past doubt—

> Of perfect *demonstration*, who yet gave
> > One clear example? Or since time began
> > What one true *forme* found out by wit of Man. . . .
> > > (I. 160)

Astronomy, philosophy, rhetoric, music, geometry—all is vanity. Practitioners of these arts are mere quarrelers for personal preeminence. If the arts and sciences, those tools of truth, are based on error, how can a man choose among truths to reach any final, ultimate truth? He is required, after all, by the reality he cannot fail to recognize, to put the dangerous, destructive, Skeptical question:

> A *Science* never scientificall,
> A *Rhapsody* of questions controverted;
> In which because men know no truth at all,
> To every purpose it can be converted:
> > Judge then what grounds this can to others give,
> > That waved ever in it selfe must live? (I. 166)

Greville was too religious—and too Stoical—a man to
rest upon the Skeptical question; nor, like Montaigne, did
he make the leap directly from Skepticism into fideism
without concern for the truth of physical "reality." In
Greville's view, however insecure a man might be among
the paradoxical pieces of information afforded him by his
limited sources of knowledge, he must never allow himself to contemplate only the inevitable flux of things; for
contemplation (says this Platonist!) destroys, "Trans-
formes all beings into Atomi:/ Dissolves, builds not."
Social reality demands that the sciences be reformed along
empirical lines, according to Bacon's doctrine of utility
(1. 171). The universities, the law courts, medicine, logic,
rhetoric—all must be stripped of their wayward terminology to conform to man's immediate and simple needs.
Only by the way of humility can man hope to reverse, or
even to modify, the general doom incurred for his original
intellectual pride. His soul must "raise herselfe again,/
Ere she can judge all other knowledge vaine" (1. 191).
By knowing all things, without being puffed up, a man may
legitimately come to reject his knowledge in order to come
into perfect knowledge.

Greville's paradoxes, like those of the two Davies', are
the traditional ones of Stoical, Skeptical, and Christian
self-examination. What is interesting about these poems
is the richness of the traditional paradoxes of content, as
well as the poetic tentative toward their proper expression.
The poems deal, after all, with the major unanswerable
questions of human speculation, the nature of the transcendent God and the nature of human thought; and they
deal with them, albeit awkwardly, in poetry. The subject
demanded and the poets attempted to supply a rhetoric
appropriate to the complications of such speculation. Without some realization of the nature and variety of the traditional paradoxes of epistemology which exercised such

fascination for these poets, we run the risk of overstating the poets' philosophical and rhetorical originality and thereby of failing to recognize their peculiar and original solutions to the poetic problems raised by the subject of transcendence. These poets were engaged in an heroic enterprise—to make as plain as possible the mysteries of human understanding. It remained for another poet to do more, to dramatize rather than to describe human understanding, to bring his readers into that understanding by performing the poetic act of understanding rather than by outlining the process in verse: John Donne in his Anniversaries.

II. JOHN DONNE'S ANNIVERSARY POEMS AND THE PARADOXES OF EPISTEMOLOGY

Donne's Anniversary Poems have been greatly illuminated by having been read against the various traditions which they exploit and of which they are a part. They are poems of meditation,[28] with medieval, reformation, and counterreformation analogues; they are poems of the old[29] and the new science;[30] they are cosmic eulogies of a dead maiden and (perhaps, though perhaps not) of a dead Maiden Queen;[31] they are a document in Skepticism[32] and in natural law;[33] they are companion pieces drawn to a

[28] Louis L. Martz, *The Poetry of Meditation*, pp. 211-48.

[29] Joseph A. Mazzeo, "Notes on John Donne's Alchemical Imagery," *Renaissance and Seventeenth-Century Studies*, pp. 60-89.

[30] Marjorie Hope Nicolson, *The Breaking of the Circle*, pp. 81-122.

[31] Nicolson, p. 96; Marius Bewley, "Religious Cynicism in Donne's Poetry," *Kenyon Review*, XIV (1952), 619-46.

[32] Louis I. Bredvold, "The Naturalism of Donne in Relation to Some Renaissance Traditions," *JEPG*, pp. 471-502; see also his "The Religious Thought of Donne" previously cited.

[33] Robert M. Ornstein, "Donne, Montaigne and Natural Law," *JEPG*, pp. 213-29.

pattern, the *quaestio* and *responsio* of medieval argument.[34]
They are, too, a body-soul debate, the first poem a *contemptus mundi* and the second a *consolatio philosophiae*,
or *consolatio spiritualis*. They are poems about sacred love,
the power of which in part derives from the poems' delicious reference to profane love—they are, then, well-
disguised poems in the traditional line of the *dolce stil
nuovo*.[35] Anti-Petrarchan, the poems outdo the Petrarchan
rhetoric which they exploit.[36]

What is remarkable about these poems is that, though
all these readings concern such very different sets of ideas,
they do not contradict, but rather enhance each other. The
poems' extraordinary quality resides in their resistance to
final definition: when all the separate explications and interpretations are added up, the Anniversary Poems prove
to be more than the sum of their parts. They hold in balance many oppositions and contradictions: they are, in
short, paradoxical poems, poems about paradoxes and
poems within the paradoxical rhetoric.

It is in two traditions of paradox, the self-conscious reflections of classical and Renaissance epistemology and the
meditative Christian paradoxes of mystery, that I propose
to read the Anniversary Poems. Like Sir John Davies'
Nosce teipsum and Fulke Greville's *Treatie of Humane
Learning*, Donne's poems are about the difficulties inherent
in understanding one's self, the world, and God. As Mr.
Bredvold has demonstrated, all these poems derive a

[34] George Williamson, "The Design of Donne's Anniversaries,"
MP, LX (1963), 183-91.
[35] I owe the suggestion for this reading to Professor Maurice
Valency of Columbia University. See also *John Donne: The Anniversaries*, ed. Frank Manley (The Johns Hopkins Press, 1963),
introduction, pp. 37-40.
[36] Donald Guss, "Donne's Conceit and Petrarchan Wit," *PMLA*,
LXXVIII (1963), 308-14; "Donne's Petrarchism," *JEGP*, LXIV
(1965), 17-28.

great deal from Montaigne's "Apologie" and from the Skeptical tradition in general; Mr. Ornstein's argument grounds them thoroughly in their Stoic background of natural law (to which, of course, the Stoical-Skeptical Montaigne owes much).[37] Like the epistemological poems of his contemporaries, Donne's Anniversary Poems work within the contradictory traditions of Stoicism and Skepticism; like the poems of Davies and Greville, they deal with the paradoxes necessarily attendant upon epistemological speculation. Like them, too, Donne exploits the traditions of Christian self-knowledge, with its paradoxes of the transcendent spirit. But where Davies and Greville reflect chiefly upon the intellectual difficulties involved in understanding the human understanding, Donne operates within an additional paradoxical area as well, that of individual psychology. Assuming the existence of a tradition of epistemological poetry, this chapter attempts to point to Donne's many-sided use of a many-sided tradition and to his peculiar mastery of an expression appropriate to it, especially in comparison to the rather tentative poetic experiments of his contemporaries engaged upon the same problem.

The Anniversary Poems consistently work within the most obvious kind of rhetorical paradox, since they regularly cheat the reader's expectation. For example, in the first poem, after a beginning conventional in its elegiac despair, Donne springs it on his readers that it is not the death of a lady only that he laments, but the death of the whole conceivable world. The poem, with its companion-piece, propounds a lament for a world mortally wounded because of the death of one particularly gracious spirit. The subject of the poem had, in her life, been in her bodily

[37] Bredvold, "The Religious Thought of Donne," and Ornstein, "Donne, Montaigne, and the Natural Law."

form the soul of the world, its "Cyment," its "intrinsique balme," the "preservative" that kept it sweet, the "Magnetick force" that gave coherence to its parts. The soul gone, the world's body has no choice but to die. The decay of the world, presented with such *Schadenfreude* in Greville's *Treatie*, actually takes place in Donne's poem: Donne's "anatomy" is performed upon a crooked and putrid corpse. In every way, the world has lost its nature—it is unbalanced, disproportionate, colorless, askew. Man has a shorter life, a smaller stature, a narrower mind than ever before. He is still the measure of all things, but by that fact all things have lost their glory: crooked and shrunken himself, he measures a world correspondingly skewed. That "stedie and settled order" of Creation, celebrated by Du Plessis Mornay,[38] the cheerful study of which he enjoined his readers to undertake, served to demonstrate to variable and doubting man that God's purpose was fixed in the beautiful patterns of natural law operating upon created nature. Donne's animate, anthropomorphized universe has partaken to the last degree of man's sin, has become as variable as wicked man himself.

A crooked mind cannot measure a crooked world; man's ways of knowing are as skewed as the world they seek to know. The nets man throws over the firmaments, those astronomical charts designed to fix the heavenly patterns, prove worthless, both because they are the inadequate inventions of weak minds and because the firmament itself has lost its originally regular pattern. None of the sciences has an ordering value any more—astronomy, medicine, natural philosophy progressively reveal how awkward the creation is, just as the arts and sciences reveal the mistakes of human life. Amidst all this, as Davies and Greville com-

[38] *The Trewnesse of the Christian Religion,* "Epistle Dedicatorie."

plained, knowledge is impossible—for Donne, it seems, impossible for the soul as well as the mind.

"Poore soule, in this thy flesh, what dost thou know?" Where Davies had asserted that it was possible for the soul to know, and organized his theory of knowledge around the soul, Donne denied the soul knowledge even of itself:

> Thou know'st thy selfe so little, as thou know'st not,
> How thou didst die, nor how thou wast begot.
> Thou neither know'st, how thou at first cam'st in,
> Nor how thou took'st the poyson of mans sinne.
> Nor dost thou, (though thou know'st, that thou art so)
> By what way thou art made immortall, know.
> Thou art too narrow, wretch, to comprehend
> Even thy selfe.   (*Progress of the Soul*, 255-62)

The most the world can do is to set riddles. All kinds of apparently ordinary questions appear to have no answer—who knows how the stone came into the bladder, or how the blood circulates? In the world of learning, nothing can be known either:

> What *Caesar* did, yea, and what *Cicero* said.
> Why grasse is greene, or why our blood is red,
> Are mysteries which none have reach'd unto.
>   (*P.S.*, 287-89)

The world "dissolves into its Atomies," particles of disorganized matter; and its forms dissolve into an eternal mutability, until men are not, genuinely, what they are. The fact that lovers' vows are impermanent—as Donne elsewhere emphasized, that impermanence is the only permanent thing about lovers—is appropriate enough, since lovers' vows are the utterances of bodies terrifyingly fluid:

> Poore cousened cousenor, *that* she, and *that* thou,
> Which did begin to love, are neither now;

> You are both fluid, chang'd since yesterday:
> Next day repaires, (but ill) last dayes decay.
> Nor are, (although the river keepe the name)
> Yesterdaies waters, and to daies the same.
> So flowes her face, and thine eyes, neither now
> That Saint, nor Pilgrime, which your loving vow
> Concern'd, remaines. . . .   (*P.S.*, 391-99)

Even lovers cannot know one another, though the idiom may dupe them into thinking that they can: and lovers are not the only variable people on the planet. No man has constant qualities—that man who "thinkes that he hath got/ To be a Phoenix" has not even a personal identity. Like everything else, man is an illusion:

> whilst you thinke you bee
> Constant, you'are hourely in inconstancie. (*P.S.*, 399-400)

In this attack upon individual and personal integrity, Donne owes a considerable debt to Montaigne's "Apologie," and some to Heraclitus. Donne administers, though, a thoroughly Christian warning to men: his is an Augustinian and "counter-Renaissance"[39] antidote to man's pride in himself.

For willy-nilly man unmakes himself.[40] The blind passage of time is not the only thing that produces irrevocable decay; man connives at his own decadence. Man is "borne ruinous," comes "headlong" upon an "ominous precipitation," all brought upon himself by his inherited behavior. Woman, "sent for mans reliefe," is the instrument of his destruction, the "cause of his languishment." With its legacy of mortality, "that first marriage was our funerall" —the day of joy is the day of death. Love, elsewhere a

[39] The phrase is taken from Hiram Haydn's *The Counter-Renaissance*.

[40] See below, Chapter 16.

redeemer, in these poems merely hastens the lover's inevitable death—

> One woman at one blow, then kill'd us all,
> And singly, one by one, they kill us now.

In this particular suicide, man can be counted on to cooperate enthusiastically:

> We doe delightfully our selves allow
> To that consumption; and profusely blinde,
> We kill our selves to propagate our kinde.
> (*The Anatomy of the World*, 106-10)

The paradoxes of love are turned upside down, in an ominous precipitation of their own—in "The Canonization," the act of love, called "death" in the voluptuary's slang, brought ecstasy and resurrection; in the Anniversary Poems, a man seeking to secure his future in an heir simply shortens his life.

In every other way, man seeks his own annihilation. He takes pride in his ingenuity and works perversely to his own end:

> Wee seeme ambitious, Gods whole worke t'undoe;
> Of nothing hee made us, and we strive too,
> To bring our selves to nothing backe ... (*A.W.*, 155-57)

All this, from the creature who even in his fallen state is the object of God's extraordinary love:

> This man, whom God did wooe, and loth t'attend
> Till man came up, did downe to man descend,
> This man, so great, that all that is, is his,
> Oh what a trifle, and poore thing he is! (*A.W.*, 167-70)

Death is hidden everywhere in life; spring times are tombs, and, in a fine pun, "false-conceptions fill the generall wombes." Man is doomed by his situation and further doomed by his behavior.

There appears to be no room for anything but despair in the picture Donne draws. However prepared readers are to expect death in an elegy, few could have been ready for so complete an elaboration of that morbid theme as these poems afford, evidently offering no way out from general and total condemnation. At the end of the First Anniversary, the world has had its qualities and attributes stripped off, like the gradually reduced man of Vesalius' drawings, until it is a dry cinder, lifeless, without substance, and without future.

But just at this point the paradoxist takes hold. We reasonably expect the poem to end, for the worse, on the grim note so long sustained, of death and annihilation. Our expectation is cheated, though, not merely by the reversal of tone and message, but by the simplicity of the reversal. By a rhetorical *topos* and a doctrinal paradox so familiar as to be commonplace, Donne turns the poem around, upon a future whose existence he has apparently hitherto denied. His own works, he says,

> Will yearely celebrate thy second birth,
> That is, thy death. . . ,

until, in truth, kingdom come.[41] All Donne's readers, trained to the paradoxes of orthodoxy, knew that death was not death, knew that

> though the soule of man
> Be got when man is made, 'tis borne but then
> When man doth die; our body's as the wombe,
> And, as a Midwife, death directs it home.
>
> (*A.W.*, 450-54)

This particular paradox was no longer a "wonder," in Puttenham's word,[42] by the early seventeenth century.

[41] O. B. Hardison, Jr., *The Enduring Monument* (North Carolina University Press, 1962), pp. 166-86.

[42] George Puttenham, *The Arte of English Poesie*, p. 189.

What is remarkable is Donne's manipulation of so "simple" a paradox—for, in fact, we discover rather to our chagrin, we have been prepared for just this turning from the very beginning of the poem, listening to a ground bass of argument accompanying the whole catalogue of disease, decadence, death, and despair. Donne tells us at the start that the lady's death raised "a perplexed doubt,/ Whether the world did lose or gaine in this"; but the poem moved so fast through such sensational images and speculations that the reader was not permitted to linger over the perplexities of that doubt. Though Donne appears to have been in no doubt that the world lost and lost mortally by the lady's death, his question could be answered another way. The title of the first poem, *An Anatomy of the World*, implies a limited optimism, since anatomies are undertaken in the hope of an ultimate understanding of the body, even of a cure for other bodies not yet dead. At the heart of one simile, fairly early in the poem, lies the promise of resurrection:

> For as a child kept from the Font, untill
> A prince, expected long, come to fulfill
> The ceremonies. . . ;   (*A.W.*, 33-35)

baptism promises the chance of a future state of bliss. Even the lines suggesting total annihilation carry deep within them their hope of a better life—

> We'are scarce our Fathers shadowes cast at noone:
> Onely death addes t'our length: nor are wee growne
> In stature to be men, till we are none. (*A.W.*, 144-47)

The Second Anniversary begins with the death so fully described in the first poem; this death is particularly suitable to the moral condition of the world, since it is the violent retributive death of a criminal:

> Or as sometimes in a beheaded man,
> Though at those two Red seas, which freely ranne,
> One from the Trunke, another from the Head,
> His soule be sail'd, to her eternall bed,
> His eyes will twinckle, and his tongue will roll,
> As though be beckned, and cal'd backe his soule,
> He graspes his hands, and he pulls up his feet,
> And seemes to reach, and to step forth to meet
> His soule. . . .   (*P.S.*, 9-17)

The long meditation, so brilliantly established in its traditional form by Professor Martz' analysis of the poem, follows properly upon the simile of the executed criminal. Each man dies for his mortal sin, but even so he may "step forth to meet / His soule," trusting that "th'immaculate blood" of a far greater victim of execution will "wash his score." Indeed, the terrible death of Donne's lady, which has reduced the world and all its wonders to a dry cinder, is seen to be the exemplum of a proper death. Man is exhorted to "thinke" himself into a good death, like the lady's, with all the strength he has. No matter how closely a man may be in possession of righteousness while he lives (and some men are, as even Donne admits), "Death must usher, and unlocke the door" for the imprisoned soul. Death is the birth into eternal life, into beatitude, into real knowledge. The soul's curious perplexed doubt in the First Anniversary—

> For who is sure he hath a Soule, unless
> It see, and judge, and follow worthinesse,
> And by Deedes praise it?   (*A.W.*, 3-5)

—comes to resolution in the Second Anniversary, where in the very symptom of its illness lies the hope of a cure. "O my insatiate soule," the poet cries out,

> Be thirstie still, and drinke still till thou goe
> To th'only Health, to be Hydroptique so.
>   (*P.S.*, 47-48)

Man's ignorance turns in his hand to become a weapon of his salvation ("To be thus stupid is Alacritie" in the search for God); his very lethargy is actually memory disguised. The lady has proved stronger in her going than in her staying, for though in her life she had preserved the world, in her death she was still medicinal, "More Antidote, than all the world was ill." She was impossibly miraculous, that lady

> To whose proportions if we would compare
> Cubes, th'are unstable; Circles, Angular . . .
> $(P.S., 141\text{-}42)$

Because of her transcendent qualities, literally, her perfection, she had left behind "a kinde of world remaining still," a new world of the imagination with new creatures settled in a "weedlesse Paradise": or, the image of a future heaven.

That image was literally regenerative. Under the prevailing narrative of death and anatomy run the images of creation and re-creation. As Davies had said,

> Then doth th'aspiring *Soule* the bodie leave,
> > Which we call *death*; but were it knowne to all,
> > What life our *Soules* do by this death receave;
> > Men would it *birth*, or *Gaol-delivery* call.[43]

Death is the midwife to the soul's birth, sending it into its newly perceived world. In the Second Anniversary, the lady is invoked as the poet's cooperative muse:

> Immortall Maid, who though thou would'st refuse
> The name of Mother, be unto my Muse
> A Father, since her chast Ambition is,
> Yearely to bring forth such a child as this. $(P.S., 33\text{-}36)$

In such a context, poetry, the living victor over time, is of consummate importance, in particular for a poet de-

[43] *Nosce teipsum*, p. 100.

termined to paint the hyperbolical ills of the world. Rhetoric as an instrument of paradox becomes the instrument
of transcendent meaning. In Davies' and Greville's epistemological poems, Donne might have found, had he
needed it, some rudimentary suggestion of his own technique. In a rather elementary use of simile and metaphor,
for example, Davies reinforced his concept of the truth of
poetry: God is at once "the rising Sunne" (which in one
of His hypostases He actually is) and is like the sun; the
soul-as-substance is "a *Vine*" and "a Starre," in illustration
of its form and function.[44] For the soul-as-spirit, a concept familiar to his readers, Davies needed no particular
metaphorical support, and could simply explicate his view,
as a prose writer might do. Greville, like his friend Francis
Bacon, the Lord Chancellor, distrusted the arts, including
rhetoric, in which he considered that words were too often
merely drugs, and language an imprecise and misleading
means of communication. But the friend of Sir Philip
Sidney could not denounce words altogether, and in the
end he permitted to poetry (as well as to music) a particular place in the worship and service of God. Poetry is
"like a Maker"; like the Maker, poetry creates worlds
and states of mind.[45]

In spite of his friendship for Sidney, who endowed
poetry with the highest powers, one feels a certain niggard-
liness in Greville's praise of the art of verse. Donne invests poetry with unqualified power. For him, the "name"
of a thing, its *logos*, glorified in both Stoic and Christian
traditions, was all-important.[46] From the *logos*, the originating word of God, all things took their form; the lady
whose death had robbed the world of its soul, and thus of
its life, had a name whose divine properties exceeded the

[44] *Ibid.*, p. 13.
[45] Greville, 1. 182.   [46] See above, Chapter 6.

"naming-magic" of Agrippa. Her name, Donne tells us, defined the world, gave it form and grace; when the world forgot her name, it forgot its own and thus ceased to know itself. Lost to the world though the sovereign power of her name is—and in a splendid practical illustration of his notion, Donne never assigns the lady a name, nor ever calls by their proper names her subsidiary representatives, Astraea, Queen Elizabeth, and the Virgin Mary[47]—that secret name has the power, in poetry, to "refine coarse lines, and make prose song." Across the wastes of despair in both poems echoes the image of song. The First Anniversary begins with the image of the lady in the angelic choir. Throughout the dirge for the world's ugliness, colorlessness, lack of taste, and bad smell, there is no hint that sound and speech have lost their power. So at the end of the First Anniversary the prose of complaint turns into song, the particular proud song of the Renaissance that sounded louder than mortality, and the religious song from which all spiritual life derives:

> Vouchsafe to call to minde that God did make
> A last, and lasting'st peece, a song. He spake
> To *Moses*, to deliver unto all,
> That song, because hee knew they would let fall
> The Law, the Prophets, and the History. . . .
>
> (*A.W.*, 461-65)

In emulation of that original song of revelation, the poet dared "this great Office to invade" in order to imprison in verse the lady's liberation. As the final couplet of the first poem says,

> Verse hath a middle nature: heaven keepes Soules,
> The Grave keepes bodies, Verse the Fame enroules.
>
> (*A.W.*, 473-74)

[47] Nicolson, pp. 92-102.

The poem does not ask blindly for eternal fame, as in the Horatian *topos*: his poems are not destined to live "forever." From the conjunction of the lady's spirit and his Muse, he wishes to produce a child a year, a poem in anniversary which shall create as the generations of man recreate, out of its own power, to

> worke on future wits, and so
> May great Grand children of thy prayses grow . . .
> For thus, Man may extend thy progeny,
> Untill man doe but vanish, and not die.
> These Hymnes thy issue, may encrease so long,
> As till Gods great *Venite* change the song.
>
> (*P.S.*, 37-38, 41-44)

Song is constant, but songs are made on earth, and even divine subjects share their end with death.

All the same, words have a power transcendent over things. They are, certainly, all too subject to human abuse, as Donne well knew. The "spungie, slack divines" vent falsehoods and vanity as if they were the word of God. Libellers misspeak and thus fatally distort the truth, undo the good done in the world. But words also make possible the lesson the lady teaches: her form and name make up the world's "worthiest booke," of which all human virtuous actions are "but a new, and worse, edition." That book was a bargain, too—

> rather was two soules,
> Or like to full on both sides written Rols,
> Where eyes might reade upon the outward skin,
> As strong Records for God, as mindes within . . . .
>
> (*P.S.*, 503-06)

The lady's ineffable name was properly holy, not falsely so, like the false saints of the Roman Church, but a true pattern for posterity, since

what lawes of Poetry admit
Lawes of Religion have at least the same.
(*P.S.*, 514-15)

Finally, in the conceit, the lady herself, not just the poet's description of her, becomes the lesson read to the people, with the poet as her reader: since her image "makes prose song," the poet's images become music. The final lines of the poem proclaim the lady's identity with the poem itself:

Thou art the Proclamation; and I am
The Trumpet, at whose voyce the people came.
(*P.S.*, 527-28)

The miraculous lady, alive and revivifying even in her death, is the pattern for and the image of the life to come. She is its whole idea; preparation for that life is best achieved in "reading" her, or in listening to her proclamation—in reading, then, the poet's poems. He is her trumpet, an instrument announcing her reign and the end of the old world. His poems are to go on, as the herald's trumpets resound, proclaiming the sovereign from generation to generation, "untill Gods great *Venite* change the song," and another Trumpet shall sound, to announce the great change of Doomsday.

At that final resurrection to grace, body and soul shall fuse again, this time into a permanent perfection where decay is impossible. In that state, indescribable, like all ideas of heavenly bliss, the frontiers of the senses shall be breached for the achievement of total experience. Man shall no longer be partial, but whole and indivisible. Donne's rhetoric reaches out to express such supernatural unity in, for instance, the lines so often quoted as his "metaphysical" denial of the limitations of sense:

> her pure, and eloquent blood
> Spoke in her cheekes, and so distinctly wrought,
> That one might almost say, her body thought . . . .
>
> (*P.S.*, 244-46)

But this is not simply a stylistic trick performed for its own sake, as the Sophists might have done: Donne is making a metaphysical, a theological, and a poetical statement. The lady's significant perfection permits her to think by a grosser part than is usually granted mortals to think by. The interpenetration of body and mind in this lady is not just the poet's *epideixis*: Donne means exactly what he says. The daring of his image proceeds from the concept it seeks to express. When we look at the poems closely, we see that throughout their long length, Donne makes a fusion, even a confusion, of part and whole, to indicate the total fusion of experience to which his poems are to lead. He does not rely, as most poets must, on the rhetorical devices of metonymy and synecdoche merely; from first to last, he commits significant solecisms to point to his paradoxes. In heaven, he tells us at the very beginning, "that rich Soule" is "now a part of both the Quire, and song": she is, then, both container and thing contained. Of the joys in heaven, she is both "partaker, and a part"; she has gone to heaven "as well t'enjoy, as get perfection." Nor is she a passive recipient of grace—in heaven, "shee receives, and gives addition."

Such devices are rhetorical modes of expressing supernal unity, and that perfect knowledge promised in heaven, where the sight of God unites object and subject, "is both the object and the wit," and where beatitude is at once "a full, and filling good." In spite of terrestrial evidence to the contrary, the container and the thing contained, by logical predestinarianism forever separate, must in ultimate salvation be one. Single is double, multiple is single. So the world, which took its form from the lady and which once contained her body and soul as the human body contains its immortal soul, may expect to live in her dying and to die into her new life. At her death, the world sings its swan's song, which is the poem; but the poet, good Christian that he is, does not sing all alone, as the dying swan does. He sings specifically to other men, utters his "full, and filling good" for their salvation as well as his own. The poem, moving from a single death to the general judgment, moves toward the fulfillment of human understanding. It moves from a moment in time, one year after a certain lady's mortal death, to that last moment in time when time, the sum of parts, becomes eternity, the indivisible whole. In the Anniversary Poems the laws emulate the laws of religion, attempting to transcend the merely physical and intellectual incompatibilities that lead men into despair. The world's variety and change frighten the poet, alarm him into a Skeptical questioning of his and all men's Stoical security, and stir him to understand variety, change, and contradiction. These poems do not try to set things straight, to make contradictions orderly: they accept contradiction and paradox as the basis of limited human existence and of human understanding still more limited, and simply build upon that acceptance. The contradictions and paradoxes are the point in these poems, are the poems themselves, make up a whole at once active and passive, giving and receiving, full and filling. These poems are a dirge that lies about itself, although like a good paradox it leaves the reader in no doubt about fundamental truth: these poems are a song of triumph, both of God's glory and the art of verse.

14

Burton's Anatomy of Melancholy
and the Structure of Paradox

> Who can but pity the mercifull intention of those
> hands that doe destroy themselves?
>> Browne, *Religio Medici,* I. 53

JONATHAN SWIFT is the culprit responsible for the vulgar error that Burton's *Anatomy* is an amorphous literary
creation, an infinite digression upon an infinity of subjects.
Actually, the paradox can be defended, not only that the
book is composed of very carefully constructed parts, but
also that the parts are disposed in the decorum suitable to
Burton's material. To begin with the most obvious element
of all, Burton's material was by medical and philosophical
tradition contradictory—"The Author's Abstract of Melancholy" asserts in its stilted measure that

> All my griefs to this are jolly,
> Naught so sad as melancholy;

and that

> All other joys to this are folly,
> None so sweet as melancholy—[1]

to remind us of the conflicting traditions, symptoms, causes,
and results of the disease called Melancholy.[2] Again and

---

[1] Robert Burton, *The Anatomy of Melancholy* (3 vols., London,
Everyman's Library, 1948), I. 11. All quotations from the *Anatomy*
are from this edition, henceforth referred to as *AM*, with volume
and page numbers.

[2] Erwin Panofsky and Fritz Saxl, *Dürers Melencolia I, Studien
der Bibliothek Warburg* (Leipzig, 1923), the great study of the
etiology and iconology of the disease, must be consulted; the work

again, as Burton points out, cases of melancholy display contradiction: the same thing may, in different cases, be cause and symptom, cause and cure; or, the cure of one case may be the cause of another.[3] For a subject such as melancholy, in which cause, symptom, and cure are so confused and so confusing, decorum demands the mixture of mode and of genre. When one looks at the separate parts of the book, one sees remarkable examples of different literary genres.

Most obviously, Burton's book is an "anatomy," an analysis of a state of mind which, when examined closely, turns into many states of mind. His title of course derives from Vesalius' contribution to the new medicine in *De corporis humani fabrica*, a technical book whose subject provided a metaphor for all sorts of examinations, of "discoveries," uncovering of areas of the globe or of knowledge analogous to the anatomical uncovering of the systems of the human body. Anatomies of Renaissance subjects abounded—of wit, of abuses, of popery, of antimony, of immortality, of the world, to name only a few. Vesalius' method proceeds inward, to strip the perfect human creature of layer upon layer, until all that remains of him is an inarticulate heap of bones. It is not the bones, though, that

---

has recently been published in an enlarged English translation: Raymond Klibansky, Erwin Panofsky, and Fritz Saxl, *Saturn and Melancholy* (London and New York, 1964). Lawrence Babb's two books, *The Elizabethan Malady* (Michigan State University Press, 1951), and *Sanity in Bedlam* (Michigan State University Press, 1959), deal with literary melancholy in English, and with Burton specifically.

[3] As for example: idleness and solitariness are both causes and symptoms of melancholy (1. 245); sorrow is a cause (1. 259) and a symptom (1. 389); love a cause and a cure (III. 256); melancholy a cure for melancholy (II. 206). In a further study of the *AM*, I hope to develop this notion of interchangeability of cause, symptom, and cure.

are the *object* of the investigation: the investigation is its own object; the investigation itself is the voyage of discovery, the total process of acquiring knowledge. Though there is much in Burton's book that is encyclopedic, he does not attempt the classical circumscription of all knowledge; instead of beating the bounds of the parish of human understanding, he begins like Vesalius from the outside and proceeds on an inward voyage of discovery which, as I hope to show, is in both the literal and the spiritual sense a revelation.

On the face of it, the *Anatomy of Melancholy* is a medical book, like Timothy Bright's *Treatise of Melancholy*, like the many books of the medical writers Burton cites, Du Laurens, Fernel, and Vesalius himself. Compared with modern medical books, however, Renaissance books of medicine were themselves much more than mere compendia of symptoms and remedies or directions for treatment. Of English books, for instance, Timothy Bright, Helkiah Crooke, and Thomas Cogan all dealt with questions of both body and soul, recognizing the psychosomatic elements of disease, elements which necessitated moral and spiritual attention as well as physical care. Because medical books dealt with physical regimen and control, they habitually commented upon public and private morality, lectured on ethics, politics, economics, and society in general,[4] as Burton's *Anatomy* so conspicuously does.

In obvious ways, Burton's casebook simply exploits the material of other books in general medicine, though, as he was careful to indicate early in the *Anatomy*, melancholy

[4] The best discussion of Burton's book against its medical background is that of Naomi Loeb Lipman, "Robert Burton's *Anatomy of Melancholy* and its Relation to the Medical Book Tradition of the English Renaissance," Columbia University, unpublished master's essay, 1952, which is full of valuable material on the range of subject matter in conventional medical writing.

was by its nature not the professional consideration of
medical men alone (i. 34-35). Since it was a disease of the
soul, melancholy belonged quite literally in Burton's professional purlieu, since by his ordination he was charged
precisely with the cure of souls. Furthermore, as he pointed
out solemnly, contribution to medicine by divines was
common enough to form a legitimate tradition of its own:
he cited as authorities for this aspect of his enterprise
Ficino, Linacre, Braunus, Hemingius, Lessius the Jesuit,
Beroaldus, St. Luke, and, finally, Hercules and Aesculapius
as types of Christ Himself (i. 34-37; iii. 375).

As a practical and theoretical textbook in both physic
and divinity, Burton's *Anatomy* joined the casuist traditions stemming from both professions. His *Anatomy* is a
tremendous display of casuistry, with cases drawn not from
the practice and experience of its author only, but from
the whole range of western—for Burton, human—history.
He was engaged in the taxonomy of melancholy, and his
cases can be classified—the man who thought he was glass,
the man who thought he was butter; the predicaments of
maids, nuns, and widows are all assigned to classes of
causes, symptoms, and cure; but each case is, as Burton
continually stressed, unique, requiring particular variations
in treatment, a fact which the skilled practitioner must
realize. Burton's book, literally, is about cases of conscience,
in both senses of that word, both understanding, and moral
sensibility: it provides the intellectual historian, moreover,
with a useful demonstration of the close connection between the casuistic method and the empiricisms of the
Renaissance. In law canon, civil, and merchant; in medicine
and (gradually) in the mathematical branches of natural
philosophy; in religion, each *casus*, each case, could claim
the right to particular scrutiny.[5] For the divine, charged

[5] A sensible, ranging study of the many Renaissance "empiricisms"

with the cure of souls, *casus* has a double significance, since it is the word for "fall," and the divine's business is to deal with the particular, unique tumble by which each man recapitulates the general Fall in Eden.

Burton's scene was set in Eden:

[Man's] disobedience, pride, ambition, intemperance, incredulity, curiosity; from whence proceeded original sin and that general corruption of mankind, as from a fountain flowed all bad inclinations and actual transgressions, which cause our several calamities inflicted upon us for our sins.   (I. 131)

Since, in Burton's world, the most general of all diseases was melancholy, with its manifold forms physical and spiritual, he was able to trace without ado all cases of melancholy back to the first Fall:

. . . from these melancholy dispositions, no man living is free, no Stoic, none so wise, none so happy, none so patient, so generous, so godly, so divine, that can vindicate himself; so well composed, but more or less, some time or other, he feels the smart of it. Melancholy in this sense is the character of mortality.   (I. 143-44)

Melancholy is the mark of living: all mortal men, by the Judaeo-Christian dispensation, are marked for life by original sin, which in Burton's language is translated into melancholy.

But Christian book that it is, the *Anatomy* is also the book of a humanist, whose roots go deep into antiquity. With his striking independence in the use of sources, Burton demonstrates the typical humanist disregard of the contextual demands of those sources, pillaging for his own

---

in the professions, trades, and religions is badly needed. Burton's association with one such tradition, that of religious casuistry, has been commented on before: see William R. Mueller, *The Anatomy of Robert Burton's England* (University of California Press, 1952), p. 20.

purposes, to suit himself, to buttress his argument or to illustrate his point, however he chose to do so. As a gallimaufry of humanist wisdom and opinion, the *Anatomy* is matched only by the self-help learning of Erasmus' *Adagia* and the idiosyncratic constructions of the *Essays* of Montaigne. Like Montaigne himself, whom Burton cites as authority for his own style of writing,

This roving humor . . . I have ever had, and like a ranging spaniel, that barks at every bird he sees, leaving his game, I have followed all, saving that which I should, and may justly complain, and truly, *qui ubique est, nusquam est* . . . that I have read many books, but to little purpose, for want of good method; I have confusedly tumbled over divers authors in our libraries, and with small profit for want of art, order, memory, judgment. (I. 17-18)

Montaigne's view—or his fiction—of himself was that he too had no memory, no learning, and little judgment; that his essays, in their sequence and their philosophy, were simply the records of his undisciplined considerations; that they were, insofar as possible, the informal and direct recapitulation of a man, of himself. The master of irony and of tone, naturally Montaigne did not present "himself," though in a formal time and out of formal literary traditions, he came remarkably close, in illusion at least, to presenting himself as he "really was." Burton's book belongs in the genre to which Montaigne gave the name, the essay; like Montaigne, Burton was busy weighing, assaying, in his case the scruples of melancholy men as well as the physic by which they could be cured.

But he assayed grosser weights, too—the values of his culture, the worth of ancient and popular wisdom, of ancient and popular learning, of ancient and vulgar errors. He weighed, again and again, himself, not just in the successive editions of his book, but also as a total man, a man in sum. Montaigne's book took the weights of the various, mutable man its author was; its tones followed the needs of his moods and his subjects. Like Montaigne's book, the *Anatomy* is various by design, since it too must match the vagaries of both its author and its subject, according to Burton's whimsical application of the principle of decorum:

. . . 'tis not my study or intent to compose neatly, which an orator requires, but to express myself and readily and plainly as it happens. So that as a river runs sometimes precipitate and swift, then dull and slow; now direct, then *per ambages*; now deep, then shallow; now muddy, then clear; now broad, then narrow; doth my style flow: now serious, then light; now comical, then satirical; now more elaborate, then remiss, as the present subject required, or as at that time I was affected. And if thou vouchsafe to read this treatise, it shall seem no otherwise to thee than the way to an ordinary traveller, sometimes fair, sometimes foul; here champaign, there enclosed; barren in one place, better soil in another: by woods, groves, hills, dales, plains, etc. I shall lead thee *per ardua montium, et lubrica vallium, et roscida cespitum, et glebosa camporum,* through variety of objects, that which thou shalt like and surely dislike.   (I. 32)

That passage was written, as the book was, by a self-conscious disciple of Montaigne, but though the *Anatomy* is a long and constant weighing, it is not quite a collection of essays. Burton was bound by his material and his method to a more complicated effort, to articulate, as anatomy does, the disparate parts into a fitting whole.[6]

The passage just cited tells us a great deal—not to expect consistency, for example; to adjust to many different tones, different styles, and different genres. Following Bur-

---

[6] See F. P. Wilson, *Elizabethan and Jacobean* (Clarendon Press, 1945), pp. 46-48; John L. Lievsay, "Robert Burton's *De Consolatione*," *South Atlantic Quarterly*, LV (1956), p. 329; Northrup Frye, *Fables of Identity* (Harbinger, 1963), pp. 155-63.

ton's own leads, his appeals to various sorts of authority and tradition, I want to explore some of the range of his use of genre and of traditional tone.

To begin with an obvious example, the synopses with which each Partition begins demonstrate Burton's training in the schools: even if we are not particularly reminded of scholastic division in Burton's additive accounts, the construction of the book as a whole follows the conventional patterns of scholastic demonstration and argument, particularly as applied to books of instruction.[7] To pass from this to a more concealed genre, the book as a whole bears the message, if not the shape, of something quite different. The entire book is a *consolatio philosophiae*,[8] the promise of the limited comfort learning can give to men under the pressure of their painful daily lives. Under singular stress, Socrates remembered to award the consolation of philosophy to his friends anticipating their bereavement; Cicero's recapitulation of philosophical strength after the death of his daughter Tullia and Boethius' remarkable testament in prison have become the classics of a reflective and didactic genre. As Burton said of himself, "I writ of melancholy, by being busy to avoid melancholy" (1.20): he shakes himself out of his disease by attacking it foursquare, and he consoles his miseries by that activity. "Cardan professeth he wrote his book *de Consolatione* after his son's death, to comfort himself; so did Tully write of the same subject with like intent after his daughter's departure. . . ." (1.21)

The whole book is located within the genre, and there are two quite different integral consolations of philosophy within it. One, in the Second Partition, warns against undue mourning at the death of friends and relations, and

[7] Lipman, "Robert Burton's *Anatomy*," pp. 40-41, especially n. 7.

[8] Lievsay, "Robert Burton's *De Consolatione*," notes the principal classical consolation, but fails to show its connection either with its Christian counterpart in the book, or with the book as a whole.

provides a discourse against the fear of one's own death.
In this essay, almost all the references are classical: the
comfort given is moral rather than spiritual, and of the
whole Bible, only the Stoical Ecclesiastes is cited. Though
in general, the tone is elevated and Stoical, at the end, the
permissive, understanding doctor has his say. If the patient cannot meet the austere demands of Stoic self-control,
then he should indulge in remedial diversions such as men
in other countries do—

The Italians most part sleep away care and grief, if it un-
seasonably seize upon them; Danes, Dutchmen, Polanders,
and Bohemians drink it down; our countrymen go to plays.
Do something, something or other, let it not transpose thee. . . .

(II. 185)

In addition to this classical *consolatio*, Burton provided
a Christian consolation, in the form of a sermon, his "Consolatory Digression," where he once more enjoins his pa-
tients to "merriment" and to holy joy:

Go then merrily to heaven. If the way be troublesome, and
you in misery, in many grievances, on the other side you have
many pleasant sports, objects, sweet smells, delightsome tastes,
music, meats, herbs, flowers, etc. to recreate your senses. Or
put case that thou art now forsaken of the world, dejected,
contemned, yet comfort thyself; as it was said to Hagar in the
wilderness, "God sees thee, he takes notice of thee": there is
a God above that can vindicate thy cause, that can relieve
thee. . . . For thy part then rest satisfied, "cast all thy care
on him, thy burden on him, rely on him, trust on him, and
he shall nourish thee, care for thee, give thee thine heart's desire"; say with David, "God is our hope and strength, in
troubles ready to be found" (Ps. xlvi, i). "For they that
trust in the Lord shall be as Mount Zion, which cannot be
removed. As the mountains are about Jerusalem, so is the
Lord about his people, from henceforth and forever" (Ps.
cxxv, 1, 2).   (II. 132-133)

One might expect at this point a pendant to the *consolatio*, the *contemptus mundi*, such as that provided in Donne's Anniversary Poems;[9] but Burton gives us no such thing. He was certainly under no illusions about the pains of this world—the book, after all, delineates them in often tedious detail: but the solitary scholar, the spectator of other men's activities, whose Egeria was melancholy herself, nonetheless never gladly renounced the world into which he was born, never for one moment underestimated the values conferred by the painful, beautiful, various world. "Solitariness," the great cause and symptom of melancholy, is always suspect: hermits are to be reintegrated into human society, and private men brought forth into community again. The world itself Burton could regard as a great box of simples from which to select the remedy proper to one's own kind of melancholy.

Burton followed Aristotle and Ficino in believing that melancholy is an heroic disease; that its principal sufferers were endowed with perceptions far more intense, more poignant, often more obsessive and more painful than those of ordinary men, but perceptions at the same time more authoritative and significant than those granted to the healthy or to sufferers from melancholy to a lesser degree. Melancholy was the malady of creative people: a bad case heightened the melancholiac's perceptions overwhelmingly, so that he might be reduced to folding his arms and pulling his hatbrim over his face, or she to sitting with her head on her hand, her elbow on her knee, staring into space, paralyzed by the grandeur of her inward vision of the outward world.[10] The melancholiac is in very interesting symbiosis with the world. His perceptions of its multiplicity may overwhelm him with fear of his own meaning-

[9] For Donne's Anniversary Poems, see above, Chapter 13.
[10] Panofsky and Saxl, *Dürers Melencolia I*, passim.

lessness; but his perceptions of the world are precisely what make him heroic, and he appreciates his perceptive power even when in the grip of his pains. The world is the melancholiac's dear enemy, and as such cannot be disposed of by *contemptu mundi*. Burton never attempted rejection of the world: his whole book is informed by respect for its vigor and variety, not by a sense of its decay.

This is not to say that Burton wrote a paean to the world's wonders like that of Pico della Mirandola, for the world was not, in Burton's vision, a friendly place or a haven for the sufferer. Burton's own attitudes toward the world varied, as he himself said. Though he attempted, like Democritus, to see it as comedy, all too often he was forced, like Heraclitus, to see it as tragedy:

Fleat Heraclitus, an rideat Democritus? in attempting to speak of these symptoms, shall I laugh with Democritus, or weep with Heraclitus? they are so ridiculous and absurd on the one side, so lamentable and tragic on the other: a mixed scene offers itself, so full of errors and a promiscuous variety of objects, that I know not in what strain to represent it.

(III. 346)

In his Heraclitan mood, Burton was capable of jeremiad. His humanist discourse on the horrors of war is an example of this, the horrors particularly of the recent wars fought, he felt, on religious pretexts rather than religious grounds (1.56; III.346-53). More specifically, Burton wept for the victims of melancholy; his sensitivity to cases of suffering is, at this long distance, very touching:

. . . [S]o by little and little, by that shoeing-horn of idleness, and voluntary solitariness, melancholy, this feral fiend, is drawn on . . . it was not so delicious at first, as now it is bitter and harsh; a cankered soul macerated with cares and discontents, *tedium vitae*, impatience, agony, inconstancy, irresolution, precipitate them into unspeakable miseries. (1 . 406-07)

Of men driven by sleeplessness upon despair, he wrote,

> They can take no rest in the night, nor sleep, or if they do slumber, fearful dreams astonish them. In the day-time they are affrighted still by some terrible object, and torn in pieces with suspicion, fear, sorrow, discontents, cares, shame, anguish, etc., as so many wild horses, that they cannot be quiet an hour, a minute of time, but even against their wills they are intent, and still thinking of it, they cannot forget it, it grinds their souls day and night, they are perpetually tormented, a burden to themselves, as Job was, they can neither eat, drink, nor sleep. (I. 431-32)

Naturally enough, in someone who chose to call himself "Democritus junior," Burton attempted to maintain a tone of ironic criticism for the better part of his work, to laugh at foolish foibles rather than to denounce human depravity. The figure of Democritus played a part in the mixed play of the Renaissance satirist;[11] Burton's choice of the laughing philosopher of antiquity as his *persona* gained him entrance into another legitimately mixed genre, that of satire. He certainly wrote more satirical passages than jeremiads: it is difficult, however, to maintain a tone of humorous detachment for the melancholy man, predisposed to weep like Heraclitus; and difficult for Burton, too, with his extraordinary sympathy for the almost infinitely varied excruciations inevitable to the condition he described. All the same, for Burton as for Juvenal, *difficile est satiram non scribere*:[12]

[11] See Lila Hermann Freedman, "Satiric Personae. A Study of the Point of View in Formal Verse Satire in the English Renaissance from Wyatt to Marston," unpublished doctoral dissertation, University of Wisconsin, 1955, pp. 326-30; Northrup Frye, *Anatomy of Criticism* (Princeton University Press, 1957), pp. 311-12.

[12] See William R. Mueller, "Robert Burton's 'Satyricall Preface,'" *MLQ*, xv (1954), 28-35.

If Democritus were alive now, he should see strange altera-
tions, a new company of counterfeit vizards, whifflers, Cuman
asses, maskers, mummers, painted puppets, outsides, fantastic
shadows, gulls, monsters, giddy-heads, butterflies.   (1. 52)

If Democritus were alive now, and should but see the superstition of our age, our religious madness. . . , so many pro-
fessed Christians, yet so few imitators of Christ; so much talk
of religion, so much science, so little conscience; so much
knowledge, so many preachers, so little practice; such variety
of sects, such absurd and ridiculous traditions and ceremonies;
if he should meet a Capuchin, a Franciscan, a pharisaical Jesuit,
a man-serpent, a shave-crowned monk in his robes, a begging
friar, or see their three-crowned Sovereign Lord the Pope,
poor Peter's successor, *servus servorum Dei*, to depose kings
with his foot, to tread on emperors' necks, make them stand
bare-foot and bare-legged at his gates, hold his bridle and
stirrup, etc. (O that Peter and Paul were alive to see this!);
if he should observe a prince creep so devoutly to kiss his toe,
and those red-cap cardinals, poor parish priests of old, now
princes' companions, what would he say?   (1. 54)

Had he seen, on the adverse side, some of our nice and curious
schismatics in another extreme abhor all ceremonies, and rather
lose their lives and livings than do or admit anything papists
have formerly used, though in things indifferent (they alone
are the true Church . . .); formalists, out of fear and base
flattery, like so many weather-cocks turn round, a rout of
temporizers, ready to embrace and maintain all that is or shall
be proposed in the hope of preferment; another Epicurean
company, lying at lurch as so many vultures, watching for a
prey of Church goods, and ready to rise by the downfall of
any: as Lucian said in like case, what dost thou think Democritus would have done, had he been spectator to all these
things?   (1. 55)

Certainly Burton's material lent itself to satire, and
satire had its uses, both in the general essay and in specific

moral essays. In the long introduction to his work, Burton's description of his society—the falseness of rulers, of laws and lawyers, the fragility of family ties and all other bonds of trust, the dubious relations between the sexes—recalls its major source, Raphael Hythlodaye's picture of England in the first book of More's *Utopia*.[13] As in that book, in which satire and utopian prescription were mutual requirements, Burton provides us with a utopian remedy for Stuart abuses:

I will yet, to satisfy and please myself, make an Utopia of mine own, a New Atlantis, a political commonwealth of mine own, in which I will freely domineer, build cities, make laws, statutes, as I list myself. And why may I not? *Pictoribus atque poetis*, etc.—you know what liberty poets ever had, and besides, my predecessor Democritus was a politician, a recorder of Abdera, a law maker, as some say; and why may I not presume so much as he did? (1. 97-98)

Like More's, Burton's utopia both was and was not a "witty fiction" merely; like Plato's, Andreae's, Campanella's, and Bacon's, it dealt with the realities of social and political organization, and provided generously for health, education, and welfare in England; like More's, his commonwealth was a humanist prescription rather than a scientific or political fantasy.[14] Burton's vision is in itself interesting: his observations can be matched again and again in the grievances laid before king and parliament; his eye was in for the good of England. Like More and unlike parliament, though, Burton was far from radical in his plans

[13] For Burton's utopianism, see J. Max Patrick, "Robert Burton's Utopianism," *PQ*, xxvi (1948), 345-58. As hardly needs pointing out by now, More's title, "Utopia," or nowhere, designates his book as a paradox, an assertion in its own terms self-contradictory or self-denying.

[14] J. H. Hexter, *More's Utopia: The Biography of an Idea*; see Mueller, *The Anatomy of Robert Burton's England*, passim.

for reform. More's pastoralism and communism have their roots in an early Christian spiritual arcadia, and Burton shared the spiritual if not the communal ideals of his predecessor. Both men were conservative, therefore: neither realized the beneficent implications in the spectacular industrial revolution going on about them. In certain respects, however, Burton was more modern in his social outlook than More; for example, his utopians were not protectionists, as More's had been, but mercantilists organized for trade free of the monopolies of which all England, except the monopolists, complained. Economically Burton was modern, but socially he was not: "I will have several orders, degrees of nobility, and those hereditary," said Burton. "My form of government shall be monarchical" (1. 101).

One might think that Burton wrote his utopia merely to gratify a whim or to demonstrate his stylistic facility and imaginative ingenuity. There is, though, a contextual justification for this odd section, embedded so deeply in the preface to the book that many readers have not recognized what they were reading. As Democritus had license to write of public matters as a law-maker in Abdera, so had Burton as a physician license to write of the ills of the commonwealth as well as the ills of the people in it. In the ancient metaphor, the body politic is likened to the human body: society is seen as diseased or disordered, its diseases and disorders are diagnosed, remedies are prescribed.[15] By extension of this metaphor, political analysis is part of the physician's correspondent task.

Burton's political commentary is closely linked to his commentary on religious institutions. The Church is, as the state is, a body, with habits and traditions. As a divine,

[15] See Lipman, "Robert Burton's *Anatomy*," passim; Mueller, *The Anatomy of Robert Burton's England*, p. 9.

Burton wrote much of *The Anatomy of Melancholy* within the generic traditions appropriate to his Church and about the ecclesiastical problems, public and private, of his time. Sometimes his satire turns to jeremiad, as in his strictures on Roman Catholic "superstition":

When I see a priest say mass, with all those apish gestures, murmurings, etc., read the customs of the Jews' synagogue, or Mahometan meskites, I must needs laugh at their folly: *Risum teneatis amici?*; but when I see them make matters of conscience of such toys and trifles, to adore the devil, to endanger their souls, to offer their children to their idols, etc., I must needs condole their misery . . . when I see grave learned men rail and scold like butterwomen, methinks 'tis pretty sport, and fit for Calphurnius and Democritus to laugh at. But when I see so much blood spilt, so many murders and massacres, so many cruel battles fought, etc., 'tis a fitter subject for Heraclitus to lament. (III. 346)

Like most Anglican priests, Burton was aware of the debt of his Church to the Roman one. He saw the Anglican Reformation as the restorer of the true religion, the English Church as the true balance between the superstitions of an overinstitutionalized Rome and the individual eccentricities of sectarians (III. 324, 423). Withal, Democritus laughed and Heraclitus wept over the state of divinity in early Stuart England, in language matched by many a Presbyterian and Independent divine:

This is that base and starveling class, needy, vagabond, slaves of their bellies, worthy to be sent back to the plough-tail, fitter for the pigsty than the altar, which has basely prostituted the study of divinity. These it is who fill the pulpits and creep into noblemen's houses. Having no other means of livelihood, and being incapable both mentally and physically of filling any other post, they find here an anchorage, and clutch at the priesthood, not from religious motives, but, as Paul says, "huckstering the word of God." (I. 328)

A divine himself, Burton had chosen not to take the conventional track to preferment:

. . . had I been as forward and ambitious as some others, I might have haply printed a sermon at Paul's Cross, a sermon in St. Mary's Oxon, a sermon in Christ Church, or a sermon before the right honourable, right reverend, a sermon before the right worshipful, a sermon in Latin, in English, a sermon with a name, a sermon without, a sermon, a sermon, etc. But I have ever been as desirous to suppress my labours in this kind, as others have been to press and publish theirs.   (1. 35)

Like all Oxford divines, Burton was obliged to deliver sermons, both for his college chapel (the cathedral of the diocese), and in the Church of St. Mary the Virgin that served the university community. He was able to make up a fine sermon, too, as the consolatory digression demonstrates, as well as the first section in the book, "On Man's Excellency, fall, Miseries, and Infirmities."

Burton certainly excelled in hortatory rhetoric. Viewed another way, the parts of the *Anatomy of Melancholy* dissolve into a treatise on education, *de regimine hominis*, a mirror of man. Once more, the genre itself, of which Erasmus' *Enchiridion* and Machiavelli's *Prince* are the most notable Renaissance examples, was closely related both to the medical treatise and to the dissertation in political theory. The most trivial Renaissance behavior book derives from the highest ancient tradition of moral discourse, in which it is assumed that the commonweal depends upon the health, physical and spiritual, of each participant.

The descriptive, prescriptive, and remedial sections of the *Anatomy* naturally refer to the moral tradition of which they are a part; Burton's book was a "macaronicon," as he said, but a macaronic not of genres territorially divided, but of genres mutually serviceable. So his remarkable chapters on the origin and etiology of melancholy, "Parents, a Cause" (1. 211), and nurses as a cause (1. 330ff.), "Education a Cause of Melancholy" (1. 333), favorite chapters of twentieth-century readers, may be seen as genre recapitulations of the *de regimine principis* (itself, incidentally, a paradoxical title, the ruler ruled), drawing upon ethical, educational, political, and medical traditions all at once, but laying stress on the negative rather than the positive formation of human beings. Burton's long, careful chapters on the "rectifications" of melancholy, by diet, air, exercise, and moderation of the passions make up a behavior book for every fallen man and woman. What distinguishes his book from most of those in the tradition is his assumption that all educations, all growings-up, must take place against a background and often in the foreground, of spiritual or nervous malady.

Burton's Third Partition, the section on love and religious melancholy, falls into a particular subtype of Renaissance behavior book, the love dialogue, or love treatise, of which Landino, Ficino, Bembo, Castiglione, and Leone Ebreo are only the most famous composers. Because the better part of Burton's discourse on love deals with the afflictions of the condition it is easy to overlook the fact that Burton the solitary scholar, celibate by reason of his post, also wrote a praise of love the more moving because he was so manifestly acquainted with love's complicated pains. He knew the power and the extent of the passion of love, so strong that the mightiest have dutifully gone down before it; he knew the self-hatred that unworthy love induces in the lover; he knew the equivocations of jealousy —all that his anatomy lays bare. Like Rabelais in his *Tiers Livre*, Burton presents the humanist defense of women and marriage, but not without the counterevidence for Chaunticler's position. Like Pantagruel, Burton (or Democritus junior) is detached during the marriage debate;

the case is far from a clear ruling, however: though marriage can bring the greatest of earthly joys, for the most part it seems not to do so. Panurge seems to have hesitated indefinitely between the joys and the frustrations anticipated in marriage, but the fact that love went attended by pain was not, for Burton, a sufficient argument to reject either love or marriage. Venus, as he thoroughly explained, was a cause of much melancholy; but she is also its cure, as maids, nuns, and widows conspicuously know.

Like Plato, Ficino, Leone Ebreo, and the rest, Burton passes up the scale from Aphrodite Pandemos, Venus Vulgaris, to Aphrodite Ouranos, Venus Coelestis, or from physical to spiritual, human to divine love. His dissertation is, however, radically different from the conventional love treatise, in which increased contentment is promised to the lover progressing from stage to stage on the ladder of love. Burton's treatise is a Renaissance love dialogue turned inside out: the *Anatomy* describes the dark side of the Platonic scale, with all the sufferings involved in every step up it.[16] The most heroic form of melancholy, and therefore the most serious case of the malady, is the melancholy suffered in loving God Himself.[17] Not only does passage up Burton's ladder of love give no assurance of

[16] Burton did not by any means invent the anti-love treatise, a form Italian in origin, with (so far as I know) Battista Fregoso's *Anteros* (Milan, 1486), translated into French and published in 1581 by Thomas Sébillet, *Contramours. L'Antéros, oux contramour de Messire Baptiste Fulgose, iadis Duc de Gennes* (Paris, Martin le Jeune, 1581); the translation is dedicated to Pontus de Tyard.

[17] *AM*, III. 311-24; though a discussion of Bruno's *Gli heroici furori* has not been included in this chapter, it properly should have been. Bruno's work is important for heroic suffering and heroic madness, and therefore belongs in a consideration of melancholy; furthermore, the metaphysical love of God prescribed in that treatise may have provided Burton with some of his ideas in the last section of the *Anatomy*.

general happiness, but it also carries with it the greatest
threat of all, the despair lurking in every case of religious
melancholy.

One form of religious melancholy proceeded directly
from the cure of love melancholy. Appreciation of God's
extraordinary beauty was the most reliable cure for sufferers from love of an earthly object; but contemplation of
God's perfection characteristically reinforced awareness of
human imperfection. Since God Himself was not always
accurately presented to His worshippers, His distorted
figure might induce or increase the fear or the madness of
religious despair: the crime of misleading Christians in
the worship of God Burton attributed particularly to the
priests of the Roman Church (III. 331-36).

Albeit in some ways a moderate one, Burton was a product of the Protestant Reformation: the Augustine he selected as authority for his views is the Augustine of *Contra
Pelagianos*, quite a different Augustine, for example, from
the one Milton selected as his authority. For Burton men
were less powerful than passions. Though medical and
humanist tradition both required that every possible remedy be devised to help men in their unequal fight against
themselves, only God's grace could really bring men
through, and even God's grace was no warranty for earthly
happiness:

So that affliction is a school or academy, wherein the best
scholars are prepared to the commencements of the Deity. And
though it be most troublesome and grievous for the time, yet
know this, it comes by God's permission and providence; He
is a spectator of thy groans and tears, still present with thee;
the very hairs of thy head are numbered, not one of them can
fall to the ground without the express will of God.

(III. 425-26)

Religious fear could also come and go in the mind of man

without effectively contaminating it: not even the most timorous need be damned by their terrors. When Christ Himself knew something very like religious despair in the garden, common men might take some comfort in their affliction:

'Tis no new thing this, God's best servants and dearest children have been so visited and tried. Christ in the garden cried out, "My God, my God, why hast Thou forsaken me?" His son by nature, as thou art by adoption and grace.   (III. 426)

By theological definition, grace is beyond understanding, though not beyond recognition. All divinity is above reason; faced with the paradoxes of divinity, one is supposed to lose one's self in "O altitudo!" Divinity is, practically speaking, unknowable and therefore unknown. For the medical man, accustomed to the vagaries of disease, for a divine trained on cases of conscience, for a literary man brought up on Montaigne, *unknowing* is a familiar condition. Recognition rather than knowledge is the most such men can hope for. For the Christian, recognition is just that: the *most* one can hope for. Discovery brings revelation; the revelation it brings is of irresistible grace.

No amount of human knowledge has the slightest effect upon God's grace, of course: but human knowledge can help to identify and to recognize conditions. Burton's book is a paradoxical exercise in many ways, but chiefly because it is about paradoxical subjects, about divinity, about epistemology, about medical problems at the frontiers of research, and therefore at the limits of discourse. Further, as one is increasingly aware in reading the medico-spiritual matter of *The Anatomy of Melancholy*, the material is itself full of contradiction. God is the first cause of melancholy and its only sure cure; love is cause and cure; idleness, solitude, sorrow, and fear are cause and symptom; melancholy itself is both the disease and its own cure. Elsewhere I hope to discuss some of the significance of these duplicities and multiplicities: here I want merely to stress the composed, contradictory, paradoxical nature of the disease itself.[18]

The practitioner treating melancholy, finding himself faced by, say, a patient exhibiting sorrow, must somehow determine the relation of this sorrow to the total disease, must sort out the contradictions of this case from others, must discover each paradox of the disease. To find out, for example, whether sorrow is the cause or the symptom in any particular case, the physician must undo the disease, determining the disorders of each layer, just as Vesalius uncovered the layered subsystems of the human body. Each case becomes a separate investigation, a separate discovery; the whole enterprise, made up of all the cases, is a voyage of intellectual discovery.

Any voyage of discovery involves the interdependent enterprises of map-making and taxonomy, as Burton recognized in his attempts both to organize melancholy as a whole and to classify its subdivisions. The metaphor of the voyage attracted him, as the preface early notes—

I never travelled but in map or card, in which my unconfined thoughts have freely expatiated, as having ever been especially delighted with the study of cosmography. (I. 18)

The book is chock-a-block with the rich comparative material brought home to Europe by the voyagers into the geographical new world.[19]

Not only the real but the imaginary voyage also has its tradition,[20] from Lucian's Icaromenippus to space fiction,

---

[18] See Panofsky and Saxl, passim.

[19] See especially, *AM*, I. 80-81; II. 35, 48, 171, 173-75.

[20] Marjorie Hope Nicolson, "Cosmic Voyages," *ELH*, VII (1940), 83-107; and *Voyages to the Moon* (New York, 1948), especially p. 225. For Burton's cosmology, see Robert L. Brown, "Robert Burton and the New Cosmology," *MLQ*, XIII (1952), 131-48.

often related to or overlapping with the utopian tradition and the satiric one. In the "Digression of the Air," Burton sets out on his imaginary journey:

As a long-winged hawk, when he is first whistled off the fist, mounts aloft, and for his pleasure fetcheth many a circuit in the air, still soaring higher and higher till he be come to his full pitch, and in the end when the game is sprung, comes down amain, and stoops upon a sudden: so will I, having now come at last into these ample fields of air, wherein I may freely expatiate and exercise myself for my recreation, awhile rove, wander round about the world, mount aloft to those ethereal orbs and celestial spheres, and so descend to my former elements again.   (II. 34-35)

This time, the trip is around the world and through the conjectural cosmos. Burton's voyage is particularly interesting, because it is not the usual fantasy of the planetary voyage, like Lucian's or Cyrano's; it is an imaginary voyage about the real world. In other words, it is not what it seems: it is a paradox. More than this, it is a double paradox, since it is also and equally a real voyage about the imaginary world, or the world of the imagination. To put it another way, the book belongs to still another genre of discovery, of venturing into the unknown, namely, the picaresque. Instead of a fictional hero, Democritus and his reader go hand in hand through the hills and valleys, the deserts, the seas, and the airy spaces of this book. He takes us in picaresque disorder from one consideration, one intellectual incident to the next, evidently at random, though with a randomness corresponding to real experience and consequently, in the *Bildungsroman* tradition, a randomness at once significant and constructive.

The picaresque is the generic privilege of every man. Every man is, before God, a rogue: every man makes his way at hazard through the journey of his life—and only some men are, like Odysseus, lucky enough to find their way home. Burton's technique, like that of Cervantes in *Don Quixote*, is to assimilate landscape—in Burton's case, the landscape of the entire universe—to mood, to inward need. The actual voyage of discovery is only apparently through the sensible world. Actually the voyage is inward, through the fantastic worlds the imagination creates, a world like that of Bruegel's "Mad Meg," where an entire landscape is made up by the action of one picaresque, errant, wandering mind.

The climate of Burton's book is of opposites and oppositions, contradictions and paradoxes: we become so acclimated to these anomalies that we tend to overlook their meanings in the large. Burton never presents his readers with a choice between one explanation for melancholy and another different or contradictory explanation. He does not present us with either the Galenical or the homeopathic remedy for any symptom. He does not present us with the choice between being and not being melancholy. His is a pluralist world, accommodating all the alternatives, even some which in conventional logic close one another out. Since Bacon, kicking stones *can* refute Berkeley: experience can make logical and metaphysical systems seem irrelevant. Burton is not dialectic, for all the rigidly imposed organization of his matter; he is like the philosopher whose name he took, ready to assume the existence of mutual contradictions, and to assume that they are the material of which the world is made up. As one perceives this, one perceives as well the fundamental way in which Burton's whole book is a medical paradox, introducing a new psychology. Ostensibly within the frame of the old faculty and humoral psychology, Burton argues against the old narrow concepts of melancholy and of human nature, providing a new way of regarding both those things.

Necessarily, in so various a world as Burton's, paradox

becomes domesticated, becomes a homely mode of perception. Because we come to regard Burton's paradoxes as
normal, the *Anatomy* has been overlooked, I think, as a
major document in the genre of paradox. In the very
simplest sense, it is a rhetorical paradox, since it is designed
to cheat the reader's expectation. We are led to expect a
straightforward medical treatise, like Bright's, and we get
a great many utterly different things thrown in—a spiritual
treatise, an atlas, a book of meteorology, a behavior book,
and so forth, and so forth. As the paradoxist is supposed
to, furthermore, Burton misleads his readers exactly: speaking of Democritus, he warns us not to expect

> a pasquil, a satire, some ridiculous treatise. . . , some prodigious
> tenent, or paradox of the earth's motion, of infinite worlds,
> *in infinito vacuo, ex fortuita atomorum collisione,* in an infinite
> waste, so caused by an accidental collision of motes in the sun,
> all which Democritus held, Epicurus and their master Leucip-
> pus of old maintained, and are lately revived by Copernicus,
> Brunus, and some others.   (I. 15)

Each of these things, from pasquil to the notions of Bruno,
is of course displayed in the treatise, and each of them
more than once. Burton sets out to contradict himself; he
has produced by calculation a series of rhetorical paradoxes
within the limits of his book as a whole. The rhetorical
paradox furthermore is the form most suited to Burton's
material, which is, quite literally, anything and everything:
the paradox, even more than the permissive satirical form,
allows for anything, encourages *genera mixta* and the
breaching of all limits established by any convention.
Under paradox's protection, pasquil, satire, jeremiad, eu-
logy, sermon, utopia, behavior book, and so on and so on,
may be—even should be—juxtaposed.

There is more to Burton's paradoxology than this. It has
seemed possible, for example, to collect Burton's comments

on himself and to subject them to psychiatric scrutiny.[21]
Burton's self-references, then, provide genuine autobiographical data. This might seem to be direct, empirical self-
reference on the model of Montaigne, had not Burton
specifically said that he "would not be known" (1.15). Not
to have recognized him, however, would have been impossible in the limited world of the seventeenth-century
English gentry, since he registered his father's and
mother's names, the place of his birth, the name of his
brother's only book and the only such book then in print,
as well as his own present occupation and habitation.[22]
Rather more like Erasmus' figure of Folly than like Montaigne, Burton refers to himself sometimes sharply and
frankly, sometimes implicitly or by denial, within the fiction he sets up. "I have laid myself open (I know it)," he
says, "in this treatise, turn'd mine inside outward. . . ."
(1. 27) Reflection in mirrors is the infinite regression in the
language of things, the "real" correlative of the intellectual
construct of self-reference. Burton's self-references are in a
dark glass, but they reflect him right enough, his face
shadowed by the disease which he served.

On closer scrutiny, Burton's service to the disease turns
out to be more unconventional than at first sight it appears.
The title of the book, the vocabulary in which the descriptions were cast, are those of the humoral psychology. But
Burton's extraordinary fragmenting of the categories of
phenomena, together with the extensive generalization he
makes of the melancholy phenomena he describes, his
identification of cause, symptom, and cure, the very univer-

---

[21] Bergen Evans and George Mohr, M.D., *The Psychiatry of
Robert Burton* (New York, 1944).

[22] *AM*, 1. 36; his birthplace: 11. 68, 250; his school: 11. 63;
Oxford, Christ Church, and the Bodleian: 1. 17, 417; 11. 66, 91,
97, 214; his brothers: 1. 36; 11. 68; his mother: 11. 251; his living
at Segrave: 11. 63-64; his patroness, 11. 68.

salization of the disease into the whole condition of humanity: all this pulverizes the structural schemes of the psychology of humors, removes the medical and spiritual problems of melancholy into a far wider area of consideration and reference. In other words, the book turns out to be paradoxical about its very material: ostensibly a treatise well within the traditional psychology and medicine, it breaks through the boundaries of that tradition to universalize for common understanding and insight what had been a technical and restricted medical problem. In the simplest sense, the achievement of the book is paradoxical, the presentation of a proposition contrary to popular opinion. In a deeper sense, the fact of that commonplace paradox is in turn paradoxical in practice: the melancholiac's anatomy of melancholy determines melancholy to be other than it appeared. In Burton's dark mirror, melancholy saw herself as she really was, as quite different from what she had been thought, perhaps even quite different from what she had thought herself before her long scrutiny.

Erasmus' Folly refers not only to Erasmus, her creator, but always to herself: *The Praise of Folly* is a huge self-reference, Folly's shameless praise of herself, as she tells us, an exercise in *philautia*, or self-love. In moral theology, *philautia* is usually translated as pride, the root sin of all the rest. True to his custom, Burton supplied several words to translate the shades of meaning involved in the concept of *philautia*: "Philautia, or Self-love, Vainglory, Praise, Honour, Immoderate Applause, Pride, overmuch Joy, etc." (1. 292). Immediately following this section is Burton's longest digression, in many ways his most touching and personal essay, the "Digression of the Miseries of Scholars" (1. 300ff.). By the end of the digression, Burton has slid into using the first-person plural, identifying himself with all miserable, all naturally and properly melancholy scholars. Even then, though, he contradicts the implications in that use of "we," ultimately agreeing with his invoked impartial observer that the clergy, of whom he is a member, make up "a rotten crowd, beggarly, uncouth, filthy, melancholy, miserable, despicable, and contemptible" (1. 330).

To degrade one's class is of course to degrade one's self, to deny one's importance and significance. The paradox, a linguistic self-denial or self-contradiction, may well ask for this kind of fictional attitude toward one's self—as, for example, Folly herself so classically demonstrates. The extreme acting-out of such self-denial in life is the act of suicide, the all-too-common close to cases of melancholy.[23] Burton provides us with his brief *biathanatos*, or debate upon the lawfulness of suicide (1. 435-39). As a divine and a physician, we might expect him to condemn suicide outright and without equivocation; but once more, he cheats our expectation by the sympathy, and even the hope of divine pardon, which he extends to men led by desperation to risk their salvation as well as their bodily health.

Actually, Burton's toleration of suicides is but another mark of his general comprehension of melancholy and of all spiritual ills. He never underestimated melancholy's miseries and tortures: but also, he never underestimated the benefits melancholy may grant to her victims. Creation is deeply involved in melancholy—the muses are melancholy, as he wrote in his digression on scholarly miseries (1. 300). The proposition is reversible: melancholy is the muses, too. Intensity of human perception, creativity in all fields are in the gift of melancholy: or, melancholy favors the gifted. Melancholy distinguishes men, one from another, and most of all those particularly qualified as men. Melancholy, as "Albertus Durer" had depicted her,

[23] See below, Chapter 16.

was an angel fixed upon the point of her own contemplation, arrested by the intensity and depth of her understanding.

Burton's book is, first and last, a paradox of the fundamental kind, a praise of folly.[24] The melancholy man
knows how to praise melancholy because of the perceptions
his melancholy gives him, because it is melancholy that
drives a man to seek solitude and to contemplate truth.
Burton's vision was as arresting and complete as that of
Dürer's intellectual giantess: for him, melancholy itself
became the organizing principle of the world. Primarily
his book belongs in the tradition of Nicholas of Cusa, who
praised *docta ignorantia*; of Montaigne, who provided a
learned proof of universal ignorance and uncertainty; of
Henry Cornelius Agrippa, who learnedly proved the in-
adequacies of all branches of learning; of Erasmus, who
praised at once folly and, by indirection and darkly, a wisdom beyond that of men; of Sebastian Brandt, for whom
the world was a ship full of fools. All these works were, in
varying degrees, didactic essays aimed at human error and
pride, at human *philautia*; all were paradoxical encomia,
praising what most men were accustomed to think vile.
Taking their texts from Ecclesiastes and Paul, all, even
Brandt, reinterpreted ignorance, uncertainty, folly, and
melancholy as the true wisdom and means to grace. The
paradoxist denies dialectic, forbids a choice between one
absolute and another; he insists upon *et*, upon the simultaneity of double and plural truth.

Like Montaigne, who calls doubt upon the method of his
"Apologie" just as he is about to lunge home, like Folly
who questions her whole oration, Burton is critical of his
own discourse. Again and again he refers to Erasmus and

[24] Irene Samuel, "The Brood of Folly," *N&Q*, cciii (1958),
430-31; Walter J. Kaiser, *Praisers of Folly*.

his *Encomion*;[25] like Folly, Democritus junior warns the reader of his own unreliability:

I have overshot myself, I have spoken foolishly, rashly, unadvisedly, absurdly, I have anatomized mine own folly. And now methinks upon a sudden I am awaked as it were out of a dream; I have had a raving fit, a phantastical fit, ranged up and down, in and out, I have insulted over most kind of men, abused some, offended others, wronged myself; and now being recovered, and perceiving mine error, cry with Orlando, *Solvite me*, pardon, *O boni*, that which is past, and I will make you amends in that which is to come; I promise you a more sober discourse in my following treatise. (I. 122)

The following treatise may be more sober, but Democritus promises no more than sobriety. That treatise too may give offense, and if it does, it does:

I hope there will no such cause of offense be given; if there be, *Nemo aliquid recognoscat, nos mentimur omnia*. I'll deny all (my last refuge), recant all, renounce all I have said, if any man except, and with as much facility excuse as he can accuse; but I presume of thy good favour, and gracious acceptance (gentle reader). Out of an assured hope and confidence thereof, I will begin. (I. 123)

So begins the book proper, calling doubt on its own matter; but the book ends quoting Augustine, who turns doubt itself into opportunity for salvation:

Do you wish to be freed from doubt? do you desire to escape uncertainty? Be penitent while of sound mind: by so doing I assert that you are safe, because you have devoted that time to penitence in which you might have been guilty of sin. (III. 432)

Those are the book's last words, in the tradition of para-

---

[25] *AM*, I. 27, 28, 29, 39, 52, 59, 247, 310, 325, 343; II. 92, 126; III. 3.

dox, an anticlimax: one is not sure that the end has been reached, one is tempted to turn the page for the climax proper to such a book. But this end is a proper ending, all the same, for the paradox does not conclude, does not close off for good. The book does not quite end, and yet it does end, realistically speaking, as any intimate discourse ends, in the expectation of continued life and continued discourse. Spiritually speaking, too, the book has come to its end, which is the assertion of belief in the life to come, in both the rest of mortal life and in a life in heaven; it ends in an assertion of trust, amidst a dangerous and mutable world, in the flexible, tolerant, comprehensive grace of God. Melancholy is simply the condition of mortality, or of living; like life itself, it is the only medium in which anyone can become a man or hope for a life after death. As in Cusanus', Montaigne's, and Erasmus' books, out of acknowledged folly grace has grown; melancholy proves to be a heavenly as well as an earthly muse.

15

"Reason in Madness"

> . . . I cannot behold a Beggar without relieving his
> necessities with my purse, or his soule with my
> prayers; these scenicall or accidentall differences
> betweene us cannot make mee forget that common
> and untouch't part of us both; there is under these
> *Centoes* and miserable outsides, these mutilate and
> semi-bodies, a soule of the same alloy with our
> owne. . . .
>
> Browne, Religio Medici, II. 13

THE following topics come from the table of contents of
the first book of paradoxy in a European vernacular,
Ortensio Lando's *Paradossi Cioè, Sententie fuori del comun
parere; Novellamente in luce*,[1] a book which, translated,
imitated, and adapted in other European languages,[2] became the reference and source for a mass of paradoxical
exercise.

> That poverty is better than riches.
> It is better to be ignorant than learned.
> It is better to be blind than to have sight.
> It is better to be mad than wise.
> It is not a bad thing for a prince to lose his state.
> It is better to live in exile than to languish in
>   one's native land.
> It is better to weep than to laugh.

[1] (Venice, 1544; 1st edition, Lyons, 1543).

[2] Charles Estienne did the French translation, with additions of
his own: *Paradoxes, ce sont propos contre la commune opinion*
(Paris, 1553). The full English translation was made by Anthony
Munday: *The Defence of Contraries. Paradoxes against common
opinion* (London, 1593).

It is better to live in a cottage than in a great palace.
It is neither shameful nor odious to be a bastard.
It is better to be in prison than at liberty.
A frugal life is better than a splendid and sumptuous one.
It is better to have no servants than to have them.

Lando's paradoxes are conventional enough, efficient expositions of views contrary to received opinion, carefully constructed on the ancient pattern, supported by proper authorities and by empirical anecdote. Even for paradoxists who never held Lando's book in their hands, his list provided the *Ur*-manual of their subjects. Lando set the tune to which scores of paradoxists wrote their careful variations.

The paradoxes on this list, selected from the whole contents of Lando's book, deal chiefly with socio-economic status and with moral condition; though many of them plainly contradict the usual assumptions of ordinary men ("Poverty is better than riches"; "It is better to live in a cottage than in a great palace"; "A frugal life is better than a splendid and sumptuous one"), they are, in different wording, restatements of the themes of the *Paradoxa Stoicorum*, assertions of the freedom of the human spirit from worldly bonds. Other paradoxes in this list tend the opposite way, inverting Stoic axioms: "It is better to be ignorant than learned"; "It is better to be mad than wise." Still others depend upon unspoken Stoic axioms for their authority, though one must think for a moment to realize what the underlying assumptions are. The defense of "It is better to be in prison than at liberty," for instance, turns on the notion that the mind must be free of its environment. In the same way, "It is better to live in exile than to languish at home," or "It is better to have no servants than to have them," all refer to the Stoic value system which rejects the complications of worldly ceremony. Quite another set of assumptions is drawn upon for "It is neither shameful nor odious to be a bastard," where Epicurean "nature" is called up to defend the condition of illegitimate (or natural) birth. Another paradox defends Heraclitus against Democritus: "It is better to weep than to laugh." Such generalizations as these paradoxes, though always in some measure directed against the clichés of received opinion, can never be absolute. The paradoxist's rhetorical task, hardly a very difficult one, was to make them seem, one way or another, absolute and fixed.

Three of the topics, ignorance, blindness, and madness, are dealt with morally and epistemologically, with something of the witty hypallage of Folly's oration. In all three cases, Lando's defenses rely on the unspoken rejection of normal worldly opinion to make a moral point about the relation of goodness to *docta ignorantia*. Goodness and salvation, he suggests, do not rest upon received opinion of what goodness and salvation are.

All the paradoxical topics on this list soon became clichés of particular interest only because they were so widely imitated and adapted by paradoxists learning their craft. They were the most obvious, the most shop-worn articles in the paradoxist's stock—it comes as some surprise, then, to realize that these hard nuggets of paradoxy are all melted into the thematic pattern of one of the most complicated and sophisticated pieces in the literary repertory of the Renaissance, that is, *King Lear*. Crudely, the paradoxes are obvious enough:[3] the play turns, after all,

---

[3] The themes of *King Lear* have been the subjects of endless discussion; and the play's paradoxes have by no means passed unnoticed. Robert B. Heilman's *This Great Stage* (Louisiana State University Press, 1948) is by far the most exhaustive image-study of *King Lear*, a book which necessarily deals with many of the paradoxes handled here (see especially p. 309, n. 5). His treatment of the Lear paradoxes is new-critical and poetic, without reference to traditions of formal paradoxy: my brief comments, a fly to Heilman's elephant, rely for their existence upon the principle of parsimony.

on the notion of a ruler's losing his state. In spite of Kent's direct "Reserve thy state,"[4] the old king divides his land between his elder daughters and as a result passes from riches to poverty, loses his servants until he is followed only by a fool and a disguised volunteer, comes to crouch in a hovel rather than lord it in the great house to which he is entitled. In the course of his reduction from his former splendor and sumptuousness to this narrow life, Lear loses his clothes, tearing them off, a madman, to become naked humanity itself. Just before his ultimate death, Lear, who had been king in his country, is thrust into prison—where, following the *topos*, he is happier than he

---

Besides Heilman's book other books and articles drawn on for this chapter are: Theodore Spencer, *Shakespeare and the Nature of Man* (New York, 1943); Geoffrey Bush, *Shakespeare and the Natural Condition* (Harvard University Press, 1956); John F. Danby, *Shakespeare's Doctrine of Nature* (London, 1949); Enid Welsford, *The Fool* (New York, 1936); William Rosen, *Shakespeare and the Craft of Tragedy* (Harvard University Press, 1960); J. A. Barish and Marshall Waingrow, "Service in *King Lear*," *Shakespeare Quarterly*, IX (1958), 347-55; O. J. Campbell, "The Salvation of Lear," *ELH*, xv (1948), 93-109; Hardin Craig, "The Ethics of *King Lear*," *PQ*, IV (1925), 97-109; W. R. Keast, "Imagery and Meaning in the Interpretation of *King Lear*," *MP*, XLVII (1949), 54-64; Julian Markels, "Shakespeare's Confluence of Tragedy and Comedy: *Twelfth Night* and *King Lear*," *Shakespeare 400*, ed. James G. McManaway (New York, 1964), pp. 75-88; Sears Jayne, "Charity in *King Lear*," *ibid.*, 277-88; Winifred Nowottny, "Lear's Questions," *Shakespeare Survey*, x (1957), 90-97; Irving Ribner, " 'The Gods are Just,' " *Tulane Drama Studies*, II (1958), 34-54; and Virgil K. Whitaker, *Shakespeare's Use of Learning* (Huntington Library, 1953); Maynard Mack, *King Lear in Our Time* (University of California Press, 1965).

[4] *King Lear*, I.i.149: here I cite the Arden edition, ed. Kenneth Muir (London, 1952), instead of the Kittredge edition cited elsewhere.

had been when at liberty, since he there enjoys Cordelia's company.

Kent goes gladly into exile—"Freedom lives hence, and banishment is here," he says as he is ordered, on pain of death, from the kingdom (1.i.181). He is shortly followed into banishment by Edgar, who has also lost estate, who comes from a great house to the same poor hovel on the heath, who exchanges the garments proper to the heir of an earldom for a barely sufficient blanket. Gloucester, ignorant of human character, is blinded, driven into exile, maddened into a suicide attempt before he finds "himself" at last. Edgar feigns madness, Lear goes mad and achieves understanding, the Fool apes madness, as his calling requires. At the end of the play, it is obviously "better" to weep than to laugh; furthermore, tears have purged many of the characters in the play ("Howl, howl!"), at whose lives and deaths the audience must weep as well. The weeping is itself ambiguous, too, for there are moments in the play so grotesque as to be almost comic. The whole play operates at the edge of what is by convention ridiculous, not tragic—ranting king, madmen, plain-speaking servingman mocking the pretensions of his "betters."

On the other side, Edmund is Gloucester's bastard son; his speaking up for bastards to question their inferior position, rests on the same naturalistic ground of Lando's (and many others') paradoxes on natural children:

> Why bastard? wherefore base?
> When my dimensions are as well compact,
> My mind as generous, and my shape as true,
> As honest madam's issue? Why brand they us
> With base? with baseness? bastardy? base, base?
>   (1.ii.6-10)

Gloucester confirms two points made by conventional defenses of bastards, the pleasure and healthy conception from which they spring: on the face of it, Edmund's defense of his rights seems legitimate enough, until the paradox itself is turned inside-out after Edmund's revelations of his real intentions. Not even he seeks to excuse his nature by the conditions of his birth—"Fut, I should have been that I am, had the maidenliest star in the firmament twinkled on my bastardizing" (1.ii.139-41).

When one looks closely at the play for stock paradoxes, one sees several more not included in Lando's repertory, especially in the Fool's speeches—the codpiece, for example, and the variations upon "all" and "nothing." As one checks them off, the traditional paradoxes of *King Lear*, once noted, are quite as obvious as those paradoxes embedded in *Gargantua and Pantagruel* and *The Anatomy of Melancholy*. The difference between the paradoxes in those works, displayed each intact and shining, and the paradoxes in *King Lear* is that the *Lear* paradoxes are submerged beneath the moving surface of the play, worked into one another in a substructure that itself keeps the surface moving in its irregular but recurrent patterns. To change the metaphor, the paradoxes in this play are wound into a strong twist spiraling in to converge upon one essential consideration. Whichever paradox one begins by examining—blindness, state, cottage—or at whatever point in the play one begins the examination, one is soon drawn into all the other paradoxes, narrowing together upon the central theme of the play, the discovery that individual self-discovery is also the revelation of the human predicament.

Both schematically and in detail, the paradoxes work together to this end. Schematically, poverty, loss of state, exile, servantlessness, hovels, rags, nakedness, prison, and tears all conjoin so that it is impossible to keep the separate topics apart. So also with blindness, ignorance, folly, and madness, inextricably knotted together. The spiral continues to turn in, imperceptibly passing from level to level, always involving more than one character in the play, involving them all ever more deeply with one another. Paradox denies boundary and category, so individual conditions overlap. Kent, Lear, Gloucester, and Edgar are all exiled or outlawed by the lawless law of handy-dandy. Lear and Edgar are both "the thing itself, unaccommodated man." Lear, figuratively blind, mocks Gloucester, actually blinded; both men begin to "see" only in the depths of their personal darkness. Lear and Gloucester share despair and the terrors of oncoming madness; both die of a double mind, Gloucester's heart "burst smilingly" as he is reunited with his true son, Lear knowing and not knowing that his true daughter is dead. The old men are, literally, driven out and toward madness by their children, who also seek to kill them outright.

Edgar by no means seeks deliberately to harm Lear, but his feigned madness contributes to the real madness, so long resisted, of the king. To the king's final folly the Fool also makes his contribution, though the Fool's relation to Lear is at the same time (and thus paradoxically) supportive also. His underlying fidelity and the truth of his sharp words play their part in strengthening Lear's grasp upon a reality cruelly double-faced. The truth is never, as the whole play demonstrates, kind. Like the Fool, Kent and Cordelia do Lear enormous pain by speaking the truth to him.

In turn, their plain speaking is not absolutely true either. Cordelia, for example, *is* far truer than her word. In her fatal interview with her father, though she does not lie, Cordelia certainly equivocates. Clearly, neither Lear nor any of his daughters is exactly as he or she seems, Cordelia no less than the others. Her pride prevents her from lying, as her sisters so readily do, and is also too great to permit full expression of her feelings for Lear. As for Kent,

> who in disguise
> Follow'd his enemy king, and did him service
> Improper for a slave. . . ,   (v.iii.219-21)

true as his word is, it is not so true as his deed. Furthermore, fitting the irony of the whole play, to act "true,"
Kent must go in disguise. The Fool follows an old man
down to disgrace in the terrible hovel on the heath: of not
even a professional fool is it required to show such extreme folly. All three faithful ones are, in the world's
eyes, fools.

   In that hovel, Lear, the Fool, Gloucester, and Kent meet
another deceiver, Edgar, forced to don the disguise of
madman and beggar too. From that confrontation and because of it, Lear finally emerges mad. With a little critical
distance from which to observe them, the fools can be seen
to be as duplicitous in their way as the knaves in theirs:
the knaves, Goneril, Regan, and Edmund, all find words to
~~distance from which to observe them, the fools can be seen~~
The fools speak harshly and are true. Their love is in fact
more than tongue can tell; they cannot heave their hearts
into their mouths. By the criteria laid down by Erasmus'
Folly, all three—Cordelia, Kent, the Fool—are true fools
of God, both because they are true to Lear in his extremity
and because of their utter selflessness, which worked to
their own worldly undoing. The three also replace one
another in the action, do one another's offices. Disguised
Kent stands in for Cordelia in France; the Fool is unmannerly to Lear after Kent's banishment: Lear himself,
truly mad, takes over from the Fool, who, his office done
when the king goes mad, without explanation fades from
the play.

   On the evil side of the morality, the elder sisters and
Edmund are also inextricably intertwined, Edmund be-
trothing himself to both sisters, to the one while her hus-

band lived. Though Goneril poisons the widowed Regan to get her out of the way, all three die as one, as Edmund says with pardonable pride (v.iii.228-29). The "marriage" of the three to which he refers is patently a social and moral "impossibility." Albany's bitter comment on his wife's betrothal to Edmund (v.iii.85-90) returns us, from a far deeper level, to the theme with which the play began, the upheaval in social regulation on which Gloucester and Kent commented in the play's first lines. When one looks back to those opening lines, the significance of the paradoxical commonplaces becomes ever clearer. Meeting just before the division of the kingdom, the Earls of Kent and Gloucester touch on two "paradoxical" and therefore touchy topics, the division of the kingdom itself and the matter of Edmund's bastardy. Throughout the short scene, the social order is conspicuously observed: the earls are polite about the general situation and to each other, and a subdued Edmund imitates the manners of his elders. Through the honeyed exchanges between Lear and each of his elder daughters, courtesy is maintained, only to be broken by Lear's ungoverned rage at Cordelia's refusal to ape her sisters. At this point, Kent speaks roundly to the king: he is unmannerly when Lear is mad. With the desertion of elementary courtesy, the action takes its course toward elemental barbarity.

Immediately after this scene, Edmund begins the disruption of the household of which he is a part, his slander of his brother bringing his father to the famous comment on collapsing social and moral structure:

. . . Love cools, friendship falls off, brothers divide: in cities, mutinies; in countries discord; in palaces, treason; and the bond crack'd 'twixt son and father . . . there's son against father . . . there's father against child. (i.ii.110-17)

Too often (and too easily) taken as evidencing the destruction of a significant "Elizabethan world picture," this speech points as well to the topsy-turvydom of parodist and paradoxist. Between the worlds upside down of most paradoxical literature—in Rabelais' book, for example, or in "Upon Appleton House"—and the world upside down in *King Lear* there is a great difference, the difference between detachment and involvement, between satiric and tragic irony. Hamlet's words in another connection mark this boundary between Cloud-cuckooland and the true territory of tragedy: in Cloud-cuckooland "they do but poison in jest, no offense *in the world.*" In tragedy—in *Hamlet*, in *King Lear*—the offense is precisely *in* the world, not merely in some witty mirror image of it. The paradoxist's inversion is in tragedy not so much an intellectual as a factual inversion: the paradox is itself contradicted, the metaphor un-metaphored, as irony turns into truth.

In turn, this new "truth" has paradoxes of its own. Working inward, the paradox once more turns inside out, to reveal that this very reversal of moral values, the upheaval in society and the elements, is what brings men back to rights. In the storm, losing his mind, Lear learns that he has "ta'en too little care of this"—and of this, and of this, and of that as well. He has let himself fall into that elementary trap against which all political counselors, from Aristotle to Machiavelli, warn rulers: flattery. That his chief flatterers were his daughters simply intensifies the poignancy of an otherwise trite situation. In many ways— part of the paradoxy of all tragedy—Lear gets his deserts. He has not "ta'en care," he has not "seen" the world right side up. He has in consequence, as the Fool tells him, made his daughters his mothers and thus deserves the beating they give him.

The world of *King Lear*, upside down and right side up, like many formal paradoxes, turns on the logical polar axis of "all" and "nothing." All Lear's troubles come from Cordelia's firm "Nothing, my lord," in answer to her father's formal request for a record of her affection. Edmund starts the troubles in Gloucester's family with exactly the same words, "Nothing, my lord," in answer to his father's request for a report on the false letter in Edmund's hand. Both Cordelia and Edmund, for quite different reasons, equivocate with that traditionally equivocal word "nothing." And neither lies.

"Nothing will come of nothing," Lear warns Cordelia, perhaps never so plainly showing his unwisdom; he repeats the orthodox truism to the Fool, who asks Lear if the king can "make no use of nothing." The double negative gives warning of the Fool's intent: Lear should have made use of "all" his holdings while he still had them. In the Fool's words, Lear has become "an o without a figure . . . a nothing" (i.iv.200-201). The sovereign who had been "all" in the kingdom is reduced to a cipher. By giving "all" away —state, palace, servants—Lear has denied himself, figuratively stripped himself as he later physically strips himself. Without a right to do so, he tries to deny others, telling Regan that "her sister's naught" (ii.iv.135)—again, a significant misjudgment of the actualities of the case. Fleeing from his father's rage, Edgar similarly denies himself —"Edgar I nothing am" (ii.iii.21).

By his rash deed, King Lear has in fact reversed God's great act of Creation: he has brought "all" to "nothing," turned form back into chaos. As he himself rightly says, pathetically often (ii.iv.252; iii.iv.20, 48-49, 64), he has given all away, until the Fool can rightly taunt him that he has pared his "wit o' both sides, and left nothing i' th' middle" (i.iv.204-05). These dramatic self-denials parallel the self-contradictory action of logical and rhetorical paradoxes, particularly of those paradoxes that deal with "all" and "nothing" as their subjects. "All" and "nothing" are not subjects for rhetorical play only, however; again and again, the echoes of the words remind us of the stakes in this play. Even the words in the mouth of a nameless gentleman at the beginning of the storm-scene sound out the total risk (III.i.9-15).

To compare *King Lear*'s "all" with another invocation of cosmic totality is to bring out the passionate affirmation beneath the unrelieved *terribilità* of Lear's chaotic "all." In *Paradise Lost*, Milton's vision of the total length of created time from Genesis to Judgment is always safely under God's inspection: all the disorder is evened out at the end, and disorder as it happens is made bearable by the expectation of ultimate ordering. For King Lear, the same span of time was all chaos, a projection of the dreadful pudder in his head and the society he himself had so significantly failed to regulate. Lear's chaos is, however, always an active one, always filled with personality. It is absolutely unlike Macbeth's chilling apprehension of infinite points of time before and after, quite unlike Pascal's disinterested, inhuman, mathematical time sequence. Lear's time is as unredeemable as theirs, but the people in it are not unredeemable, as it turns out. Lear's "time" is filled, and filled to overflowing, with passionate recording of the untold importance of human choice, human action, and human nature. "Undoing" can extend throughout the realms of both nature and grace, but it is specific human undoing of which Lear speaks.

In his eschatological cursing, Lear leaves no room for anything but human misbehavior. The judgment he invokes falls upon everyone alike; no one will escape annihilation, no one will escape to grace:

> Crack nature's moulds, all germains spill at once,
> That make ungrateful man.　　　　　　(III.ii.8-9)

Close pent-up guilts,
   Rive your concealing continents, and cry
   These dreadful summoners grace.   (III.ii.57-59)

By the end of the play, there is somewhat more hope than at this moment, but not much. In the canon of Shakespeare's tragedies, *King Lear* affords the barest restoration of grace. What must be said for the play, in spite of the austerity of its ending, is that its universe is always entirely human; no matter how dreadful, it remains a great stage where fools act out their inevitable disaster, a stage of enormous human actions and reactions, of enormous human motions and emotions.

"Nothing" paradoxes tend to turn inside-out; beneath the linguistic paradox of "nothing" in this play lies the moral anomaly reversing the first meaning of the paradox, for King Lear is not, as we painfully learn with him, "nothing." Nor is any man, no matter how close to nothing he may come. The examination of naked human nature takes place when destitution and nakedness converge in the persons of Tom and Lear, the beggar and the king. Of Tom, Lear says in the familiar language of satire on sumptuary luxury:

Consider him well. Thou ow'st the worm no silk, the beast no hide, the sheep no wool, the cat no perfume. Ha! Here's three on's are sophisticated—

that is, three of us still covered with clothes, according to our stations. But those three are in fact only "sophisticated," or, their clothes are sophistries, concealing their true natures. For all three of them are disguised—Lear, dressed as a king, is king no more. Kent, dressed as a rough servant, is an earl. The Fool, properly dressed in motley, is far from a fool. Nor is Tom less deceitful—neither madman nor beggar, he only seems to be what Lear calls him: "Thou art the thing itself: unaccommodated man is no

more but such a poor, bare, forked animal as thou art"
(III.iv.105-11). Attempting to become "the thing itself,"
Lear becomes like one of his destitute subjects—"You
houseless poverty"; "Poor naked wretches" (III.iv.26-28)
—of whom in his great house, clad in fine robes, he had
never thought.

The paradoxy works on, and inward. As he loses the
vestments of his earlier self, as he loses even his unreason-
able reason, Lear becomes more and more a man, more and
more himself. His undoing is his re-creation as a man.
Distracted, he is far wiser than he had been in his "perfect
mind." Edgar too is the better for having been Tom.
Strengthened in vision and in courage, he can honestly
say to his father, in spite of the long deception, "In nothing
am I chang'd/ But in my garments" (IV.vi.9-10).

The critical comment on clothes, normally in Renaissance writing reserved to satire on social aspirations (as in
Hamlet's remarks about Osric, or Lafeu's to Parolles), in
King Lear is so deeply integrated into the theme of human
nature as to become a clothes philosophy. Kent begins,
sounding like Lafeu to Parolles in *All's Well*, saying to the
pretentious Oswald, "a tailor made thee." Simply, Oswald
is dressed above his proper social station, and Kent refers
thus to the falsity of his appearance. Gradually we learn
that Oswald's appearance in fact does not belie him: he is
as false as the clothes he wears. A tailor cannot make a
man, and Oswald is not a man. Kent knows, and Lear
learns, that other things make a man's life, by itself as
cheap as a beast's, into something dearer than that.

Nature does not "accommodate" man; it is society that
dresses men up beyond their reality. When Goneril and
Regan outdo each other in stripping Lear of his retinue,
he answers them, not in terms of men, but in terms of
clothes—

> Thou art a lady:
> If only to go warm were gorgeous,
> Why, nature needs not what thou gorgeous wear'st,
> Which scarcely keeps thee warm.   (ii.iv.269-72)

At this point, servant theme, clothing theme, and palace-hovel theme overlap and fuse. In the next exchange Regan says,

> This house is little: the old man and 's people
> Cannot be well bestow'd.   (ii.iv.290-92)

Kent, seeing his master bareheaded on the heath, urges him to the hovel, himself returning for succor to the same "hard house" from which they have all been barred. The hovel takes them in: where, each man for himself, they face what it is to be truly unaccommodated, with Tom in his near-nakedness serving as their emblem and text. In this case, too, we find that with whatever paradox we begin, we are drawn from one into all the rest, and then on into the inevitable consideration on which all the paradoxes focus, irreducible human nature.

From the hovel the figures emerge to the world again, building back to some kind of human connection. Gloucester remembers Tom simply by his exceptional nakedness —"Is this the naked fellow?"—but he is not too proud to ask that naked fellow to set him on the Dover road. The old man leading Gloucester into Tom's company is also a figure of charity. Long a Gloucester tenant, he responds to the plight of his disaccommodated lord and of poor Tom, promising the beggar "the best 'parel that I have." With this giving-taking of kindness, mankind takes leave of its alternate, manunkind, to face the consequences of self-recognition.

Man is not nothing, as the characters show, but he is naked. Nakedness is essential mortality, standing against hypocrisy and semblance. Lear, "fantastically dressed with weeds," makes his great speech of "reason in madness":

> Through tatter'd clothes small vices do appear;
> Robes and furr'd gowns hide all. . . .
>
> (iv.vi.166-67)

and comes out of his heartlessness to identify the man on whose infirmity he has so painfully harped:

> I know you well enough; thy name is Gloucester.
> Thou must be patient. We came crying hither;
> Thou know'st, the first time that we smell the air
> We wawl and cry.   (iv.vi.180-82)

The naked baby, true-born or bastard, has no choice about his coming hither, and the defenseless old man as little in his going hence: between the first cry and the last, unaccommodated man must make his choices as best he can. Not until he recognizes himself as unaccommodated, though, is he able to recognize others and to make legitimate choices; though once he has done so, even a foolish fond old man, far from his perfect mind, can choose right: folly is never altogether fool.

Just as Lear recovers right reason by enduring madness, so Gloucester recovers vision by the loss of his eyes. He stumbled when he saw, and he had not, he thought, then needed spectacles to see "nothing"—though in fact he had seen something where nothing was. Still, Gloucester was never entirely benighted, even before the blinding, for he had recognized Edgar in Tom when he first caught sight of him, though he had not realized his recognition. His darkness is never allowed to envelop him altogether, even though he seems to wish that it would. When he seeks to destroy himself, Edgar's charity prevents him, and Edgar's Stoicism persuades him to stand the course until

> his flaw'd heart—
> (Alack, too weak the conflict to support!)
> 'Twixt two extremes of passion, joy and grief,
> Burst smilingly.   (v.iii.196-99)

Dramatically, Gloucester bears both for himself and for
Lear the penalty of moral blindness, thereby relieving
Lear to bear more fully the pain of madness. From the
beginning, the images of folly and blindness have been
connected. Lear refuses to "see" in the play's first scene.
"Hence, and avoid my sight!" he cries out to Cordelia;
and "Out of my sight!" to Kent, who (making the situation worse) answers back,

> See better, Lear, and let me still remain
> The true blank of thine eye.   (i.i.158-59)

In his towering rage at Cordelia, Lear loses his sense of
himself, sending all his friends away and leaving himself
naked to the charity of his elder daughters. As Regan observed of him, "He hath ever but slenderly known himself" (i.i.293-94); all the more remarkable that he "ripens" to self-knowledge at all. In the huge task of self-
identification, Lear's courage is terrifying. "Who is it who
can tell me who I am?" he asks after Goneril's first descent upon him, only to hear the Fool respond, "Lear's
shadow" (i.iv.239). Terrible though it is that a king in
substance is reduced to the dark flat pattern of himself,[5]
by paradoxical convention, even a shadow carries some
hope of substantiation. Donne noted in his apocalyptic
"Nocturnall" that some body must always have existed to
have cast a shadow, a body which might once more be in-
vested by that shadow. Even in the pathos of his madness,
Lear comes to "embody" the shadow that he has been.

In spite of his inexperience in self-examination, Lear

[5] See above, Chapter 7, p. 230-231.

recognizes the danger in which he stands, and tries to direct himself away from his own obsessions—

> O Lear, Lear, Lear!
> Beat at this gate, that let thy folly in
> And thy dear judgment out! (ɪ.iv.279-81)

> O, let me not be mad, be mad, sweet heaven!
> Keep me in temper; I would not be mad.
> (ɪ.v.47-48)

> O fool, I shall go mad. (ɪɪ.iv.288)

> O that way madness lies. (ɪɪɪ.iv.21)

Two scenes after that last cry, though, Lear has come to face and to proclaim the madness that claims him. In answer to the Fool's "Prithee, nuncle, tell me whether a madman be a gentleman or a yeoman?" Lear answers unequivocally, "A king, a king!" (ɪɪɪ.vi.11). The Fool this time tries to temper the bitter self-revelation, but this time the king has spoken with the Fool's fearless truthfulness, though his wits have had to turn to let him learn plain speaking at last. After his fit near Dover, he wakens in Cordelia's presence, to honesty:

> For, to speak plainly,
> I fear I am not in my perfect mind.
> (ɪv.vii.62-63)

He comes to the truth without equivocation; long past the normal age limit for regeneration by psychological insight, in the midst of excruciating stress, Lear ripens to recognize things as they are, to recognize himself, his family, and his society. That he, so far from the truth, should come to recognize it at its bitterest, is precisely what makes the old madman heroic. Cordelia had always known about human nature—in this, as in their equivocation, she and Edmund are alike. From her no secrets are hid: "I know you what you are," she roundly takes leave of her sisters. Edmund, the machiavel, also knows both himself and others, recognizes the real characters beneath the seeming. The true daughter and the false son stand in this paradoxical equilibrium in the play: it is proper, at the end, that Edmund pay his belated respects to Cordelia's truth by trying to save her from the death to which he had sent her.

He fails, of course. At exactly the moment that Albany promises conventional rewards to the virtuous and conventional punishments to the wicked, Lear appears with Cordelia's body in his arms. For all his intermittent delusion that she lives, he must die knowing that she is dead. His madness is not the kindly delusive folly that makes most things bearable in Erasmus' *Encomion*: madness enforces that Lear see all the horrible truth. Only death affords any protection against human sufferings from human folly. Kent speaks the words of release at Lear's death, and himself promises his own Stoical self-disposal; Edgar must take up his office in the gored state without prospect of satisfaction or reward. At the cost of almost total destruction, some order is restored to a society utterly jeopardized by Cordelia's proud integrity and her father's wildness. For their faults of excess, her intransigent truth and his unbridled foolishness, Cordelia and Lear must, as surely as the evil characters must, drain the cup of their deservings. Folly turned wisdom acknowledges that folly has privileges only in spiritual life. In moral life, folly pays for herself like everyone else.

In paradox, folly is characteristically treated critically rather than crucially: the folly theme permits the protection of ironical distance from relative human frailties. In *King Lear*, the examination of folly is in fact also the examination of moral perception, moral value, and moral action. Man's one distinguishing human characteristic, his reason, is scrutinized, the questions posed and acted out:

how little reason may a man have, and still be a man? how much must a reasonable man know of his reasons? In this play, self-examination is not scientifically treated, the self displayed as its own neutral subject of scrutiny, as in Montaigne's lifelong cool presentation. Rather, self-examination is dramatized as a passionate process toward a moral end, toward understanding as action. Certainly this is the humanist conviction, the message (more gently taught) of Erasmus' *Encomion*, which deepened from game to the serious preoccupation with salvation. As her irony began to thicken into the tragic theme, Folly backed away into her anti-epilogue to preserve the decorum of self-contradiction proper to pure paradoxy. In *King Lear* there is no backing away from the relentless moral paradoxes of self-knowledge.

Twisting normally separate paradoxical topics into one tight skein of theme and character would be a remarkable enough achievement if *King Lear* were not also an even greater *tour-de-force* of paradoxy. The essence of paradox is its doubleness, with its concomitant detachment and postponement of commitment. Such engagement as formal rhetorical paradoxes have, is with themselves: they are, and are supposed to be, ultimately self-regarding and self-referential. Though they must call forth "wonder" from their audience, paradoxes do not require—indeed, normally they repel—identification on the part of their audience. The specific paradoxes of *King Lear* might, had they somehow stood alone, have induced the same detached marveling to be got from the brilliant paradoxical passages in *Gargantua*, or in Sidney's or Donne's lyrics, or in the fine formal dispraise of virginity that Parolles reels off to Helena. But the paradoxes in *King Lear* are not by any means self-sufficient, self-referential, entities, encysted perfectly within the whole work. Defying their boundaries, they flow together to draw the beholder into the experience of contradiction, operating much more like the paradoxes of religious transcendence exploited in *Paradise Lost* and in Donne's Anniversary Poems than like the forensic paradoxes of Lando's *epideixis*. The paradoxy of *King Lear* transforms the intelligence into the understanding, transforms the rhetorical into the psychological, the intellectual into the moral. Lando's archetypal paradoxes are formal stimuli, to chafe minds into detached consideration of the validity of received opinion. The very same paradoxes in *King Lear* invade areas of the mind normally inviolate, forcing the critical intelligence into a crucial affirmation of the profound duplicities of moral life. In *King Lear* Shakespeare has made the common currency of paradox pay the wergild of human nature which, in this play, affirms itself exactly in its display of the terrible consequences of being human.

16

"Mine own Executioner"

> Nay, further, we are what we all abhorre, *Anthro-*
> *pophagi* and Cannibals, devourers not onely of men,
> but of our selves; and that not in an allegory, but
> a positive truth; for all this masse of flesh which
> wee behold, came in at our mouths: this frame wee
> looke upon, hath beene upon our trenchers; In
> briefe, we have devoured our selves.
>
> Browne, *Religio Medici,* I. 37

S PEAKING of his own argument in his "Apologie," and
within that work itself, Montaigne likens his paradoxical
enterprise to the last desperate trick of a fencer who, to
disarm his opponent (or to kill him), disarms himself, for
victory's sake, hazarding his own destruction:

> You for whom I have taken the paines to enlarge so long a
> worke (against my custome) will not shun to maintaine your
> *Sebond,* with the ordinary form of arguing, whereof you are
> daily instructed, and will therein exercise both your minde and
> study: For this last trick of fence, must not be employed but as
> an extreme remedy. It is a desperate thrust, gainst which you
> must forsake your weapons, to force your adversary to re-
> nounce his, and a secret slight, which must seldome and very
> sparingly be put in practise. *It is a great fond-hardnesse to lose*
> *our selfe for the losse of another.*[1]

Montaigne involves the readers in his own theoretical and
philosophical problems in the "Apologie," the risk involved
in any paradox—the self-contradiction and self-cancellation implied by that deliberately indeterminate genre.
Though paradox certainly encourages postponement of

[1] Montaigne, *Essayes,* II.xii.502.

commitment, it can also work, as in *King Lear*, to an exactly opposite end. Like all examples of showing off, the epideictic paradox must either succeed or fail—if it succeeds, it demonstrates the kind of self-contradiction proper to paradoxy. If it fails, it eliminates itself. In other words, the paradox takes a risk simply by its own existence. Its self-contradictions and self-references must remain integrally ambiguous, otherwise its rhetorical and stylistic failure cancels whatever meaning it has. Without resonance, paradox is dead.

And it has, then, killed itself by overreaching. The paradox that has overreached has failed at "the last trick of fence," at the "extreme remedy" and the "desperate thrust." The analogy between paradoxy and fencing recalls the risks involved in living at a time when by the code of honor a man was expected regularly to bring his life into hazard. Richelieu's ban on dueling may have offended hotheads among the king's *mousquetaires*, each anxious to prove himself the bravest of men; but Richelieu thought of his measure as a mercantilist protection against the prodigal waste of a major national resource, the lives of brave men. The dueling code itself had been a restriction upon wholesale slaughter for passion's sake, since it laid down very strict regulations for proper behavior in cases of honor; once established, in other words, the dueling code regulated risk in a society given to extravagant risk. A man could easily die by the sword, either publicly in warfare or privately, seeking satisfaction of honor. Since he himself lent himself to that risk, he often acquiesced, if not in his own death, at least in the possibility of his own death.

There were therefore a great many books on the art of defense written and published during the Renaissance, of which one, George Silver's *Paradoxes of Defence*,[2] pro-

---

[2] George Silver, *Works*, ed. Cyril G. R. Matthey (London,

vides a useful point of departure. Even the title is relevant to this discussion, since the word *problema* means,
among other things, "defense." The title is, then, about
paradoxes and problems, or paradoxes of problems.[3] In
the second place, the book is "paradoxical" in that it is
written against the accepted opinion, namely, that the Italian was the best fencing style. Finally, the book is paradoxical in that it is *not* in fact paradoxical: the mode of
fighting Silver advocates is the reasonable and sensible
English one. Though the book is primarily about fencing,
it is a paradox, and therefore its *"Epistle Dedicatorie"* is
properly concerned with the differences between truth and
opinion.

The mind of man is a greedie hunter after truth, finding the
seeming truth but chaunging, not alwayes one, but alwayes
diverse, forsakes the supposed, to find out the assured certaintie:
and searching every where save where it should, meetes with
all save what it would. . . . So in Fencing . . . But though
we often chop and change, turne and returne, from ward to
ward, from fight to fight, in this unconstant search, yet wee
never rest in anie, and that because we never find the truth:
and therefore we never find it, because we never seeke it in
that weapon where it may be found.

It can be found "in short Swords, short Staves, the halfe
Pike, Partisans, Gleves, or such like weapons of perfect
lengths, not in long Swords, long Rapiers, nor frog-pick-
ing Poiniards . . . ," can be found, in short, in weapons
"tending . . . to the honor of our English nation." Silver
(p. 21) minced no words about the risks involved in the
art: "the blow being strongly made, taketh sometimes

1898). See Stone, *The Crisis of the Aristocracy,* pp. 242-50, for
dueling in England between 1558 and 1641.

[3] The phrase casts some light on the fact that Donne's *juvenilia*
in this genre were called *Paradoxes and Problemes.*

cleane away the hand from the arme, hath manie times
bene seene. Again a full blow upon the head or face with
the short sharpe Sword, is most commonly death." As opposed to "the thrust," "the blow" gives the best service:

> The blow hath manie parts to wound, and in everie one of
> them commaundeth the life; but the thrust hath but a few, as
> the bodie or face, and not in everie part of them neither. (p. 22)

Silver (p. 25) lays his stress on winning: his method of
defense is really offense. He warns particularly about overreaching with long weapons; however attractive they may
seem, they lead a man to the risk of losing his guard and
of being stabbed by the opponent's dagger. Silver's "overreaching" is not metaphorical. After his early discussion of
relative and receding truth, his book is sternly devoted to
positive injunctions in practice. Behind the whole discourse,
however, hangs the dark curtain of danger and risk which
Silver's "paradoxes" design to shorten.

In engaging in a duel, a man also ran the risk of mortal
sin, perhaps of two mortal sins, murder and suicide, the
one active, the other, in Donne's usage, passive or "negative." The hazard was, like Pascal's spiritual wager, total:
every time he engaged to defend his honor, a man risked
his mortal and his immortal life. "Fencing" was properly
a metaphor not for intellectual debate only, but also for
total risk, in the sense in which Montaigne used his figure
of speech.

However achieved, death certainly ends the experiential
life of man: even the believer knows that to die is to abandon all experience, to give up the tenaciously held pleasures
and pains of existence, to cease to be "all," to become perhaps "nothing" or nobody. "We entertaine and carry all
with us: whence it followeth," Montaigne wrote, "that we
deeme our death to be some great matter. . . ."[4] Even the

---

[4] Montaigne, *Essayes*, ii.xiii.548.

believer, presumably convinced of the ultimate rewards of heaven, inclined to draw back from the finality of death. Cases of suicide intensified the poignancy of the general problem death presented; suicide, death by one's own hand, was a self-referential act of annihilation, a decision to undo, to unmake, to eliminate one's self by one's own act. Suicide is the paradox of self-contradiction at its irrevocable extremity, as exemplified, once more, in Steinberg's drawing of a man crossing himself out,[5] or the similar terrible gesture of Jean-Louis Barrault in *Les enfants du paradis*, the mime crossing out his own reflection in the green-room mirror. The act of self-cancellation that suicide is, deals with ends, rather than with beginnings. On the whole, suicide tends to be an escape from worldly situations too grave to be endured, a release of the self from the indentures of responsibility and pain: such was, for instance, the Stoical suicide officially condemned by Renaissance Christianity but clandestinely admired by many Christian Stoics. Sometimes also suicide is the result of a self-disgust so intense that one can only reduce the hopeless self to not-being, a kind of self-punishment in which a man acts as his own judge—in Donne's phrase, as his own executioner, or in Browne's, as his own assassin.[6] That disgust with the worldly self may be the desire simply to annihilate one's self altogether, a desire motivated by deep self-disapproval; or it may be to rid one's self of sinfulness and temptation, to atone for one's sins by the destruction of the sinner—and, perhaps thereby, as a reward for one's stringent self-judgment, to become better—thereby, to be spiritually rewarded.

In a mild form, all martyrs were involved in bringing about their own destruction, were, in Donne's terminology, "negatively" their own murderers, running to embrace

[5] Steinberg, *The Passport*.
[6] Sir Thomas Browne, *Religio Medici*, ed. L. C. Martin, p. 41.

death in order to reach as quickly as possible the supernal delights of union with God. The Roman administrative talent of St. Augustine had been severely taxed in *The City of God*, when he had had to discourage the practically regrettable tendency of Christians eager for heavenly bliss to embrace martyrdom. In *Pseudo-martyr*, Donne concerned himself with the problems of genuine martyrdom and substantial suicide, concluding, like T. S. Eliot long after, that many apparently genuine martyrdoms would be adjudged quite differently on the Last Day.

Intellectually speaking, to condone the idea of suicide is in itself paradoxical: that is, Christian doctrine had set so heavily against it that, in the received opinion, suicide was an irrevocably and eternally unforgivable sin. The popularity of Roman Stoicism, however, certainly reactivated the idea of the "noble suicide"—as a victory over the trials of living and over the passions of the self, and as an admirable expression of man's conquest of himself.[7] Though Renaissance orthodoxy could not approve the practice of suicide, the literature of sixteenth-century Stoicism is full of overt or covert admiration for many suicides: Cato and Lucretia constantly recur as commendable stock suicides. Formal tragedy naturally relied on the Stoical self-reliance exhibited by heroic characters to demonstrate the good fortune involved in apparent fall, or destruction, or self-destruction.[8] As a literary form, tragedy domesticates the terrors of violence, orders the horror until it can con-

[7] Schopenhauer's paradox of suicide as the supreme expression of the will-to-live may owe more than a little to the Stoical formulation: as it stands, it is a most paradoxical statement about a paradoxical subject.

[8] Weisinger, *Tragedy and the Paradox of the Fortunate Fall.* The whole question of Senecan tragedy and Senecan influence upon Elizabethan tragedy has been discussed at length: see especially Madeline Doran, *Endeavors of Art* (Wisconsin University Press, 1954), pp. 15-16, 120-35, 353-59, and p. 396, n. 25.

form to certain patterns of expectation, among them, adjustment to the idea of a "good"—that is, a virtuous or courageous or altruistic—suicide. Enobarbus is one example of the sympathetic suicide: and both Kent and Horatio seem to promise to follow the antique Roman custom after their masters have died.

Both Hamlet and Macbeth come to the tragic realization that death is not only inevitable for each breather on earth but also immanent in every separate moment of breath: every second contains potentially the extinction or the annihilation of a man's whole and only earthly life. A man is very tender, as the *topos* ran. In Donne's words,

There is scarce anything that hath not killed somebody; a hair, a feather hath done it; nay, that which is our best antidote against it hath done it; the best cordial hath been deadly poison.[9]

And in Browne's,

. . . I that have examined the parts of man, and know upon what tender filaments that Fabrick hangs . . . doe thanke my God that we can die but once . . . 'tis in the power of every hand to destroy us, and we are beholding unto every one wee meete, hee doth not kill us.[10]

In the midst of life we are in death—and, further, death at one's own hand:

. . . every man is his owne greatest enemy, and as it were, his owne executioner. *Non occides,* is the Commandement of God, yet scarse observed by any man; for I perceive every man is his own *Atropos,* and lends a hand to cut the thred of his owne dayes.[11]

[9] John Donne, *Devotions upon Emergent Occasions* (University of Michigan Press, 1959), p. 44.
[10] Browne, *Religio Medici*, ed. Martin, p. 42.
[11] *Ibid.*, p. 61.

Just before he goes to the duel in which he loses his life, Hamlet recognizes the inevitability of death and the part each man plays in preparation for that death: "If it be now, 'tis not to come; if it be not to come, it will be now: if it be not now, yet it will come: the readiness is all" (v.ii.231-34). The suicide problem is not left at that in *Hamlet*, however, but is twice debated at length, once by Hamlet in his set speech, the second time by Hamlet and the gravedigger just before Ophelia's burial. Hamlet dies, too, in a duel to which he has submitted himself fully conscious of the risk, his *pari* of all against nothing. As he acknowledges, Hamlet has shot his arrow o'er the house and hurt his brother; ironically, it is Laertes, directing *his* arrow o'er the house to shoot his brother, who becomes another case on the spectrum of self-slaughter when his stratagem is fatally used against himself. The metaphor of fencing is written directly into the action of the play: after Lamond's testimony to Laertes' skill, the final device Claudius chose by which to slay Hamlet seems to be foolproof. Lamond, he says to Laertes,

> gave you such a masterly report
> For art and exercise in your defence,
> And for your rapier most especially,
> That he cried out 'twould be a sight indeed
> If one could match you. The scrimers of their nation
> He swore had neither motion, guard, nor eye,
> If you oppos'd them. (iv.vii.97-104)

In spite of his skill, Laertes fell into the trap and forfeited his own life: the wager the king seemed to enter upon was never a real wager, since Laertes had poisoned his sword and the king the cup from which Hamlet was to drink. Hamlet, as Horatio thought too, had not the slightest chance of success. The purposes mistook fell on their inventors' heads—and, though Hamlet died, so did

everyone else. Because he had finally been able to sub-
ordinate his private ends to the general good, Hamlet managed to die in the name of that general good: therefore,
though he died, he was not destroyed. The others, because
they were identified only with their ends, were destroyed
utterly.

Hamlet was also "ready" in the simplest sense. Having
heard of Laertes' skill at the fence, he had practiced mean-
while. Talented though he was, Laertes had not studied
Silver's paradoxes or noted Montaigne's warning against
overreaching and the desperate thrust. Like his father and
his sister, Laertes put himself in the way of death, to
acknowledge as he died the justice of his death—"I am
justly kill'd with mine own treachery"; and, "The foul
practice/ Hath turn'd itself on me" (v.ii.317,328-29).

In *Hamlet*, everyone of importance is hoist with his
own petard. Rosencrantz and Guildenstern, who made love
to their employment, found that their weapon turned in
their hand to put a quick end to them. The Queen's blindness led to her too deep involvement in the schemes of her
second husband and therefore to her death. Polonius and
his children stumbled upon their own destruction; and
Hamlet, in the tragic hero's fashion, went through various
stages of irresolution and mistimed resolution to the final
resolution for, among other things, his own death.

In the course of the play, Hamlet reassesses himself, his
own life, the nature and purposes of life in general, the
nature and purpose of his own life in particular. At many
levels, the play is the tragedy of knowing: Hamlet knows
all along, and begins to act upon what he knows, long before
he beats his conscious mind into recognition of what he
knows. For him, the terrible fact is that what he knows is
true: he tested the ghost by way of probation in the mouse-
trap play, but long before that play had taken place, he
knew that the ghost was a true ghost and the test is really

of Claudius and of Gertrude. The Skeptical, empirical Hamlet tests everything and everyone—Ophelia, who is found wanting and who lies about her father's whereabouts in the nunnery scene; Rosencrantz and Guildenstern, who turn out to be unable to play the recorders; the King and Queen—even Polonius and Osric. He tests Horatio, who alone turns out to be, simply, true; he tests himself for his sanity, for his resolution, for his loyalty, and for his honor.

Hamlet is concerned with what reality "really" is, with the moral reality of human nature, with the moral role of roles, with the relation of illusion to reality, and of deception to illusion and reality. He himself adopts various roles both passively, for defense, and actively, for offensive action. He is *homo sapiens et ludens*: he plays, he acts out parts and scenes before he can undertake to act in earnest.[12] Partly to test the situation, partly, like the tiger kitten or wolf pup playing with its fellows, exercising in preparation for the exigencies of real life, Hamlet plays his parts until those parts he plays have their own designs and serve to turn his acting into doing.

Though Hamlet's soliloquies are often excerpted from the play as if they had little necessary connection with it, the fact is that they are removed from the action of the play in several ways. In the first, they afford the audience some perception into the extraordinary estrangement of Hamlet from his situation; in the second, they show the privacy of Hamlet's working mind; in the third, they show the difference in time between Hamlet's decisions and his awareness of having taken decisions; in the fourth, they show the difference in quality between Hamlet's mind and the other minds working throughout this highly devious play about intelligence. In the first soliloquy Hamlet discusses being and not-being; he considers the merits of

[12] See Maynard Mack, "The World of Hamlet," *Yale Review*, XLI (1948), 502-23; on play, Huizinga, *Homo ludens*, passim.

nonexistence, or of being dead, but evidently without serious impulse to arrange his own death. It appears sufficient deterrent to suicide that the Everlasting *had* fix'd His canon 'gainst self-slaughter: in any case, however elegant his intellectual consideration of not-being, his emotional preoccupation with incestuous sheets overwhelms his scholarly presentation of suicide.

In the second soliloquy, "O what a rogue and peasant slave am I," Hamlet berates himself both as an un-Stoical slave of passion and an ignoble man of honor, a man who "can say nothing" to his situation, in contrast to the player, who weeps and falters in his speech—"and all for nothing!" That curious soliloquy marks a real shift in Hamlet's control over his emotions, through his awareness of the controlling function of roles and of acting. At the end of his self-acknowledged hysterics, he comes to the mousetrap experiment, by which he, his father's ghost, and his uncle are to be tested.

The third soliloquy is Hamlet's most eloquent discussion both of the meanings of being itself and of the values of life and death. It is a Stoical disputation on death, perhaps in part dependent upon Cicero's commonplaces in the *Tusculan Disputations*; and an essay, à la Montaigne, on the relations of death to life—a Stoical disputation, then, balancing the advantages of life and of death, and in the play's economy, balancing an overtly Stoical expression against the empirical, Skeptical experiment of the mousetrap. Wittenberg has served Hamlet well: he proves in the event to be neither committed Stoic nor committed Skeptic, but manages to balance the two, to manipulate the two attitudes of mind, in concert and in opposition, toward his own self-realization and the realization of his ultimate end.[13]

---

[13] See above, Chapter 13.

For Hamlet appearances turn out to be real: the "reality" is exactly as horrible as his suspicions had led him to believe, so horrible that mere living becomes a burden—a fardel—almost too heavy to bear. *Almost*: if Hamlet had really believed that death was utterly different from life, he might indeed have made his quietus with that bare bodkin. But he could not, because it was only in terms of life, with all its excruciations, that Hamlet could conceive of death. It was not fear of not-being that held him back from taking his life as much as it was fear of some continued exacerbation of consciousness ("conscience," in the older idiom) in the sleep of death. If the dreams of death are like those of life, then it is wise to postpone the sleep of death as long as possible.

Hamlet's view of suicide is, partly, that it is an escape from the pains of life, partly that it is the last resort of the Stoical gentleman intent upon his integrity: in either case, it offers no solution to his dilemma. Caught as he is between "all" and "nothing," a totally painful being and a terrifying nightmarish not-being, Hamlet waits to hazard his "all" with a fair chance of success. As in Pascal's wager, Hamlet may lose his life, but all is by no means lost thereby.

Unlike Othello, Hamlet never regards his soul as "perfect"; as he says to Horatio about the mousetrap, if he is proved wrong, then "my imaginations are as foul/ As Vulcan's stithy." His treatment of his mother is far from ideal, as he himself recognizes; and the effects of his perturbed spirit on Polonius and Ophelia are far from innocent, as he himself ever more deeply realizes. Because of Hamlet's rashness, it is Ophelia, not Hamlet, who actually commits suicide, passively, it is true, but suicide nonetheless. Ophelia dies, indeed, of privation: insufficiently strong to help Hamlet in his undefined turbulence of mind, she is deprived of his company and of his love, deprived of her father by Hamlet's violence, deprived of her wits and thus of her life. Ophelia teaches the lesson, to the audience and to Hamlet, that one must not lose one's wits, whatever one's losses: her madness is not feigned, and it brings her to nothing. The plays on the word "nothing," so grossly applied to Ophelia early in the play, cut with extra poignancy as she loses her mind: Laertes speaks the truth of her wandering utterance when he says, "This nothing's more than matter."[14]

And Ophelia becomes, in the gravedigger's paradox, nobody. Her corpse is denied the full honors of Christian burial, though her rank is sufficient to ensure burial in holy ground—near, note well, the grave that housed the court fool. In the exchange between Hamlet and the absolute gravedigger, the close relationship among paradox, equivocation, and lie is revealed once more: after all, it *is* the gravedigger's grave because he lies in it. But because he lies, it is not his, by the inevitable rule of the Liar paradox —and yet he does not altogether lie, any more than the clown in Othello lies about Cassio's whereabouts. He lies and he doesn't, or, he speaks a paradox, properly about nobody, since the grave is for no woman and for no man, but for one that was a woman. Actually, by the strictest interpretation, Ophelia has destroyed her soul by allowing herself to die, therefore she "is not"; though most readers prefer Laertes' opinion and consider that the merciful God will indeed accept her as a ministering angel. In other words, the positive values of life insist that Ophelia is not reducible to nobody or to nothing; sad though her life was, deprived as she was of personal strength and of external support, Ophelia was someone who could not, even in suicide, entirely obliterate herself.

Still less could Hamlet obliterate himself, thaw and re-

[14] See above, Chapter 7.

solve himself into a dew—who with his last words asks
Horatio to refrain from Stoical suicide in order to repair
Hamlet's wounded name: in other words, Horatio's life
is impressed into the service of Hamlet's fame, because for
Hamlet the true story of his having lived was important.
Horatio acts as chronicler, and also as poet, projecting
Hamlet's painful life and heroic death into human story.

In the event, Hamlet hazarded all, knowing that the
most he could lose was his life, which finally he had learned
to value for its potential service to the general good rather
than for itself alone; knowing that he could lose nothing
not already lost, even if he should die. In the last fencing
match, Hamlet could bet as safely as Pascal, without fear
of total annihilation. Between the beginning of the play's
action, when to Hamlet the world seemed without value,
to the end, when the restoration of value seemed worth
the hazard, Hamlet had learned to distinguish between
intellectual and actual extremes and to direct himself out
of his own extremity.

In Hamlet's case, the death to which he came was not
the negation of the self and of personal values it had
seemed to him early in the play. Hamlet's death was something quite opposite—the paradoxical affirmation of the
right to live well. His death was only literally a self-
destruction, since the life of the "real" Hamlet—that is,
of his values—is guaranteed by Horatio's "story" and by
the honorable man of action to whom Hamlet entrusts
Denmark's future. At his death, Hamlet requests that of
his wounded name a paradigm be made for life—than
which no more, in the Renaissance, no more could be asked.
He died "ready" for death, whenever it might come.

Long ago, Theodore Spencer noted the similarities between the literary creation Hamlet, the melancholy, frustrated, speculative, paradoxical, witty, active Prince of Denmark, and the actual man John Donne, the melancholy,

frustrated, speculative, paradoxical, witty, active office-seeker.[15] Certainly in these respects the imaginary and the real young men shared many characteristics and interests: different as their ultimate solutions were to the problems of life, both young men spent a considerable amount of time debating, from both Stoical and Skeptical points of view, the problems of life and of death.

Donne's early images of suicide in his poems are syntactical and logical paradoxes, self-cancellations, pointed toward the psychological paradoxes of love and living. In "The Legacie," the lover dies as often as he must leave his lady's company; a dead man, that lover is at once his own executor and his own legacy. The poem fuses and confuses the identities and sexes of lover and beloved, so that mutual possession of the lovers becomes exactly their identity. He kills himself because "he" is "she," who is cruel; because "she" is also kind, he is revived from death, promptly to experience, within the metaphorical structure of the poem, another death upon that revival. In "The Flea," the lady commits at once murder and suicide in the destruction of the flea that is three-in-one, consubstantial with the lovers; in the First Anniversary, each man kills himself to propagate his kind, and all men

> seeme ambitious, Gods whole worke t'undoe;
> Of nothing hee made us, and we strive too,
> To bring our selves to nothing backe. . . .　(ll. 155-57)

In a letter written about 1609, Donne wrote that he had "tried how I can induce to be mine own grave,"[16] and, very famously in his *Devotions upon Emergent Occasions,*

[15] Theodore Spencer, "Donne and His Age," *A Garland for John Donne* (Gloucester, Mass., 1958), pp. 187-90.

[16] Donne, *Letters to Severall Personages of Honour* (London, 1651), p. 19.

not only that he was involuntarily his own executioner[17] but also that he simultaneously destroys himself and presages "that execution upon himself."[18]

Characteristically, Donne came to terms with death, well within the Christian tradition of which he was an official representative: like Shakespeare, he too paraphrased the Pauline *topos*, "death once dead, there's no more dying then" in his great Holy Sonnet, "Death be not proud":

> Thou art slave to Fate, chance, kings, and desperate men,
> And dost with poyson, warre, and sicknesse dwell,
> And poppie, or charmes can make us sleepe as well,
> And better than thy stroake; why swell'st thou then?
> One short sleepe past, wee wake eternally,
> And death shall be no more; Death thou shalt die.
>
> (ll. 9-14)

According to Christianity, a good man's death falls on "the first day of his Jubilee," as Browne's phrase put it; Donne agreed, in the *Devotions*, at least: "this great festivall, my dissolution," he called his own prospective death.

But Donne did not arrive automatically or easily at his ultimate acceptance of death as a festival: throughout his work he plays with the notion of suicide, nowhere more equivocally than in his *Biathanatos*.[19] As the subtitle states, *Biathanatos* is officially a paradox—*A Declaration of that Paradoxe, or Thesis, that Self-homicide is not so naturally Sin, that it may never be otherwise*. That the book is an argument against received opinion is quite clear, of course:

[17] Donne, *Devotions*, p. 78.

[18] *Ibid.*, p. 8.

[19] John Donne, *Biathanatos*, ed. J. William Hebel (Facsimile Text Society, 1930): the title is usually taken as a barbarous combination of *bios* and *thanatos*, thus a play on life-and-death; it is likely that the title is also a play on *bia*, or violent, as well, a barbarism, this time, for *biaithanatos*. All references in text are to this edition.

suicide was, in most men's minds, a settled sin. Donne knew how "paradoxical" his book was, as his letters to Sir Robert Carr and Edward Herbert make plain. In the letter to Carr, he gave specific orders for the preservation of the little book, but not for its publication:

It was written by me many years since; and because it is upon a misinterpretable subject, I have always gone so near suppressing it, as that it is onely not burnt: no hand hath passed upon it to copy it, nor many eyes to read it; onely to some particular friends in both Universities, then when I writ it, I did communicate it: And I remember, I had this answer, That certainly, there was a false thread in it, but not easily found: Keep it, I pray, with the same jealousie; let any that your discretion admits to the sight of it, know the date of it; and that it is a Book written by *Jack Donne*, and not by *Dr Donne*: Reserve it for me, if I live, and if I die, I only forbid it the Presse, and not the Fire: publish it not, but yet burn it not; and between those, do what you will with it.[20]

He certainly did not want the book destroyed, as he indicated to Herbert, too: nor did he want it (and thus himself) abused; hence he never jeopardized his paradox by defending it openly.

I make accompt that this book hath enough performed that which it undertook, both by argument and example. It shall therefore the lesse need to be it self another example of the Doctrine. It shall not therefore kill it self; that is, not bury it self; for if it should do so, those reasons, by which that act should be defended or excused were also lost with it. Since it is content to live, it cannot chuse a wholsomer aire then your Library, where Authors of all complexions are presented. If any of them grudge this book a room, and suspect it of new or dangerous doctrine, you who know us all, can best moderate. To those reasons which I know your love to me will make in my favour and discharge, you may adde this, that though this

---

[20] Donne, *Letters to Severall Persons*, p. 19.

doctrine hath not been taught nor defended by writers, yet they, most of any sort of men in the world, have practised it.[21]

In his excellent study of *Biathanatos*,[22] unhappily still unpublished, A. E. Malloch (pp. 37-38) called the book "two hundred purposely enigmatic pages," and connected its composition with Donne's trying years of poverty and frustrated ambitions at Mitcham, when the poet was occupied, as he put it, with "aimless business." During the Mitcham years Donne did his hackwork for the cause of English Protestantism, working as researcher for Thomas Morton's polemical writings and producing his own *Pseudomartyr*, a brilliant, bitter, and witty casuistic argument against Jesuit casuistry. Two of the preoccupations of *Pseudo-martyr* are related to *Biathanatos*, the substantive problem of voluntary self-destruction and the technique of equivocation. Once martyrdom became a relatively easy course of action, its motivation became suspect, even among devout Christians; many officially styled martyrs—as Donne, in common with other reformers, was fond of saying—did not deserve the name.

Biathanatos is a book of casuistry in both neutral and pejorative senses. Neutrally, it is a book of casuistry because of its heavy reliance upon "cases," seeking to establish, of course, the autonomy, variety, and precision involved in argument by case. Pejoratively, the book is casuistic, since though it never overtly argues the case for suicide—no single sentence or passage in the book precisely states the unequivocal case for suicide—it is clear that Donne, like Hamlet and Laertes, and like Burton after him, counsels charity for suicides.

There are many kinds of paradox in the book—first, its

[21] *Ibid.*, pp. 17-18.
[22] A. E. Malloch, "A Critical Study of Donne's *Biathanatos*," unpublished doctoral dissertation, University of Toronto, 1958.

argument against an officially authorized opinion; second, the equivocation by which the author defers his own judgment so that no decision is ever firmly expressed on the question debated; third, the conflict between the avowed intention never to publish the book (which in fact was published by his son only after Donne's death)[23] and the care and clarity of the presentation, clearly for an audience of concerned readers; fourth, the self-protectiveness of its presentation, evidently relying upon the conventional view that paradoxes are written to elicit refutation rather than to propound their ostensible thesis; and, probably not last, but as far as I am able to go into this infinite regression, the absence of any reasoned conclusion to the voluminous materials displayed in polemical patterns.

Like the Anniversary Poems, *Biathanatos* has been adduced as argument both for the Skepticism (and, therewith, the libertinism) and for the Stoicism of John Donne:[24] in both cases, rightly enough. But, as in the case of the Anniversary Poems and the case of Hamlet, the Skepticism Donne evinces about the Stoical concepts of natural law and right reason is counterbalanced, perhaps even overweighed, by an ultimate sympathy for Stoical suicide. That is, natural law is shown by Skeptical empirical evidence to reveal the "lawfulness" of suicide; and therefore Stoical suicide, sheared away from concepts of natural law and right reason by Christian hands, is restored to its important position in the Stoical moral system. But not altogether, of course; Donne never permitted his argument overtly to support that view, but rather merely made it very difficult for any counterargument to overcome his data. In this sense, too, the convention of paradox is (para-

[23] S. E. Sprott, *The English Debate on Suicide from Donne to Hume* (La Salle, Illinois, 1961), pp. 1-29, 56-67.

[24] George Williamson, "The Libertine Donne," *PQ*, XIII (1934), 276-91; see also material cited in Chapter 13, nn. 32 and 33.

doxically) denied, since this paradox in fact is *not* a fair
invitation to refutation,[25] but anticipates counterarguments
and undercuts them as it goes.

The method of argumentation is slippery, too, even to
internal self-contradiction. In Professor Malloch's words
(p. 48), "In a series of objections, qualifications, and distinctions Donne gnaws away at one premise of his opponent's argument, and then when its force has been consid-
erably reduced, he suddenly allows that premise of his
opponent's argument on quite other grounds." More than
this, Donne conceals the simplicity of his logical and syntactical strategy so that one loses the impetus of both his
unimpeachable and his false logic.[26]

Donne considers the relation of martyrdom and pseudo-
martyrdom to death in general, which, though the body
perish, leads to heaven and a better life (*Biathanatos*, p.
49); he manages to classify all good deaths as the self-
preservation assumed as a fundamental tenet of natural
law (pp. 48-50). By this argument, all deaths are good,
and the self-sought death, presumably, more intelligently
good than the accidental or natural one. To that theme he
recurs, in other contexts (p. 111); "Death it selfe therefore is not evill, nor is it evill to wish it, is it evill to further
that with more actuall helpe, which we may lawfully wish
to be done?" (p. 119) Euthanasia, defended by "Sir
Thomas Moore a man of the most tender and delicate conscience," was permitted in Utopia, and suicide urged by
priests and magistrates upon the incurably ill in that state

[25] —in spite of the efforts, cited by Sprott (pp. 29-93), to refute the book's argument.

[26] In her otherwise extraordinarily perceptive book, Joan Webber
seems to have missed at least half the point of *Biathanatos*; see her
Contrary Music (University of Wisconsin Press, 1963, pp. 11-12,
and p. 206, nn. 14-16). It is quite clear that Donne knew *exactly*
what he wanted to do in this successfully confusing work.

(p. 74). A young man of fashion, Donne recognized the suicidal impulse in duels, and observed that legislation against dueling betrays the high incidence of deaths by that means:

For wheresoever you finde many and severe lawes against an offense it is not safe from thence to conclude an extreame enormity or hainousnesse in the fault, but a propensnesse of that people, at that time, to that fault . . .

So in *France* the lawes abound against Duells, to which they are headlongly apt.   (pp. 93-94)

Fencing in Donne's argument is not just a fact but a metaphor for the developing argument, a metaphor directed, like Montaigne's, to the risk of self-destruction:

But as in Fencing, Passion layes a man as open as unskilfulnesse, and a troubled desire to hirt, makes one not onely misse, but receive a wound; so out of an inordinate fervour, to strike home, hee which alledgeth this place, overreacheth to his own danger. . . .   (p. 179)

The overreaching is both the lopping-off, by suicide, of a member of the body of which Christ is the head, and the beginning of a long stretch to the argument's extreme. Hercules and Samson are types of Christ (pp. 199-201) who permitted their own destruction, connived at destroying themselves, for other people and for the truth as they saw it. In the case of Saul, too, though disputed in exegetical interpretation, the man himself was not denied sanctity by reason of his suicide.[27] The question turns, of course, not on Hercules, Saul, or Samson, but on Christ Himself, who unquestionably acquiesced in His own death. Donne does not force that point, but neither does he let it go. He merely mentions the case in his casuistic praise

[27] The ambiguities of the suicide of Saul account perhaps for the subject's being one of the famous sixteenth-century anamorphoses: see Baltrušaitis, Plate IV.

of suicides, making of Saul (and not, one notes, of Samson), his main argument just at its end: "for though the phrase of Scripture impute nothing to him [Saul] for that fact of killing himselfe, yet I have found none that offer any particular excuse in his defence" (p. 204).

Christ Himself is adduced in support of forgiving suicides: Christ is charity, and charity argues the forgiveness of crimes, therefore Christianity enjoins charity for the extremity of suicide. And furthermore, since Hercules and Samson are types of Christ and brought about their own deaths, the death of Christ, self-willed, is regarded also as a kind of suicide. According to this interpretation, Christ's death is proved to be charity precisely by the altruism of His end. By a careful selection of texts (John 12:25; Luke 14:26; I John 3:16) Donne arrives (pp. 191-92) at the meaning of Christ's exemplary self-homicide:

And as these informe us how ready we must be, so all those places which direct us by the example of Christ, to doe it as he did, shew, that in cases when our lives must be given, we neede not ever attend extrinsique force of others, but as he did in perfect charity, so we in such degrees of it, as this life, and our nature are capable of, must dy by our owne will, rather then his glory be neglected, whensoever, (a) as *Paul* saith, Christ may be magnified in our bodies, or the spirituall good of such another as wee are bound to advance, doth importune it.   (p. 193)

And thus retaining ever in our minds, that our example is Christ, and that he dyed not constrained, it shall suffice to have learned by these places, that in Charitie men may dye so, and have done, and ought to doe.   (p. 194)

It is noticeable that in both passages, one must know the subject discussed to perceive the force of the point being made: grammatically, Donne protects himself so that neither passage, so plain in its context, taken alone betrays its import. In other words, he equivocates consistently. The verbal paradox on which the argument turns is that of *mors negativa*, a phrase which, understood one way, is simply descriptive—death is a negative thing; understood another, the phrase is an oxymoron, in which death (a negative thing) is negated—or, two negatives lead to a positive conclusion. *Mors negativa* in scholastic terminology is the "passive death" of which Donne says, citing Jerome, fasting is a type (pp. 128-29).

> I must not kill my selfe but I may let my selfe dy. . . . And if the matter shall bee resolved and governed only by an out-ward act, and ever by that; if I forbeare to swimme in a river and so perish [like Ophelia], because there is no act I shall not bee guilty, and I shall bee guilty if I discharge a Pistoll upon my selfe, which I knew not to be charged, nor intended harme, because there is an act.   (p. 132)

In a way, the whole *Biathanatos* is an argument, not so much for suicide, as for voluntarism, for the responsibility of each man to make conscious decisions about his life and therefore about his death.[28] *Biathanatos* is an extension of Hamlet's short debate on suicide, with the sources cited and explicated, as in the lawyer's brief. That Donne personally inclined toward voluntarism is made clear by many comments throughout his works, most particularly by a passage in a letter to Sir Henry Goodere:

> I would not that death should take me asleep. I would not have him meerly seise me, and onely declare me to be dead, but win me, and overcome me. When I must shipwrack, I would do it in a Sea, where mine impotencie might have some excuse; not in a sullen weedy lake, where I could not have so much as exercise for my swimming. There I would fain do something; but that I cannot tell what, is no wonder. For to

---

[28] Cf. Introduction, above, pp. 36-39; this is one of Malloch's major points: pp. 81, 138-40, 150.

chuse, is to do: but to be no part of any body, is to be nothing.[29]

"To chuse, is to do: but to be no part of any body, is to be nothing." The paradox turns back upon itself, as paradoxes should. To die, even to die by one's own hand, and thus, as in the great mimic act of Jean-Louis Barrault, to cancel one's self out, is a kind of self-assertion more determined than living without will or decision. Donne's paradox is, at this point, a paradox of a paradox of paradoxes, as well as a paradox about a paradox—in other words, his paradox is a member of its own class. The *Biathanatos* ends equivocally, and appropriately, by discussing lying:

> For, it is certainly true of this, which *Cassianus* saith of a ly, *that it hath the nature of* Ellebore, *wholsome in desperate diseases, but otherwise poyson*. . . .   (p. 217)

This paradox, however, asserts more than its contradictory action in cases of health and of disease: it manages, by a long casuistic train of argument from authority, to entwine Calvinist predestinarianism inextricably with the doctrine of voluntarism, so that the highest expression of individual will becomes, simply, acceptance of God's will—as Browne had put it, "Thy will bee done, though in my owne undoing."[30]

At its core, this paradox, like the others, is epistemological. Examination of human motives leads in an infinite regress which, in the Christian system, can be checked only by reference to a paradox of a greater kind, the paradox involved in deity itself. Epistemology, the study of human knowing rather than of human knowledge, constantly deals in nescience, even about itself—and especially about itself. Epistemologists under allegiance to a transcendent meta-

---

[29] Donne, *Letters to Severall Persons*, p. 43.
[30] Browne, *Religio Medici*, ed. Martin, p. 75.

physics must yield to the idea of a suprarational deity whose knowledge not only surpasses and encompasses all human knowledge, but whose knowledge also by definition—in this case, the phrase must be taken literally—cannot be known. The paradoxist, whose consistent intellectual effort, whether undertaken lightly or gravely, is to break down limits, boundaries, and terms arranged by the conventions of human understanding, turns out to be paradoxical in this respect also, since he postulates a higher understanding, by definition beyond limitation, which in its integrity cannot be broken down. In other words, the paradoxist's view of ultimate knowledge is paradoxical, since that knowledge is both beyond the reach and the idea of definition. For such an ideal transcendent knowledge, all human definitions are trivial and parochial: by this arrangement, it is easy to conceive that opposites can be one. So the two negatives in the final sentence of *Biathanatos*—

Against the reasons whereof, and against charity, if prejudice, or contempt of my weaknes, or misdevotion have so precluded any, that they have not beene pleased to tast and digest them, I must leave them to their drowsiness still, and bid them enjoy the favour of that indulgent Physitian, *Qui non concoxit, dormiat.*   (pp. 217-18)

—are both two negatives and a positive statement, between which the human mind must either choose or must forever oscillate, recognizing the autonomy of both. "To chuse, is to do": Donne's paradox seems *not* to choose, not to do, since it never unequivocally commits itself on the merits of the great question it debates; but, as a good paradox should, it directs its readers to choice and therefore to action. *Biathanatos* is a self-denial and a self-cancellation which seems to annihilate itself as it actually creates; it concerns a subject, self-homicide, which seems to annihilate but which, by the complex arguments of this paradox, actually ends by creating a new life. *Biathanatos* depends upon the certain knowledge that life is uncertain, and that human interpretations of what happens in that uncertain life are themselves untrustworthy, that a given cause may produce a given effect, but that cause-and-effect explanation is liable to error, especially as a general law to which life—to say nothing of deity—might be bound. *Biathanatos* assumes that material and spiritual worlds operate in ways beyond the resources of human understanding, and that events demonstrate again and again the topsy-turvydom of human efforts to explain them. Written in a riddling syntax, with an equivocal style and method, *Biathanatos* is a paradox about paradoxy, matching[31] its form to its matter so that the one cannot be separated from the other, and thereby making its subject both autonomous and real. *Biathanatos* manipulates the psychological implications of the end of life and of all things precisely in order to deny the existence of such an end.

[31] E. H. Gombrich, *Art and Illusion*, p. 29 and passim.

Epilogue

UNLIKE Folly, I dare not let the book go without an epilogue, especially because there may be need for something even more final, an epitaph. As a major mode of expression, paradoxy certainly went out of favor at the end of the Renaissance—the decline of paradoxy in literature is one indicator of a new style. The formal paradox did not entirely disappear, of course: a book like John Dunton's *Athenian Sport: or, Two Thousand Paradoxes merrily argued to Amuse and Divert the Age* appeared in 1701, and was much imitated, much pillaged. Though in eighteenth-century literature there is more than one great paradox, not the least of them Diderot's, on the whole, paradox either turned into a trifling amusement, as in Dunton's gargantuan collection, or was submerged back into figurative language, where paradoxes always silently dwell. Paradox ceased to inform imaginative literature. The epidemic was over.[1]

Historically considered, the epidemic of formal paradoxy in the Renaissance reveals a good deal about the life of thought and image. During the epidemic, paradox was recreative in the highest sense of that term, ever attempting the imitative recovery of a transcendent "truth," with all of its ambivalences. Because paradox manages to be at once figure of speech and figure of thought, appropriate to a view of the universe profoundly metaphysical—and, more often than not, profoundly religious—it served to mediate all sorts of ideas and things which, under strict categorical arrangements, do not at first glance appear to "fit." Because of its deliberate lack of limitation, its conscious blur-

[1] For another discussion, from a different point of view, of the radical shift in literary, especially poetic, styles, see Earl R. Wasserman, *The Subtler Language* (The Johns Hopkins Press, 1959), Chapter v.

ring of distinction and difference, the asymptotic mode of
paradox managed to bear the burden of doubleness imposed by a metaphysical world view: in a world increasingly dedicated to the pursuit of exact knowledge, however,
paradoxy lost its transcendent sense of "re-creation" to become mere "recreation," trivial diversions such as Dunton
served up. With increasing distrust of "words," paradoxes
degenerated into mere puzzles, whose answers were no
longer expected to lead into the experience of real truth.

Degradation of paradox is one result of a revolution in
thought which valued clarity and exactness above the
tricky duplicities of comprehension induced by paradox.
In *The Dialogue concerning the Two World Systems*,
Galileo's Simplicio points to the dangers involved in favor-
ing "words" over "things" as guides to truth: ". . . [O]nce
you have denied the principles of the sciences and have
cast doubt upon the most evident things, everybody knows
that you may prove whatever you will, and maintain any
paradox."[2] For Simplicio, then, "paradox" has come to
mean *only* any arbitrary or haphazard odd notion, true or
false, unverifiable by experience; preference for "words"
over "things" implied, for him, that a good rhetorician was
always technically capable of defending "whatever you
will," regardless of the truth of the proposition. In these
terms, paradox could never be a mode of establishing immutable and transcendent truth. Galileo was no less complicated a thinker than many an official paradoxist, but he
rejected outright the validity of paradox as a method or
criterion of truth. The successful translator of the principle
of cause-and-effect from logic to physics and great propa-
gandist for empirical validation, Galileo regarded the self-

[2] Galileo Galilei, *Dialogue Concerning the Two Chief World
Systems*, trans. Stillman Drake (California University Press, 1953),
p. 4.

confirming operations of paradox as both time-wasting and misleading. Of the Liar paradox, he makes Simplicio say:

Did I not tell you it could be nothing but a sophism? This is one of those forked arguments called "sorites," like that of the Cretan who said that all Cretans were liars. It follows therefore that the Cretans were not liars, and consequently that he, being a Cretan, had spoken truth. And since saying that Cretans were liars he had spoken truly, including himself as a Cretan, he must consequently be a liar. And thus, in such sophisms, a man may go round and round forever and never come to any conclusion.[3]

The beauty of the Liar construction did not concern Simplicio, interested as he was in a progressive demonstration rather than in the inevitable self-envelopment of the snake-eating-its-tail. Galileo's deity was quite a different figure from Milton's, or Herbert's; his was an intellectual God, with an infinite quantum of knowledge, some of it packaged in ways which the human mind could "fully" understand. Galileo's model, as well as his subject in this passage, was mathematics, with its inexorable proofs and its equally inexorable self-impelled "progress":

. . . the human intellect does understand some propositions perfectly, and thus in these it has as much absolute certainty as Nature itself has. Of such are the mathematical sciences alone; that is, geometry and arithmetic, in which the Divine intellect indeed knows infinitely more propositions, since it knows them all. But with regard to those few which the human intellect does understand, I believe that its knowledge equals the Divine in objective certainty. . . .[4]

In *"objective certainty"*: such a definition of knowledge denies the validity of self-confirming, revelatory paradox. For Galileo, human knowledge of this sort is "certain" in

[3] Galileo, *Dialogue*, p. 42.
[4] *Ibid.*, pp. 103-104.

a way entirely alien to the paradoxical mode—and, further-more, human ignorance is itself never valuable. Mathe-matics is progressive and linear; it is also accumulative—that is, propositions once certainly known cannot be un-known thereafter, and they lead to further propositions and to further solutions. According to this view, human knowledge once gained cannot be diminished.

Locke's great *Essay on Human Understanding* pro-pounds a neat contrast to the *O altitudo* of Sir Thomas Browne, content to praise God for His enormous mystery. Locke might have written this passage in answer to Browne —"*Credo, quia impossibile est*: I believe, because it is im-possible, might, in a good man, pass for a sally of zeal, but would prove a very ill rule for men to chose their opinion of religion by."[5] Though Locke acknowledged the inviola-ble privacy of a man's religious opinions, he would not countenance a principle of irrationality to be adduced in validation of opinion—still less, in validation of the truth. The defender of the reasonableness of Christianity, Locke admitted no contradiction to revelation:

For if the light which everyone thinks he has in his mind, which in this case is nothing but the strength of his own per-suasion, be an evidence that it is from GOD, contrary opin-ions may have the same title to be inspirations; and GOD will be not only the father of lights but of opposite and contradic-tory lights, leading men contrary ways; and contradictory propositions will be divine truths, if an ungrounded strength of assurance be an evidence that any proposition is a divine revelation. (IV. xix. 11)

For once, Hobbes was on Locke's side:

That which taketh away the reputation of wisdom, in him that formeth a religion, or addeth to it when it is already formed,

[5] John Locke, *Essay Concerning Human Understanding*, IV. xviii. 11.

is the enjoining of a belief of contradictories: for both parts of a contradiction cannot possibly be true: and therefore to enjoin belief of them, is an argument of ignorance.[6]

Tertullian's axiom is here reversed: *non credo, quia impossibile est*—since, as Hobbes went on to assert, "revelation a man may indeed have of many things above, but of nothing against natural reason."

Commonsense apperception replaces wonderment, and, as investigation into the natural world continued, many former "wonders" yielded their marvelous aspects to become simple "truth." For Locke, "facts" themselves could simplify paradoxical contradiction. As he wrote in his *Essay*, "darkness visible" was no miracle, but rather the common experience of any observant man:

. . . the picture of a shadow is a positive thing. Indeed, we have *negative names* which stand not directly for positive *ideas* but for their absence, such as *insipid, silence, nihil*, etc., which words denote positive *ideas*, e.g., *taste, sound, being* with a signification of their absence.

And thus one may truly be said to see darkness. (I. vii. 5, 6)

In much the same way, Locke dealt with the problem of the vacuum, so troublesome to his predecessors: "those who dispute for or against a *vacuum* do thereby confess they have distinct *ideas* of *vacuum* and *plenum.* . . ." (II.xiii. 142). Infinity presented no terrors for him, either: in his word, one comes by the idea "historically." The idea of infinity is come by as naturally as "the *idea of finite*":

Everyone that has any *idea* of any stated lengths of space, as a foot, finds that he can repeat that *idea*; and *joining* it to the former, make the *idea* of two feet; and by the addition of a third, three feet; and so on, without ever coming to an end

[6] Thomas Hobbes, *Leviathan*, ed. Michael Oakeshott (Oxford, 1955), p. 77.

of his addition . . . he finds that, after he has continued his doubling in his thoughts and enlarged his *idea* as much as he pleases, he has no more reason to stop, nor is one jot nearer the end of such addition than he was at first setting out. . . .

(II. xvii. 3)

The laws of natural science, furthermore, were invariably grounded on reason. Catoptrics and anamorphoses provided him with an example, not of mystification, but of clarification:

There is nothing more proper to make us conceive this confusion than a sort of pictures usually shown as surprising pieces of art, wherein the colours, as they are laid by the pencil on the table itself, make out very odd and unusual figures and have no discernible order in their position. This draught thus made up of parts wherein no symmetry nor order appears is, in itself, no more confused thing than the picture of a cloudy sky wherein, though there be as little order of colours or figures to be found, yet nobody thinks it a confused picture. What is it then that makes it be thought confused, since the want of symmetry does not? . . . I answer, that which makes it be thought confused is the applying it to some name to which it does no more discernibly belong than to some other. . . . But when a cylindrical mirror, placed right, hath reduced those irregular lines on the table into their due order and proportion, then the confusion ceases and the eye presently sees that it is a man or *Caesar*. . . . Just thus it is with our *ideas* which are, as it were, the pictures of things. (II. xvii. 3)

Science brings order to the most apparently disordered view of things. Locke's reaction to the intellectual puzzles of paradox was either to ignore them or to rearrange them in terms of sensible fact and experience; either way, he tended to drain the mystery out of paradoxes, to deny transcendence to that mode of expression. It might be pointed out that Locke was "wrong" to have done so, since there is a sense in which all philosophy, including his own, is always paradoxical—both because philosophy restates accepted opinion in a new way, and because philosophy deals in questions which seem, to the historian, perpetually irresolute.

The objection to Locke's view is valid; but more must be said in its defense. The point is that some philosophers deal paradoxically with their inevitable paradoxes, as for example, Nicholas of Cusa and Bruno, so deliberately paradoxical in their formulations; and others reject the style altogether. Spinoza is a case in point. It would be impossible to deny that Spinoza dealt in extraordinary paradoxes and effected extraordinary tautologies. After all, few philosophers have so completely devoted themselves to the rationalization of the infinite as he did. All the same, the infinite universe of Spinoza, filled with an infinite number of an infinite variety of things, was always orderly; his logic led progressively and inexorably to the total unity of mind and matter, in spite of the infinite puzzles involved in validating such a paradoxical union. Self-reference is inevitable in Spinoza's system. Proposition xxxvi of the final book of the *Ethics* resounds to the familiar paradoxical tone: "The intellectual love of the mind towards God is that very love whereby God loves himself, not in so far as he is infinite, but in so far as he can be explained through the essence of the human mind regarded under the form of eternity; in other words, the intellectual love of the mind towards God is part of the infinite love whereby God loves himself."[7] But the proposition is not just left therewith, to dazzle readers and to convince them by means of dazzle; Spinoza goes on to explicate and analyze the meanings contained within his proposition. He required his readers to understand the ineluctable logic of his views, since, for him, those views were the truth.

[7] Benedictus de Spinoza, *Chief Works*, ed. R.H.M. Elwes (New York, 1951), ii. 264-65.

Though about a subject naturally paradoxical, the philosophy of Spinoza is rigorously organized upon the principles of linear logic; it is noticeably stripped of verbiage, of puns, and, insofar as possible, of double meanings. The remarkable thing about the structure of Spinoza's book is its aesthetic classicism, its genuine geometrizing of both the infinite varieties of matter and the infinite modes in which that infinite matter was also spiritual. His subject might well have encouraged paradoxy, but for Spinoza conviction had to be intellectual rather than emotional. The shortcuts of paradox were as unacceptable to him as they were to Galileo and to Locke: rationalist and empiricist alike turned away from the method of paradox.

Paradox was no longer rhetorical for them: it could not persuade. Locke made fun of Sir Robert Filmer's *Patriarcha* by saying that he would have taken the book for "such another exercise of wit, as was his who writ the Encomium of *Nero*, rather than for a serious Discourse meant in earnest, had not the Gravity of the Title and Epistle, the Picture in the Front of the Book, and the Applause that followed it, required me to believe, that the Author and the Publisher were both in earnest."[8] Addison's papers on true, false, and mixed wit need only glancing reference here, as the *locus classicus* for the rejection of visual and spoken punning. Using Locke's distinction between wit and judgment,[9] Addison categorized as false

[8] John Locke, *Two Treatises of Government*, ed. Peter Laslett (Cambridge, 1960), p. 159.

[9] Joseph Addison, *Spectator* 35, 58-63. Compare Locke, *Essay*, II. xi. 2: "For *wit* lying most in the assemblage of *ideas*, and putting those together with quickness and variety, wherein can be found any resemblance or congruity, thereby to make up pleasant pictures and agreeable visions in the fancy: *judgment*, on the contrary, lies quite on the other side, in separating carefully, one from another, *ideas* wherein can be found the least difference, thereby to avoid being misled by similitude, and by affinity to take one thing

wit all puns, anagrams, rebuses, lipogrammatic writing, *imprese*, echo-refrains (especially macaronic echoes), *bouts rimés*, and shape poems ("which resemble the Figure of an Egg, a Pair of Wings, an Ax, a Shepherd's Pipe, and an Altar"), for which "Mr. Herbert" was particularly taken to task. Stylistically, so to speak, the gaming spirit was disqualified as a poet's proper tool.

Of course paradoxes could not be legislated out of existence, even though formal paradoxes were treated so harshly. A brief comparison of formal with "natural" paradox might now be helpful in the recapitulation and concentration of this book's long argument. Paradox cannot ever be suppressed by *homo loquens*, given the peculiarities inherent in matching words to things. In some measure, language always limits, even where it strives for the greatest precision; it is never fully adequate to its referent, and therefore in some sense always a lie. Figurative language flaunts this very disability: its trick is to create the illusion of accuracy by means of an instrument acknowledged to be inadequate. When Sidney praised rhetorical paradoxes, he remarked that in them "good lye hid in neerenes of the evil,"[10]—a comment on the contradictory merits of the disability under which all language, and all figures, must work.

When one looks sharply at them, formal paradoxes can be seen as very stylized examples of figurative language, examples deliberately drawing attention to their own skill at harmonizing "impossibles" and radical contradictions. In paradox, as in all metaphor, something is declared to be what it manifestly is not—"my love" (either the feeling

for another. This is a way of proceeding quite contrary to metaphor and illusion. . . ."

[10] Sir Philip Sidney, *Apology for Poetry*, *Elizabethan Critical Essays*, ed. Gregory Smith (Oxford, 1937), I. 181-82.

or the girl) is *not* a red, red rose; an Alexandrine line is *not* a snake, after all. Both metaphor and paradox, it turns out, narrow alternatives sharply: faced with Gombrich's rabbit-duck drawing,[11] we concern ourselves only with seeing rabbits and ducks. Wolves, wolverines, palm trees, engines, and all other things are automatically barred by the terms in which the problem is set. In Donne's line, "Until I labour, I in labour lie," forces us to select the exactly appropriate meanings for "labour," not to allow our minds to run at random over plowing, carpentry, construction work, or whatever. Indeed, it comes as a bit of a surprise in the context to realize that these activities are "labor" too, so preoccupied are we with the "labours" appropriate to the line. So with paradoxes: we are invited to consider either that Epimenides is a liar or that he isn't —our puzzlement, our paralysis comes from the fact that we are not permitted a third alternative. In twentieth-century "real" life, after all, Epimenides' statement seems both obvious and trivial, so general is the truth expressed in it. Montaigne arranged his "Apologie" so that we feel we must choose between reason and faith—but many spokesmen for a tradition more central to Renaissance philosophy insisted upon mediating between these two "extremes."

The formal structure of the paradox is of course dialectic: therefore it inevitably is a figure of thought. Because most paradoxes are also metaphorical, or figures of speech (folly is wisdom; "Until I labour, I in labour lie"; "Buried in a sea of yce, and drown'd amidst a fire") as well, they illustrate their own fusion of different categories. Paradox exists to reject such divisions as those between "thought" and "language," between "thought" and "feeling," between "logic" and "rhetoric," between "logic,"

[11] E. H. Gombrich, *Art and Illusion*, p. 4.

"rhetoric," and "poetics," and between all of these and "experience." In paradox, form and content, subject and object are collapsed into one, in an ultimate insistence upon the unity of being. Thinking in terms of paradox, or thinking about paradox, one cannot rely upon conventional categories; one must not accept, in Parmenides' formulation, the separate existences of the Many; or, in the scholastic formulation, the ineffability of each individual thing. One is forced to fuse categories, since paradox manifestly manages at once to be creative and critical, at once its own subject and its own object, turning endlessly in and upon itself.

No wonder Galileo, Locke, and Spinoza turned away from paradoxy and, because we are willy-nilly educated by Enlightenment values, no wonder paradoxy is so difficult for us to "read." We are trained to expect "development" in argument and in art; we naturally read in terms of beginning, middle, and end. In paradox, beginnings and ends are usually deceptive: "In my end is my beginning"—that is, the whole meaning of a paradox is involved at any of its particular points, so that both in its rhetorical arrangements and in its philosophical message, it has no end: or, to switch meanings a little, its means are always ends. Paradox is not evolutionary, nor yet logically sequential. Paradox envelops rather than develops, folding all its parts into one unbroken, if asymmetrical, whole. In this sense, paradox is self-regarding, self-contained, and self-confirming; it attempts to give the appearance of ontological wholeness. The paradox of paradoxy persists even here, however, since paradoxes are, in fact, of all the rhetorical and literary forms the least self-contained. Paradox relies utterly upon its action in audience or beholder or reader. Paradox requires a beholder willing to share in its action and by thus sharing in it to prolong that action. Always "about" being, the paradox is not fully ontological, since by drawing attention to its own form and technique it demands a "wonderer," a reader to admire it and to wonder about it. Paradox must, in short, generate thought and even understanding. In yet another sense, paradox is paradoxical: each paradox begins an infinite activity, which, from Zeno on, has forced new minds to consider afresh the irresolute problems of the human understanding. Because of their almost imperceptible reaching out to involve their beholders and readers, paradoxes fit particularly that style called "baroque," in which a slanted perspective, a hand extended from a picture toward the beholder, or an actor turning directly to the audience were common devices appealing across conventional limits between "art" and "reality." But paradoxes are by no means confined to baroque practice: they persist in the history of thought, the history of arts, their infinite action stimulating the mental activity of quite different, quite independent, quite separate men.

Paradox begins an infinite *action*, not an infinite progress: characteristically, paradox reveals and reinforces very simple truths—perhaps, really, only one simple truth, that Truth is One. It does not *argue* that this is so (though it often may seem to); it demonstrates that fact by its own operation, circling and spiraling about its central fixed point, always deepening, thickening, reinforcing our awareness of how multiplex any simple truth is. So, for example, a reader vicariously lives through the experience of understanding how time and eternity can coexist by reading *Paradise Lost*; the infinite regress of self-regard is gained from reflection upon, and reflection from, the *Essayes* of Montaigne. In Rabelais' *Tiers Livre*, the moral meanings of being a man are lightheartedly set out; the paradoxes of debt, codpiece, marriage, and folly fuse to demonstrate the doubleness involved in any human enterprise. In *King*

Lear the same paradoxes, really, inexorably tighten upon one lesson—the same lesson as that of the *Tiers Livre*, but this time taught in relation to tragedy—that moral life cannot be lived alone.

It is fair to say that all paradoxes attempt the same kind of fusion, though not all paradoxes attempt the fusion in terms so elevated as that of *Paradise Lost* and *King Lear*. But, certainly, Cornwallis' paradoxes attempt to show the doubleness of human perception as surely as Burton's subtler uses of the same tricks. The difference in value between Cornwallis and Lando on the one hand, and Milton and Shakespeare on the other, indicate how much *techne* does count, that very *techne* which is both subject and object of all paradoxy. Art must be sufficiently developed to exploit the possibilities of a form so vulnerable to wounds from its own misuse. To work in paradox requires the utmost artistic tact, as a comparison of Donne's poetic use of paradox with, say, that of Henry King, makes blindingly clear. Equally, within Donne's own canon, the *Biathanatos* makes far more complex and interesting use of paradox than his own juvenile exercises in *Paradoxes and Problemes*. Whoever works in paradox knows that the choice of mode does not guarantee the success of the work—on the contrary, the work is conspicuously endangered by the very difficulty paradox entails. The paradoxist knows, none better, that paradox tends toward self-contradiction and thus toward self-destruction: only confident men can contemplate paradoxes in the first place, and only the most secure technicians can accept its risks. Within the tradition of paradoxy, very few artists have been able to outplay paradox by its own rules.

Bibliography

Aall, A.A.F. *Der Logos. Geschichte seiner Entwicklung in der griechischen Philosophie und der christlichen Litteratur.* Leipzig, 1896, 1899, 2 vols.

Ackerman, James. "Science and Visual Art," *Seventeenth-Century Science and the Arts,* ed. Hedley H. Rhys. Princeton, 1961.

Addleshaw, G.W.O. and Frederick Etchells. *The Architectural Setting of Anglican Worship.* London, 1948.

Admiranda rerum admirabilium encomia. Nijmegen, 1666, 1676.

Agrippa, Henry Cornelius. *Apologia adversus calumnias propter declamationem de vanitate scientiarum.* Cologne, 1533.

———. *De incertitudine et vanitate scientiarum, et artium.* Antwerp, 1530.

———. *De nobilitate foeminei sexus. The Commendation of Matrimony.* Trans. David Clapam. London, 1545.

———. *Three Books of Occult Philosophy.* Trans. J. F. London, 1651.

Albright, E. M. "Spenser's Cosmic Philosophy and his Religion," *PMLA,* XLIV (1929), 715-759.

———. "Spenser's Reason for Rejecting the Cantos of Mutability," *SP,* XXV (1928), 93-127.

Alvarez, A[lfred]. *The School of Donne.* London, 1961.

Angelus Silesius. *Sämtliche Poetische Werke.* Ed. Hans Ludwig Held. München, 1949-52, 3 vols.

Arbuthnot, John. *Of the Laws of Chance.* London, 1692.

Argumentorum ludicrorum et amoenitatum scriptores varij. Leiden, 1623.

Auerbach, Erich. *Mimesis.* Trans. Willard Trask. Garden City: Anchor Books, 1957.

Augustine, Aurelius, St. *Confessions.* Trans. William Watts. London, 1631.

Babb, Lawrence. *The Elizabethan Malady.* East Lansing, Mich., 1951.

———. *Sanity in Bedlam.* East Lansing, Mich., 1959.

Bacon, Francis. *Selected Writings.* Ed. Hugh G. Dick. New York: Modern Library, 1955.

————. *Sylva Sylvarum.* London, 1627.

————. *The Twoo Bookes of the Proficiencie and Advancement of Learning, divine and humane.* London, 1605.

Baker, John Tull. "The Emergence of Space and Time in English Philosophy," *Studies in the History of Ideas,* III (1935), 273-293.

————. *An Historical and Critical Examination of English Space and Time Theories from Henry More to Bishop Berkeley.* Bronxville, N.Y., 1930.

Baltrušaitis, Jurgis. *Anamorphoses.* Paris, 1955.

Barish, J. A. and Marshall Waingrow. "Service in *King Lear,*" *SQ,* IX (1958), 347-355.

Barker, Arthur. "Structural Pattern in *Paradise Lost,*" *PQ,* XXVIII (1949), 17-30.

Barrow, Isaac. *The Usefulness of Mathematical Learning.* London, 1734.

Bennett, Josephine Waters. "Spenser's Garden of Adonis," *PMLA,* XLVII (1932), 46-80.

————. "Spenser's Venus and the Goddess Nature of the *Cantos of Mutabilitie,*" *SP,* XXX (1933), 160-192.

————. "The Theme of Spenser's *Fowre Hymnes,*" *SP,* XXVIII (1931), 18-57; *SP,* XXXII (1935), 131-157.

Berger, Harry, Jr. "Spenser's Gardens of Adonis: Force and Form in the Renaissance Imagination," *UTQ,* XXX (1961), 128-149.

Bergström, Ingvar. *Dutch Still-life Painting in the Seventeenth Century.* Trans. Christina Hedström and Gerald Taylor, London, 1956.

Bettini, Mario. *Apiaria universae philosophiae mathematicae.* Bologna, 1642, 2 vols.

Bewley, Marius. "Religious Cynicism in Donne's Poetry," *Kenyon Review,* XIV (1952), 619-646.

Blunt, Wilfrid. *The Art of Botanical Illustration.* London, 1950.

Boas, George. *The Limits of Reason.* New York, 1961.

Bolzano, Bernard. Paradoxes of the Infinite. Trans. Fr. Přihonsky. Introduction by Donald A. Steele. London, 1950.

Boyd, George. "George Herbert: a Revaluation." Unpublished doctoral dissertation, Columbia University, 1957.

Boyle, Robert. *Hydrostatical Paradoxes*. Oxford, 1666.

————. *The Skeptical Chymist*. London, 1661.

Bredvold, Louis I. "The Intellectual Milieu of John Dryden," *University of Michigan Publications in Language and Literature*, XII (1934).

————. "The Naturalism of Donne in Relation to Some Renaissance Traditions," *JEGP*, XXII (1923), 471-502.

————. "The Religious Thought of Donne in Relation to Medieval and Later Traditions," *University of Michigan Publications in Language and Literature*, I (1925), 193-232.

————. "The Sources Used by Davies in *Nosce Teipsum*," *PMLA*, XXXVIII (1923), 745-769.

Brooks, Cleanth. *The Well-Wrought Urn*. New York, 1947.

Brown, Robert L. "Robert Burton and the New Cosmology," *MLQ*, XIII (1952), 131-148.

Browne, Sir Thomas. *Religio Medici and Other Writings*. Ed. L. C. Martin. Oxford, 1964.

————. *Works*. Ed. Sir Geoffrey Keynes. London and Oxford, 1964, 4 vols.

Bruno, Giordano. *Opera latina conscripta*. Eds. F. Fiorentino *et al*. Napoli, 1879-86, 3 vols.

————. *Opere italiane*. Ed. B. Croce, G. Gentile, and V. Spampanato. Bari, 1923-27, 3 vols.

Buffum, Imbrie. *Studies in the Baroque from Montaigne to Rotrou*. New Haven, 1957.

Burckhardt, Jacob. *The Civilization of the Renaissance in Italy*. Trans. S. G. C. Middlemore. London and New York, 1951.

Burgess, Theodore. *Epideictic Literature*. Chicago, 1902.

Burton, Robert. *The Anatomy of Melancholy*. London: Everyman edition, 1949, 3 vols.

Burtt, E. A. *The Metaphysical Foundations of Modern Physical Science*. Garden City: Anchor Books, 1954.

Bush, Geoffrey. *Shakespeare and the Natural Condition*. Cambridge, Mass., 1956.

Calman, Gerta. "The Picture of Nobody," *JWCI*, XXIII (1960), 60-104.

Campbell, O. J. "The Salvation of *Lear*," *ELH*, XV (1948), 93-109.

Cardanus, Girolamo. *De rerum varietate*. Basel, 1557.

————. *De subtilitate*. Nürnberg, 1550.

Carpenter, Nathanael. *Philosophia libera*. Oxford, 1622.

Cassirer, Ernst. *Individuum und Kosmos in der Philosophie der Renaissance*. Leipzig, 1927.

Castiglione, Baldassare. *The Book of the Courtier*. Trans. Sir Thomas Hoby. London, 1900.

Caus, Isaac de. *New and Rare Inventions of Water-works*. Trans. John Leak. London, 1659.

Caus, Salomon de. *Les raisons des forces mouvantes*. Frankfurt-am-Main, 1615.

Chapuis, A. and E. Droz. *Les automates*. Paris, 1949.

Charron, Pierre. *De la sagesse*. Bordeaux, 1601.

————. *Of wisdome*. Trans. Samson Lennard. London, 1608.

Clarke, Samuel. *A Collection of Papers, which passed between the late Learned Mr. Leibnitz, and Dr. Clarke*. London, 1717.

Clements, A. L. "On the Mode and Meaning of Traherne's Mystical Poetry: 'The Preparative,'" *SP*, LXI (1964), 500-521.

Colie, R. L. "Constantijn Huygens and the Metaphysical Mode," *GR*, XXXIV (1959), 59-73.

Colie, R. L. "*Some Thankfulnesse to Constantine*." The Hague, 1956.

Conklin, George Newton. *Biblical Criticism and Heresy in Milton*. New York, 1949.

Conway, Anne. *The Principles of the Most Ancient and Modern Philosophy*. London, 1962.

Cope, Jackson I. *The Metaphoric Structure of Paradise Lost*. Baltimore, 1962.

Cornford, Francis. *Plato and Parmenides*. London, 1939.

Cornwallis, William. *Essayes of Certaine Paradoxes*. London, 1617.

Craig, Hardin. "The Ethics of King Lear," *PQ*, IV (1925), 97-109.

Cudworth, Ralph. *The True Intellectual System of the Universe*. London, 1678.

Cumming, W. P. "Ovid as a Source for Spenser's Monster-Spawning Mud Passages," *MLN*, XLV (1930), 166-168.

————. "The Influence of Ovid's *Metamorphoses* on Spenser's 'Mutabilitie' Cantos," *SP*, XXVIII (1931), 241-256.

Curtius, Ernst Robert. *European Literature and the Latin Middle Ages*. Trans. Willard Trask. London, New York, 1953.

D., E. *The Prayse of Nothing*. London [1625?].

Danby, John F. *Shakespeare's Doctrine of Nature*. London, 1949.

Davies, Sir John. *Nosce Teipsum*. London, 1599.

Davies of Hereford, John. *The Complete Works*. Ed. Alexander B. Grosart. London, 1878, 2 vols.

De Morgan, Augustus. *A Budget of Paradoxes*. London, 1872.

Dionysius the Areopagite. *On the Divine Names*. Trans. C. E. Rolt. Ed. W. J. Sparrow-Simpson. London, 1920.

————. *Opera*. Strassburg, 1503.

————. *Works*. Trans. John Parker. London, 1897.

Dissertationum ludicrarum et amoenitatum scriptores varij. Leiden, 1638, 1644.

Donne, John. *The Anniversaries*. Ed. Frank Manley. Baltimore, 1963.

————. *Biathanatos*. Ed. J. William Hebel. New York, 1930.

————. *The Courtier's Library, or Catalogus Librorum Aulicorum*. Ed. E. M. Simpson. London, 1930.

————. *Devotions upon Emergent Occasions*. Ann Arbor, Mich., 1959.

————. *The Divine Poems*. Ed. Helen Gardner. Oxford, 1952.

————. *Letters to Severall Persons of Honour*. London, 1651.

————. *Paradoxes, Problemes, Essayes, Characters*. . . . London, 1652.

Donne, John. *Poems.* Ed. H.J.C. Grierson. Oxford, 1912, 2 vols.

Doran, Madeline. *Endeavours of Art.* Madison, Wis., 1954.

Dornavius, Caspar. *Amphitheatrum sapientiae socraticae joco-seriae.* Hannover, 1619.

Drayton, Michael. *Poems.* Ed. John Buxton. London, 1953, 2 vols.

Drebbel, Cornelis. *Een Kort Tractaet van de natuere der ele-menten.* Haarlem, 1621.

Dulles, Avery. *Princeps Concordiae. Pico della Mirandola and the Scholastic Tradition.* Cambridge, Mass., 1941.

Du Plessis Mornay, Philippe. *De la vérité Chrestienne.* Antwerp, 1581.

————. *The True Knowledge of a Mans owne Selfe.* Trans. A[nthony] M[unday]. London, 1602.

————. *A Woorke concerning the Trewnesse of the Christian Religion.* Trans. Sir Philip Sidney and Arthur Golding. London, 1587.

Du Vair, Guillaume. *A Buckler against Adversitie.* Trans. Andrew Court. London, 1622.

————. *De la constance.* Rouen, 1604.

————. *The Moral Philosophie of the Stoicks.* Trans. Thomas James. London, 1598.

English Madrigal Verse (1558-1623). Ed. E. H. Fellowes. Oxford, 1929.

Epigrammata et poemata vetera. Ed. P. Pithou. Paris, 1590.

Erasmus, Desiderius. *Adagiorum opus.* London, 1529.

————. *Christiani matrimonii institutio.* Basel, 1526.

————. *The Praise of Folie.* Trans. Sir Thomas Chaloner. London, 1549.

————. *Sileni Alcibiadis.* Paris, 1527.

An Essay Concerning a Vacuum. London, 1697.

Escher, M. C. *Graphic Work.* London, 1961.

Evans, Bergen, and George Mohr, M.D. *The Psychiatry of Robert Burton.* New York, 1944.

Facetiae. I. *Musarum Deliciae, or the Muses Recreation* (1646). II. *Wit Restor'd* (1658). III. *Wits Recreations* (1640). London, 1817, 2 vols.

Facetiae facetiarum. Frankfurt-am-Main, 1615.

Faerber, Hansruedi. *Das Paradoxe in der Dichtung von John Donne.* Zürich, 1950.

Ferry, Anne Davidson. "Innocence Regained: 17th-Century Reinterpretations of the Fall of Man." Unpublished doctoral dissertation, Columbia University, 1956.

Ficino, Marsilio. *Opera omnia.* Ed. M. Sancipriano and P. O. Kristeller. Torino, 1959.

Flegel, Georg. *Sechs Acquarelle.* Ed. Friedrich Winkler. Berlin, 1954.

Floia, de magna humani gestis Floga. . . [n.p., n.d.: early 17th-century].

Foss, Martin. *The Idea of Perfection in the Western World.* Princeton, 1946.

Frame, Donald M. *Montaigne's Discovery of Man.* New York, 1955.

Freccero, John. "Donne's 'Valediction: Forbidding Mourning,' " *ELH*, XXX (1963), 335-376.

Freedman, Lila Hermann. "Satiric Personae. A Study of Point of View in Formal Verse Satire in the English Renaissance from Wyatt to Marston." Unpublished doctoral dissertation, University of Wisconsin, 1955.

Freeman, Rosemary. *English Emblem Books.* London, 1948.

Fregoso, Battista. *Anteros.* Milan, 1496.

———. *Contramours.* Trans. Thomas Sébillet. Paris, 1581.

Freud, Sigmund. "The Antithetical Sense of Primary Words," *Collected Papers*, IV, 184-196. New York, 1959.

Friedlaender, Max J. *Landscape, Portrait, Still-life.* Trans. R.F.C. Hull. New York, 1963.

Frye, Northrop. *Anatomy of Criticism.* Princeton, 1957.

———. *Fables of Identity.* New York, 1963.

Galilei, Galileo. *Dialogue Concerning the Two Chief World Systems.* Trans. Stillman Drake. Berkeley, Calif., 1953.

Gang, Theodor. "Nature and Grace in *The Faerie Queene*: the Problem Reviewed," *ELH*, XXVI (1959), 1-22.

Geiger, Benno. *I Dipinti ghiribizzosi di Giuseppe Arcimboldi.* Firenze, 1954.

Geraldine, Sister M., C.S.J. "Erasmus and the Tradition of Paradox," *SP*, LXI (1964), 41-63.

Glazier, Lyle. "The Nature of Spenser's Imagery," *MLQ*, XVI (1955), 300-310.

Goldscheider, Ludwig. *Johannes Vermeer*. London and New York, 1958.

Gombrich, E. H. *Art and Illusion*. London, 1960.

————. "Icones Symbolicae," *JWCI*, XI (1948), 163-192.

————. "Moment and Movement in Art," *JWCI*, XXVII (1964), 293-306.

————. "Light, Form, and Texture in XVth Century Painting," *Journal of the Royal Society of the Arts*, October, 1964, 826-849.

————. *Meditations on a Hobby Horse*. London, 1963.

Gracian, Baltasar. *The Critick*. Trans. Paul Rycaut. London, 1681.

Greenlaw, Edwin A. "Spenser and Lucretius," *SP*, XVII (1920), 439-464.

————. "Spenser's 'Mutabilitie,' " *PMLA*, XLV (1930), 684-703.

Greville, Fulke. *Poems and Dramas*. Ed. Geoffrey Bullough. London, 1945, 2 vols.

Guss, Donald. "Donne's Conceit and Petrarchan Wit," *PMLA*, LXXVIII (1963), 308-314.

————. "Donne's Petrarchism," *JEGP*, LXIV (1965), 17-28.

Hagstrum, Jean H. *The Sister Arts*. Chicago, 1958.

Hale, Matthew. *Difficiles Nugae*. London, 1674.

————. *Observations Touching the Principles of Natural Motions*. London, 1677.

Haller, William. *The Rise of Puritanism*. New York, 1938.

Hardison, O. B., Jr. *The Enduring Monument*. Chapel Hill, 1962.

Harington, Sir John. *A New Discourse of a Stale Subject called the Metamorphosis of Ajax*. Ed. Elizabeth Story Donno. New York, 1962.

Harris, Victor. *All Coherence Gone*. Chicago, 1949.

Hartman, Geoffrey H. "Milton's Counterplot," *ELH*, XXV (1958), 1-12.

Hawkins, Sherman. "Mutabilitie and the Cycle of the Months," *Form and Convention in the Poetry of Edmund Spenser*. Ed. William Nelson. New York, 1961.

Haydn, Hiram. *The Counter-Renaissance*. New York, 1950.

Heath, Robert. *Paradoxical Assertions and Philosophical Problems*. London, 1659.

Heilman, Robert B. *This Great Stage*. Baton Rouge, La., 1948.

Heinze, F.F.M. *Die Lehre vom Logos*. Leipzig, 1872.

Helmont, F. M. van. *The Paradoxical Discourses concerning the Macrocosm and the Microcosm*. London, 1685.

Helmont, J. B. van. *A Ternary of Paradoxes*. Trans. and ed. Walter Charleton. London, 1650.

————. *Works*. London, 1664.

Herbert, George. *Works*. Ed. F. E. Hutchinson. Oxford, 1953.

Hexter, J. H. *More's "Utopia." The Biography of an Idea*. Princeton, 1952.

Hobbes, Thomas. *Leviathan*. Ed. Michael Oakeshott. Oxford, 1947.

Hocke, Gustav-René. *Die Welt als Labyrinth*. Hamburg, 1957.

Hollander, John. *The Untuning of the Sky*. Princeton, 1961.

Hoopes, Robert. *Right Reason in the English Renaissance*. Cambridge, Mass., 1962.

Hudson, Henry. *Divers Voyages and Northerne Discoveries, Purchas his Pilgrimes*. London, 1625.

Huizinga, Johan. *Homo Ludens*. London, 1949.

Hunt, Clay. *Donne's Poetry*. New Haven, 1954.

Huntley, Frank L. " 'Macbeth' and the Background of Jesuitical Equivocation," *PMLA*, LXXIX (1946), 390-400.

Huret, Grégoire. *Optique de portraiture et peinture*. Paris, 1670.

Hurtlaub, G. F. *Zauber des Spiegels. Geschichte und Bedeutung des Spiegels in der Kunst*. München, 1951.

Huygens, Christiaan. *De ratiociniis in ludo aleae*. In Franciscus van Schooten, *Exercitationum mathematicarum libri quinque*. Leiden, 1657.

Huygens, Constantijn. *Briefwisseling*. Ed. J. A. Worp. *Rijksgeschiedkundige Publicatien*. The Hague, 1911-1918, 6 vols.

Huygens, Constantijn. *Gedichten.* Ed. J. A. Worp. Groningen, 1892-1899, 9 vols.

―――. *De Jeugd van Constantijn Huygens, door hemzelf beschreven.* Trans. A. H. Kan. Rotterdam and Antwerp, 1946.

Iredale, Hilda Queenie. *Thomas Traherne.* Oxford, 1935.

Jackson, Thomas. *A Treatise of the Divine Essence and Attributes.* London, 1628.

Jammer, Max. *Concepts of Space.* Cambridge, Mass., 1954.

Jayne, Sears. "Charity in *King Lear*," *Shakespeare 400.* Ed. James G. McManaway. New York, 1964.

Jocorum atque seriorum, tum novorum, tum selectorum atque memorabilium centuriae. Nürnberg, 1643.

Jones, R. M. "Ideas as Thoughts of God," *CP*, XXI (1926), 317-326.

Jones, Rufus M. *Spiritual Reformers in the 16th and 17th Centuries.* London, 1914.

Jorgensen, Paul A. "Much Ado about *Nothing*," *SQ*, V (1954), 287-295.

Kaiser, Walter. *Praisers of Folly.* Cambridge, Mass., 1963.

Keast, W. R. "Imagery and Meaning in the Interpretation of *King Lear*," *MP*, XLVII (1949), 45-64.

Kelley, Maurice. *This Great Argument.* Princeton, 1941.

Kermode, Frank. *John Donne.* London, 1957.

Kivette, Ruth Montgomery. "Milton on the Trinity." Unpublished doctoral dissertation, Columbia University, 1960.

Klemm, Gustav. *Zur Geschichte der Sammlungen für Wissenschaft und Kunst in Deutschland.* Zerbst, 1837.

Klibansky, Raymond. *The Continuity of the Platonic Tradition.* London, 1939.

―――. "Plato's *Parmenides* in the Middle Ages and the Renaissance," *Medieval and Renaissance Studies*, I (1943), 281-330.

Kneale, William and Martha. *The Development of Logic.* Oxford, 1962.

Knowles Middleton, W. E. *The History of the Barometer.* Baltimore, 1964.

Knowles Middleton, W. E. "The Place of Torricelli in the History of the Barometer," *Isis*, LIV (1963), 11-28.

Knowlton, E. C. "Spenser and Nature," *JEGP*, XXXIV (1935), 366-376.

Koyré, Alexandre. *Epiménide le menteur. Ensemble et catégorie. Actualités scientifiques et industrielles.* Paris, 1946.

———. *From the Closed World to the Infinite Universe.* Baltimore, 1957.

———. "Le vide et l'espace infini au XIVe siècle," *Etudes d'histoire de la pensée philosophique. Cahier des Annales*, XIX. Paris, 1961.

Krailsheimer, A. J. *Studies in Self-Interest.* London, 1962.

Krieger, Murray. *The New Apologists for Poetry.* Bloomington, Ind., 1963.

———. *A Window to Criticism. Shakespeare's Sonnets and Modern Poetics.* Princeton, 1964.

Kris, Ernst. *Psychoanalytic Explorations in Art.* New York, 1952.

Kuhn, Thomas S. *The Structure of Scientific Revolutions.* Chicago, 1962.

Lando, Ortensio. *Paradossi Cioè, Sententie fuori del commun parere.* Lyons, 1543; Venice, 1544.

———. *Paradoxes, ce sont des propos contre la commune opinion.* Trans. Charles Estienne. Paris, 1553.

———. *The Defense of Contraries.* Trans. Anthony Munday. London, 1593.

Lebreton, Jules. "Les théories du Logos au début de l'ère chrétienne." *Etudes*, CIV (1906).

Lee, Rensselaer W. "*Ut Pictura Poesis*: The Humanistic Theory of Painting," *Art Bulletin*, XXII (1940), 197-269.

Legrand, Francine-Claire and Felix Sluys. *Arcimboldo et les archimboldesques.* Aalter, 1955.

Lemmi, C. W. "Monster-spawning Nile-Mud in Spenser," *MLN*, XLI (1926), 234-238.

Leonardo da Vinci. *Notebooks.* Trans. Edward Macurdy. London, 1954.

Leurechon, Jean. *Mathematical Recreations.* Trans. William Oughtred. London, 1633.

Leurechon, Jean. *Les recréations mathématiques.* Lyons, 1629.

Lewalski, Barbara K. "Structure and the Symbolism of Vision in Michael's Prophecy, *Paradise Lost,* Books XI-XII," *PQ,* XLII (1963), 25-35.

Lewis, C. S. *A Preface to Paradise Lost.* London, 1942.

Lievsay, John L. "Robert Burton's De Consolatione," *SAQ,* LV (1956), 329-336.

Lipman, Naomi Loeb. "Robert Burton's *Anatomy of Melancholy* and its Relation to the Medical Book Tradition of the English Renaissance." Unpublished Master's Essay, Columbia University, 1952.

Locke, John. *An Essay Concerning Human Understanding.* Ed. John W. Yolton. London, 1961, 2 vols.

————. *Two Treatises of Government.* Ed. Peter Laslett, Cambridge, 1960.

Lovejoy, A. O. *Essays in the History of Ideas.* Baltimore, 1948.

————. *The Great Chain of Being.* Cambridge, Mass., 1936.

Lucian. *Works.* Ed. A. M. Harmon. Loeb Classical Library, 1913.

McColley, Grant. *Paradise Lost.* Chicago, 1940.

Macdonald, Hugh, and Mary Hargreaves. *Thomas Hobbes. A Bibliography.* London, 1952.

Mack, Maynard. *King Lear in our Time.* University of California Press, 1965.

————. "The World of Hamlet," *Yale Review,* XLI (1948), 502-523.

MacLure, Millar. "Nature and Art in *The Faerie Queene,*" *ELH,* XXVIII (1961), 1-20.

Maier, Michael. *Jocus severus, hoc est, tribunal aequum, quo noctua, regina avium, phoenice arbitro.* Frankfurt-am-Main, 1617.

Malloch, A. E. "A Critical Study of Donne's *Biathanatos.*" Unpublished doctoral dissertation, University of Toronto, 1958.

————. "John Donne and the Casuists," *SEL,* II (1962), 57-76.

Malloch, A. E. "The Technique and Function of the Renaissance Paradox," *SP*, LIII (1956), 191-203.

Markels, Julian. "Shakespeare's Confluence of Tragedy and Comedy: *Twelfth Night* and *King Lear*," *Shakespeare 400*. Ed. James G. McManaway. New York, 1964.

Martz, Louis L. *The Poetry of Meditation*. New Haven, 1954.

Marvell, Andrew. *The Poems and Letters*. Ed. H. M. Margoliouth. Oxford, 1952.

Mazzeo, Joseph A. *Renaissance and Seventeenth-Century Studies*. New York, 1964.

Meiss, Millard. "Light as Form and Symbol in Some Fifteenth-Century Paintings," *Art Bulletin*, XXVII (1945), 175-181.

Miller, Henry Knight. "The Paradoxical Encomium with Special Reference to its Vogue in England," *MP*, LIII (1956), 145-178.

Miller, Milton. "Nature in *The Faerie Queene*," *ELH*, XVIII (1951), 191-200.

Milton, John. *Complete Poetry and Selected Prose*. Ed. Merritt Y. Hughes. New York, 1957.

———. *Of Christian Doctrine. Works*. Ed. Frank Allen Patterson, *et al*. New York, 1933.

Mirollo, James V. *The Poet of the Marvellous: Giambattista Marino*. New York, 1963.

Moeller, Liselotte. *Der Wrangelschrank und die verwandten süddeutschen Intarsienmöbel des 16. Jahrhunderts*. Berlin, 1956.

Montaigne, Michel de. *Essayes*. Trans. John Florio. Ed. J. I. M. Stewart. New York, 1933.

More, Henry. *An Antidote against Atheisme*. London, 1653.

———. *The Complete Poems*. Ed. Alexander B. Grosart. Chertsey Worthies Library, 1878.

———. *Enchiridion Metaphysicum*. London, 1671.

———. *Remarks upon Two Late Ingenious Discourses*. London, 1676.

Mourgues, Odette de. *Metaphysical, Baroque, and Précieux Poetry*. Oxford, 1953.

Mueller, William R. *The Anatomy of Robert Burton's England*. Berkeley, Calif., 1952.

———. "Robert Burton's 'Satyricall Preface,'" *MLQ*, XV (1954), 28-35.

Musei Kircheriani in Romano Societatis Jesu Collegio Aerea. Rome, 1763.

Museum Wormianum, seu historia rerum rariorum. Leiden, 1655.

Nagel, Ernest and James R. Newman. *Gödel's Proof*. New York, 1958.

Nelson, William. *The Poetry of Edmund Spenser*. New York, 1963.

Newton, Isaac. *Mathematical Principles of Natural Philosophy*. Ed. Florian Cajori. Berkeley, Calif., 1934.

———. *Opticks*. New York, 1952.

Nicéron, Jean-François. *La perspective curieuse*. Paris, 1638.

———. *Thaumaturgus opticus, seu admiranda optices, catoptrices, et dioptrices*. Paris, 1646.

Nicholas of Cusa. *Of Learned Ignorance*. Trans. Fr. Germaine Heron. New Haven, 1954.

———. *Prohemium in hoc volumine continentur certi tractatus*. . . . Strassburg, 1490[?].

Nicolson, Marjorie Hope. *The Breaking of the Circle*. Evanston, Ill., 1950.

———. "Cosmic Voyages," *ELH*, VII (1940), 83-107.

———. "Milton and the Telescope," *Science and Imagination*. Ithaca, New York, 1956.

———. *Mountain Gloom and Mountain Glory*. Ithaca, N.Y., 1959.

———. *Voyages to the Moon*. New York, 1948.

——— and Nora Mohler. "The Scientific Background of Swift's 'Voyage to Laputa,'" *Annals of Science*, II (1937), 299-334.

———. "Swift's 'Flying Island' in the 'Voyage to Laputa,'" *Annals of Science*, II (1937), 405-430.

Noël, Père Etienne. *Le plein du vuide*. Paris, 1648.

Nowottny, Winifred. *The Language Poets Use*. London, 1962.

Nowottny, Winifred. "Lear's Questions." *Shakespeare Survey*, X (1957), 90-97.

Ore, Oystein. *Cardano, the Gambling Scholar*. Trans. Sydney Henry Gould. Princeton, 1953.

Ornstein, Robert M. "Donne, Montaigne, and Natural Law," *JEGP*, LV (1956), 213-229.

Ozanam, Jacques. *Recreations Mathematical and Physical*. London, 1708.

Padelford, F. M. "Spenser's 'Fowre Hymnes,'" *JEGP*, XIII (1914), 418-433; *SP*, XXIX (1932), 207-232.

Palmer, Herbert. *Memorials of Godlinesse and Christianitie*. London, 1657.

Panofsky, Erwin and Fritz Saxl. *Dürers Melencolia I. Studien der Bibliothek Warburg*. Leipzig, 1923.

Panofsky, Erwin. *Early Netherlandish Painting*. Cambridge, Mass., 1953.

Pascal, Blaise. *Expériences nouvelles touchant le vuide*. Paris, 1647.

————. *Oeuvres*. Ed. Jacques Chevalier. Paris, 1949-50.

————. *Oeuvres*. Eds. Léon Brunschvicq and Pierre Boutroux. Paris, 1908.

————. *Pensées, The Provincial Letters*. Trans. W. F. Trotter and Thomas M'Crie. New York, 1941.

Passerat, Jean. *Le Bon-iour de R. de B. . . .* Paris, 1599.

Patrick, J. Max. "Robert Burton's Utopianism," *PQ*, XXVII (1948), 345-358.

Pease, A. S. "Things without Honour," *CP*, XXI (1926), 27-42.

Pelikan, Jaroslav. *The Light of the World*. New York, 1962.

Petrarca, Francesco. *Canzoniere, Trionfi, Rime varie*. Eds. Carlo Muscetta and Daniele Ponchiroli. Torino, 1958.

————. *Lettere di Francesco Petrarca della cose familiari*. Ed. G. Fracassetti. Firenze, 1892, 5 vols.

————. *Sonnets and Songs*. Trans. Anna Maria Armi. New York, 1946.

Peyre, Henri. *Literature and Sincerity*. New Haven, 1963.

Pico della Mirandola, Giovanni. *Conclusiones nonagentae in omni genere scientiarum*. [?Rome], 1532.

Plato. *The Sophist.* Loeb Classical Library, 1912.

―――. *Symposium.* Loeb Classical Library, 1912.

Pont-Aymery, Alexandre de. *Paradoxe apologétique, ou il est fidèlement démonstré que la femme est beaucoup plus parfaicte que l'homme en toute action de vertu.* Paris, 1596.

Popkin, Richard. *The History of Scepticism from Erasmus to Descartes.* Assen, Holland, 1960.

Popper, Karl. "Self-reference and Meaning in Ordinary Language," *Conjectures and Refutations.* London, 1965.

Porta, Giovanni Battista. *Natural Magick.* London, 1658.

Poulet, Georges. *Etudes sur le temps humain.* Paris, 1950.

Primaudaye, Pierre de la. *Académie Françoise.* Paris, 1610. *The French Académie.* Trans. Thomas Bowes [?]. London, 1618.

Prince, F. T. "Adam Unparadis'd," *The Living Milton.* Ed. Frank Kermode. London, 1960.

―――. "On the Last Two Books of *Paradise Lost,*" *Essays and Studies.* London, 1958, pp. 40-51.

Puttenham, George. *The Arte of English Poesie.* London, 1589.

―――. *The Arte of English Poesie.* Eds. Gladys Doidge Willcock and Alice Walker. Cambridge, Mass., 1936.

Pyles, Thomas. "Ophelia's 'Nothing,' " *MLN,* LXIV (1949), 322-323.

Quarles, Francis. *Complete Works.* Ed. Alexander B. Grosart. Chertsey Worthies Library, 1881, 3 vols.

Quine, W. V. "Paradox," *Scientific American* (April 1962), pp. 84-96.

Rabelais, François. *Gargantua and Pantagruel.* Trans. Sir Thomas Urquhart and Peter le Motteux. London, 1954, 2 vols.

Rajan, B. *Paradise Lost and the 17th Century Reader.* London, 1947.

Ramsey, Frank Plumpton. *The Foundations of Mathematics and Other Logical Essays.* Ed. R. B. Braithwaite. London, 1931.

Ribner, Irving. " 'The Gods are Just,' " *Tulane Drama Review,* II (1958), 34-54.

Rice, Warner G. "The *Paradossi* of Ortensio Lando," *Michigan Essays and Studies in Comparative Literature*, VIII (1932), 59-74.

Ridlon, Harold G. "The Function of the 'Infant-Ey' in Traherne's Poetry," *SP*, LXI (1964), 627-639.

Robbins, Frank Egleston. *The Hexaemeral Literature*. Chicago, 1912.

Roche, Thomas P., Jr. *The Kindly Flame*. Princeton, 1964.

Rosen, William. *Shakespeare and the Craft of Tragedy*. Cambridge, Mass., 1960.

Rudio, Ferdinand. "Das Problem von der Quadratur des Zirkels," *Vierteljahrsschrift der Naturforschenden Gesellschaft in Zürich*, 1890, pp. 1-51.

Rüstow, Alexander. *Der Lügner. Theorie, Geschichte, und Auflösung*. Leipzig, 1910.

Russell, Bertrand. *The Principles of Mathematics*. London, 1937.

Sackton, Alexander. "The Paradoxical Encomium in Elizabethan Drama" [University of Texas] *Studies in English*, XXVIII (1949), 83-104.

Salkeld, John. *A Treatise of Paradise*. London, 1617.

Samuel, Irene. "The Brood of Folly," *N&Q*, CCIII (1958), 430-431.

Saxl, Fritz. "Veritas Filia Temporis," *Philosophy and History*. Eds. Raymond Klibansky and H. J. Paton. New York, 1963.

Scaliger, J. C. *Exotericarum exercitationum liber*. Paris, 1557.

Schlosser, Julius von. *Die Kunst- und wunderkämmern der Spätrenaissance*. Leipzig, 1908.

Schoock, Marten. *De nihilo*. Groningen, 1661.

Schott, Gaspar. *Joco-seriorum naturae et artis, sive magiae naturalis centuriae tres*. Würzburg, 1677.

———. *Magia universalis naturae et artis*. Nürnberg, 1657.

———. *Physica curiosa*. Nürnberg, 1662.

———. *Technica curiosa*. Nürnberg, 1664.

Schultz, Howard. *Milton and Forbidden Knowledge*. New York, 1955.

Screech, M. A. *The Rabelaisian Marriage*. London, 1958.

Shakespeare, William. *Complete Works*. Ed. George Lyman Kittredge. Boston, 1936.

————. *King Lear*. Ed. Kenneth Muir. London, 1952.

Sidney, Sir Philip. *An Apologie for Poetrie*. *Elizabethan Critical Essays*. Ed. G. Gregory Smith. Oxford, 1937, 2 vols.

————. *Poems*. Ed. William A. Ringler. Oxford, 1962.

Silver, George. *Works*. Ed. Cyril G. R. Matthey. London, 1898.

Simon, Theodor. *Der Logos. Ein Versuch erneuter Würdigung einer alten Wahrheit*. Leipzig, 1902.

Simpson, Evelyn M. *A Study of the Prose Works of John Donne*. Oxford, 1948.

Spencer, Theodore. "Donne and his Age," *A Garland for John Donne*. Gloucester, Mass., 1958.

————. *Shakespeare and the Nature of Man*. New York, 1942.

Spenser, Edmund. *Poetical Works*. Ed. J. C. Smith and E. de Selincourt. London, 1963.

Spinoza, Benedictus de. *Chief Works*. Ed. R.H.M. Elwes. New York, 1951, 2 vols. in 1.

Spitzer, Leo. *Linguistics and Literary History*. Princeton, 1962.

Spivack, Bernard. *Shakespeare and the Allegory of Evil*. New York, 1958.

Sprott, S. E. *The English Debate on Suicide: from Donne to Hume*. La Salle, Ill., 1961.

Stambler, Elizabeth. "The Unity of Herbert's 'Temple,'" *Cross Currents*, X (1960), 251-266.

Stampfer, Judah L. "The Cantos of Mutabilitie: Spenser's Last Testament of Faith," *UTQ*, XXI (1952), 140-156.

Stapleton, Lawrence. "Milton's Conception of Time in *The Christian Doctrine*," *Harvard Theological Review*, LVII (1964), 9-21.

Steinberg, Saul. *The Passport*. New York, 1954.

Sterling, Charles, *Still-life Painting from Antiquity to the Present Time*. Trans. James Emmons. New York, 1959.

Stirling, Brents. "The Concluding Stanzas of *Mutabilitie*," *SP*, XXX (1933), 193-204.

Stirling, Brents. "Two Notes on the Philosophy of *Mutabilitie.*" *MLN*, L (1935), 154-155.

──────. "The Philosophy of Spenser's 'Garden of Adonis,'" *PMLA*, XLIX (1934), 501-538.

Stone, Lawrence. *The Crisis of the Aristocracy, 1558-1641.* Oxford, 1965.

Summers, Joseph H. *George Herbert. His Religion and His Art.* London, 1954.

Surtz, Edward L. *The Praise of Pleasure.* Cambridge, Mass., 1957.

Svendsen, Kester. *Milton and Science.* Cambridge, Mass., 1956.

Swift, Jonathan. *Travels into Several Remote Nations of the World.* London, 1747.

Tarski, Alfred. *Logic, Semantics, Metamathematics.* Trans. J. H. Woodger. Oxford, 1956.

Thompson, E.N.S. "The Philosophy of Thomas Traherne," *PQ*, VIII (1929), 97-112.

Tillyard, E.M.W. *The Elizabethan World-Picture.* London, 1943.

Tinbergen, Nikolaas. *A Study of Instinct.* Oxford, 1951.

Toulmin, Stephen. *Seventeenth-Century Science and Arts.* Ed. Hedley Howell Rhys. Princeton, 1961.

Traherne, Thomas. *Centuries, Poems, and Thanksgivings.* Ed. H. M. Margoliouth. Oxford, 1958, 2 vols.

──────. *Christian Ethicks.* London, 1675.

Trapp, J. B. "Owl's Ivy and the Poet's Bays: an Enquiry into Poetic Garlands," *JWCI*, XXI (1958), 227-255.

Tuve, Rosemond. *A Reading of George Herbert.* London, 1952.

──────. "Spenser and the Zodiake of Life," *JEGP*, XXXIV (1936), 1-19.

Tuveson, E. L. "Space, Deity, and the 'Natural Sublime,'" *MLQ*, XII (1951), 20-38.

Tymme, Thomas. *A Dialogue Philosophicall.* London, 1612.

Valentini, M. B. *Museum museorum.* Frankfurt-am-Main, 1714, 2 vols.

Venning, Ralph. *Orthodox Paradoxes, Theoreticall and Experimentall.* London, 1647 (1650, 1652, 1657).

Vives, Joannes Ludovicus. *De institutione foeminae Christianee.* Antwerp, 1524.

Wade, Gladys I. *Thomas Traherne.* Princeton, 1944.

Walker, J. D. "The Architectonics of George Herbert's *The Temple*," *ELH*, XXIX (1962), 289-305.

Wallace, John Malcolm. "Thomas Traherne and the Structure of Meditation," *ELH*, XXV (1958), 79-89.

Ward, Richard. *The Life of the Learned and Pious Henry More.* London, 1710.

Warnke, Frank J. "Play and Metamorphosis in Marvell's Poetry," *SEL*, V (1965), 23-30.

————. "Sacred Play: Baroque Poetic Style," *JAAC*, XXII (1964), 455-464.

Wasserman, Earl. *The Subtler Language.* Baltimore, 1959.

Watkins, W. B. C. *An Anatomy of Milton's Verse.* Baton Rouge, 1955.

Webber, Joan. *Contrary Music.* Madison, Wisconsin, 1963.

Weisinger, Herbert. *Tragedy and the Paradox of the Fortunate Fall.* East Lansing, Mich., 1953.

Weiss, K. "Der Prolog des heiligen Johannes. Eine Apologie in Antithesen," *Strassburger Theologische Studien*, III (1899).

Welsford, Enid. *The Fool.* New York, 1936.

Whitaker, Virgil K. *Shakespeare's Use of Learning*, San Marino, Calif., 1953.

White, Helen C. *The Metaphysical Poets.* New York, 1936.

Whiting, George Wesley. *Milton and This Pendant World.* Austin, Tex., 1958.

Wiley, Margaret. *The Subtle Knot.* Cambridge, Mass., 1952.

Wilkins, John. *Mathematical Magick.* London, 1648.

Wilkinson, Elizabeth M. "The Inexpressible and the Unspeakable: Some Romantic Attitudes to Art and Language," *German Life and Letters*, N.S., XVI (1963), 308-320.

————. "The Theological Basis of Faust's *Credo*," *German Life and Letters*, N.S., X (1956), 229-239.

Willett, Gladys. *Traherne: an Essay*. Cambridge, Mass., 1919.

Williams, Arnold. *The Common Expositor*. Chapel Hill, N.C., 1948.

Williams, Kathleen. " 'Eterne in Mutabilitie': The Unified World of *The Faerie Queene*," *ELH*, XIX (1952), 115-130.

Williamson, George. "The Design of Donne's Anniversaries," *MP*, LX (1963), 183-191.

—————. "The Libertine Donne," *PQ*, XIII (1934), 276-291.

—————. "Mutability, Decay, and Seventeenth-Century Melancholy," *ELH*, II (1935), 121-150.

Willoughby, L. A. " 'Name ist Schall und Rauch,' " *German Life and Letters*, N.S., XVI (1963), 294-307.

Wilson, F. P. *Elizabethan and Jacobean*. Oxford, 1945.

Wind, Edgar. *Pagan Mysteries in the Renaissance*. London, 1958.

Wittkower, Rudolf and Margot. *Born under Saturn*, London, 1963.

Wolfson, Harry A. "Extradeical and Intradeical Interpretations of Platonic Ideas," *JHI*, XXII (1961), 3-32.

Woodhouse, A.S.P. "Nature and Grace in *The Faerie Queene*," *ELH*, XVI (1949), 194-228.

—————. "Nature and Grace in Spenser: a Rejoinder," *RES*, N.S., VI (1955), 284-288.

—————. "Notes on Milton's Views on the Creation: the Initial Phases," *PQ*, XXVIII (1949), 211-236.

Wotton, Henry. *Life and Letters*. Ed. Logan Pearsall Smith. Oxford, 1907, 2 vols.

Yates, Frances A. *John Florio*. Cambridge, 1934.

—————. *Giordano Bruno and the Hermetic Tradition*. London, 1964.

Index

Aall, A.A.F., 28, 521
Ackerman, James, 285, 521
Addison, Joseph, 515-516
Addleshaw, G.W.O., 192, 521
Aertsen, Pieter, 286, 289
Aesculapius, 433
Agrippa, Henry Cornelius, 102,
    400-401, 402, 425, 458, 521
Alabaster, William, 170
Albertus Magnus, 150
Albright, E. M., 342, 521
Alcibiades, xiii, 16, 47
"all," 27, 40, 115, 119, 205, 208,
    221, 223, 225-229, 234, 236,
    238, 244, 247, 252-272, 393,
    465, 470-472, 493
Alvarez, Alfred, 200, 521
anamorphosis, 63, 286-289, 307,
    312-314, 317, 323, 513
anatomy, 431-432
Angelus Silesius, 223, 521
aporia, 12. See also *insolubilia*
Arbuthnot, John, 322-323, 325,
    521
Archimedes, 306
Arcimboldo, Giuseppe, 286-288,
    307
Aristotle, xiii, 319, 329, 439, 470
Auerbach, Erich, 69, 375, 521
Augustine, St., 78, 173, 180, 235-
    237, 241, 249, 252, 319, 392,
    418, 449, 459, 487, 521

Babb, Lawrence, 431, 521
Bacon, Francis, 221, 278-279, 280,
    300-304, 306, 311, 325, 330,
    331, 412, 424, 443, 453, 522
Bailly, David, 292
Baker, John Tull, 148, 522
Baltrušaitis, Jurgis, 285, 289, 312,
    502, 522
Barish, Jonas A., 464, 522
Barker, Arthur, 170, 182, 522

baroque, xii, xiv, 519
Barrault, Jean-Louis, 486, 505
Barrow, Isaac, 159-160, 522
"becoming," xiii, 39, 194, 291,
    300-352
"being," xiii, 39, 60-61, 161, 194,
    237-249, 300-352
Beeckman, Isaac, 253
"beholder's share," 35, 134-135,
    518-519
Bell, Millicent, 170
Bembo, Pietro, 447
Bennett, Josephine Waters, 331,
    335, 339, 342, 522
Berger, Harry, Jr., 335, 522
Bergström, Ingvar, 277, 289, 291,
    522
Berkeley, George, 35, 453
Beroaldus, Pierre, 433
Bettini, Mario, 305-306, 316, 326,
    522
Beuckelaer, Joachim, 289-290
Bewley, Marius, 413, 522
Blunt, Wilfrid, 285, 522
Boas, George, 190, 522
Boethius, 437
Bolzano, Bernard, 11, 146, 319,
    523
Boxhoorn, Marcus Zuerius, 122
Boyd, George, 192, 523
Boyle, Robert, 221, 255, 273, 308-
    310, 311, 327, 330, 331, 364,
    369, 523
Brandt, Sebastian, 458
Braunus, Georgius, 433
Bredvold, Louis I., 405-406, 413,
    415, 523
Bright, Timothy, 432, 454
Brooks, Cleanth, 130, 523
Brown, Robert L., 451, 523
Browne, Sir Thomas, xi, 23-24,
    43, 72, 96, 145, 169, 170, 173,
    190, 219, 227-228, 232, 252,